W9-BES-301

THE GILDED AGE

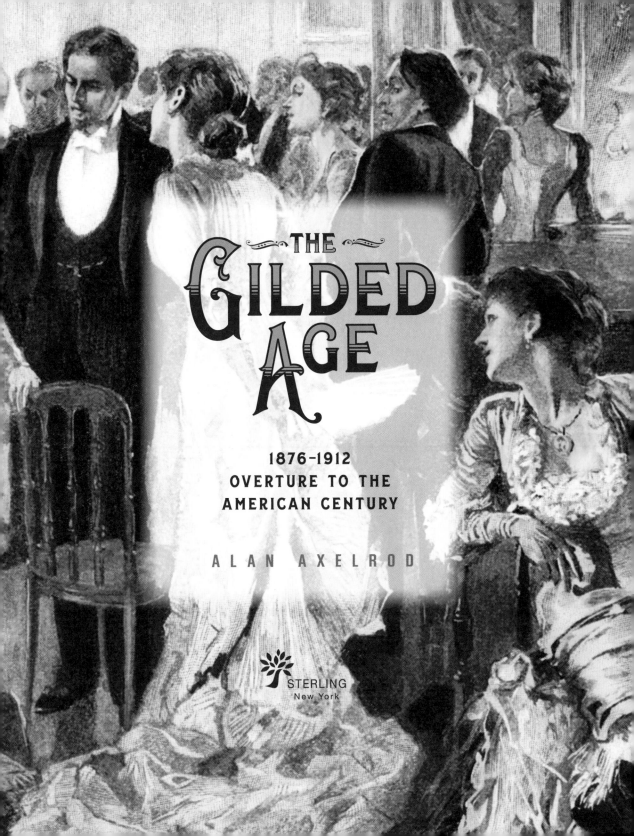

THE GILDED AGE

1876–1912
OVERTURE TO THE
AMERICAN CENTURY

ALAN AXELROD

STERLING
New York

STERLING
New York

An Imprint of Sterling Publishing Co., Inc.
1166 Avenue of the Americas
New York, NY 10036

STERLING and the distinctive Sterling Logo are registered trademarks
of Sterling Publishing Co., Inc.

Text © 2017 Alan Axelrod

All rights reserved. No part of this publication may be reproduced, stored in a
retrieval system, or transmitted in any form or by any means (including electronic,
mechanical, photocopying, recording, or otherwise) without prior written
permission from the publisher.

Any trademarks are the property of their respective owners, are used for editorial
purpose only, and the publisher makes no claim of ownership and shall accquire no
right, title, or interest in such trademarks by virtue of this publication.

ISBN 978-1-4549-2575-0

Distributed in Canada by Sterling Publishing Co., Inc.
c/o Canadian Manda Group, 664 Annette Street
Toronto, Ontario, Canada M6S 2C8
Distributed in the United Kingdom by GMC Distribution Services
Castle Place, 166 High Street, Lewes, East Sussex, England BN7 1XU
Distributed in Australia by NewSouth Books
45 Beach Street, Coogee, NSW 2034, Australia

For information about custom editions, special sales, and premium and
corporate purchases, please contact Sterling Special Sales at 800-805-5489
or specialsales@sterlingpublishing.com.

Manufactured in China

10 9 8 7 6 5 4 3 2 1

sterlingpublishing.com

Design by Lorie Pagnozzi
Image credits - see page 372

CONTENTS

Strollers traverse Manhattan's Grand Army Plaza, the Hotel New Netherland (opened in 1892–93) prominent in the background. That hotel was replaced in 1927 by the Sherry-Netherland.

ALL THAT GLITTERS

"The flames of a new economic evolution run around us, and we turn to find that competition has killed competition, that corporations are grown greater than the State and have bred individuals greater than themselves, and that the naked issue of our time is with property becoming the master instead of servant, property in many necessaries of life becoming monopoly of the necessaries of life. . . . Our industry is a fight of every man for himself. The prize we give the fittest is monopoly of the necessaries of life, and we leave these winners of the powers of life and death to wield them over us by the same 'self-interest' with which they took them from us."

—HENRY DEMAREST LLOYD,
WEALTH AGAINST COMMONWEALTH (1899)[1]

In 1890, 73 percent of America's wealth was held by the top 10 percent of the population. In 2013 (per data released by the Congressional Budget Office in 2016), the top 10 percent of families held 76 percent of total wealth. As Mark Twain is often credited with having said, "History doesn't repeat itself but it often rhymes."[2] Googling the phrase "new gilded age" on December 26, 2016, returned "about 9,040,000 results," including the farewell speech of retiring Senate Minority Leader Harry Reid, who left office warning of "a new gilded age."[3]

Many of today's economists and historians believe they have found a kind of handbook of the new gilded age. It is *Capital in the Twenty-First Century* (English edition, 2014) by French economist Thomas Piketty, a work the Nobel laureate economist Paul Krugman calls a "magnificent, sweeping meditation on [wealth] inequality."[4] Piketty argues that when the rate of return of capital is greater than rate of economic growth, concentration of wealth results. A nearly identical concentration occurred during the post–Civil War nineteenth century and during the last quarter of the twentieth century into the opening of the twenty-first. The numbers support the assertion that we have both a First and a Second Gilded Age. Perhaps by understanding the First, we can understand and—as a democracy—more effectively manage the Second. Perhaps.

———————— ◆ ————————

IF PIKETTY'S *CAPITAL IN THE TWENTY-FIRST CENTURY* is *the* book of the New or Second Gilded Age, its counterpart in the original Gilded Age—the American period between the end of the Civil War and the dawn of the twentieth century—is perhaps more importantly remembered for being an eponym of the period itself: an 1873 novel written by Mark Twain in collaboration with the journalist-editor Charles Dudley Warner, titled *The Gilded Age: A Tale of Today.* Twain borrowed that title from one of William Shakespeare's least-read and least-performed plays, *The Life and Death of King John*, based on the life of John, king of England (1166–1216), who was forced by his kingdom's rebellious barons to guarantee them certain legal rights as set out in the Magna Carta. Act 4, Scene 2 begins with the king pleased after commanding a second coronation to force his

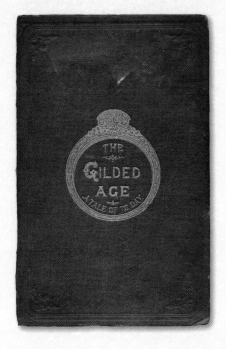

The original cover of the 1873 satirical novel by Mark Twain and Charles Dudley Warner that gave the era its name.

barons to swear their allegiance anew. One baron, Lord Salisbury, compares this to a brief catalog of other superfluous and extravagant acts:

To gild refined gold, to paint the lily,
To throw a perfume on the violet,
To smooth the ice, or add another hue
Unto the rainbow, or with taper-light
To seek the beauteous eye of heaven to
garnish,
Is wasteful and ridiculous excess.

Thus Twain and Warner saw their own era—an epoch of excess, of consumption not merely conspicuous but pornographic, as a "gilded age." It was an age of robber barons and political bosses; of obscene wealth acquired and disposed of in total disregard to "how the other half lives"; an age of industrial expansion at the expense of the land; an age of American imperial adventurism culminating in the Spanish-American War, annexation of the Philippines, and annexation of Hawaii, all in 1898. Most of all, Twain, Warner, and many others regarded the Gilded Age as an amoral epoch of exuberant political cynicism and chronic political mediocrity. As Senator and Republican National Committee Chairman Mark Hanna (R-Ohio) remarked in 1895, "There are two things that are important in politics. The first is money and I can't remember what the second one is."[5]

Having elected in 2016 a combination magnate and reality television star to the presidency—especially one whose signature show, *The Apprentice*, embodied the social Darwinism Andrew Carnegie defined in his 1889 essay "Wealth" (see page 86)—Americans may be forgiven for seeing the nineteenth-century Gilded

Age through a twenty-first-century lens. Both Gilded Ages are steeped in the same lily-gilding self-indulgence of what reality TV pioneer Robin Leach (host of the 1980s *Lifestyles of the Rich and Famous*) called "champagne wishes and caviar dreams."[6] But to go no further than visions of bubbly and roe is to do great injustice at least to the original Gilded Age.

True, Twain and Warner's novel is about the greed, excess, and corruption in post–Civil War America. True, also, is the hint that the "Gilded Age" was something of a pun on "Guilty Age," a period of American history criminal at its core and steeped in original sin. There is also the notion that it was an era marked by stark contrasts between insiders and outsiders and populated by a profusion of "guilds," as it were—monopolies, crony-capitalist cartels, political parties, labor unions, and other special interest groups, including lodges, secret societies, and a host of reform organizations. Those who could not identify themselves with any particular "guild" were the outsiders, the masses, the feckless victims.

Finally, it is also true that the most obvious connotation of a "gilded age" is that it must be a much-degraded imitation of a true "*golden age*." For Twain and Warner, the robber baron capitalist was a Midas whose touch was so shallow that it produced not solid gold but only a thin veneer barely covering the rot and corruption that had spawned it.

Twain and Warner were not mistaken

Andrew Carnegie was an impoverished child laborer in Scotland who became a ruthless industrialist in America. Having made his fortune, he gave most of it away to finance works for the public good. "The man who dies rich," he wrote, "dies disgraced."

about the age they named. But they hardly told the whole story. Pursue the metaphor of a *gilded* age further and you will find that, whatever its symbolic and moral implications, *gilding* is an artificial process, a means of transforming the world through human invention, industry, artifice, and will. In this sense, America's "Gilded Age" was an era of unprecedented creativity, not confined to a few extraordinary geniuses as in the Renaissance—an era popularly seen as a true golden age—but creativity disseminated to a burgeoning new American middle class in a kind of manufactured utopia, a demi-Eden predicted in the dazzlingly optimistic Centennial Exposition of 1876 (which we will cover in chapter 1) and in the World's Columbian Exposition of 1893 (chapter 15), an even more dazzling display.

In the chapters that follow, we will neglect none of the lurid negatives of post–Civil War America, but we will also celebrate the positives, the myriad inspirations from which our own beleaguered and materially unequal age may draw inspiration.

"America's 'Gilded Age' was an era of unprecedented creativity, not confined to a few extraordinary geniuses as in the Renaissance."

⬥

WAR IS USUALLY RUINOUS TO PEOPLES AND NATIONS, especially civil war, but the bloody conflict between the American North and South from 1861 to 1865 made fortunes and laid the foundation for even more fortunes to come. Although it brought devastation to the South, the war rapidly accelerated industrial development in the North, and it occasioned two great national initiatives. One was the opening of public lands in the trans-Mississippi West to settlement and development by the Homestead Act of 1862, and the other was the federally subsidized building of a transcontinental railroad by the Pacific Railway Acts of 1862 and 1863. All three pieces of legislation were demonstrations of bold faith in a nation torn apart by the biggest, costliest, bloodiest war in its history. The Homestead Act affirmed the American dream of property ownership in what white Americans thought of as "virgin land," quite disregarding the Native

Americans' age-old residence in the West. The Homestead Act also encouraged foreign, specifically European, immigration to the United States, and it opened up vast new markets for the fruits of American invention and industry.

As the Homestead Act began the transformation of the United States into a great consumer economy, the building of the transcontinental railroads, enabled by the legislation of 1862 and 1863, made western expansion practical, even as it stimulated American industrialization—which, by the 1870s, pulled far ahead of the original epicenter of the Industrial Revolution, Great Britain. The American railroads spawned many heavy industries and created a vast demand for coal that expanded coal mining, especially in the Far West.

Western settlement and western railroads drew domestic as well as international investments in American business. New York was added to London and Paris as a global capital of finance and soon eclipsed both European cities in this regard. Indeed, while America grew as an industrial giant, its growth as a center of capitalism—investment in industry, real estate, and banking—began to overshadow even manufacturing, mining, and railroad building.

"The business of America is business," President Calvin Coolidge would say in the 1920s. But it was much earlier, during the final quarter of the nineteenth century, that the business of American business had become, quite simply, wealth. This meant that "building" businesses was something more than a matter of brick and mortar. As great wealth became increasingly concentrated in a relatively few families during the Gilded Age, so corporations began to coalesce into massive and monopolistic "trusts" (see page 88), especially in the petroleum, steel, meat, sugar, and farm machinery sectors. The largest of these trusts were not only horizontal—a Standard Oil, for instance, gobbled up many smaller oil companies—but vertical as well. Standard Oil's John D. Rockefeller came to control the extraction, refining, transportation, and retail distribution of petroleum products, and his friend Andrew Carnegie, founder of Carnegie Steel, not only operated steel mills, but also owned the iron mines that fed them and the coal mines that fed the ovens, which processed the coal into coke to fuel the mill furnaces. Carnegie also invested in research and development to create advanced steel-making techniques, which were disseminated to Carnegie Steel managers and employees through classes conducted at a Carnegie industrial institute.

The great capitalists not only revolutionized the structure of corporations, they redesigned work itself. At the lower levels, factory workers were subject to training

Dubbed the "Smoky City," Pittsburgh was the center of the burgeoning American steel industry during the Gilded Age. This stereograph from c. 1905 shows a plant along the Monongahela River.

in efficiency, and their labor was closely integrated with specialized machinery, to which they were effectively subordinated. The era of the unskilled manual laborer gave way to the trained machine tender, even as the era of the craftsman gave way to the semiskilled factory worker. A new class of middle-management employees developed as well, many of them trained in engineering colleges, which began to appear across the country. America became a center of innovation and led the world in the creation of patents.

As the American economy grew during the 1870s and 1880s at the fastest rate in its history, the so-called robber barons[7] ruled over the working class sometimes ruthlessly, sometimes paternalistically, and, often, even philanthropically. Men like John D. Rockefeller, Andrew Carnegie, and Leland Stanford, ruthless in business, used a large portion of their wealth to finance vast philanthropic endeavors, including centers for medical research, hospitals, public museums and libraries, universities, opera houses, and other noble institutions. Yet they never abandoned the social Darwinism of nineteenth-century English philosopher Herbert Spencer, who transferred Charles Darwin's concept of the "survival of the fittest" from the realm of biological evolution to that of social development. Capitalism, Spencer argued, winnowed out the socially weak and elevated the socially strong, thereby justifying social stratification and inequality of wealth distribution.

The rise of the capitalist class did not go unchallenged. The Gilded Age saw the rapid development of large labor unions, beginning with the Knights of Labor, established in 1869. Strikes were frequent and sometimes violent, with violence directed by strikers against employers and, even more viciously, by employers against strikers. In 1886, a labor demonstration in Chicago's Haymarket Square was bombed, killing seven police officers and four demonstrators, and wounding sixty other people. On June 26, 1892, Andrew Carnegie's Homestead Steelworks in Pennsylvania was struck by workers protesting a wage cut. Ten days later, on July 6, a battle erupted between the strikers and Pinkerton guards hired by the company. Ten strikers and three Pinkerton operatives were killed, prompting Pennsylvania's governor to call out the state militia. The strike dragged on until November 20. On May 11, 1894, workers at the Pullman Palace Sleeping Car factory in Chicago went on strike to protest cuts wage cuts that had been made without reductions in rents at company-owned housing. Eugene V. Debs, president of the American Railway Union, called for a boycott on trains carrying Pullman cars on June 26, and violence related to the strike and the boycott resulted in some thirty deaths and fifty-seven injuries.

Along with strikes, Progressive activists and politicians moved to improve conditions for workers, increase wages, and regulate or eliminate child labor. In the meantime, immigration, which had been encouraged by both political and business leaders to stimulate westward expansion, was becoming an increasingly contentious political and economic issue. Workers were concerned that immigrant labor would "steal" their jobs by undercutting their salary demands. Labor interests lobbied for restrictions and quotas on immigration, even as many capitalists lobbied for liberalized immigration policies. In the big cities, the influx of immigrant labor led to the construction of cheap tenement apartment buildings, which, on the one hand, created culturally diverse and intellectually rich communities while, on the other, resulted in the development of unhealthy and sometimes crime-ridden slums.

Racial and ethnic discrimination became major issues in American life. Irish, Italian, and Jewish immigrants were often targeted for discrimination, as were African Americans. In the South, the end of post–Civil War Reconstruction in 1876 (see chapter 10), brought a racist backlash against freed slaves and their descendants, ranging from employment restrictions that created a permanent black underclass in the South to outright terrorism, as practiced by

The Carnegie Steel plant at Homestead, Pennsylvania, was the site of a labor lockout and strike that turned into a bloody battle between strikers and Carnegie's Pinkerton guards in 1892.

such groups as the Ku Klux Klan. Many African American working men and families migrated to the cities and factory towns of the North, where racial segregation was not decreed by law, but was nonetheless a fact of life.

The clashing interests of wealthy capitalists and struggling workers reshaped American politics, promoting both audacious corruption—which reached its height during the two-term administration of Ulysses S. Grant (1869–77)—and the ambitious reform initiatives of the Progressive movement. In the cities, machine government, run by political bosses, became rampant as the "spoils system" exerted a powerful hold on state and local governments. The bosses curried favor and exerted control by rewarding their faithful with lucrative government positions and government contracts.

> ## "We Do Not Ask for Sympathy or Pity. We Ask for Justice."
>
> —POPUPULIST PARTY
> BANNER, 1892

On the national level, the spoils system expressed itself in special interest lobbying and in political patronage. Paralleling this was the emergence of what many have called ethnocultural politics: party adhesion based on ethnic, immigrant, religious, and racial affiliation or origin. In 1891, the People's Party—sometimes called the Populist Party—was founded in Cincinnati, Ohio, mainly as an agricultural third party aligned against the two major political parties, the Republicans and Democrats. On July 4, 1892, the party nominated former Union general James Baird Weaver, an Iowan, for president, under a banner proclaiming, "We Do Not Ask for Sympathy or Pity. We Ask for Justice."

Four years later, the Populists endorsed Democratic agrarian candidate William Jennings Bryan, who spoke against the monetary gold standard and in favor of the coinage of silver in a move to increase the money supply and free up credit for farmers. "You shall not crucify mankind upon a cross of gold," he declared on July 7, 1896, to the delegates assembled at the Democratic National Convention. Bryan was defeated for the presidency by Republican William McKinley; however, the Populists would be replaced by the Progressive Party, which, in 1912, would nominate Theodore Roosevelt as its candidate. Before the Gilded Age came to an end, both Populism and Progressivism emerged as important forces challenging the political status quo.

———◆———

THE GILDED AGE SAW THE URBANIZATION OF AMERICA, but it also created a massive expansion of farming. Between 1860 and 1905, the number of American farms increased from two million to six million and the number of people living on farms during that time from ten million to thirty-one million.[8] Unfortunately, however, farmers were subject to the whipsaw effect of agricultural booms and busts, especially when demand for and prices of wheat and cotton would skyrocket, only to plummet during the numerous crises of economic instability to which the nation was subject during this period. Farmers'

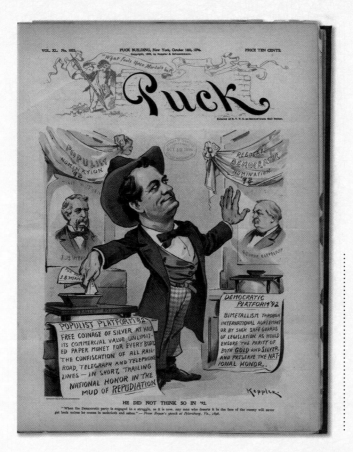

This *Puck* magazine chromolithograph depicts Populist apostle William Jennings Bryan, who, having electrified the Democratic National Convention with his "Cross of Gold" speech, won that party's 1896 presidential nomination, only to be defeated by Republican William McKinley.

troubles were compounded by the predatory freight pricing of rail carriers, who fixed prices among themselves to avoid competition and thereby were often in a position to gouge farmers in the regions served by a single railroad. Farmers responded by embracing mechanization of farming, which increased productivity while reducing costs, and, in 1867, by organizing themselves into the politically powerful Grange movement (a fraternal organization that still exists on a smaller scale today). The Grange successfully pressured Congress for passage of so-called Granger Laws, which set limits on railroad and warehouse fees. On February 4, 1887, Congress enacted the most sweeping piece of Gilded Age regulatory legislation, the Interstate Commerce Act, which required railroads to charge reasonable rates and barred them from granting "preferred" (that is, big and powerful) customers reduced rates.

Indian chiefs and U.S. officials meet at the Pine Ridge Reservation on January 16, 1891, in the aftermath of the Wounded Knee Massacre of December 29, 1890. Among those pictured here are Crow Dog and Short Bull, standing second and third from the left; standing sixth from the left is William F. "Buffalo Bill" Cody.

The Homestead Act of 1862 was followed by the Southern Homestead Act of 1866, the Timber Culture Act of 1873, the land rushes in Oklahoma in 1889 and the 1890s, and the Enlarged Homestead Act of 1909. Together with the expansion of the transcontinental rail lines, these accelerated white settlement in the West, triggering the so-called Indian wars, beginning in the late 1860s and culminating in the Wounded Knee Massacre in South Dakota on December 29, 1890.

Along with abuse of African Americans in the South and the urban North, the war against and the displacement of Native Americans in the West are tragic and shameful aspects too often glossed over in discussions of the Gilded Age, which typically focus on conflicts between labor and capital. In fact, the injustices committed against African Americans, Native Americans, farmers, and labor were all intimately related to the economic growth that drove the Gilded Age. It was this explosive growth that also contributed to the rise of American imperialism, yet another dimension of the Gilded Age.

The combined energy of capital and political ambition sought out new outlets for profit and power in the 1890s. On July 12, 1893, an obscure history professor from the University of Wisconsin rose to deliver a paper at the Art Institute of Chicago during the World Columbian Exposition. Based on his interpretation of the 1890 census, in which the United States Bureau of the Census had decided that it could no longer designate the boundaries of a western frontier by means of population statistics, Professor Frederick Jackson Turner announced that the frontier, the source of so much of America's distinctive identity, was now, in effect, statistically "closed." Although uniformly rejected by modern historians as a distorted and inadequate explanation of the early modern history of the American West, Turner's "frontier thesis," as it was called, not only made him America's foremost historian at the close of the nineteenth century, it profoundly influenced the way most Americans thought of themselves. It explained much about the popular mythology of the American West, and it suggests a reason why American political and business leaders turned from the West to lands beyond the North American continent to expand both nation and markets.

"What the Mediterranean Sea was to the Greeks," Turner told his Chicago audience, "breaking the bond of custom, offering new experiences, calling out new institutions and activities, that, and more, the ever retreating frontier has been to the United States." He continued: "And now, four centuries from the discovery of America, at the end of a hundred years of life under the Constitution, the frontier has gone, and with its going has closed the first period of American history." He argued that the expansive character of American life—"that restless, nervous energy; that dominant individualism . . . that buoyancy and exuberance which comes from freedom"—created by the frontier would not end with its closing. Instead, he asserted, "American energy will continually demand a wider field of exercise."[9]

Some of Turner's fellow historians called his "frontier thesis" the "safety valve" thesis. Anyone living in the Gilded Age, an era driven by steam power, would have appreciated the metaphor. Steam was a tremendous force—indispensably useful when properly managed, but catastrophically explosive when it was not. For this reason, all steam devices were equipped with a safety valve to relieve pent-up pressure before it became dangerous. In Turner's formulation, the frontier had served as a "safety valve" for the relentless energy of Americans. Now that this outlet was closed, where would the nation's expansionist drive find release?

Turner predicted that Americans would be impelled to undertake imperialist ventures overseas. Whether or not the frontier/safety valve thesis truly explains why the 1890s were indeed an era of American imperialism, the Spanish-American War (1898), the annexation of Hawaii (1898), the Hay-Bunau-Varilla (Panama Canal Zone) Treaty (1903), and the Roosevelt Corollary to the Monroe Doctrine (1904) pushed American national interest beyond U.S. borders. This, too, is a legacy of the Gilded Age.

<hr/>

ABOUT NINE O'CLOCK ON THE EVENING OF SUNDAY, OCTOBER 8, 1871, fire broke out in or near a barn belonging to the O'Leary family on Chicago's Near South Side. With astonishing speed, a conflagration tore through the city's masses of wood-frame buildings, and by Tuesday, almost four square miles (10 km²) of the city lay in charred ruins, at least 300 lives had been lost, and 100,000 Chicagoans out of a population of some 300,000 were homeless.

In at least one way, the Great Chicago Fire was the best thing that ever happened to a city widely condemned as a blighted example of careless, ramshackle growth, spurred by the industrialization of the Midwest. A "Great Rebuilding" followed the fire, and, fortunately for the city and the nation, Chicago drew on a cadre of remarkably forward-looking architects, including William Le Baron Jenney, John Wellborn Root, Louis Sullivan, and Dankmar Adler. These and others introduced the skyscraper, a distinctive American building type, to world architecture, along with the radically innovative steel-cage construction that made it possible. What is more, the work of these individuals was set in the context of a great modern urban-design plan masterminded by Daniel Burnham. Chicago thus became a showcase of unique and uniquely influential American architecture, arrayed along the magnificent shore of Lake Michigan.

A phoenix risen from the ashes, post-fire Chicago came to symbolize the creative energy that was as much a part of the Gilded Age as all its excess, conflict, and corruption. The innovative buildings were of a piece with American innovation in areas of applied technology. Alexander Graham Bell patented his telephone in 1876 and Thomas Edison filed for a patent on his incandescent electric light in 1879 (awarded in 1880). From these developed two national and global

A Gilded Age vision of the American city as a New World utopia—the World's Columbian Exposition of 1893 in Chicago. Most of the magnificent structures were built of "staff," a cheap concoction of plaster of Paris, cement, and a few other materials intended for the erection of temporary buildings and monuments.

economic and technological networks, the telephonic communication network and the electrical power grid. Other inventors, including George Westinghouse and Nikola Tesla, further established electricity as the basis of a whole new mode of civilization, and both industry and markets grew in ways unimagined before the Civil War.

There was an explosion of commerce in the high-tech Gilded Age, and consumerism rose as the principal driver of the American economy. Great department stores opened in New York, Philadelphia, and Chicago, along with humbler "five-and-dime" stores in towns and cities across the nation. Rural America was served by new catalog-based mail-order enterprises introduced by Montgomery Ward (1872) and Richard Warren Sears (1888). Despite growing income inequality, consumerism in the Gilded Age was the product of a rising middle class, and it shaped both personal economic aspirations and politics. The mass of

Americans had entered the Gilded Age as seekers of nothing more or less than the means of sustenance. Before they emerged from the era, they were dedicated consumers. As the nation crossed the threshold of the twentieth century, the products and the iconography of corporate America vied for mindshare with the traditional patriotic symbols of the republic itself.

This new American materialism was reflected in the art, literature, and philosophy of the era. In American literature, the decade prior to the Civil War—the 1850s—is often called the American Renaissance. It was an intense literary period that saw the rise of some of the nation's greatest authors and poets, including Ralph Waldo Emerson, Henry David Thoreau, Nathaniel Hawthorne, Herman Melville, Walt Whitman, and Emily Dickinson. Although they grappled with the realities of American life and life in general, they shared a certain

Mark Twain, second from left, celebrates his seventieth birthday in 1905 at New York's famed Delmonico's restaurant. With him (from left) are children's book author Kate Douglas Wiggin, his close friend Reverend Joseph Twichell, Canadian poet Bliss Carmen, authors Ruth Stuart and Mary Wilkins Freeman, author Henry M. Alden, and industrialist Henry H. Rogers.

romantic, often idealistic and even spiritual vision. The subsequent generation of post–Civil War authors, who came to dominate the Gilded Age, had a harder edge to their outlook. Such writers as Mark Twain—who gave the era its name— William Dean Howells, Henry James, Edith Wharton, and Hamlin Garland were unapologetically immersed in the material realities around them. Those who entered the literary arena toward the end of the era, including Stephen Crane, Kate Chopin, Frank Norris, and Theodore Dreiser, took the materialism to a more radical level, developing a distinctly American version of what such novelists as Honoré de Balzac, Gustave Flaubert, and Emile Zola had created in France. It was called naturalism, and it brought to literary realism the cool, sometimes brutal, rigor of scientific observation. Whereas the pre–Civil War generation had focused on spirit, the first writers of the Gilded Age concentrated on the material surface of things, and the later writers went even further. They clawed beneath the surface in search of the operation of natural law, a force indifferent to the sensibilities and sufferings of humanity. These writers produced memorable, dynamic, amoral, and even shocking characters as they delved into the phenomena of corruption, vice, disease, poverty, racism, and social violence.

The intellectually and morally challenging aspects of Gilded Age literature were matched by the emergence of a fresh vision in American visual arts. Painters such as John Singer Sargent specialized in the splendors of high society, whereas Mary Cassatt absorbed French Impressionist influences and turned them into a unique vision of domesticity. Others took visual art in bolder directions. Thomas Eakins and Winslow Homer developed intense, even dark, visions of the world around them with an aesthetic that sometimes paralleled the literary naturalists. James McNeill Whistler had ideas different from Singer and Cassatt as well as from Eakins and Homer. He sought to reclaim art for itself—"art for art's sake"—by producing what he called "compositions," which were to be appreciated less as renderings of external reality than as new creations that deserved to take their place in the world in their own right and on their own merits. Whistler opened the door, albeit just a crack, to abstract as well as the nonrepresentational art of the mid- and late twentieth century.

The technology, enterprise, architecture, literature, and visual art of the Gilded Age created a legacy of a new and distinctly American "realism." It has proved to be enduring and deep, rather than superficial or "gilded." For all the undeniable moral and physical ugliness of the era, the period from the end of the Civil War to the opening of the twentieth century produced some of the greatest intellectual and aesthetic monuments of American civilization. We need to appreciate these works, just as we need to accept that it was the injustice, exploitation, excess, and corruption of the Gilded Age that provoked and incited a generation of American reformers to launch the Progressive movement.

Acknowledge though we must that the Gilded Age is justifiably synonymous with political corruption, we must further recognize that this view, by itself, is far too simplistic and far too narrow. Still, there is truth in it, and the greatest political scandal of the many that characterized the era was the "stolen election" of 1876, in which Democratic Party leadership agreed to concede the disputed outcome of the presidential contest between Samuel Tilden and Republican Rutherford B. Hayes in exchange for Hayes's pledge to end the regime of post–Civil War Reconstruction throughout the South. Duly installed in the White House in 1877, Hayes kept his pledge, and African Americans were thereby relegated to persecution and second-class citizenship throughout the former Confederacy. While this situation endured until the civil rights movement of the 1960s, the Gilded Age itself produced foundational reforms in racial justice, including ratification of the Fourteenth Amendment (1868) and the Fifteenth Amendment (1870), as well as the Civil Rights Act of 1875 and the founding of the Tuskegee Institute in 1881.

The Gilded Age also saw the revolt of many American women against social marginalization and forcible confinement to the domestic sphere. This rebellion laid the foundation for what would emerge as the "women's movement" nearly a hundred years later. Indeed, the last quarter of the nineteenth century saw the rise of what some have called a "maternal commonwealth" of female reformers and female-led reforms. These ranged from the full flowering of the temperance movement, to the ongoing struggle for women's voting and property rights, to relief and uplift of the poor. The latter was embodied most dramatically by the settlement house movement organized by Jane Addams, who founded Chicago's Hull House in 1889. The maternal commonwealth unfolded within the context of the changing roles of women of all socioeconomic levels during the Gilded Age. Although feminist leadership was drawn chiefly from the upper, upper-middle, and so-called educated classes during the era, the rank and file of the growing movement was drawn from laboring women, both married and single.

Stereograph photo of President Theodore Roosevelt promoting the expansion of the U.S. Navy in a 1902 speech at Haverhill, Massachusetts.

As a political movement, Progressivism developed in opposition to the apparent triumph of an oligarchic class and an unholy alliance between government and big business in an unapologetic orgy of crony capitalism. Not since the American Revolution was an American political movement so thoroughly joined and led by nonpoliticians. It was crusading journalists, novelists, educators, philosophers, social scientists, and all-around activists who inspired reform among the political class. In the end, however, it was a great politician and political leader, Theodore Roosevelt, who finally transformed the Gilded Age into the Progressive era, the heyday of which overlapped the Gilded Age and went beyond it, spanning roughly 1890 to 1920. In one way or another, Progressivism endured to both influence and infuse American civilization through two world wars, the Great Depression, and the liberal movements of the 1960s. Today, as we embark upon what many are already calling a Second Gilded Age, it remains to be seen whether a new Progressivism will reemerge into political relevance.

A panoramic chromolithograph of the 1876 Philadelphia Centennial Exposition, built in the city's Fairmount Park—then and now one of the largest urban parks in the United States.

PART 1

PEOPLE AND THINGS

"Never before have the achievements of the industrial arts, the fine arts, and the sciences generally, shone with such lustre as gilds this epoch of the nineteenth century."

—J. S. INGRAM, *THE CENTENNIAL EXPOSITION, DESCRIBED AND ILLUSTRATED* (1876)[1]

Illustrated

Historical Register of the Centennial Exposition 1876

CHAPTER I

CENTENNIAL

It was officially called the International Exhibition of Arts, Manufactures, and Products of the Soil and Mine and was accurately billed as the first American "world's fair." Unofficially, it was known simply as the "Centennial," a title that reflected its origin in an idea presented to the mayor of Philadelphia in 1866 by John L. Campbell, a science professor at Wabash College in Crawfordsville, Indiana. He wanted to celebrate a hundred years of American progress on the hundredth anniversary of the Declaration of Independence, the founding document composed, debated, and adopted in Philadelphia's premier landmark, Independence Hall.[1]

Was the exhibition to be a patriotically pious, backward-looking centennial commemoration or a forward-leaning celebration of an American materialist utopia, an orgy of "Arts, Manufactures, and Products" versus a "Centennial"? From its inception, the Philadelphia exposition embodied two opposing purposes and visions. Campbell, a physicist with an interest in electricity, found a ready sponsor in Philadelphia's esteemed museum of science and technology, the Franklin Institute. Other early supporters, including members of the city's Republican political machine, were more interested in promoting Philadelphia's central role in the nation's

The cover of *Frank Leslie's Illustrated* historical register of the Centennial Exposition of 1876. Columbia, goddess of Liberty (symbolizing America in red, white, and blue) reveals to figures representing Europe, Asia, and Africa (plus a submissively kneeling Native American) the wonders of American industry, commerce, and government, on display at the exposition.

founding.[2] Both purposes drove the exhibition throughout its six-month run, and because it was simultaneously forward-looking and backward-looking, the Philadelphia Centennial provides a convenient portal by which we may enter the Gilded Age—an intense era of anxiety and uncertainty masked by blithe self-confidence. It was marked both by a longing for golden days gone by and by rapacious visions of a glittering future shaped by the thoroughly tamed forces of science, industry, finance, and empire. As the "Publisher's Preface" to *The Centennial Exposition, Described and Illustrated* crooned, "Never before have the achievements of the industrial arts, the fine arts, and the sciences generally, shone with such lustre as gilds this epoch of the nineteenth century. Being the fruits of prosperity and peace, and in our case certainly due in no small measure to the high civilization which our glorious institutions secure, they will be specially memorable to the American people."[3]

At a door-stopping 770 pages, *The Centennial Exposition* was no mere souvenir pamphlet, but an exhaustive description of the exposition, kicked off by a recitation of the historical context in which it appeared, starting with "The Exhibitions of Imperial Rome" and "The International Fairs of the Middle Ages" and going up to "The Vienna Exposition of 1873." All of this preamble was to show off the Philadelphia display as "the grandest and most complete" of all, the "largest in area, widest in scope, and the most numerously attended of all its predecessors," from ancient Rome onward.[4]

No flimsy souvenir, this guide to the Centennial Exposition was a hefty 770 pages and placed the Philadelphia fair in company with the "Exhibitions of Imperial Rome," among others.

The exposition tome describes the "principal buildings . . . erected for the Centennial Exhibition, beginning with the Main Building (with a floor space of 21.47 acres [8.6 ha] and a cost of $1.6 million), the Machinery Hall (1,402 x 360 feet [427 x 110m], built at a cost of $792,000), the Agricultural Hall (540 x 820 feet [165 x 250m], $300,000), and the Horticultural Hall (383 x 193 feet [117 x 59m], $252,937). "The most imposing and substantial of all the Exhibition structures," however, "was Memorial Hall [1.5 acres (0.6 ha)], built at a cost of $1,500,000 by the State of Pennsylvania and the city of Philadelphia." Here were displays of traditional fine art as well as "engraving and lithography, photography, industrial and architectural designs, models and decorations, ceramic and vitreous works, and mosaic and inlaid executions." The exhibition also featured a U.S. government building and, last though presumably not least, the Women's Pavilion, "originated and paid for by the women of America, and devoted to the exclusive exhibition of the products of woman's art, skill and industry."[5]

In all, the Centennial occupied 285 acres (114 ha) of Philadelphia's Fairmount Park. A massive Corliss engine, powered by steam, was not only the most

The great Corliss engine, apotheosis of the American age of steam power, was manufactured in Providence, Rhode Island. Not only was it the most popular attraction in Machinery Hall, but it provided the power for the entire exposition.

This stereograph shows the Main Building of the Philadelphia Exposition as viewed "From South East Tower Looking N. E."

popular attraction in Machinery Hall—perhaps even in the entire fair—but was also the source of power for the Centennial.[6] In addition, Machinery Hall also exhibited a dazzling array of highly specialized, American-manufactured, American-patented devices, from the mundane to the magnificent, including, the "Little Wonder" mechanical embroidery machine, shoe- and boot-making machines, large picture frames made by machines, sewing machines by Howe and by Singer, a machine for rifling gun barrels, type-casting machines for printing, the Lockwood Envelope Machine for "making envelopes by the million," gumming and folding machines for envelopes, lathes for fancy wood turning, silk-weaving machines, a giant grapple dredge for excavation, a pile driver powered by gunpowder, glue and other products made from industrial waste products, "florists' goods," decorative gas fittings, a sugarcane mill, a hydraulic cotton press, a pin-making machine, a wallpaper printer, a machine for cutting gears, a vacuum pan to clarify sugar, a steam-driven "tailor" to manufacture pants and other clothing, a giant stone and ore crusher, an "Archimedean brick-making machine," railroad car wheels, a Nevada quartz mill, a diamond stone saw, a diamond drill, a shingle-cutting machine, a belt-making tool, a band saw, a display of steam locomotives, Gatling guns, the Campbell rotary printing press, an exhibit of gold pens, an array of hardware and cutlery, screws, hand files and rasps, and a catalog of chemicals of all kinds and for all purposes. Fire engines were exhibited in abundance, as were hoisting apparatus, weighing machines, scroll saws, and adjustable miter machines. Rutland marble from Vermont, slate, Japanese paperware, and terra-cotta ware were all on display. Druggists' and perfumers' glassware could be seen, along with soda water fountains, "telegraphic apparatus," an electromagnetic mallet, and an electric burglar alarm.[7]

And so it went, exhibit after exhibit, with exhibitors demonstrating "their processes of manufacturing while also offering their products for sale."[8]

Beyond the glorification of innovation, technology, sheer productivity, and the evocation of a paradise for consumers, two additional elements figured prominently in the Centennial. The first was a celebration of consumer goods and their consumption. The second was "a desire to forgive and forget the Civil War."[9]

Housed in the Main Building, whose west end is depicted in this lithograph, was a dazzling array of manufactured goods, most of them produced by American factories.

WANAMAKER'S

Among the initial backers of the world's fair was John Wanamaker, proprietor of Oak Hall, a Philadelphia men's clothing store he founded with his brother-in-law in 1861, near Franklin Square. In 1876, Wanamaker relocated to the cavernous and lavishly ornate former terminal of the Pennsylvania Railroad. He renovated it, fitting out the building in the manner of two European precursors of the modern department store, Les Halles in Paris and the Royal Exchange in London. Wanamaker opened his "Grand Depot" just in time for the start of the Centennial. With its impressive size, vast interior spaces, and eccentric Moorish façade, Wanamaker's emporium was a monument to emerging American consumerism and was also a building that fit right into the world's fair cityscape. From a central circular counter, 129 counters radiated, each thickly laden with merchandise.

In 1876, the great iron network of American railroads was a symbol of limitless energy harnessed for industry, commerce, and the freedom of high-speed travel. How fitting, then, that Wanamaker transformed a great railway station into the Grand Depot, a veritable cathedral of consumerism. While the building was repurposed rather than new, Wanamaker made it a center of unique innovation in retailing. He commissioned advertisements so special that they were copyrighted (completely unheard of in advertising at the time) as well as rigorously factual (*nearly* unheard of among Wanamaker's contemporaries). Everything the Grand Depot sold was guaranteed in print, money back. Wanamaker even invented the price tag, which meant that customers no longer had to ask a cashier or a floorwalker about the cost of a contemplated purchase. Not only did the price tag increase transparency, it avoided potential embarrassment, helped make the sale, and subtly yet certainly discouraged time-consuming haggling. It was not that Wanamaker wanted to reduce contact between his employees and customers. On the contrary, he hired his personnel selectively and with great care. Criteria for a successful hire included appearance, poise, and courtesy. In an era in which workers were often driven, pushed, and even abused, Wanamaker paid top dollar, insisted that managers treat every employee with the utmost respect, created the John Wanamaker Commercial Institute (where employees could develop their retail skills), offered free medical care, and even maintained profit-sharing and pension plans. The innovative approach to human resources extended to technology as well. In 1878, the Grand Depot became the first department store to be lit electrically, and, a year later, it was the first to install telephones. To improve efficiency in the store's grand spaces, Wanamaker set up a system of pneumatic tubes to move cash, receipts, and other documents from sales floor to back offices.

The spectacular Grand Depot turned out to be but an overture to something yet more grand, the two-million-square-foot (185,800 m²), twelve-story Wanamaker's, completed in 1910 on the site of the Grand Depot building. It would be a literal cathedral of commerce, complete with a 28,000-pipe organ. The store is still a much-visited landmark today.

The Gilded Age saw the transformation of America from a nation of modest shoppers at the local general store to a country of consumers catered to by a new institution: the department store. Wanamaker's, in Philadelphia, was among the first such emporiums—and a prelude to much greater cathedrals of commerce to come.

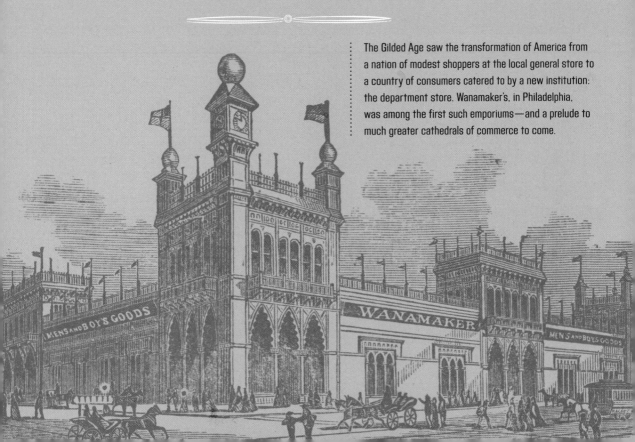

A HEALING GESTURE

The final element of the 1876 Centennial was a gesture rather than an exhibition. Those who staged the fair arranged for a grand meeting of one-time enemies—former Union and former Confederate soldiers—in Philadelphia, site of the nation's birth and, thanks to the exposition, epicenter of Gilded Age progress. In the planning of the Centennial, former Union generals, including Philadelphia native and Gettysburg victor George Gordon Meade, were awarded all the important positions on the United States Centennial Committee. Singled out for special honors during the opening ceremony were none other than William Tecumseh Sherman, Philip Sheridan, and Winfield Scott Hancock—with President Ulysses S. Grant officiating. Yet Confederate veterans were prominently featured among the ten thousand Civil War soldiers who paraded through the streets of Philadelphia on July 4, 1876. A special unit of troops from the thirteen original states were put under the joint command of former Union and Confederate generals as the Centennial Legion, and the former First Virginia Artillery, whose members had fought in every major Eastern Theater battle from First Bull Run to Five Forks and Sayler's Creek, marched by Independence Hall while its band played "Dixie."[10]

Although faded, this stereograph suggests the immensity and excitement of the opening ceremony of the 1876 Centennial Exposition, which sought to heal the nation a decade after the Civil War by inviting both Union and Confederate veterans to march in an opening parade.

The Centennial was not only the first world's fair staged in the United States, it was also unique not only in its message of commemoration and innovation, but of national healing. Watching Union and Confederate march together in a city sacred to the nation's birth, an observer could be forgiven for thinking that the Civil War was finally over, eleven years after Appomattox. Yet this closing chord of the celebration was not quite pitched in a triumphal major key. One month after the Centennial closed, the most closely contested presidential election in American history took place.

DEMOCRACY

November 7, 1876, was election night, and Lucy Hayes, wife of Ohio governor and Republican presidential candidate Rutherford B. Hayes, busied herself serving refreshments. She smiled, struggling to put the best face on what looked to be the certain defeat of her husband at the hands of Democrat Samuel Tilden. A parade of downcast politicos shuffled in and out of the gas-lit parlor of the governor's Columbus home. The family's closest friends remained, waiting, fidgeting, nervous until the final late-evening returns, which suggested that even the vote count from Ohio was not breaking the governor's way. At this discouraging news, Lucy kissed her husband, pleaded a headache, and climbed the stairs to their bedroom.[11]

In contrast to his somber guests, Governor Hayes appeared composed, even cheerful. Back in June, at the Republican National Convention in Cincinnati, he hadn't thought he stood a chance against Speaker of the House James G. Blaine. Hayes, solid and modest, paled beside the inexhaustibly orotund Gilded Age speechifying that gushed forth from the celebrated "Plumed Knight." It was a sobriquet bestowed by orator Robert G. Ingersoll, who nominated him at the Republican National Convention. "Like an armed warrior," Ingersoll declaimed, "like a plumed knight, James G. Blaine marched down the halls of the American Congress and threw his shining lance full and fair against the brazen foreheads of the defamers of his country and maligners of his honor."

Hayes had to admit to himself that no one would ever *think* of making a

> *"Hayes had to admit to himself that no one would ever think of making a speech like that about him."*

James G. Blaine, speaker of the House—hailed as "a plumed knight" who "threw his shining lance . . . against the brazen foreheads of the defamers of his country"—lost the 1876 Republican nomination for president to dark horse candidate Rutherford B. Hayes.

speech like that about him. True, he had served his nation bravely in the Civil War, and his governorship was free from the taint of scandal—no mean feat in the outrageously corrupt years of the Ulysses S. Grant administration. There was even a trace of outright reform about Hayes, but, mostly, he was careful to offend no one, and his overriding self-restraint bathed him in the bland light of harmless irrelevance. In the convention's first ballot, Hayes, not surprisingly, ran fifth in a field of six. After four more ballots, Hayes made a significant gain on the fifth. Yet he still trailed Blaine, as well as others. The sixth ballot threw more votes Hayes's way, but Blaine gained as well. And so, as polling for the seventh ballot began, supporters of Rutherford Hayes held out little hope for their candidate.

Despite its appetite for the fiery and the florid, the Gilded Age ultimately preferred its politics lightly seasoned, bland, even flavorless. For politicians on the make, there is a certain virtue in harmless irrelevance. By ballot seven, the Ohio governor began to look like an increasingly attractive prospect. After all, the Plumed Knight had recently been accused of having received $64,000 from the Union Pacific Railroad in return for worthless Little Rock & Fort Smith Railroad bonds. It was common knowledge that, as speaker of the house, Blaine was in an excellent position to help the UPRR, and, amid the cigar smoke of the waning evening, the whiff of scandal began to stink. As for the other prospective nominees, each had significant drawbacks. Oliver P. Morton of Indiana was ailing and, in any case, far too radical on the subject of Reconstruction, which meant that nobody anywhere close to the Mason-Dixon line would ever vote for him. New York boss Roscoe Conkling? He could barely walk for pants pockets bulging heavily with the spoils of Grant-era patronage and favor buying. There was always Benjamin H. Bristow, President Grant's current secretary of the treasury. His problem, however, was that the Republican machine, not to mention President Grant himself, despised him ever since he had exposed the infamous Whiskey Ring, a band of corrupt schemers who used U.S. revenue agents—the officials charged with enforcing the federal excise tax on liquor—to extort campaign funds from distillers. The final nominee, Pennsylvania governor John F. Hartranft, had done nothing wrong (or right, for that matter), but he *was* guilty of being from Pennsylvania. Since *any* Republican candidate would carry that staunchly Republican state, why waste a valuable nomination on Hartranft in an election predicted to be a close one?

As polling on the seventh ballot proceeded, the Indiana delegation chairman suddenly withdrew Morton's name and bestowed 25 of his state's votes on Hayes. Next, Kentucky withdrew Bristow from the race and gave Hayes all 24 of its votes. Buckling under the burden of scandal, the candidacy of Conkling could not hold onto a sufficient number of New York votes to prevail. Conkling had to settle for taking revenge on his personal and political enemy Blaine, who had once mocked what he called his "turkey-gobbler strut." Roscoe Conkling persuaded his state's delegation to cast 61 votes for Hayes, leaving only a die-hard 9 for Blaine.

Blaine, however, was not easy to eliminate. Pennsylvania, with 58 votes, was his native state. But that state's Hartranft champions withdrew their support from him and split their vote—30 to Blaine, 28 to Hayes—and when the polling was finally completed at 5:30 in the afternoon of June 16, Hayes had won his

The Republican National Convention of 1876 was rife with mediocre candidates who, typical of the period, stirred no enthusiasm and were tinged with corruption. In this cartoon, the whole group of potential nominees are tossed into a hopper: "Who'll come out first?"

> ## *"I still think that Democratic chances [are] the best."*
>
> —RUTHERFORD B. HAYES
> ON ELECTION DAY

party's nomination by a scant 5 votes. With that, he took on Governor Samuel J. Tilden, a conservative—or so-called Bourbon—Democrat, who had the support of the corrupt Tammany Hall Democratic machine, yet remained untouched by scandal himself. Tilden's ability to live in two worlds—conservative yet able to work with party bosses—made him a formidable contender, and Hayes consistently predicted that the odds were against him because the Democrats would resort to crime and bribery in the North and intimidation in the Reconstruction-era South to get their man into the White House. On Election Day, Hayes told a demonstrably optimistic well-wisher, "I still think that Democratic chances [are] the best," and when the news reached him after midnight that Tilden would probably carry New York City by 50,000 votes, Hayes ushered the last of his guests out the door and joined his wife in bed. The couple consoled one another with the shared thought that defeat would at least make their lives simpler, and they "soon fell into a refreshing sleep and the affair seemed over."

DAN SICKLES: A MAN FOR A GILDED AGE

As Hayes lay beside his wife in Columbus, at least one of his supporters, Daniel E. Sickles, was wide awake in New York City. He had spent the evening not in Republican National Committee Headquarters, but at the theater followed by a late supper. Only now, on his way home, did he drop by the all-but-deserted party headquarters. His lower leg, shattered by a cannonball at the Battle of Gettysburg, had been amputated in a field hospital. Sickles never quite relinquished the leg, however, but instead donated it to an army medical museum, where he is said to have visited it frequently. Now he settled into a chair. Taking the weight off his prosthetic limb, rubbing his knee, Sickles studied the returns.[12]

At first glance, the numbers seemed incontrovertible—final. The returns gave Tilden New York, New Jersey, Connecticut, Indiana, and the entire South. This meant that Samuel J. Tilden was the next president of the United States by a plurality of at least 250,000 popular votes and 203 electoral votes (185 being required for victory). But if Dan Sickles had learned anything from his own life, it is that very few things are truly incontrovertible and final.

For example, there was what he had done at the Battle of Gettysburg. A major general of volunteers, Sickles didn't like the sector that George Meade, commanding general of the Army of the Potomac, had assigned him along Cemetery Ridge. Without asking, he impulsively advanced his III Corps to Houck's Ridge and the Peach Orchard northwest of the two hills known as Big and Little Roundtop. This blunder not only exposed III Corps to attack, but laid bare the left flank of the entire Army of the Potomac. Confederate major general John Bell Hood hit Sickles hard through an area called the Devil's Den, and started caving in the Union's flank. Had it not been for the heroic intervention of the battle-battered 20th Maine, commanded by Colonel Joshua Lawrence Chamberlain, Gettysburg would almost certainly have been lost by the North and, with it, very likely, the Civil War. Had this happened, the finger of blame would have pointed with incontrovertible finality at Daniel Edgar Sickles.[13]

Daniel Sickles: serial philanderer, cuckold, murderer, Union general who almost single-handedly lost the Battle of Gettysburg, and a political fixer who masterminded the "corrupt bargain" by which the GOP stole the election of 1876.

But Chamberlain, months earlier a mild-mannered professor of rhetoric at Maine's Bowdoin College and a most unlikely military hero, led an even more unlikely charge against the Rebel attackers—unlikely because he was not only outnumbered, but also clean out of ammunition. Nevertheless, the day was saved, giving Sickles an opportunity to catch a cannonball in the leg, lose that leg, and be deemed a hero instead of face a court-martial. In 1893, he would even be awarded a Medal of Honor for the action.

If few expected heroism from a Joshua Chamberlain, no one had looked for it from Dan Sickles. A notorious boozer and womanizer, he was the target of official complaints that he had turned every one of his headquarters into a cross between a brothel and barroom. Of course, some people didn't complain about this at all. Agnes Leclerc, a Baltimorean who had starred in the circus as a trick rider before marrying Austrian Prince Felix zu Salm-Salm (he served as colonel of the 8th New York Regiment), recalled the festivities at a Sickles encampment near Washington in the winter of 1863:

I especially remember [a party] given by General Sickles, in a hall improvised from canvas by uniting a dozen or more large hospital tents in a convenient manner.

This immense tent was decorated inside and outside with flags, garlands, flowers and Chinese lamps in great profusion, and offered a fairy-like aspect. The supper laid under the tent for about two hundred persons, ladies and gentlemen, could not have been better in Paris, for the famous Delmonico from New York had come himself to superintend the repast, and brought with him his kitchen aides and batteries, and immense quantities of the choicest provisions and delicacies, together with plate and silver, and whatever was required to make one forget that it was a camp supper. The wines and liquors were in correspondence with the rest, and no less, I suppose, the bill to be paid.[14]

Indeed, few had expected that a man like Sickles would ever receive a brigadier's commission in the Union Army. But, then, he had friends in high places. Abraham Lincoln personally nominated him for a commission in September 1861, and the Senate indignantly rejected it. Lincoln caused some arms to be twisted and forced through a second nomination. Still, "a man like Sickles" was decidedly not the kind of man expected to ally himself with prim, proper, and blandly moderate Rutherford B. Hayes. President Andrew Johnson appointed Sickles military governor of the Carolinas after the war, but removed him because of the sadistic zeal with which he carried out the policies of Reconstruction. In 1869, under President Grant, he became U.S. minister (ambassador) to Spain, but was forced to resign in 1873 because he had become romantically involved with Isabella II, the deposed queen of that country.

And these were the least of his scandals. The first and most spectacular occurred two years before the Civil War, on February 27, 1859. The nation's newspapers would dub it the "Washington Tragedy." Although Sickles's career began well before the Gilded Age, he developed into an exuberant caricature of Gilded Age moral and political excess. Born October 20, 1819, in New York City, an only child, he was spoiled rotten—truly rotten. Educated in private schools, he attended New York University, obtained a law degree, and quickly concluded that his opportunities for greatest advancement lay in politics. He struck up acquaintances with movers and shakers like droopy-eyed, droopy-mouthed lawyer, labor activist, and future Civil

War general Benjamin Butler, who switched political parties whenever the spirit moved him, and with former president Martin Van Buren. It was such connections that ushered Sickles into Tammany Hall, the New York political machine, which won him election to the state legislature in 1847.

For the next few years, young Sickles earned a reputation as a man about town, never hesitating to push the envelope of propriety by frequently appearing in company with Fanny White, a notorious bordello madam. In 1852 at the age of thirty-three, he suddenly married Teresa Bagioli, pretty, pregnant, and sixteen years old. If this created even the whiff of scandal, in the corrupt era of Tammany Hall, it hardly mattered. The very next year, Sickles was named corporation council of the city of New York, the top lawyer in the city government. When James Buchanan, future president of the United States, was appointed ambassador to the Court of St. James's (the diplomatic title of the ambassadorship to the United Kingdom), Sickles pulled strings to obtain an appointment as his assistant, and he and Teresa were off to London. There they both became intimate friends of Ambassador Buchanan.

At length, Teresa grew to dislike England, and Sickles obliged her by returning to Tammany Hall. Uncharacteristically, he challenged the city bosses by championing the idea of transforming a large, shabby swath of Manhattan, occupied mostly by shanties and ramshackle farmhouses, into a magnificent city park. Central Park would be Dan Sickles's enduring legacy to his hometown. (He also hoped it would prove a real estate bonanza for himself, but that dream came to nothing.)

In 1856, the year voters elected James Buchanan president, they sent Sickles to Congress. He and Teresa rented a house on Lafayette Square, in the shadow of the White House, and the couple soon cut dashing figures in Washington social circles. *Harper's Weekly Magazine* proclaimed "Mr. and Mrs. Sickles . . . universal favorites; nowhere is there a more refined or generous welcome," and the New York Herald noted that Teresa Sickles's receptions were "always attended by the most presentable people in town." Among these was President Buchanan, of course, and one Philip Barton Key, a man of smooth wit and incredibly good looks.

Key was the son of Francis Scott Key, a prominent lawyer who served as district attorney in Washington from 1833 to 1841. During that time, he unsuccessfully prosecuted a would-be assassin of President Andrew Jackson, but lost to a defense attorney who, for the first time in an American court, successfully argued innocence by reason of insanity. Of course, Francis Scott Key is today far more famous for the verses he penned while he was detained on a British

Philip Barton Key (top), prominent Washington attorney, man about town, and son of the author of "The Star-Spangled Banner," slept with Daniel Sickles's wife, Teresa Bagioli (bottom), and paid for it with his life.

warship in Baltimore Harbor during the War of 1812. Key watched through the night as the British bombarded Fort McHenry, September 13–14, 1814, and, at dawn's early light, saw that the "Star-Spangled Banner" yet waved. Set to an old English tavern tune, Key's poem enjoyed immediate popularity and eventually became our national anthem.

Philip Barton Key studied law in Annapolis and, by means of his father's connections, became a prominent lawyer in Washington. By 1859, Key had three children of his own and was a highly eligible widower, his wife having died four years earlier. The combination of his social prominence, charming conversation, physical appeal, and widower status made him a sought-after dinner guest, and he was frequently at the table of Dan and Teresa Sickles. Sickles used his own influence to obtain political appointments for Key, and, like other busy congressmen, on more than one occasion he tapped Key to escort his wife to events he could not attend himself.

Between Philip Key and Teresa Sickles a friendship developed, which ripened into romance. The two were seen together more and more frequently. Eventually, Key began visiting Teresa alone in the Sickles house on Lafayette Square. At first they made love in the parlor of that house, but soon Teresa was stopping by the shabby apartment Key had rented on a squalid block that neither Dan Sickles nor anyone of his social station would be likely to stumble upon. The couple worked out a system. Key would take a window seat at his gentleman's club on Lafayette Square, which afforded a view of the Sickles house. When Teresa was ready to meet him at the apartment, she would signal with a scarf from the second-story window of the house. Key carried opera glasses in his coat, the better to watch for the signal. Key would then go to the apartment and hang a ribbon or string out the window to indicate that he was waiting.

Their assignations continued over the course of several months. For whatever reasons—perhaps he was simply absorbed in the hectic business of a nation on the verge of civil war, perhaps he himself was involved elsewhere, or perhaps he was just that thick—Sickles remained unsuspecting. Then, on February 24, a letter arrived at his Capitol office. Its author, known only by initials, has never been identified:

DEAR SIR WITH DEEP REGRET I ENCLOSE TO YOUR ADDRESS THE
FEW LINES BUT AN INDISPENSABLE DUTY COMPELS ME SO TO DO
SEEING THAT YOU ARE GREATLY IMPOSED UPON. THERE IS A FELLOW
I MAY SAY FOR HE IS NOT A GENTLEMAN BY ANY MEANS BY THE [NAME] OF
PHILIP BARTON KEY & I BELIEVE THE DISTRICT ATTORNEY WHO RENTS A
HOUSE OF A NEGRO MAN BY THE NAME OF JNO. A GRAY SITUATED ON 15TH
STREET BTW'N K & L STREETS FOR NO PURPOSE THAN TO MEET YOUR WIFE
MRS. SICKLES. HE HANGS A STRING OUT OF THE WINDOW AS A SIGNAL TO
HER THAT HE IS IN AND LEAVES THE DOOR UNFASTENED AND SHE WALKS IN
AND SIR I DO ASSURE YOU HE HAS AS MUCH THE USE OF YOUR WIFE AS
YOU HAVE. WITH THESE FEW HINTS I LEAVE THE REST FOR YOU TO IMAGINE.
MOST RESPFLY [SIC] YOUR FRIEND R. P. G.

For months, Sickles had heard rumors, and, for months, he dismissed them as rumors. But this letter was different. It named names, and it gave an address. The lawyer in Dan Sickles recognized evidence when he saw it. He asked his closest friend, Samuel Butterworth, to make some inquiries in the neighborhood of 15th Street between K and L. Butterworth reported that the rumors were all too true.

Sickles tumbled into profound depression, then reemerged just as quickly in fury. He stormed at his wife, who, terrified, wrote out a full confession on Saturday, February 26: "a true statement, written by myself, without any inducement held out by Mr. Sickles of forgiveness or reward, and without any menace from him. This I have written with my bed-room door open, and my maid and child in the adjoining room, at half past eight o'clock in the evening. Miss Ridgely is in the house, within call." On Sunday, Sickles invited Butterworth to his house on Lafayette Square. As the two talked, Sickles caught a glimpse of Key coming out of the gentleman's club across the square. In court, Butterworth swore that he left the Sickles house, ran into Key without planning to, and engaged him in conversation about the health of a mutual friend who happened to be a club member. Newspaper reports, however, claimed that Sickles had purposely sent his friend out to detain Key while he armed himself.

It was a mild day for February, more early spring than late winter, and many people strolled the square in front of the White House. All the witnesses agree: Butterworth and Key were talking when a third man, Congressman Daniel Sickles, ran up to them and shouted. Butterworth reported the words as these: "Key, you scoundrel, you have dishonored my house—you must die!"

With that, Sickles drew a revolver and fired. It is uncertain whether Sickles missed or the weapon misfired. Key's reaction was to rush Sickles as if to tackle him. But the congressman stepped back, drew a second pistol, and leveled it. Key backed away, taking, as he did so, something out of his pocket. He threw the object at Sickles.

It was a pair of opera glasses.

The congressman stepped toward Key and fired again. Key recoiled with the impact, staggered, then fell.

"Don't shoot me!" he cried, belatedly.

Sickles took out a *third* pistol, walked over to the now prostrate Philip Barton Key, and shouted—according to Butterworth's testimony—"You villain! You have dishonored my house, and you must die!"

He fired a third time, shooting Key in the chest, mortally wounding him. Some witnesses say he tried to fire a fourth or even fifth time. Butterworth, however, testified that, after shot number three, he took his friend by the arm and advised him either to walk up 16th Street to the home of the attorney general and turn himself in there or go back to his own house and wait for the police.

"Homicide of P. Barton Key by Hon. Daniel E. Sickles, at Washington, on Sunday, February 27, 1859." The murder stirred less public outrage than the murderer's willingness to take his wife back.

Still other witnesses claimed that Sickles pressed yet another gun to Key's head, but apparently did not fire it. All witnesses agreed that Sickles and Butterworth walked off together, and that Butterworth turned back to where Key lay and retrieved the hurled opera glasses. The two friends then called on the attorney general, to whom Sickles surrendered himself.

Sickles was jailed, comfortably enough, not in a cell, but in the apartment of the DC head jailer, there to await trial amid an avalanche of sensational publicity—almost all of it sympathetic to the act of an aggrieved husband against "the man who had dishonored his bed."

At trial, Sickles's attorney, Edwin M. Stanton, did not depend on mere sympathy, however. Stanton had earned a reputation as a brilliantly resourceful practitioner of the law—a profession he would later leave to serve as Abraham Lincoln's ruthless secretary of war—and he devised a boldly innovative defense. For the first time in American legal history, a plea of not guilty by reason of temporary insanity was entered. Remarkably enough, the jury was persuaded, and Daniel Edgar Sickles, incontrovertibly a murderer, walked out of court a free man.

That was one lesson in the nonfinality of finality and how even the incontrovertible may be controverted. The next lesson created a bigger scandal than the murder of his wife's lover: Dan Sickles took Teresa back. Her adultery and his act of homicide hadn't put an end to their marriage.

STEALING THE CENTENNIAL ELECTION

This, then, was the Daniel Edgar Sickles who contemplated election returns as he sat in Republican National Headquarters, after midnight, massaging his knee. To Hayes and to party chairman Zach Chandler, both sound asleep now, those returns seemed final. But what the wakeful Sickles saw was a steely glimmer of hope. The returns of far-off Oregon were not yet in. Of the Southern states, the returns of South Carolina, Florida, and Louisiana were not yet beyond salvaging. This, however, would require the application of some highly creative vote counting, but Sickles was confident that it would take very little prompting to elicit the requisite creativity from the Republicans who controlled the election boards in those Reconstruction-era states.

Sickles did not bother to send anyone to awaken Chairman Chandler. Instead, over Zach Chandler's signature, he himself sent telegrams to leading Republicans in Oregon and the three Southern states: "With your state sure for Hayes, he is elected. Hold your state."

None of the prominent Republican recipients questioned the meaning of orders to "hold your state" on the night *after* the election. They understood what was meant: whatever the count turned out to be, make sure it was in favor of Hayes.

By six in the morning, Sickles had encouraging replies from Oregon and South Carolina. Before he himself continued home and to bed, he sent another telegram to all four states. He worded this message in the language of the general he used to be, writing of "the enemy" who claimed victory and proclaiming that, with "vigilance and diligence, that enemy could be defeated yet."

With these telegrams, the nation plunged into an electoral crisis equaled only by the Civil War itself. The popular vote gave Tilden a 250,000-ballot lead over Hayes. Sickles persuaded his fellow Republican leaders not to concede. By contesting electoral votes in Oregon, Louisiana, South Carolina, and Florida, the disputed electoral votes could be delivered to Hayes. But it wasn't easy converting numerical defeat into numerical victory, and the resulting dispute raged

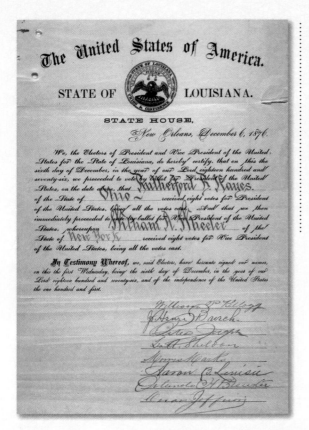

The United States of America.

STATE OF LOUISIANA.

STATE HOUSE,

New Orleans, December 6, 1876.

We, the Electors of President and Vice President of the United States for the State of Louisiana, do hereby certify, that on this the sixth day of December, in the year of our Lord, eighteen hundred and seventy-six, we proceeded to vote by ballot for President of the United States, on the date above, that Rutherford B. Hayes *of the State of* Ohio *received eight votes for President of the United States, being all the votes cast. And that we then immediately proceeded to vote by ballot for Vice President of the United States, whereupon* William A. Wheeler *of the State of* New York *received eight votes for Vice President of the United States, being all the votes cast.*

In Testimony Whereof, we, said Electors, have hereunto signed our names, on this the first Wednesday, being the sixth day of December, in the year of our Lord eighteen hundred and seventy-six, and of the independence of the United States the one hundred and first.

Republican manipulation of the vote in Oregon, South Carolina, Florida, and Louisiana set up the "corrupt bargain" that put Rutherford B. Hayes in the White House. Pictured is Louisiana's certification of eight electoral votes awarded to Hayes. The price of the "stolen election" was the abrupt end of Reconstruction and the opening of many decades of racial persecution in the states of the former Confederacy.

wildly. As the March 4 Inauguration Day neared without a president having been elected, there was talk of authorizing the current secretary of state to serve as interim chief executive. Many in the South had begun talking about secession and were already setting up rival governments.

Just two days before the inauguration deadline, Congress intervened by authorizing a bipartisan Electoral Commission. Seemed fair enough, but, while this was going on, lawmakers from both parties negotiated an entirely behind-the-scenes deal to decide the issue. What it came down to was this: The Democratic South would give the election to Republican Hayes in return for his solemn pledge to bring full home rule to the Southern states and an immediate end to the Reconstruction regime, especially the U.S. military–run state governments.

Since the end of the Civil War, shaking off the shackles of Reconstruction had been a single-minded goal throughout the white South. President Lincoln's assassination on April 14, 1865, brought into office Tennessee Democrat Andrew

Johnson, who was irascible, crude, blunt, and even uncouth, entirely lacking Lincoln's dignity, charisma, judgment, eloquence, and general political savvy. His implementation of Lincoln's liberal and lenient Reconstruction policies alienated Congress, especially the Radical Republican wing, which wanted to punish the South. The Thirteenth Amendment, abolishing slavery in the United States, was passed by the Senate on April 8, 1864, and by the House (after a fight) on January 31, 1865, and was ratified by the states on December 18, 1865. The Fourteenth Amendment, which defined citizenship to include blacks, was passed by Congress in June 1866 and ratified on July 28, 1868, although most Southern states rejected it. This rejection, along with a series of racist laws passed by Southern legislatures and relentless violence perpetrated against Southern blacks, persuaded a majority of voters in the North that the South was incorrigible. Furthermore, Johnson's refusal to yield to the Radical Republicans exacerbated the social and political gulf between North and South and tended to radicalize both Northerners and Southerners. The result was an overwhelming victory for the Radical Republicans in the congressional elections of 1868. Under their control, Reconstruction became an overtly military operation, with state governments administered by Northern military officers and enforced by federal troops. Some states were readmitted to the Union between 1868 and 1870, after each accepted the Fourteenth Amendment. Others were not readmitted until passage and ratification of the Fifteenth Amendment, guaranteeing the civil rights of the former slaves. As typically constituted under Radical Republican supervision, the civil governments of the restored states consisted exclusively of Republicans and included blacks (freed slaves, most of whom were uneducated and unprepared to administer or govern anything), "carpetbaggers" (Northerners who emigrated to the South to reap the political and material spoils of the restoration government), and "scalawags" (native Southerners who collaborated with blacks and carpetbaggers in government). These new civil governments were universally unpopular and were seen by Southern whites as tyrannically imposed upon them by the North. Resentment drove the creation of white-supremacist organizations, including the Ku Klux Klan (KKK) and the similar Knights of the White Camelia (the spelling was idiosyncratic), groups that terrorized blacks (and whites who collaborated with blacks), as well as the carpetbaggers and scalawags. In many parts of the South, the KKK and similar organizations functioned as shadow governments, bent on undermining Radical Reconstruction.

PUCK.

THE "STRONG" GOVERNMENT 1869—1877.   THE "WEAK" GOVERNMENT 1877—1881.

Puck contrasts the "strong" government under Reconstruction with the "weak" government of "Carpetbagger" Rutherford B. Hayes.

As he had promised the Democrats, President Hayes summarily ended Reconstruction and fully restored home rule as soon as he took office. The result of what was widely condemned as a "corrupt bargain" was the institutionalization of racial segregation and abuse of Southern blacks. Oppressive Jim Crow laws and "Black Codes" would endure throughout the South, in one form or another, well into the 1960s. The corrupt bargain that sent Rutherford B. Hayes to the White House was sometimes poorly disguised as an effort to "forgive and forget" the Civil War. It only succeeded, however, in widening the rift between North and South and deepening the bitter gulf between white and black Americans. As for Hayes, he was doomed to bear throughout his single term the mocking title of "His Fraudulency," which came to symbolize corruption and illegitimacy as the new American status quo. It was a dispiriting counterpoint to the innovation, economic progress, national building boom, and air of optimism that otherwise characterized the dawning Gilded Age.

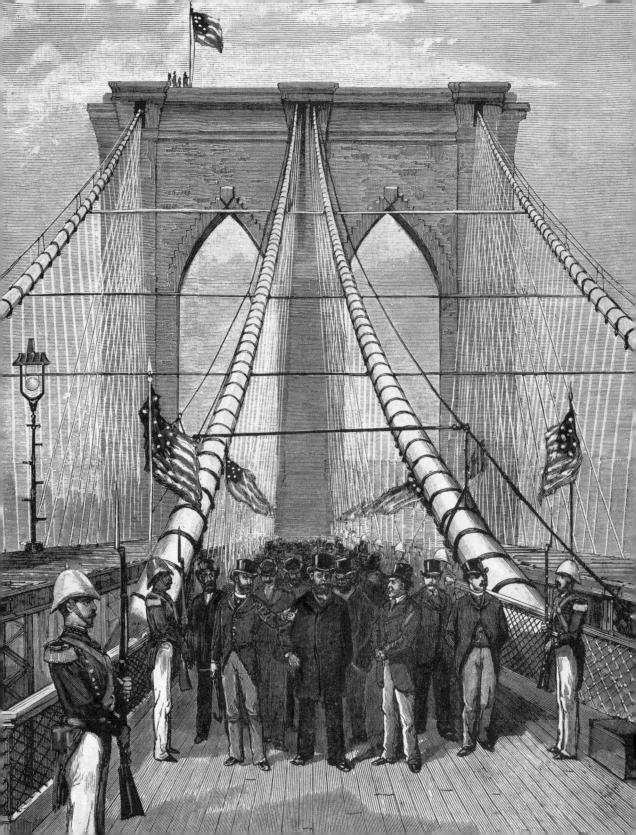

CHAPTER 2

THE DYNAMO, THE VIRGIN, AND THE BRIDGE

No American child ever came into the world with more of an insider edge than Henry Brooks Adams. Born in Boston in 1838, he was the descendent of two American presidents. His great-grandfather, John Adams, was not only the second U.S. chief executive, but also a central founding father and George Washington's vice president. John Quincy Adams—John Adams's son and the sixth U.S. president—was Henry's grandfather. Thrown into the mix was another great-grandfather, Nathaniel Gotham, who was a signer of the Constitution; a grandfather, Peter Chardon Brooks, who was a fabulously wealthy Boston merchant; and a father, Charles Francis Adams Sr., who was a congressman, Abraham Lincoln's ambassador to the United Kingdom, and the first biographer of his father, John Adams. Armed with this pedigree, young Henry matriculated at Harvard College, graduated, and then served his ambassador father as private secretary in London. After this, he launched his own career as the author of numerous works of history, including the epic and much-praised nine-volume *History of the United States*

President Chester A. Arthur and an entourage of dignitaries inaugurate the Brooklyn Bridge by walking across it on Opening Day ceremonies, May 24, 1883.

Henry Brooks Adams in his Harvard graduation photo.

During the Administrations of Thomas Jefferson and James Madison (1889–91).

His histories were highly respected and, for academic volumes, widely read. But while he was earning his public reputation as a historian, Adams quietly issued in 1907 a privately printed memoir with a title that befit its wry third-person approach, *The Education of Henry Adams.* Among the cadre of intellectual and political elite who obtained one of the one hundred copies, the book became a sensation, a sort of instant cult classic, and almost immediately after Adams died in 1918, at the age of eighty, *The Education* hit the commercial presses. Despite its esoteric content and tone, it was a best seller on publication and, ever since, has occupied a place on college required-reading lists for history, American civilization, literature, sociology, and even science courses.

The book's attraction? It put into words the unease and alienation of people living in a modern age, many of whom—even the privileged American classes—had come to feel that all they had learned was being made irrelevant by an environment transformed at incredibly high speed by science and technology. Take Adams himself. The world of 1838, the year of his birth, was moved by horses and lit by candles, kerosene lanterns, and gas. Samuel F. B. Morse transmitted his first telegram (across two miles [3 km]) just two months before Adams was born, but the telephone would not arrive until Alexander Graham Bell's patent of March 7, 1876, and the radio at the very end of the nineteenth century. Automobiles appeared, here and there, in the 1880s, but mass production did not begin until 1901 when Ransom Olds started turning out Oldsmobiles. Two years after that, the Wright Brothers flew at Kitty Hawk. While it was true that rudimentary forms of electronic communication, of automotive technology, and of powered flight made their appearance during Adams's adulthood, these were all outliers. The fact is that Henry Adams, like his early readers, came of age in an industrial epoch run on steam. It was a power source symbolized by the great Corliss engine featured at the Philadelphia Centennial.

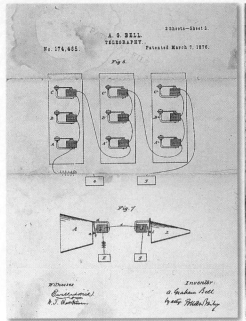

The title of the patent (above left), awarded on March 7, 1876, is "A. G. Bell. Telegraphy." It was, in fact, for the telephone, perhaps *the* breakthrough invention of the Gilded Age.

The mammoth Corliss engine (above right), which was a big hit at the 1876 Philadelphia Centennial Exposition, symbolized steam power, which drove just about everything in the last quarter of the nineteenth century.

AGE OF DISRUPTION

By 1876, steam power was impressive yet also ubiquitous and comforting in its familiarity. Everyone saw steam engines in action all the time. The force that powered them and thus drove the nineteenth century was visible and obvious and could be summoned up by anyone with a teakettle and a flame. All around, machines smoked, bellowed, whistled, and pounded. Americans were accustomed to this and proud of it, and much that was on display at the Centennial celebrated it.

Less apparent to most visitors to the 1876 exposition was evidence suggesting that this very year was a tipping point, a threshold, a passage between the familiarity of steam energy and the emerging mysteries of electric power. Already, on March 6, Alexander Graham Bell had patented his telephone. Within three years, on November 4, 1879, Thomas Alva Edison would patent his incandescent electric lamp. Between these two inventions, civilization-transforming

This Currier & Ives print illustrates the progress of the nineteenth century in four inventions—the "lightning" steam-powered printing press, the locomotive, the steamboat, and the electric telegraph. Three of these ran on long-familiar steam power, but the fourth—and most prominently featured—was powered by a mysterious new energy source: electricity.

industries and global networks would be created—and quickly, too—interconnecting vast populations for purposes of communication and the transmission of power. America's Gilded Age, simultaneously backward-looking and forward-looking, would witness this elemental transformation, even against a backdrop of intense moral, political, and economic disruption.

Henry Adams wrote his *Education* just after his life had crossed from the nineteenth to the twentieth century. With the crossing, this insider, whose career had been all about explaining the world by telling its story through history, realized he no longer understood the world around him. He focused on this personally felt disruption in the most famous chapter of his memoir. "The Dynamo and the Virgin" begins with a tour he took in 1900 of a world's fair that opened in Paris nearly a quarter-century after the Philadelphia Centennial. Adams was guided through the Exposition Universelle by American scientist and aviation pioneer Samuel Pierpont Langley, whom Adams called "the best-informed man in the world." Where steam energy—as represented

A stereograph of the Hall of Dynamos at the Exposition Universelle, Paris, 1900. Beholding the dynamo, a bewildered Henry Adams asked Samuel Pierpont Langley, "the best-informed man in the world," how the dynamo worked. Langley was at a loss.

by the mammoth Corliss engine housed in Machinery Hall and powering the whole 1876 exposition—was the star in Philadelphia, the dynamo, which transformed steam power into electricity, was the central artifact of the 1900 Paris extravaganza. Instead of a Machinery Hall, there was a Hall of Dynamos, and when Langley led Adams into it, the scientist admitted frankly "how little he knew about electricity or force of any kind." All he could manage was the glib explanation that (as Adams recalled) the dynamo was "an ingenious channel for conveying somewhere the heat latent in a few tons of poor coal hidden in a dirty engine-house carefully kept out of sight." Adams wrote that, until the exposition closed in November, he "haunted it, aching to absorb knowledge, and helpless to find it."[1]

The enigma set Adams to thinking. He looked back to English philosopher and statesman Francis Bacon (1561–1626), who "took a vast deal of trouble in teaching King James I and his subjects, American or other, towards the year 1620, that true science was the development or economy of forces; yet an elderly American in 1900 knew neither the formula nor the forces." Adams had "looked at most of the accumulations of art in the storehouses called Art Museums; yet he did not know how

Held in Paris in 1900, the Exposition Universelle brought nineteenth-century technology to a close and raised the curtain on that of the twentieth. Bearing witness was Henry Adams, renowned American historian, who struggled to understand the future on whose threshold he unsteadily stood.

to look at the art exhibits of 1900. He had studied Karl Marx and his doctrines of history with profound attention, yet he could not apply them at Paris."[2]

The message of the 1876 Centennial was equal confidence in the past and in the innovations anticipated in the future. Twenty-four years later, the generation that had been young during the Philadelphia fair could not even comprehend what was shown at the 1900 exposition. The sum total of the Gilded Age? Incomprehension.

Faced with mystery, Adams found himself resorting to religion:

> The dynamo became a symbol of infinity. As he grew accustomed to the great gallery of machines, he began to feel the forty-foot dynamos as a moral force, much as the early Christians felt the Cross. The planet itself seemed less impressive, in its old-fashioned, deliberate, annual or daily revolution, than this huge wheel, revolving within arm's-length at some vertiginous speed, and barely murmuring—scarcely humming an audible warning to stand a hair's-breadth further for respect of power—while it would not wake the baby lying close against its frame. Before the end, one began to pray to it; inherited instinct taught the natural expression of man before silent and infinite force. Among the thousand symbols of ultimate energy, the dynamo was not so human as some, but it was the most expressive.[3]

Steam drove the turbine of the dynamo, which generated electricity, yet Adams could discover no "more relation . . . between the steam and the electric current than between the Cross and the cathedral." Although in both cases, the "forces were interchangeable if not reversible," all he could discern was "an absolute *fiat* in electricity as in faith." When he turned to Langley for help, the scientist "seemed to be worried by the same trouble, for he constantly repeated that the new forces were anarchical, and especially that he was not responsible for the new rays"—a reference to the high-energy radiation the German physicist

Wilhelm Röntgen called X-rays in 1895 and that were emitted from radium, an element first isolated by Marie and Pierre Curie in 1898. These "new rays . . . were little short of parricidal in their wicked spirit towards science." For, as Langley saw it, "Radium denied God—or, what was to Langley the same thing, denied the truths of his Science. The force was wholly new."[4] Roughly between the two world's fairs, from 1876 to 1900, force had emerged as central to civilization. But there was a major difference. The physical force of the steam engine could be measured in the clearly comprehensible unit the Scottish engineer James Watt had devised back in the eighteenth century: horsepower. Steam power could be seen and heard and measured in terms of the work a good draft horse produced. This not only created understanding in a physical sense, it created understanding in an economic sense. People understood the value of a draft horse, the value of what it took to feed and shelter it, and the value of the work it could produce. Watt transferred this understanding to steam—and that understanding held firm in 1876. But by 1900, Adams "lost his arithmetic in trying to figure out the

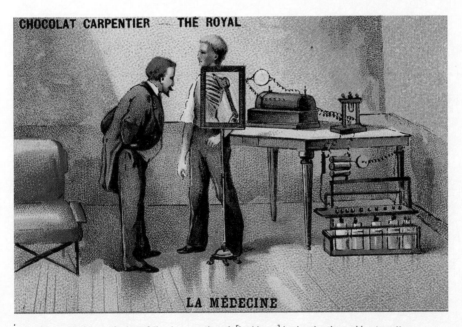

X-rays made Adams feel as if "his historical neck [had been] broken by the sudden irruption of forces totally new." The German-Dutch physicist Wilhelm Röntgen, shown here in a chromolithograph, discovered (and named) X-rays in 1895 and very quickly recognized their diagnostic value to medicine.

equation between the discoveries and the economies of force." Force was still central to civilization, but the meaning of that force, the new "economies ... were absolute, supersensual, occult; incapable of expression in horse-power. ... Frozen air, or the electric furnace, had some scale of measurement, no doubt, if somebody could invent a thermometer adequate to the purpose; but X-rays"—unlike the draft horse—"had played no part whatever in man's consciousness, and the atom itself had figured only as a fiction of thought." Between 1876 and 1900, mankind had somehow "translated himself into a new universe which had no common scale of measurement with the old." Adams felt that "he could measure nothing except by chance collisions of movements imperceptible to his senses, perhaps even imperceptible to his instruments, but perceptible to each other, and so to some known ray at the end of the scale."[5]

Henry Adams was a historian, which he defined as someone who "undertake[s] to arrange sequences—called stories, or histories—assuming in silence a relation of cause and effect." Standing in the Hall of Dynamos at the end of the Gilded Age, however, he found himself left with nothing but force, unmeasurable by any human being and without human or moral sense. He felt that "his historical neck" had been "broken by the sudden irruption of forces totally new." His former conception of human, moral, economic cause and effect seemed artificial and inadequate. Only force remained, and so, for the sake of understanding, he "made up his mind to . . . risk translating rays into faith." He recalled that when he "was a boy in Boston, the best chemist in the place had probably never heard of Venus except by way of scandal, or of the Virgin except as idolatry; neither had he heard of dynamos or automobiles or radium; yet [Adams's] mind was ready to feel the force of all, though the rays were unborn and the women were dead." He understood that the Virgin and the dynamo—religion, electricity, or X-rays—were "two kingdoms of force which had nothing in common but attraction. . . . The force of the Virgin was still felt at Lourdes, and seemed to be as potent as X-rays; but in America neither Venus nor Virgin ever had value as force—at most as sentiment. No American had ever been truly afraid of either."[6]

In force, Adams saw attraction. In the Middle Ages, religious objects and ideas and personages—the Virgin especially—drew and motivated certain portions of humankind, giving them direction, purpose, and a sense of both order and value. In

America, this degree of attraction to the Virgin and other such mystical religious symbols never quite took hold, but in the span of the last quarter of the nineteenth century—a span that saw his own maturity—Adams now realized that a new force had indeed seized the minds and hearts of his fellow Americans. It was the force of discoveries and devices that harnessed energy and "rays" hitherto unknown to produce light, heat, and motive force; a force that would move people to invent more and more devices to convert supersensual forces into an array of useful work, work for which men and women would pay money; a force that elected governments would use to their perceived advantage, willingly going to war against other peoples who would deny them the use of these forces; and a force capitalists would use to build great business enterprises that created wealth for the few while subjugating the many. In the past, religion—as mysterious a source of force as invisible electricity or X-rays—drove all these processes of history. In this new age, and nowhere more than in America, it was science acting through industry that seized and converted force into something compelling to human beings—something that made them labor; made them elevate some people and denigrate others; made them go to war, obey some, rebel against others, make sacrifices, and even sacrifice their very lives.

"In America neither Venus nor Virgin ever had value as force—at most as sentiment. No American had ever been truly afraid of either."

—HENRY ADAMS, *THE EDUCATION OF HENRY ADAMS*, 1907

There was no morality but force, Henry Adams concluded. Was it mere coincidence that this amorality would be, among commentators as diverse as Mark Twain and Theodore Roosevelt, condemnation of what Twain called the Gilded Age? Had he answered this question (which he did not), Adams might have said that it was no coincidence at all. On the contrary, it was an accurate analysis of what drove the last quarter of the nineteenth century in America. Having answered this way, however, Adams would doubtless have continued by pointing out that this state of affairs deserved no condemnation—or, rather, that it was as useless and meaningless to condemn the worship of the Dynamo as it was to condemn the worship of the Virgin. Both merely channeled force, and it is the nature, the property, of force, as any physicist knows, to attract and to compel.

The acts and monuments of the Gilded Age, though often clad in a veneer of righteousness as thin as gold leaf, were amoral but nevertheless irresistible. As the magnificent Cathedral of Chartres—an object of special study for Henry Adams—was the inevitable product of faith in the Virgin, so the telephone, the electric light, electric motors, and X-rays were the products of faith in everything the Dynamo represented. In both cases, force was the cause of the effects that defined a civilization at a certain time and place. What those effects were, at that time and place, depended on what force humanity felt drawn to worship.

Many living in late nineteenth-century America found it difficult or even impossible to reconcile themselves to this vision. For them, the Dynamo could never furnish the spiritual sustenance of religious faith. For others, however, the innovative spirit drove a new morality of social justice and social reform, as we will see in part II. Others found ample spirituality in the aesthetics of a new architecture (chapter 8) and new enterprise (chapters 3, 4, and 5).

A NEW AGE, A NEW VISION, A NEW BRIDGE

At least two men of the gilded age, father and son, found a way to build a Chartres for their own time and, like that sublime cathedral, for all time.

On May 24, 1883, New York mayor Franklin Edson joined Chester A. Arthur (who had become president in 1881 after a disgruntled office seeker fatally shot the elected president, James A. Garfield) in a procession from Manhattan to Brooklyn to inaugurate the newly completed Brooklyn Bridge linking the two cities. (The bridge was initially called the "New York and Brooklyn Bridge"; Brooklyn would not become part of New York City until 1898.) Thousands of New Yorkers and Brooklynites gathered to witness the walk, and cannons were fired in salute and celebration.

Conspicuously absent from the ceremonies was the forty-six-year-old builder of the bridge, Pennsylvania engineer Washington Roebling, who had become a semi-invalid, partially paralyzed and nearly blind, as a result of decompression sickness—what undersea divers call the "bends" and what a physician who treated those who built the bridge called "caisson disease." To build the underwater portions of the East River suspension bridge, workers descended into specially built caissons, massive chambers that were pressurized to keep out the river water and sustain the lives of the laborers. Unfortunately, the caissons—an untested innova-

New Yorkers celebrated the opening of the Brooklyn Bridge on May 24, 1883, the same way they celebrated American independence—with "fireworks and illuminations," as depicted in this Currier & Ives print commemorating the occasion.

tion—were insufficiently pressurized to prevent nitrogen gas bubbles from forming in the workers' blood vessels and tissues. As a result, some developed nothing more serious than joint pains and severe rashes. Some, like Washington Roebling, suffered paralysis, pain, and other neurological effects of varying degrees of permanence. (In time, Roebling recovered much of his sight and some of his mobility, but he contended with the lingering effects of the bends for the rest of his life.) Others died an excruciating death.

Washington Roebling sacrificed his health to the bridge. His father, John Augustus Roebling, a civil engineer trained in his native Germany, sacrificed his life. Born in 1806, he studied architecture and engineering in Berlin while also developing an intense interest in what was called at the time "natural philosophy." His curiosity produced a thousand-page manuscript on nothing less ambitious than the nature of the universe. In the 1820s, Roebling turned his attention to studying the architecture and engineering of suspension bridges, a field that was very new at the time. He and his brother Carl left Prussia for the United States in 1831, intending to establish a German utopian community in Butler County, Pennsylvania. The result was Saxonburg, but John Roebling soon abandoned utopianism to build canals and

Washington Roebling contended his whole life with the effects of "decompression sickness" caused by insufficiently pressurized underwater caissons used in suspension-bridge construction. A semi-invalid, he was forced to supervise much of the work from his Brooklyn Heights apartment, which overlooked the construction site.

survey routes for railroads. In 1841, he began manufacturing innovative wire rope to be used to pull canal boats, and in 1844 he adapted this technology to build a suspension aqueduct across the Allegheny River. The next year, he built a suspension bridge over the Monongahela at Pittsburgh. More suspension structures followed, and in 1848, Roebling founded a major wire-and-cable production enterprise in Trenton, New Jersey. In 1851, he began building a two-level combination railway and wagon suspension bridge over the Niagara River, completed in 1854. Its central clear span was a then-spectacular 825 feet (250 m). But just five years later, in 1859, he completed work on a 1,030-foot-long (314-m) bridge in Pittsburgh and in 1867, completed the magnificent Covington-Cincinnati Bridge, today called the John A. Roebling Suspension Bridge, which was at the time the longest in the world, with a main span of 1,057 feet (322 m).

Having established the suspension bridge as the solution to building across bodies of water previously too wide to span, and having established himself as the master designer-builder in this form, Roebling began planning the Brooklyn Bridge in 1867. His designs for the structure were approved in 1869, but on June 28 of that year, while surveying to determine the exact location of the bridge, his foot slipped between the dock on which he stood and an arriving ferryboat. His foot was badly mangled. After his toes were amputated, Roebling stubbornly refused further conventional medical treatment and attempted instead to promote healing by what he called "water therapy," which consisted of nothing more than continuously pouring water over his injury. He contracted tetanus and died on July 22, 1869, on a bed in the Brooklyn Heights house of his son, Washington Augustus Roebling.

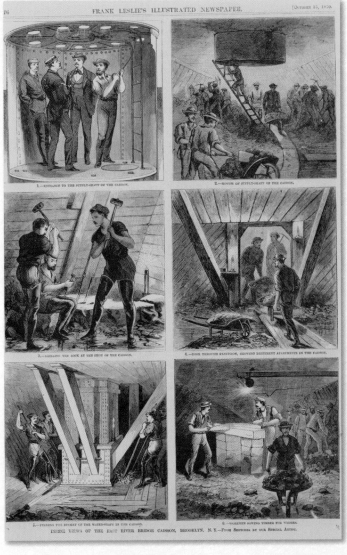

1.—ENTRANCE TO THE SUPPLY-SHAFT OF THE CAISSON.

2.—MOUTH OF SUPPLY-SHAFT OF THE CAISSON.

3.—DRILLING THE ROCK AT THE EDGE OF THE CAISSON.

4.—DOOR THROUGH PARTITION, SHOWING DIFFERENT APARTMENTS IN THE CAISSON.

5.—FILLING THE BUCKET OF THE WATER-SHAFT IN THE CAISSON.

6.—WORKMEN SAWING TIMBER FOR WEDGES.

INSIDE VIEWS OF THE EAST RIVER BRIDGE CAISSON, BROOKLYN, N. Y.—FROM SKETCHES BY OUR SPECIAL ARTIST.

Underwater construction was a new field when work began on the Brooklyn Bridge, and Washington Roebling designed the caissons—pressurized structures to shelter workers deep underwater—that made construction possible. *Frank Leslie's Illustrated Newspaper* featured detailed lithographs of life inside a caisson.

The junior Roebling had followed in his father's footsteps, studying engineering. At Rensselaer Polytechnic Institute in Troy, New York, his graduate thesis was a design for a suspension aqueduct. After graduating in 1857, he assisted his father on several projects until he enlisted in the Union Army during the Civil War, rising by gallantry in action from private to brevet colonel. At war's end, he rejoined his father and was appointed assistant engineer on the Brooklyn Bridge project. His father's death promoted him to chief engineer.

John A. Roebling had created the design for the bridge. Washington Roebling was left to build it. The project was an epic struggle among men, materials, and the elements. Crucial to its success were the revolutionary caissons Washington Roebling designed to make feasible the underwater construction of the foundations for the two great towers. Extraordinary though they were, the caissons were imperfect, and workers were menaced, injured, and killed by cave-ins, blowouts, and "caisson disease." Building the bridge cost at least twenty-seven lives and injured even more workers, some of whom were disabled for life. When Roebling himself was crippled by caisson disease, he oversaw construction from the very bed in which his father had died; his bedroom overlooked the building site. He relied on his wife, Emily, to serve as his in-person, on-site representative.

The product of Gilded Age vision, technology, optimism, and grit, the Brooklyn Bridge was also plagued by Gilded Age corruption, the worst instance of which was the criminal behavior of a supplier of steel cable who charged top dollar for inferior wire. When Washington Roebling discovered that at least some of the cables had been fashioned of below-spec wire, he responded by redesigning the cable system, adding many more strands to them to compensate for the substandard steel.

At the time of its completion, the Brooklyn Bridge was 50 percent longer than any other suspension bridge in the world, with a total length of 5,989 feet (1,825 m), over a mile (1.6 km), its longest single span measuring 1,596 feet (486 m). Not everyone had perfect faith in this expression of engineering and imagination. On May 30, 1883, less than a week after it was opened, a wild rumor spread among the throngs crossing the bridge. A frenzied warning that the bridge was giving way was conveyed across the milelong span, and a stampede began, resulting in a dozen deaths by trampling. A year later, on May 17, 1884, Roebling and others, anxious to build full confidence in the structure, induced showman P. T. Barnum to demonstrate the strength of the bridge by driving a parade of twenty-one elephants, including the legendary Jumbo, across the span. Not only was faith restored in the Brooklyn Bridge, Barnum succeeded in attracting record crowds to what he called "The Greatest Show on Earth."

The Brooklyn Bridge embodied cutting-edge technology, much of it invented expressly for this unprecedented structure. The very look of any large suspension bridge was ultramodern—and yet the towers from which the Brooklyn Bridge cables were suspended had been designed in the neo-Gothic mode, so

The Brooklyn Bridge was designed for pedestrians as well as vehicles. A stroll on its Promenade was as great a thrill and pleasure in 1900, when this photograph was published, as it is today.

that this monument to advanced engineering and high-speed commerce recalled the cathedral architecture that had so inspired Henry Adams. Formed of vision, genius, science, engineering, sweat, courage, and life itself—tainted as well by greed, graft, and corruption—the Brooklyn Bridge was also an expression of a new faith, a kind of secular religion. The technology of forces that scarred so much of the Gilded Age landscape with the grim artifacts and dismal living conditions of the Industrial Revolution had at last been channeled into an object with all the power and grace of a medieval cathedral dedicated to the worship of human ambition, aspiration, commerce, and wealth.

CHAPTER 3

TITANS, PLUTOCRATS, AND PHILANTHROPISTS

By 1859, the United States was disintegrating. Not that William Tecumseh Sherman was thinking much about this. His immediate problem was the need for a job. Since he had left the U.S. Army in 1853, his life had drifted. He struggled and failed as a bank manager. He turned to the practice of law and lost more cases than he won. So, when his old comrade-at-arms Major Don Carlos Buell told him a position was open as superintendent of the spanking-new Louisiana State Seminary of Learning & Military Academy in Pineville, Louisiana—set to open its doors on January 2, 1860—Sherman seized on it.

And everything started to go swimmingly at last. An Ohioan by birth and upbringing, Sherman nevertheless quickly adjusted to the new climate, surroundings, and people. At forty, when men of substance have already built comfortable lives, Sherman was just beginning to sense the prospect of financial stability. So, on Christmas Eve 1860, Superintendent Sherman was enjoying a collegial dinner with the institution's professor of classics—until a sharp knock on the door interrupted the two men. It was big news. The

In a *Puck* cartoon of June 1882, titled "Our Robber Barons," Corporations, Telegraph Monopoly, Railroad Monopoly, and Stock Jobbing waylay Tax-Payer and steal his Income, as Congress obligingly garrotes him with Unjust Tax.

state of South Carolina had just proclaimed its secession from the United States of America.

Sherman fixed wide, angry eyes on his dinner companion, David Boyd (future Confederate general and future president of what the Pineville institution would become, Louisiana State University) and said: "This country will be drenched in blood, and God only knows how it will end. It is all folly, madness, a crime against civilization!"[1]

There is no account of how the other man responded when Sherman pressed on: "You people"—and by this, he meant *Southern* people—"speak so lightly of war; you don't know what you're talking about. War is a terrible thing!" He pointed out most specifically that the South lacked the "men and appliances of war to contend against" the people of the North. "The North can make a steam engine, locomotive, or railway car; hardly a yard of cloth or pair of shoes can you make. You are rushing into war with one of the most powerful, ingeniously mechanical, and determined people on Earth—right at your doors. You are bound to fail. . . . If your people will but stop and think, they must see in the end that you will surely fail."

William Tecumseh Sherman, c. 1869.

Sherman would be proved right—mostly, but not completely. The South had men who were not only willing to fight but who were also very good at it. There just weren't enough of them. The region also had manufacturing, just not nearly enough of it. In the years before the war, South Carolina senator James Henry Hammond famously pronounced cotton "king of the South." And so it was. "King Cotton" claimed but a modest portion of farmland in southern North Carolina, but held sway over a broad swath in South Carolina and ate up most of Georgia, Alabama, and Mississippi. Nearly a quarter of the arable land in Tennessee was devoted to cotton, as was half of Arkansas farmland, a good deal of upper Louisiana, and most of the eastern half of Texas. The Florida panhandle was dotted with cotton plantations as well. A distant second behind cotton were three more cash crops: rice, tobacco, and sugar.

THE GILDED AGE

PICKING COTTON ON A GEORGIA PLANTATION.

The South's principal source of wealth, "King Cotton," was planted, harvested, and processed by slave labor. Without slaves, King Cotton would have been a pauper. This illustration is from the Boston periodical *Ballou's Pictorial*, 1858.

Cotton made the South's slave-owning planters wealthy, some fabulously so. They went about agriculture very differently from Northern farmers. Producers of food commodities, such as wheat, corn, and beef, the Northerners invested in farm machinery to facilitate production. The Southern planters put their money into more and more slave labor. By 1860, the average Northern farmer owned $0.89 worth of farm machinery per acre, whereas the average Southern plantation owner had just $0.42 worth. In the South, the demand for slaves drove up their price dramatically, making slave labor increasingly inefficient in terms of production costs. Northern mechanization, by contrast, made Northern farming highly efficient, which meant that the farmland of that region was more productive. This increased its value even more. On average, an acre of farmland was worth $25.67 in the North, but less than half that in the South, $10.40.[2]

Some in the South sounded the alarm, calling on planters to diversify investment to include mining, manufacturing, and railroad building. But the planters were loath to abandon what was for them—if not for the region—a very good thing. And so the South, a net exporter of the major slave crops, remained a net importer of manufactured goods during the years before the war. The North, in the meantime, made huge investments in industry, steamship transportation, railroads, and all the financial infrastructure that went with these things—banks, insurance companies, and speculative investment firms. Of the 1,642 banks and bank branches in the United States in 1860, 1,421—86.6 percent—were in the Northern states.[3]

As of 1860, the United States rail network consisted of 30,626 miles (49,277 km) of track, two-thirds of it in the North, even though the geographical area of the South exceeded that of the North by some 300,000 square miles (777,000 km^2). In that same census year, the South reported having roughly 18,000 manufacturing establishments employing 111,000 workers (white men mostly, since slaves were rarely employed in manufacturing), whereas the North had 111,000 manufacturing plants, employing 1.3 million workers. In other words, about 90 percent of the nation's manufacturing in 1860 came from the North, which entered the Civil War with a far more powerful industrial economy than the South.[4]

The South had the passion for a fight, but the North had the industry, the railroads, the massive population, and the financial resources to sustain any fight the South might bring. This watercolor by James Fuller Queen, c. 1857, depicts a Pennsylvania factory.

THE GILDED AGE

This print, published in Philadelphia shortly after the surrender of Fort Sumter in 1861, depicts the goddess of Liberty descending into the darkness of discord—a prediction of ultimate Union triumph.

For the North, this was a good thing, since the Civil War, which quickly developed into a conflict far larger and far more terrible than anyone (except perhaps William Tecumseh Sherman) had imagined, ran on the output of industrial technology. The North manufactured thirty-two times more firearms than the South—3,200 pieces to every 100 produced in the South. Although cotton was unquestionably king in the South, the North *manufactured* seventeen times more cotton and woolen textiles and thirty times more leather goods. This translated into uniforms, tents, haversacks, and army shoes—as well as goods for sale.

"The Civil War created conditions ripe for peacetime industrial expansion."

Northern mills turned out twenty times more pig iron than the South—pig iron for railroad tracks, for artillery, and for ammunition.[5]

So, the Civil War taught Americans a great deal about the power of finance and industry, and the war—mostly—stimulated the expansion of industrial capacity, at least in the North. Shoes and other leather goods underwent spectacular growth during the conflict, as did industries related to arms, ammunition, and the manufacture of wagons. Iron production actually slumped at the outset of the war, but exploded during 1863–64, rising to a level of production 29 percent higher than the nation's prewar record year of 1856. In mining, coal boomed, with production during 1861–65 rising 21 percent over that of the previous four years. It is true that the devastation of the South's cotton production hurt the North's textile manufacturing industry—but only in the area of cotton fabrics. The region's woolen industry soared some 100 percent in terms of production during the war.[6]

Of even greater importance than the rise in some areas of industrial productivity was the way in which the demands of war stimulated innovation and invention. Whereas some of the war's production demands did not outlast the duration of the conflict, the demand for new products and technologies never waned. Enduring wartime innovations included advances in machine-made interchangeable parts for manufacturing; the commercial development of Gail Borden's "condensed-milk" (patented in 1856), which became an indispensable ration item for Union troops; and improved weapons of all kinds. But dedicated wartime production also created pent-up demand for manufactured consumer goods, which stimulated industrial production and expansion after the war. During the conflict, the production of pig iron rose 10 percent, whereas from 1865 to 1870, the five years immediately following the war, the increase was 100 percent. During the war, output of American commodities increased 22 percent, but rose to a 62 percent growth rate during the postwar 1870s. The war also created pent-up demand for labor by discouraging immigration during 1861–65.[7]

In short, the Civil War created conditions ripe for peacetime industrial expansion. This was aided by postwar reduction in government regulation, a strong desire among soldiers-turned-civilians to make good lives for themselves and their families, a movement from farm to city, and a general channeling of energies from making war to making products. All these impulses boded well for the American economy; however, the assassination of Abraham Lincoln imparted a far less wholesome quality to the postwar expansion. Lincoln combined pragmatism with idealism to a degree matched by few political leaders before him or since. He committed the Union to total victory, yet he advocated a policy of Reconstruction designed to welcome the South back to the nation. His death meant that his enlightened leniency toward the former Confederacy was abruptly ended, and Reconstruction became the province of Radical Republicans intent on punishing the South and holding it in perpetual economic thrall to the North. As a result, postwar industrial growth and investment were concentrated in the North, and the South became a political pawn that acquiesced in political corruption on a grand scale. The failure of Reconstruction transformed the South into a region of racial oppression, which prompted many African Americans to migrate to the urban North and to laboring and industrial employment. The creation of a laboring underclass not only became a fixture of the Gilded Age, it also took on a racial cast.

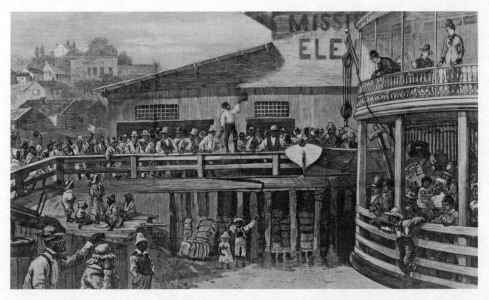

In the years following the Civil War, many African Americans migrated from the former Confederacy to the North, with its promise of better treatment and more plentiful and lucrative employment. In this illustration from 1879, hopeful migrants board a riverboat leaving Vicksburg, Mississippi, bound northward.

The Lincoln assassination had another impact on the nature of the Gilded Age. Lincoln the pragmatist did not hesitate to make bargains with profiteers and spoilsmen to advance the cause of victory during the war. He freely ventured into what today would be called crony capitalism. It was clear that such deal making was an expedient intended to win the war and that, come victory, Lincoln the idealist would have likely eclipsed his pragmatism. Of course, we can never know this for certain, but we do know that the absence of a strong and idealistic chief executive after 1865 and before the ascension of Theodore Roosevelt to the presidency in 1901 contributed to the unchecked rise of industrial capitalism under the regime of the robber barons. For all the glories of the Gilded Age, the period was marked by racial oppression—of African Americans, Native Americans, and others—by the devaluation of labor and the rise of industrial slums, and by the development of enormous income inequality. Moreover, while the period saw much economic growth—from which all classes benefited, albeit very unequally—it also endured two catastrophic depressions, one beginning in 1873 and the next in 1893, which caused profound social and political upheaval.

BARONS AND CAPTAINS

The makers of the Gilded Age got their start before the Civil War, but it was in the overheated post–Civil War social, economic, and industrial environment that the makers of the Gilded Age emerged. Both before and after the war, some celebrated them as "captains of industry," using a phrase that had been coined by the Scottish essayist and historian Thomas Carlyle in his 1843 book *Past and Present:* "The Leaders of Industry . . . are virtually the Captains of the World. . . . [I]f there be no nobleness in them, there will never be an Aristocracy more. . . . Captains of Industry are the true Fighters . . . Fighters against Chaos . . . and all Heaven and all Earth [say to them] audibly, Well-done!"[8]

However, not everyone saw them in so romantic and idealistic a light. On February 9, 1859, Henry J. Raymond, editor of the *New York Times,* wrote an editorial titled "Your Money or Your Line." It blasted Cornelius Vanderbilt, whose fabulous fortune was built on railroading and waterborne shipping—inland steamboats and seagoing steamships, a big enough fleet to earn him the nickname "Commodore Vanderbilt." Raymond detailed how Vanderbilt extorted

THE PROTECTORS OF OUR INDUSTRIES.

In this 1883 cartoon, the fat robber barons sit on piles of money and stacks of goods carried safely across the rough seas of "Hard Times" on the bent backs of the laboring masses.

large monthly payments from the Pacific Mail Steamship Company in return for his pledge not to compete in the California shipping business. He likened Vanderbilt to "those old German barons who, from their eyries along the Rhine, swooped down upon the commerce of the noble river and wrung tribute from every passenger that floated by." Raymond's comparison was to medieval German feudal bandits or "robber knights," called *Raubritter* by an early nineteenth-century German writer. After Raymond's article appeared, the term "robber baron," a loose English translation of the German word, caught on as a pejorative alternative to "captain of industry."[9] The epithet caught on and was broadly applied to an array of industrialists, financiers, and tycoons.

Whether you called them captains of industry or robber barons, their ascension, as a class of businessman, began with the railroads. After the Civil War, the American West offered huge vistas of unlimited wealth. Out there were ores: silver, gold, copper, and iron. The industrial machines needed to mine them were manufactured back East. Out there were cattle and wheat enough to feed even the millions of new factory workers back East who made those machines. The need, therefore, was to connect West with East. Those who did this could make their fortunes. So, railroads—acquiring the land for them, building them, and running them—became the first big business of the Gilded Age, the business that spawned the others.

Railroad magnates not only needed land; they needed laborers hungry enough to break their backs laying the tracks on that land. Making the tracks, first of iron and then of steel, was work for many other hungry men. Getting the land and hiring the men required money, and lots of it. As noted in the Introduction (see page 5), the Pacific Railway Act of 1862, enacted under Abraham Lincoln, had

THE GREAT RACE FOR THE WESTERN STAKES 1870

From 1868 to 1869, Cornelius Vanderbilt and James Fisk battled one another for control of the Erie Railroad and, with it, a monopoly of rail transportation in New York State. Vanderbilt sought to add the Erie to the two railroads he already controlled, the Hudson River and the New York Central, as shown here in this Currier & Ives cartoon of c. 1870.

supplied some of the money and some of the land, but it was in the corrupt climate of the Ulysses S. Grant administration (1869–77) that seemingly endless grants of cash and land were distributed. From across the Pacific came much-maligned and ostracized Chinese immigrants for whom railroading offered at least a chance to keep from starving. From across the Atlantic and the urban slums of the American East Coast came millions of Irishmen, eager for work of any kind. Loaded with land and flush with cash, the railroading robber barons had plenty of work to offer.

The train whistle was to early Gilded Age capitalism what the bugle call was to a cavalry charge. Everywhere, from the Mississippi to the Pacific, Eastern-built locomotives running on Eastern coal pulled more and more parts of the nation westward. For the rest of the nineteenth century, trains dominated the American imagination, politics, and livelihood.

In this environment of corruption, energy, and innovation, the likes of Jay Gould, Cornelius Vanderbilt, J. P. Morgan, Andrew Carnegie, John D. Rockefeller, and others built their empires and made their fortunes. In the name of efficiency, the industrialists among them introduced large-scale, specialized production in the place of earlier, decentralized methods and practiced "vertical integration," controlling not merely the manufacture and sale of a final product but also the raw resources the product required. The financiers among the group made massive loans that enabled industrialists to assemble massive trusts, or corporate conglomerates (see page 88).

In truth, one observer's captain was another's robber. Even to this day, to some, the names of many of the following men are infamous. And yet they drove the building of modern America, the nation that created

> *"Everywhere, from the Mississippi to the Pacific, Eastern-built locomotives running on Eastern coal pulled more and more parts of the nation westward. For the rest of the nineteenth century, trains dominated the American imagination, politics, and livelihood."*

A Currier & Ives print, titled "American Railroad Scene," 1874. The Gilded Age was the first great epoch of American railroading. Rail transportation tamed both time and distance, making it the foundational technology and industry of the last third of the nineteenth century.

R. ATWATER, Del.

ENTERED ACCORDING TO ACT OF CONGRESS IN THE Y

AMERICAN   RA

LIGHTNING EXPRESS TRA

AILROAD SCENE.

NS LEAVING THE JUNCTION.

the Gilded Age that took the nineteenth century into the twentieth, the era many would call the "American Century":

ANDREW CARNEGIE, steel magnate of Pittsburgh and New York

WILLIAM A. CLARK, copper king of Butte, Montana

JAY COOKE, Philadelphia-based financier

CHARLES CROCKER, railroad magnate of San Francisco

JAMES BUCHANAN DUKE, tobacco prince, Durham, North Carolina

MARSHALL FIELD, Chicago's genius of retail commerce

JAMES FISK, New York-based financier

HENRY MORRISON FLAGLER, oil, railroad, and real estate empire builder in New York and Florida

HENRY CLAY FRICK, steel magnate of Pittsburgh and New York

JAY GOULD, leading railroad developer and speculator, New York

EDWARD HENRY HARRIMAN, railroad magnate from New York

JAMES J. HILL, St. Paul–based fuel, coal, steamboat, and railroad magnate

MARK HOPKINS, railroad financier from California

COLLIS POTTER HUNTINGTON, California and West Virginia railroad man

ANDREW W. MELLON, financier and oilman, Pittsburgh

J. P. MORGAN, New York-based financier and industrial consolidator

HENRY B. PLANT, Florida railroad man

JOHN D. ROCKEFELLER, founder of Standard Oil, based in Cleveland and New York

CHARLES M. SCHWAB, steel man, Pittsburgh and New York

JOSEPH SELIGMAN, New York banker

LELAND STANFORD, railroad tycoon from California

CORNELIUS VANDERBILT, railroad and shipping tycoon, New York

CHARLES TYSON YERKES, builder of street railways in Chicago

Titans of the Gilded Age, clockwise from top left: Andrew Carnegie, c. 1913; Jay Gould, c. 1880; John D. Rockefeller, c. 1909; Cornelius Vanderbilt, c. 1860.

In their own time, bombastic apologists dubbed them industrial "statesmen" for enhancing and modernizing the American capitalist system, while strident detractors pointed to their indifference to public welfare and their ostentatious displays of wealth at the expense of their workers—living in huge mansions while their employees languished in urban squalor or bleak company towns. The reigning philosophy was summed up neatly in the phrase for which William Vanderbilt became infamous: "The public be damned!"

Surely this had seemed the attitude of William Vanderbilt's father, "Commodore" Cornelius Vanderbilt, who relentlessly built the New York Central into the largest single railroad line in America. Mark Twain, who thought him both rapacious and vulgar, excoriated him in an "Open Letter" published in the March 1869 edition of *Packard's Monthly:* "Most men have at least a few friends, whose devotion is a comfort and a solace to them, but you seem to be the idol of only a crawling swarm of small souls, who love to glorify your most flagrant unworthiness in print; or praise your vast possessions worshippingly; or sing of your unimportant private habits and sayings and doings, as if your millions gave them dignity."[10]

"The public be damned!" likewise described Jay Gould's attitude when he had used an unwitting President Grant in a scheme to manipulate the gold market in 1869 by indirectly persuading the president to suspend gold sales. Under Grant, the U.S. Treasury sold a set amount of gold each week to pay off the national debt—a heavy burden after the Civil War—and to stabilize the dollar. With his business partner James Fisk, Gould persuaded Abel Corbin, a financial speculator married to the president's sister, to introduce them to Grant so that they could obtain inside information on the gold sales, which would allow them to manipulate and corner the gold market. Gould convinced Grant that the gold sales were hurting Western farmers. Grant instructed Secretary of the Treasury George S. Boutwell to suspend sales, whereupon Gould and Fisk bought up all the gold they could lay their hands on, thereby driving up its price. Made aware of the manipulation, Grant ordered $4 million in gold to be released on Friday, September 24, 1869. Gould was foiled in his effort to corner the market, but Wall Street panicked and the gold and other financial markets crashed. It was dubbed Black Friday. In this crisis, the railroads—already ripe for disaster as a result of intense competition and a shaky economy—rather than go bankrupt, sold out to war profiteer J. P. Morgan. Morgan, who by 1900 would own half of all railroad track in America (his friends owned the rest), set exorbitant shipping rates across the country. His massive fortune grew even more massive.

John Pierpont Morgan—shown here at center, in a photograph from c. 1907—emerged from the Gilded Age as the archetypal American financier and banker, the dominant force in corporate finance as the nineteenth century turned into the twentieth.

It was Morgan who, in 1901, established United States Steel Corporation, to which Andrew Carnegie sold Carnegie Steel that year for $480 million (close to $13 billion in today's dollars) (see page 119). Confident that his steel company would be the core of a great vertical trust that would control every aspect of steel making, Carnegie had mocked Morgan's Federal Steel as "the greatest concern the world ever saw for manufacturing stock certificates," but predicted it "will fail sadly in Steel." In fact, Federal rapidly closed in on Carnegie Steel, whereupon Charles Schwab, Carnegie's number-two man and an unabashed advocate of business by monopoly, covertly met with Morgan to discuss selling him Carnegie Steel. Finding interest, Schwab next rendezvoused with Carnegie, who was golfing at the St. Andrews Golf Club in Westchester County, New York. The magnate finished his game, went home, slept on the matter, summoned Schwab, and handed him a slip of paper on which he had written "$480 million," his selling price. Schwab took the slip to Morgan, who said, "I accept this price." With that, U.S. Steel was born, and Andrew Carnegie became the richest man in the world.[11]

ANDREW CARNEGIE: BOBBIN BOY MAKES GOOD

Of all the men of business most closely associated with the Gilded Age, no one is more iconic than Andrew Carnegie. He was born in 1835, far from anything gilded, in a small weaver's cottage in the Scottish town of Dunfermline. The year

after his birth, the family moved to a larger house, thanks to a bump in the senior Carnegie's income earned as a weaver of heavy damask, suddenly much in demand for upscale upholstery and drapery. Andrew came of age in a backwater, but he benefited from a good elementary education in the town's Free School, the gift of a philanthropist named Adam Rolland. Although Rolland had died years before Andrew was born, Carnegie never forgot that the beginning of everything he knew about the larger world came because of Rolland's dedication to the public good.

The Highland Potato Famine, a blight that devastated Scottish agriculture beginning in 1846, brought the hardest of hard times when Andrew was thirteen. As the Highland economy collapsed, the demand for damask (and everything else) fell off sharply. Mrs. Carnegie eked out an income as an assistant to her cobbler brother and by selling potted meats. At last, in 1848, the struggling Carnegies, like so many other European families, sought relief through immigration to America. The four Carnegies—father, mother, Andrew, and his younger brother, Thomas—settled near Pittsburgh, where Andrew went to work as a bobbin boy, running from loom to loom in a cotton mill, replacing empty bobbins with full ones. His pay, $1.20 a week,

Andrew Carnegie (right) was thirteen when he and his younger brother Thomas were taken by their mother and father from a blighted Scotland, hard hit by the Highland Potato Famine, to the promise of America. The thirteen-year-old found work as a "bobbin boy" in a Pennsylvania cotton mill.

was vital to the support of his family, yet he still found time to devour works of history and literature at the local public library. A quick study, young Carnegie left the mill to become a messenger for the Ohio Telegraph Company, graduating to full-fledged telegraph operator after only a year. Now he became acquainted with a wealthy local businessman, Colonel James Anderson, who gave working boys like Carnegie the run of his impressive personal library. Many years later, Andrew Carnegie would dedicate a considerable part of his fortune to building public libraries in cities and towns across America.

In 1853, Carnegie became telegrapher/secretary for the Pennsylvania Rail-

In 1872, Andrew Carnegie and a group of investors built Pittsburgh's first steel mill, the Edgar Thomson Steel Works (depicted in this photograph, c. 1908), named after the president of the Pennsylvania Railroad. By the early 1890s, Carnegie Steel was biggest steel maker in the world.

road and rapidly rose to the position of superintendent of the Pittsburgh Division. In this position, he soaked up the lessons of managing a large organization, in particular the fine art of cost control. This knowledge would stand him in good stead throughout his career. At thirty, he left the Pennsylvania Railroad to start his own company, Keystone Bridge, which soon expanded from building iron bridges to operating iron and steel mills. In 1872, Carnegie and several investors built Pittsburgh's first steel mill, the Edgar Thomson Steel Works, named after the president of the Pennsylvania Railroad. Within two decades, Carnegie Steel was the biggest steel maker in the world, and Andrew Carnegie, bobbin boy from Dunfermline, found himself among the world's wealthiest men.

It was his sharply honed skill at cost cutting that drove him to the top. Invariably, he managed to underprice and outsell his competitors. But his efficiency came at a cost—to those who worked for him. Carnegie automated certain aspects of steel production, with newly designed overhead cranes to handle materials and with machines to charge his cutting-edge open-hearth furnaces. Although he hired more workers as demand for his steel grew, the modernized production reduced the need for *skilled* workers. His expanded mills relied chiefly on unskilled labor, from which he ruthlessly extracted every last ounce of effort. Their wages were the lowest in the industry, and Carnegie vigorously fought efforts to reduce his company's twelve-hour days to eight. It was an extreme example of what was nevertheless typical of late nineteenth-century American industrial labor. Owners willingly worked employees to exhaustion, if not death, and they did not hesitate to fire anyone who complained.

On June 30, 1892, Carnegie workers did more than complain. Since the early 1880s, the Amalgamated Association of Iron and Steel Workers (AA) had represented the skilled laborers in mills west of the Allegheny Mountains. After an 1889 strike at the Homestead (Pennsylvania) works, Carnegie and his management team determined that AA work rules inflated costs unacceptably. Moreover, relations between union workers and managers became increasingly belligerent, even toxic. Henry Clay Frick, an industrialist whom Carnegie had put in charge of his steel company's operations, resolved to break the union once and for all. This put Andrew Carnegie in an acutely uncomfortable position. Having grown up poor in a time and a place that routinely oppressed labor, he had publicly—and sincerely—proclaimed his support for unions. But his passion for efficient production now outweighed every other consideration. In preparation for the strike he knew would come when the current collective bargaining agreement with AA expired, Carnegie ordered a ramp-up of production so that there would be sufficient product on hand to outlast the impact of any work stoppage. The Homestead plant employed 3,800 workers, of whom only 800 were skilled men represented by AA. When the union demanded a wage increase for its 800 members, Carnegie decided to provoke a strike by directing Frick to counter not only

Strikers keep an eye out for trouble at the Homestead works of the Carnegie Steel Company during the great strike and lockout of 1892.

with a wage decrease (as much as 22 percent for many men), but also with the elimination of numerous skilled positions.

On April 30, 1892, Frick warned AA leaders that he would continue bargaining for just twenty-nine more days, after which Homestead Steel would cease to recognize the union. In a cynical show of good faith, Frick offered a token improvement in the wage scale, but the union did not back down from its original demands. On June 28, Frick imposed a partial lockout at the Homestead plant. This was followed the next day by a total lockout of union workers.

Homestead Steel became an armed fortress—"Fort Frick" it was dubbed—complete with barbed wire, sniper towers, and water cannon. On their side, the AA men, now reinforced by the huge Knights of Labor union and workers at other Carnegie mills, took steps to close the plant to *all* workers, skilled and unskilled. With both sides girding for war, Frick hired a private "army" of three hundred Pinkerton guards. This force assembled at the Davis Island Dam on the Ohio River on the night of July 5, 1892. Winchester rifles were distributed to them, and, on July 6, they sailed up the river in two barges. The guards disembarked at the plant, precipitating a pitched battle in which nine strikers and seven guards were killed before the Pinkertons surrendered.

Rioting in and around the town of Homestead continued until July 12, when Pennsylvania governor Robert E. Pattison dispatched eight thousand state militiamen to Homestead. Gradually, the militia quelled the riot, and strikebreakers began working at the plant. Over the next four months, Carnegie Steel lodged formal complaints against about a hundred strikers, many of whom (at the company's instigation) were arrested on charges of murder. Although most of the charges were subsequently dismissed and no one was convicted, the AA bled its coffers dry on legal defense costs alone, and the strike was officially called off on November 20, 1892. Carnegie Steel emerged victorious, which meant that workers continued to endure twelve-hour days for even lower wages. On the one hand, Homestead had demonstrated to the nation the determination of the labor unions. On the other, it showed that this determination had its limits.

The Homestead strike turned public opinion in two directions. Labor leaders and political reformers saw it as an occasion to condemn an unholy alliance between capital and government, whereas business leaders and many in the middle class condemned it as an instance of an arrogant labor union run amok. Only one thing was certain: the hard line between capital and labor, between big busi-

After homestead strikers and Pinkerton guards hired by Carnegie Steel fought a pitched battle on July 6, 1892, rioting spread to the town of Homestead, prompting Pennsylvania's governor to call in state militia troops, shown here in a *Harper's Weekly* illustration of July 23, 1892.

ness interests and the masses, had become that much harder, and men like Carnegie were put on the defensive. Four years before the Homestead strike, Carnegie had published in the *North American Review* an essay titled "Wealth," in which he acknowledged that the "conditions of human life have not only been changed, but revolutionized, within the past few hundred years. In former days there was little difference between the dwelling, dress, food, and environment of the chief and those of his retainers." In modern times, however, the difference between high and low was huge. Far from being inequitable, however, Carnegie argued that the "contrast between the palace of the millionaire and the cottage of the laborer with us today measures the change which has come with civilization." It is, he wrote, a change "not to be deplored, but welcomed as highly beneficial. It is well, nay, essential for the progress of the [human] race that the houses of some should be homes for all that is highest and best in literature and the arts, and for all the refinements of civilization, rather than that none should be so." There is, however, a price to be paid "for this salutary change" in civilization, and it "is, no doubt, great":

> We assemble thousands of operatives in the factory, and in the mine, of whom the employer can know little or nothing, and to whom he

is little better than a myth. All intercourse between them is at an end. Rigid castes are formed, and, as usual, mutual ignorance breeds mutual distrust. Each caste is without sympathy with the other, and ready to credit anything disparaging in regard to it. Under the law of competition, the employer of thousands is forced into the strictest economies, among which the rates paid to labor figure prominently, and often there is friction between the employer and the employed, between capital and labor, between rich and poor. Human society loses homogeneity.

The "law of competition" does create inequality, Carnegie conceded, "and may be sometimes hard for the individual," but "it is best for the race, because it insures the survival of the fittest in every department."[12]

"Survival of the fittest" became the rationale many so-called robber barons used to justify the social inequality on which their fortunes were built. This phrase summed up the doctrine of social Darwinism—the transfer of Charles Darwin's theory of evolution by natural selection (essentially, the survival of the fittest, best-adapted organisms) from the realm of biology to society. In the English-speaking world, the great proponent of social Darwinism was the British biologist/sociologist Herbert Spencer (1820–1903), whose works enjoyed a tremendous vogue during the 1880s and 1890s.

JOHN D. ROCKEFELLER AND STANDARD OIL

Perhaps even more emphatically than Carnegie, John D. Rockefeller (1839–1937) unabashedly embodied social Darwinism in business. The American oil industry was born in 1859, when Edwin Drake was hired by the Pennsylvania Rock Oil Company to investigate "oil seeps" on company-owned land. In 1859, Drake decided to drill the first commercial oil well along the banks of Oil Creek near Titusville, Pennsylvania. John D. Rockefeller, living in Cleveland, Ohio, took notice. Convinced that there was a great future in petroleum, he decided to get into this new oil business, and figured that his hometown was perfectly situated for building a major oil refinery. By 1862, he was in operation—and the refinery took off right from the start.

But Rockefeller kept looking forward. He envisioned more than a refinery. His ambition was to control all aspects of the oil industry, from extracting the raw materials through pricing and distribution. To that end, he formed a trust, the first and the largest in the country. A "trust" was a corporate conglomerate that put under unified management as many companies as were necessary to achieve end-to-end control of an industry. As Rockefeller saw it, the trust was the corporate organization "fittest" to survive and prosper in modern business. The reason was simple. A monopolistic trust crushed everyone and everything that got in the way of its growth.

A board of nine trustees ran the Standard Oil trust, managing the operations not only of Standard Oil of Ohio but also of the numerous smaller companies across America that Standard Oil gobbled up whole. The trust made ever-larger profits, which allowed Standard to undercut the competition by waging scorched-earth rate wars against them. The bigger the company got, the more power it wielded. Once again, success depended on the railroads. Rockefeller was big enough to demand—and receive—preferential freight rates and rebates from the main lines. He soon moved the headquarters of the trust from Ohio to New York City, where he could better manage relations with the nation's financial titans and from which he could, through a massive network of information gatherers and analysts, keep his fingers on the pulse of consumers and competitors alike.

The Darwinian rapacity of Rockefeller did not go challenged by reformers (see chapter 14), and, using the Sherman Antitrust Act Congress had passed in 1890, President Theodore Roosevelt directed his attorney general to bring suit against the trust with the objective of breaking it up. It was not until 1911, during the administration of Roosevelt's successor,

John D. Rockefeller, junior and senior, take a stroll in 1910. President Theodore Roosevelt invoked the Sherman Antitrust Act to break up the Standard Oil trust, but it was a Supreme Court decision in 1911, during the administration of William Howard Taft, that finally dissolved the trust into thirty-four companies.

THE GILDED AGE

William Howard Taft, that the Supreme Court—responding to a fresh wave of Progressive reforms—determined that Standard Oil was operating in violation of the Sherman legislation by monopolizing an industry and unfairly restraining free trade. The Court handed down a decision that ordered the trust dissolved into thirty-four companies.

THE GOSPEL OF WEALTH

Many considered robber barons like Rockefeller and Carnegie immoral or amoral or ruthless or just plain evil. Yet these men were hardly deaf to the public outcry against them. In fact, many of them devoted generous portions of their personal and corporate wealth to programs of philanthropy unprecedented in scope and enduring to this day. Such corporate philanthropy became as much a part of the Gilded Age legacy as corporate greed.

Both Rockefeller and Carnegie were among the leaders in nineteenth-century American philanthropy, along with J. P. Morgan, Henry Clay Frick, Leland Stanford, and, in the generation immediately following them, Henry Ford. Carnegie even wrote about it. In "Wealth," the same 1889 essay in which he defended the material prosperity of the captains of industry on the grounds of necessary and beneficial social Darwinism, Carnegie also proposed that the upper class of self-made millionaires like himself owed an absolute obligation to society to redistribute their surplus wealth not in family bequests, but in thoughtful, socially beneficial philanthropy. In 1901, when the essay was published with other Carnegie writings in book form, its title was expanded from "Wealth" to "The Gospel of Wealth."[13]

THE KING OF THE COMBINATIONS.

Rockefeller's Midas crown, depicted in this 1901 cartoon, illustrates the nature of the vertical monopoly or "combination." Standard Oil controlled not only the extraction, refining, and sale of oil, but also the very means of its transportation via a network of railroads in which he held majority shares.

"There are but three modes in which surplus wealth can be disposed of," Carnegie wrote. "It can be left to the families of the decedents; or it can be bequeathed for public purposes; or, finally, it can be administered during their lives by its possessors." Carnegie rejected the first "mode" as (among other things) "misguided affection" because "great sums bequeathed oftener work more for the injury than for the good of the recipients." He rejected the second mode, "leaving wealth at death for public uses," because it required that a person be "content to wait until he is dead before [his wealth] becomes of much good in the world." Moreover, the "cases are not few in which the real object sought by the testator is not attained, nor are they few in which his real wishes are thwarted. In many cases the bequests are so used as to become only monuments of his folly." This left the third mode:

> This, then, is held to be the duty of the man of Wealth: First, to set an example of modest, unostentatious living, shunning display or extravagance; to provide moderately for the legitimate wants of those dependent upon him; and after doing so to consider all surplus revenues which come to him simply as trust funds, which he is called upon to administer, and strictly bound as a matter of duty to administer in the manner which, in his judgment, is best calculated to produce the most beneficial results for the community—the man of wealth thus becoming the mere agent and trustee for his poorer brethren, bringing to their service his superior wisdom, experience and ability to administer, doing for them better than they would or could do for themselves.

In this mode of redistributed wealth, Carnegie wrote, "we have the true antidote for the temporary unequal distribution of wealth, the reconciliation of the rich and the poor—a reign of harmony—another ideal, differing, indeed, from that of the Communist in requiring only the further evolution of existing conditions, not the total overthrow of our civilization." If the wealthy do their duty, "we shall have an ideal state, in which the surplus wealth of the few will become, in the best sense the property of the many, because administered for the common good." The wealth of the individual, earned by being the fittest, and "passing through the hands of the few," Carnegie continued, can be made a much more potent force for the elevation of our race than if it had been distributed in small sums to the people themselves. Even the poorest can be made to see this, and to agree that great sums gathered by some of their fellow-citizens and spent for public purposes, from which the masses reap the principal benefit, are more valuable to them than if scattered among them through the course of many years in trifling amounts. . . . The laws of accumulation will be left free; the laws of distribution free. Individualism will continue, but the millionaire will be but a trustee for the poor; intrusted for a season with a great part of the increased wealth of the community, but administering it for the community far better than it could or would have done for itself.

"Thus is the problem of Rich and Poor to be solved," Carnegie triumphantly commenced the conclusion of his essay. Thus, too, is the problem of deciding whether the builders of the Gilded Age—men such as he—were robber barons or captains of industry. Anyone "who dies leaving behind many millions of available wealth, which was his to administer during life, will pass away 'unwept, unhonored, and unsung,' no matter to what uses he leaves the dross which he cannot take with him," Andrew Carnegie wrote. "Of such as these the public verdict will then be: "The man who dies thus rich dies disgraced."

Carnegie's greatest and most visible legacy to the nation that made him rich is the many public libraries he built and financed in the United States—1,759 in all. In this photograph from c. 1905, children read in the historic Pittsburgh Carnegie Library.

CHAPTER 4

SCIENCE AND INDUSTRY

"Is it a fact," Clifford Pyncheon asks in Nathaniel Hawthorne's 1851 novel *The House of the Seven Gables*, "or have I dreamt it—that, by means of electricity, the world of matter has become a great nerve, vibrating thousands of miles in a breathless point of time?"[1] Fully fourteen years after Samuel F. B. Morse patented his first system, the telegraph still felt sufficiently revolutionary to be portrayed as well-nigh magical. A little over half a century after Hawthorne, however, the Irish playwright George Bernard Shaw expressed quite a different point of view in two epigrams from his *Man and Superman*: "Those who admire modern civilization usually identify it with the steam engine and the electric telegraph" and "Those who understand the steam engine and the electric telegraph spend their lives in trying to replace them with something better."[2]

By 1876, the truth of the situation was this: The telegraph had been the last great electric invention *before* the Gilded Age and in 1851 it still seemed like a miracle. But at the very beginning of the Gilded Age, in that centennial year of 1876, Alexander Graham Bell patented "something better."

On October 18, 1892, Alexander Graham Bell himself placed a call from New York to Chicago, inaugurating the nation's first regular long-distance telephone service.

Patented in 1837 by Samuel F. B. Morse, the telegraph rapidly evolved into a civilization-altering communications technology. During the Civil War, it revolutionized both strategic and tactical communications between higher headquarters and front-line field stations. Pictured here is a Union telegraph station in Virginia in 1864.

In what way was Bell's telephone "better" than the telegraph? After all, telegraphy enabled virtually instantaneous communication, potentially in real time. True, there were delays created by the time it took to manually transcribe the electrical signals (the "dots" and "dashes" of Morse code) into more universally readable alphabetic language and numerals, and there was the time consumed in delivering messages from the telegraph office to the addressee. But in certain applications, communication was not only in real time but interactive, even conversational. A military commander at the front of a battle, for instance, could communicate telegraphically with higher headquarters in a rear echelon to report on conditions, ask for instructions, request reinforcements, or respond to orders. Indeed, during the Civil War, telegraph wire was run along the rope that tethered manned observation balloons to the ground, thereby allowing observers aloft to report in real time on enemy movements or the effect of artillery fire, so that commanders on the ground could adjust their tactics, and artillerists adjust their aim. Within years of its invention, the telegraph expanded into a vast network that one writer on the history of technology dubbed the "Victorian Internet."[3] Writers of the mid-nineteenth century were captivated by the notion of commu-

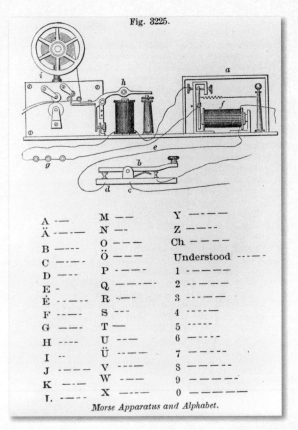

Fig. 3225.

Morse Apparatus and Alphabet.

Morse Code, which Samuel F. B. Morse began developing in 1837, the year of his telegraph patent, could be called history's first piece of software. Without it, the hardware of telegraphy would have been utterly useless. This 1877 diagram illustrates the Morse apparatus and key.

"Within years of its invention, the telegraph expanded into a vast network that one writer on the history of technology dubbed the 'Victorian Internet.'"

nicating via electricity, a force or phenomenon steeped in mystery and perceived to be so ineffably ethereal as to utterly defy physical reality. To be sure, using electricity, telegraphy actually did defy time and space, and when the "Victorian Internet" was vastly expanded from continent to continent via the submarine transatlantic cable, beginning in 1858, the degree of this defiance was almost beyond imagination.

Yet the telegraph had a major failing as a civilization-transforming technology. It offered an interface between machine and human that was greatly flawed and a poor substitute for face-to-face verbal communication. First, unless you were very wealthy or were a corporate or government entity, you could not afford to install a telegraph set in your home or place of business. You had to go to a designated telegraph office to send a message or you had to summon a messenger to pick up a handwritten message from you to deliver to that office. As for receiving a message, you generally had to wait for a telegraph messenger to deliver a transcribed hard copy to you. Second, telegraph technology required a great deal of human intervention in the form of professional telegraphers skilled at transmitting and receiving Morse code.

These two interface flaws imply a third, which is even more profound than the first two. Telegraphy was a system that required a lot of tending. Until the development of multiplexing, which allowed multiple two-way transmissions over a single line, messages had to be carefully scheduled for transmission, something that involved human judgment for prioritization and sorting of transmissions and replies. Telegraph lines were subject to interference over long distances. Transmissions were often garbled along the line. In addition, encoding analog messages into binary dots and dashes for transmission—and then, at the other end of the wire, decoding those binaries back into an analog message—required operators with considerable mental agility. Mistakes were frequently made. Because of the high incidence of errors, telegraphers continually weighed workload against speed against error checking to decide how much to retransmit to ensure a reasonable degree of accuracy. Under the best of conditions, operating telegraph equipment was demanding and fatiguing. This was exacerbated by error and retransmission.

In short, while telegraphic technology served humankind by coming close to eliminating the obstacles of time and distance, it also demanded hard labor from human beings. Yes, the machine performed useful work, but that work also required skilled personnel to devote their time, attention, and training to serving the machine. Indeed, such service was also demanded from customers. Telegrams were not cheap. Charges were assessed by the word, with an allowed maximum of fifteen characters per word for a "plain-language" telegram and ten per word for telegrams written in code. Customers were therefore compelled to adapt their style of expression to the demands of the whole electromechanical system.

So the telephone definitely offered "something better."

While the telegraph generated dots and dashes—mere electromechanical noise—the telephone carried nothing less amazing and expressive than the human voice. Why is this difference important? Unlike the fairly labor-intensive telegraph, the telephone put technology almost *entirely* at the service of human

Human operators seated at telephone switchboards were originally required to make all call-to-call connections. The profession became an iconic and much-respected source of employment for women, mostly young and unmarried. Here, a Bell office in Hamburg, New York, c. 1905.

beings. Instead of people serving a machine, it was a machine serving people. Interpreting the human voice requires no special training, talent, or skill. You don't even need to know how to read. Moreover, because no operator was required at the receiving end—no need for someone schooled and skilled in translating binary signals into analog language—the telephone was a technology easily adapted to any office, any home, any room, any place.

Think ahead for a moment, to August 12, 1981, when IBM released its model 5150 desktop computer. This was the machine they called the PC, the *personal* computer. Not long before, all computers were huge machines housed in dedicated, specially

"*Instead of people serving a machine, it was a machine serving people.*"

air-conditioned rooms that were staffed by technicians even more highly trained than telegraphers back in the nineteenth century. On August 12, 1981, however, computers became "personal," in that anyone with an office desk or a kitchen table and an electrical outlet could own and operate one. What the IBM PC did for computing, Bell had done for telecommunications 105 years earlier. His master telephone patent no. 174465 (March 7, 1876)[4] should be regarded as the first major, even iconic, invention of the Gilded Age because it made high technology accessible to ordinary people, and putting machines at the service of people would be the direction of science and industry in this era—provided that, by "people," you meant customers, or consumers. To mass-produce these new machines as consumer products required workers who, in return for a paycheck, meekly subordinated themselves to an array of automated machines, the most consequential of which was the assembly line. This was one of the paradoxes of the Gilded Age. It was the first great era of American consumerism. It opened a vast consumer culture, an age in which marvelous machines served anyone who could afford to buy them. At the same time, consumerism created a tremendous demand for unskilled, low-paid labor to tend, in the capacity of wage slaves, the machines that produced the machines.

ALEXANDER GRAHAM BELL'S "HISTORIC SHOUT"

Histories describe Alexander Graham Bell as an inventor, scientist, and engineer. Both by education and vocation, however, he was none of these. Born in Edinburgh, Scotland, in 1847, he was the son and grandson of pioneers in the field of elocution, with emphasis on working with what were then called "deaf-mutes," people with severe hearing and speech impairment. Bell, whose mother was deaf, followed in the family profession, becoming an elocutionist and a teacher of the deaf and speech-impaired as well as a student of both the physiology of speech and of acoustical physics. While studying the physiology and acoustics of speech, he experimented with the use of tuning forks to convert sound into electrical signals. He pursued this work with the thought that the musical tones of tuning forks were similar to the vowel sounds of speech. He reasoned that if he could convert tones to electrical signals, he could convert vowel sounds as well. If he could produce vowel sounds electrically, why not consonants? And if both vowels and consonants could be produced electrically, they could be transmitted electrically.

While Bell experimented, he supported himself as an elocutionist and as a tutor

Self-educated as a scientist and engineer, Alexander Graham Bell was by training and profession a teacher of elocution who specialized in helping the hearing-disabled communicate. Bell (the dark-bearded man in the center of the back row) poses with the students and teachers of the Scott Circle School for deaf children, Washington, DC, 1883.

to hearing- and speech-impaired clients in London, where his family had moved. When he was twenty-three, he moved from the UK to Canada, where he used a system of "visible speech" (developed by his father) to transcribe the previously unwritten language of the Mohawks. In 1871, he moved to Boston, Massachusetts, to introduce visible speech to instructors and students at the Boston School for Deaf Mutes. But Bell never abandoned his tuning-fork experiments, which he now struggled to transform into a practical invention he called the "harmonic telegraph." The device was intended to allow the transmission of multiple telegraph messages over a single wire by tuning each message to a different pitch. While pursuing this work, he opened his own School of Vocal Physiology and Mechanics of Speech in Boston, which drew many deaf students, including the young Helen Keller.

In 1873, Bell was appointed professor of vocal physiology and elocution at Boston University, yet even as his academic and clinical stature rose, he became increasingly consumed by his experiments in the electrical transmission of sound and harmonic telegraphy. He gave up what had become a lucrative teaching career, retaining just two private students: a profoundly deaf boy who could not speak and Mabel Hubbard, a young deaf woman he would later marry and whose father, Gardiner Greene Hubbard, a lawyer and financier, would become one of the founders of the Bell Telephone Company. This was the pattern of Bell's early career, which combined work with people in need, science, and invention.

Learning that Western Union was intensely interested in the development of a multiplexing telegraphy system capable of sending multiple messages over a single wire, Gardiner Hubbard and another backer, Thomas Sanders, agreed to finance Bell's work and to fund the hiring of an assistant, Thomas A. Watson, who was a skilled electrical technician. Bell's latest version of the harmonic telegraph used tuned reeds, one of which, on June 2, 1875, Watson accidentally plucked while working on the transmitter. Bell, stationed at the receiver in the next room, distinctly heard the reed's overtones through the device. What flashed through his mind was that the electrical transmission of speech was neither more nor less than the electrical transmission of overtones. At the moment, he had a viable harmonic telegraph, which he now called an "acoustic telegraph," and immediately filed a patent application. At the same time, he moved ahead on a patent for what he described as a "method of, and apparatus for, transmitting vocal or other sounds telegraphically." This patent was issued on March 7, 1876, and three days later, he refined his device by using not a vibrating metal diaphragm to transmit speech, but a more sensitive liquid transmitter. "I then shouted into M [the mouthpiece] the following sentence," Bell recorded in his notebook on March 10:

> "Mr. Watson, come here—I want to see you." To my delight he came and declared that he had heard and understood what I said.
>
> I asked him to repeat the words. He answered, "You said 'Mr. Watson—come here—I want to see you.'" We then changed places and I listened at S [the speaker] while Mr. Watson read a few passages from a book into the mouthpiece M. It was certainly the case that articulate sounds proceeded from S. The effect was loud but indistinct and muffled.[5]

Watson recalled the wording somewhat differently—"Mr. Watson come here I want you"[6]—and a fuller context for the first telephone message was reported in his 1934 *New York Times* obituary:

In an interview here several years ago Mr. Watson described how an accident, involving spilled acid, resulted in the first actual reception of a human voice over a wire on March 10, 1876.

Professor Bell and Mr. Watson had arranged wires leading from a room on the top floor of a Boston boarding house to a room on the floor below. The apparatus was arranged for transmission of the voice in one direction only.

A HISTORIC SHOUT.

Watson was waiting tensely in the room below, with the reception apparatus held against his ear. Suddenly he heard Dr. Bell shout excitedly:

"Mr. Watson! Come here; I want—!"

Struck with the realization that he had actually heard Professor Bell over the wire, Watson dashed jubilantly upstairs.

"I heard you! I heard you!" he gasped.

Then he noticed Professor Bell brushing frantically at his arms and clothing. He had accidentally spilled a bottle of acid upon himself. His summons over the wire, made with little hope it would be heard, was really one for assistance.

Mr. Watson said Professor Bell forgot about the acid when he learned his voice had been heard over the wire by his associate.[7]

Thus the first telephone transmission was a technological triumph but also a doubly human event. First, it was the result of an accident—nothing is more human than that. Second, it was a call for help—a 911 call before 911 was even a concept. The following year, with Hubbell's backing, the Bell Telephone Company was founded and, within less than a decade, 150,000 subscribers owned Bell telephones. By 1900, there were some 600,000, a number that exploded to 2.2 million by 1905 and 5.8 million by 1910.[8] (As of 2017, there are an estimated 5 billion mobile phone users across the globe.)[9]

Alexander Graham Bell was a man of intense humanity and curiosity, with an uncanny ability to see relations between the apparently diverse realms of sound—specifically, the human voice—and telegraphic transmission. The creation of the telephone was a work of individual genius, although other individuals had similar ideas. Between 1844 and 1876, at least five inventors—Innocenzo Manzetti (Italy, 1844), Charles Bourseul (France, 1854), Johann Philipp Reis (1861, Germany), Antonio Meucci (1871, Italian but working in the United States), and Elisha Gray (1876, United States)—built prototypes. The difference between them and Bell was that, while Bell was no businessman himself, he had the immediate backing of financiers who quickly created a corporation that was able to build the network infrastructure necessary to make the telephone "instrument" useful to people everywhere. In the Gilded Age, invention might be the work of an individual genius, but fully realizing an invention, disseminating it, selling it, and monetizing it, required big business and big industry.

THOMAS EDISON INVENTS THE "INVENTION FACTORY"

The union of science and industry, of creative genius and commercial acumen, was, if anything, even more prolifically manifested in the next great Gilded Age inventor, Thomas Alva Edison. He received his first patent (0,090,646) in 1869, for an "Electrographic Vote-Recorder," which enabled members of Congress to record votes by turning a "yes" or "no" switch. Edison promoted the device as a means of making congressional voting faster and more efficient—only to be informed by the congressional leaders to whom he demonstrated the device that the very last thing they wanted was to make voting faster and more efficient. The laborious roll-call method provided valuable time for twisting arms. Although his first invention worked, it failed to find a market, and Edison pledged to himself that, going forward, he would make sure people wanted a thing *before* he invented it. He thus instantly transitioned from inventor to inventor-entrepreneur. Within a very short time, he would evolve further into an inventor-marketer-industrialist. As such, over the next sixty-two years, he was awarded 1,093 US patents, the final one, US 1908839 A, for a "Holder for article to be electroplated," filed on January 9, 1931,[10] ten months before Edison died, at the age of eighty-four, on October 18, 1931. His record for patents held until 2015, when he was surpassed by American physicist Lowell Wood.

By the time Edison made the cover of *Scientific American* on February 27, 1909, his phonograph was enjoying spectacular commercial success.

Edison's life story became part of Gilded Age mythology and remains a cornerstone of American popular culture. Born in 1847 in Milan, Ohio, he was six years old when he and his family moved to Port Huron, Michigan, a Midwestern hamlet just beginning to enjoy prosperity through commerce with the rest of the country via the new Grand Trunk Railway, which linked it to Detroit and the world beyond. Like young Alexander Graham Bell, Edison was an intensely curious youth. Unlike Bell, his curiosity often got him into trouble and even branded him as a delinquent. Bored in the classroom, he attended school sporadically and finally received most of his elementary education at home, from his doting mother. Although his maverick ways became part of the Edison pop culture mystique, his educational experience was something Edison shared with many American boys of the mid-nineteenth century. Most children typically attended only a few years of elementary school before going to work full time. Yet young Tom Edison did not settle for just any menial job that came his way. At age twelve, he went to work as a "news butcher," a concessionaire on the Grand Trunk Railway, purveying newspapers, magazines, candy, sandwiches, and other merchandise to passengers between Port Huron and Detroit. While it is true that most news butchers of the era were youths, Edison did much more than sell copies of the *Detroit Free Press*. He wrote, edited, and printed his own paper, liberally larded with items of local interest. From an early age, he was clearly an energetic, innovative self-starter—but this attitude was more representative of America at the threshold of the Gilded Age than it was unusual. Edison's paper was one of many self-published local newspapers that came into being across the country, not a few published by mere teenagers. Still, Edison did introduce a genuinely unique wrinkle by using a small proofing press to print the paper aboard the moving train. It is likely that he did this not merely to amuse himself, but to market printed news with a freshness approaching real-time reporting. The railroad, an industrial technology foundational to the Gilded Age, was all about speed. The teenage Edison innovated a consumer product—call it real-time news—perfectly suited to the speed of rail travel. Although Edison, as a mature inventor, would create many devices for business and industry, he is best remembered for his consumer inventions—the phonograph, improvements to the telephone, motion pictures as popular entertainment, electric light for the home. These all accelerated the transformation of American society into a consumer civilization.

Exceptional though young Tom Edison was, he nevertheless had much in common with others his age, including an interest in the nation's burgeoning railroads and, something that went along with them—the telegraph. His job as a railroad news butcher brought him into contact with telegraphers along the Grand Trunk, and this led to his increasing interest in electricity and its application. In 1863, he himself started working as a telegrapher, joining a fraternity of what today would be called nerds or geeks. Most telegraphers were irrepressible technological tinkerers, who gladly devoted much of their free time to modifying and tweaking the equipment they used. Very quickly, Edison saw that telegraphy demanded more than mere tinkering. Given the growing demand for instantaneous communication nationwide, the industry needed full-scale innovation and invention. After four years as a "tramp telegrapher"—an itinerant operator who built a reputation not only for speed and accuracy, but for practical innovation, Edison found a Boston businessman willing to back him, and he set up shop in that city as a professional inventor. Although his first patent, for his electric vote recorder in 1868, was a commercial failure, it gave him confidence in his

A modern-day photograph of the heavy machine shop in Edison's laboratory–workshop–manufacturing complex in West Orange, New Jersey (now a National Historic Park).

ability to invent and innovate. The very next year, 1869, he moved to New York City and became a manufacturer of telegraph equipment, working primarily as a subcontractor for Western Union and other companies. Two years later, in 1871, he branched out into what today would be called R&D—research and development—opening a combined factory and laboratory-workshop across the Hudson, in Newark, New Jersey.

It was Edison, not Bell, who invented commercially successful multiplexing telegraphy systems, enabling the simultaneous transmission and reception of multiple messages over a single line. In 1876, Edison used profits from his quadruplex telegraph equipment, which effectively multiplied the capacity of existing telegraph lines by a factor of four, to build his most famous laboratory-workshop complex, in then-rural Menlo Park, New Jersey. Here he created nothing less than a technology village, the forerunner of the innovation campuses of modern-day Silicon Valley. He called Menlo Park an "invention factory," and from it flowed, with remarkable regularity, one wonder of technology after another. The year 1877 saw the release of his first civilization-altering consumer product—the phonograph—and, two years later, came the even more epoch-making incandescent electric lighting system.

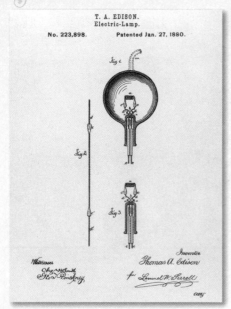

T. A. EDISON.
Electric-Lamp.

No. 223,898.   Patented Jan. 27, 1880.

Edison's most famous patent was for the "Electric-Lamp." With this simple product, the inventor created a demand for electric power that, in turn, spawned a new public utility, myriad new electrical devices, and a whole new infrastructure for a new "high-tech" global civilization.

In 1879 the prolific inventor patented an incandescent electric lamp, the "light bulb." The far greater significance of this invention, however, was its role as the fertile seed of an entire *system* of inventions. The success of the incandescent lamp instantly created a need for electric power, which spurred Edison to create an utterly new utility, a complete system for generating, distributing, and retailing electrical energy. This entirely new industry forever changed the course of civilization, and it is what made Thomas Edison the quintessential inventor of the Gilded Age.

In 1887, Edison moved from Menlo Park to a larger laboratory-workshop-manufacturing complex in West Orange, New Jersey. Here, in 1888, he made extensive improvements to the phonograph, transforming it from a charming curiosity into a commercial product of enormous influence and profitability. In 1889, he formed Edison General Electric to turn his inventions into products and appliances of all kinds. The year before, he released the "kinetograph," an early motion picture camera. It was not until 1894, however, that he paired the kinetograph with the kinetoscope, a motion picture viewer. Later that year, Edison opened the first commercial motion picture exhibition "parlor" in New York City. In a move prophetic of the computer age, having invented the hardware—phonograph and motion picture devices—he next founded a recording company and a movie production company to turn out the software for this hardware.

Not everything Edison invented turned to gold. He suffered numerous technical and commercial failures in his career, the costliest of which was a decade-long effort to develop a commercially viable process to electromagnetically separate high-grade iron from cheap, low-grade ore. Likewise, his efforts, early in the twentieth century, to develop a more reliable and practical storage battery to power electric vehicles was threatened by the sudden demise of electric car

Edison partnered with American inventor Thomas Armat on the latter's electrically powered projector, launching it as the Vitascope to project Kinetoscope films. The Vitascope, touted here in a promotional poster from c. 1896, was initially featured in vaudeville theaters and, later, in specially built movie theaters.

technology after Henry Ford, the last great innovator of the Gilded Age, successfully marketed his mass-produced Model T in 1908. The success of that vehicle ensured the triumph of the internal combustion automobile engine, fueled by gasoline. In typical Edison fashion, however, the inventor recovered from both disasters. He managed to convert much of his capital investment in the ore-separating enterprise—especially his heavy machinery—into an advanced plant for the manufacture of Portland (artificial) cement, and when his intended market for the storage battery disappeared, he innovated a host of new applications for the invention, ranging from powering electrical railway signals to providing lighting for houses and businesses isolated from electric lines.

HENRY FORD: DRIVING GILDED AGE INNOVATION

Although his world of invention made *Edison* quite literally a household name, the inventor was not made of the emotional stuff of the Gilded Age robber barons, and he never became wealthy on the scale of Carnegie or Rockefeller—or, for that

> *"Although his world of invention made Edison quite literally a household name, the inventor was not made of the emotional stuff of the Gilded Age robber barons."*

matter, Henry Ford. Yet he and Ford became the closest of friends. Their families vacationed together, and the two men even bought neighboring winter homes in Fort Myers, Florida. Clearly, Edison bore Ford no grudge for having been the first of what would be a succession of automotive industrialists to "kill" the electric car. Besides, Edison's storage battery technology eventually found its way into the gasoline-powered automobile in 1911, after inventor Charles F. Kettering was tasked by Henry M. Leland, the founder of Cadillac, to develop a practical electric starter system for automobiles; it replaced the temperamental and sometimes bone-breaking hand crank.

In some ways, Edison and Ford were quite similar in personality. They were both tinkerers with a genius for turning their tinkering into full-scale innovation and turning innovation into commercial success. They were both small-town Midwesterners with a connection to Michigan. Edison spent most of his formative years in Port Huron, and Ford was born and raised in rural Wayne County, not far from Detroit. They embodied what they thought of as the "simple" values of small-town middle America, and they shared a sincere belief in self-reliance and the potential of becoming anything you could dream of being—a belief that their own remarkable lives validated, a belief that became a driving mythos of the Gilded Age.

In other ways, the two men were very different. A childhood illness left Edison partially deaf, a disability that sometimes made him seem aloof and curt. Despite this, he enjoyed an excellent rapport with his staff of technicians, mechanics, and engineers. He encouraged them not only to come up with their own ideas and ways of solving problems, but to actually try them out. On every workbench in his laboratory/workshop, Edison distributed notebooks and pencils. He asked his "boys," as he called them, to write down any ideas or observations that occurred to them as they worked. He wanted their ideas, their input, and he clearly relished the time he spent among his staff, going so far as to install a large pipe organ at

THE GILDED AGE

Fast friends, Henry Ford and Thomas Edison formed a two-man mutual admiration society. Here, c. 1930, Ford speaks directly into the ear of the inventor, who had been hearing-impaired since childhood, perhaps the result of illness, injury, or a combination of the two. Edison believed his "handicap" gave him a creative edge by minimizing distraction from his work.

one end of the main workroom at Menlo Park to provide musical entertainment. Edison believed that the labor of invention should be joyous. Indeed, Edison's relations with his employees were marked by the same collegiality that characterized his attitude toward Henry Ford. For his part, Ford reciprocated collegial feelings to Edison—but never to his employees. It is true that Ford would, by 1914, pay his assembly line workers an unheard of $5-a-day wage, arguing that those who made Model Ts should earn enough to buy one. Yet everything about the Ford assembly line was inimical to Edison's approach to labor. It subordinated men to machinery. Creativity was taken out of the work process because it only served to reduce productivity. Instead, each worker was trained to do a single repetitive task on a vehicle that moved past each worker on a system of conveyors and pulleys. It was up to each man to keep pace with the machine.

In an era often marked by the oppression of the working class, Edison treated his employees with respect and kindness. He encouraged creativity, independent thought, and, not least of all, fun. Employees at his West Orange, New Jersey, plant are seen dancing on Lakeside Avenue in 1915.

Introduced in 1913 in Ford's plant, the moving assembly line was built to assemble Model Ts as quickly and as cheaply as possible. The first of these cars had gone into production earlier, in 1908, on a version of the assembly line that lacked the moving conveyor system. It was by no means the first automobile—the first production vehicle was built by Karl Benz, in Germany, in 1888—nor was it Ford's first car. That would be the Quadricycle, an ethanol-powered engine on a frame fitted with four bicycle wheels, completed at two o'clock in the morning on June 4, 1896 in his Dearborn, Michigan, toolshed. But the Model T was very different from any of the earlier automobiles. Whereas these had been regarded as custom-crafted luxury items for the wealthy, the Model T would be cheap enough for most people of ordinary means to afford. To reduce costs, Ford

Ford's moving assembly line—shown here in 1913—was the brainchild of William "Pa" Klann, who was in charge of the Model T assembly plant at Highland Park, Michigan. Klann was inspired by the so-called "disassembly" line at a Chicago slaughterhouse, where carcasses were systematically butchered as they moved along a conveyor belt.

designed in 1908 an assembly line along which specific workers built specific components and other workers fitted them to the vehicle. This rigorously standardized, numbingly repetitive system enabled Ford to get the per-car cost down to $950, far less than custom-built automobiles cost, but still beyond the reach of the average working family. Getting the assembly line to move past stationary workers made all the difference. In 1916, three years after the moving assembly line was introduced, the price of a Model T was down to $360. Ford had turned out 13,840 cars in 1909. In 1916, production rose to 585,388.[11] By 1927, the last year the model was made, Ford had produced 14,689,520 Model T cars.[12] It is a record that remained unbroken until the 15,007,034th Volkswagen® Beetle rolled off the line in 1972.[13]

Where Edison's consumer-focused inventions brought a kind of magic to the people—light, sound, and entertainment—and were perceived as the work of craftsmen-wizards, the Model T was an ambiguous symbol of Gilded Age industrial technology. On the one hand, it was a sturdy, reliable, generic product of the early perfection of mass production that fostered a consumer-driven society. It bestowed upon virtually all economic classes equal and unprecedented mobility, and it began the unification of the nation through a vast network of roads and transformed great swaths of rural America into suburbs of the nation's cities. But it also took the relation of labor and management to a low of worker alienation. Indeed, it changed the very nature of labor.

None of this happened by accident. In 1911, Frederick Winslow Taylor published his *Principles of Scientific Management*, which codified everything that Gilded Age industrialists, culminating in Henry Ford, did or were doing to "rationalize" production processes. A foreman at Philadelphia's Midvale Steel

"Where Edison's consumer-focused inventions brought a kind of magic to the people and were perceived as the work of craftsmen-wizards, the Model T was an ambiguous symbol of Gilded Age industrial technology."

Company during the 1880s, Taylor had observed that, despite the growing mechanization of the plant, the rate of production was still largely dependent on the pace and methods set by the more skilled workers. From this observation, he reasoned that the "excessive idiosyncrasy" of craftspeople would always impede the rate of production. To maximize productivity, therefore, managers, not workers, had to assume control of the entire production process, prescribing methods and setting the pace. Moreover, they had to do this scientifically, basing their systems on meticulous observation and analysis of each manufacturing step—indeed, of every movement made by every worker. By collating these observations, managers could determine the best method for getting a job done, whatever that job was. This was a step—a necessary step in an increasingly mechanized world— toward making human workers as efficient as machines.

Taylor invented a new profession—management consultant—and his method, soon universally called Taylorism, created controversy, excitement, and despair in the American workplace. Without question, Taylorism increased productivity, ensuring that the United States would emerge from the Gilded Age into the twentieth century an industrial titan among nations. Capitalists even argued that Taylorism bettered the lot of unskilled labor. Anyone could be trained to do the repetitive tasks assembly-line work demanded, they pointed out, and thus more jobs were made available to the growing numbers of unskilled laborers immigrating into the country during the early twentieth century. Moreover, Taylorism prescribed a system of "scaled piecework rates" as an incentive for workers to move faster and achieve higher output—so while the pace might be difficult (literally inhuman, as a matter of fact), at least compensation was commensurate with production.

Or so it was claimed. In truth, while more productive workers were rewarded— and, conversely, less productive workers penalized—both tended to make less than they would have if their pay had been hourly. The net result was a dehumanization of the workplace, as workers were deprived of autonomy and were thereby alienated from motives of craftsmanship. Widening the already yawning gulf between labor and management, Taylorism, the final flower of Gilded Age industrial civilization, was instrumental in creating the productive but paradoxical character of twentieth-century American industrial life. On the one hand, it drove production costs as low as they could possibly be driven, thus making many more consumer products available to many more consumers. Arguably, this empowered the working class and promoted the growth of a substantial middle class, thereby increasing social equality and enhancing the American democracy. Yet the hidden cost—hidden because it could not be calculated in dollars and cents—was in the sacrifice of happiness, hope, and a fulfilling sense of purpose among legions of workers who spent eight, ten, or twelve hours, six out of seven days in every week, serving a tyrant made of gears, pulleys, and moving belts.

Workers prepare subassemblies for installation on a Ford Model T in 1924.

PUCK

BILLION DOLLAR BANK MERGER

FRANK A. NANKIVELL

THE MARKETPLACE

The Gilded Age is often portrayed as the era of corporate conglomeration, of relentless mergers and acquisitions, and of monopolistic trusts designed to crush all competition. If this picture is less than accurate, it is only because the situation was often even worse. Companies such as John D. Rockefeller's Standard Oil not only bought up or squeezed out competing oil companies, they adopted so-called vertical growth strategies to acquire everything necessary to control their industry and markets end-to-end (see page 88). Thus Standard Oil not only engaged in the extraction and refining of oil, it also acquired pipelines, railroad tank cars, and terminal facilities. The company even had a subsidiary that manufactured oil barrels. In 1882, a novel corporate arrangement was established by which Standard Oil stockholders voluntarily transferred their shares to a board of trustees who controlled the entire conglomerate of companies. For this, stockholders received a share of the consolidated earnings of these jointly managed companies. Standard soon became so big that collusion among refineries to regulate output and price became business as usual. A company that defied its price-fixing scheme risked being undercut, bought out (cheap), or simply driven out of business. So successful was the Standard trust that the business model was adopted by big firms in some two hundred American industrial sectors, including sugar, coal, steel, and tobacco.

J. P. Morgan on the cover of *Puck*, February 1910. One greedy arm clutches a "billion dollar bank merger" while the other goes after a toddler's piggy bank. The caption (not visible) reads: "The Central Bank—Why should Uncle Sam establish one, when Uncle Pierpont is already on the job?"

A Standard Oil stock certificate from 1882, the year in which investors transferred their shares to a board of trustees presiding over a vast "trust," which controlled Rockefeller's entire conglomerate of companies. With this move, the vertical monopoly was born.

Certainly, Andrew Carnegie followed Rockefeller's strategy closely, although his route to transforming Carnegie Steel into a super-corporation took an even craftier, more personal turn that focused more closely on finance than on building verticals to control the market. As the nineteenth century drew to a close, Carnegie, perhaps tired of his perpetual wars with labor, began to think about selling his steel company. He would content himself with no ordinary sale, however.

In 1898, the financier J. P. Morgan absorbed a company called Illinois Steel into the company he controlled, Federal Steel. The enlarged firm then reached out to acquire other, smaller steel companies. Taking note that Morgan was obviously conglomerating, Carnegie decided to offer him his company. He hardly approached the financier hat in hand, however. Instead, Carnegie played his man, as the saying goes, like a grand piano.

Morgan had a well-deserved reputation for rapacity. Among a generation of hyperaggressive capitalists, none were more ravenous than he. That was fine with Carnegie, who used his press agent—the forerunner of a corporate publicity office—to let it be known that he was about to build a mammoth plant for the manufacture of steel pipe and tubing. It would be unprecedented in cost ($12 million) and size—the largest such enterprise in the world. Morgan, as Carnegie

THE GILDED AGE

well knew, owned a controlling interest in the National Tube Works, with which Carnegie's proposed enterprise would obviously compete. Leaving nothing to chance, Carnegie next began planting rumors that he was about to build, from scratch, a railroad to carry not only his own steel products to market but those of others as well. He knew, of course, that Morgan happened to own the Pennsylvania Railroad.

Faced with the specter of competition not in one but in two major industries, Morgan grew visibly concerned. That is when Carnegie pounced. Charles M. Schwab began as a laborer in the engineering department of one of Carnegie's steelworks and rose rapidly through the ranks to become, in 1897, president of Carnegie Steel itself. As chairman of the company, Carnegie directed Schwab to invite Morgan to a dinner party at the University Club in New York on December 12, 1900, and, over an elegant meal, persuade him to buy Carnegie Steel so that Morgan could join it to what he already owned and create the biggest steel company in the world—United States Steel. Morgan took the bait and, the

COMMERCIAL MIGHT *versus* DIVINE RIGHT.
The Modern Trust King Seems Greater to the Old Kings of Europe.

following month, in January 1901, bought out Carnegie for the price of the entire initial bond issue of U.S. Steel—$303.45 million—and a large bloc of preferred and common stock, making a total sale price of $480 million.[1]

The deal was so big and U.S. Steel itself was so big, that it could not help but become even bigger as investors gobbled up the new company's stock, driving up the price of common shares from 38 to 55 in scarcely the blink of an eye, with preferred stock exploding from 82¾ to 101⅞.[2] For

> By purchasing Carnegie Steel, J. P. Morgan created United States Steel, the biggest steel maker in the world. Already enormously wealthy, he grew mightier than kings and emperors, as illustrated in this *Puck* cartoon of 1902

a time, this single stock lifted the entire New York Stock Exchange with it; in 1901, Progressive journalist Ray Stannard Baker wrote that U.S. Steel "receives and expends more money every year than any but the very greatest of the world's national governments; its debt is larger than that of many of the lesser nations of Europe; it absolutely controls the destinies of a population nearly as large as that of Maryland or Nebraska, and indirectly influences twice that number."[3]

———◆———

EVEN AS MANY IN THE PUBLIC eagerly invested in US Steel, there was growing concern about trusts and other conglomerates. In 1902, *The Commoner,* a magazine owned by the Populist politician William Jennings Bryan, distilled the substance of this growing discontent by quoting J. P. Morgan himself: "America is good enough for me." Presumably, Morgan intended this as a benign expression of patriotism, but the editor added his own comment: "Whenever he doesn't like it, he can give it back to us."[4]

The Gilded Age was torn between admiration of big business and resentment, revulsion, and rage. Some corporate behemoths looked for ways to reconcile with the public. As discussed in chapter 3, some tycoons—such as Carnegie and Rockefeller—turned toward philanthropy. This is not to imply that they were insincere. To read Carnegie's "Gospel of Wealth" is to be convinced that his passion for philanthropy was genuine. But it is also true that a display of public-spirited philanthropy and good corporate citizenship did much to improve the image of big enterprise, defuse public anger, and thwart any federal regulatory action.

THE TOBACCO DUKES

Other businesses found different ways to win public sympathy. Tobacco had been a tremendously popular consumer product in Europe since the sixteenth century, when Jean Nicot, French ambassador to Portugal, brought tobacco plants—newly introduced to the Iberian Peninsula—to Paris. The use of snuff by the French royal court popularized tobacco throughout the continent and England. As for Nicot, the great Swedish naturalist Carl Linnaeus named the tobacco plant in his honor, *Nicotiana,* from which the modern word *nicotine* is derived.

The Dukes of North Carolina, brothers James "Buck" (left) and Benjamin, launched the American Tobacco Company and then built it into a "tobacco trust" conglomerate.

By the nineteenth century, many Europeans smoked tobacco in the form of hand-rolled cigarettes, a practice that became even more prevalent when large-scale cigarette manufacturing began in France in the 1840s. In the United States, however, cigarettes had a hard time catching on. Smoking them in private was socially questionable for women, and smoking them in public downright indecent. Men, of course, could do as they wished, but cigarette smoking by men was widely deemed effeminate. Pipes, cigars, a good chew—these were manly actions. Cigarettes? A bit too dainty.

The Duke brothers, James "Buck" Buchanan and Benjamin, joined their father, George Washington Duke, in the family cigarette business when it was no more than a North Carolina family business. The Dukes produced so-called ready-mades—hand-rolled cigarettes—in an era when most of those who smoked cigarettes at all rolled their own, using cut tobacco and rolling papers. The ready-mades were a luxury item for the few who could afford them. In 1880, however, a young man from Virginia's tobacco country, James Albert Bonsack, patented an ingenious cigarette-making machine. It fed very finely shredded tobacco onto a continuous strip of rolling paper, which the machine shaped, rolled, pasted, and

The Bonsack cigarette-making machine was the Gilded Age innovation that enabled the mass production of "readymade" smokes. Freed from the effort of "rolling their own," smokers turned in droves from pipes, cigars, and chewing tobacco to cigarettes—and American Tobacco owned the most profitable brands.

cut into individual cigarettes. In 1885, the Dukes bought the machine and put it to work. As they had hoped, bringing down the price of cigarettes through mass production enlarged the market for the product. Believing that they were on the verge of making and marketing a truly major consumer good, the Dukes decided in 1890 to clear the way by buying up several smaller competitors in exchange for stock in the new conglomerate, to be called the American Tobacco Company.

Now the family had the means to increase production and thereby lower retail cigarette prices even more. They also—for the time being, at least—controlled the market for cigarettes. The only trouble was that the market was still too small. Fortunately for American Tobacco, the Duke brothers were not only innovators in production, they proved to be innovators in marketing. The Dukes took branding beyond trademarking. Understanding that smoking was all about gratifying a personal taste, they created not just one brand, with a unique name and image, but a range of brands, each intended to convey a distinct quality and *appeal*, and each targeting a particular consumer who had a particular taste in tobacco.

THE GILDED AGE

FIRST TRADEMARKS

THE CONCEPT OF THE BRAND—A NAME, A SYMBOL, A TRADEMARK THAT CONVEYS TO THE MARKETPLACE A PRODUCT'S UNIQUE IDENTITY—DATES FROM PREHISTORY, BUT THE FIRST UNIVERSALLY RECOGNIZED TRADEMARK STILL IN EXISTENCE MAY BE THE RED TRIANGLE REGISTERED IN BRITAIN BY THE BASS® BREWERY ON JANUARY 1, 1876, NINETY-NINE YEARS AFTER THE BREWERY WAS ESTABLISHED AT BURTON-UPON-TRENT, ENGLAND. IN THE UNITED STATES, IN 1870, CONGRESS ENACTED LEGISLATION TO CODIFY THE SO-CALLED COPYRIGHT CLAUSE OF THE CONSTITUTION (ARTICLE I, SECTION 8, CLAUSE 8). AMENDED IN 1878, THE STATUTE WAS RULED UNCONSTITUTIONAL BY THE SUPREME COURT IN 1879. IN 1881, CONGRESS PASSED A NEW TRADEMARK ACT BASED ON THE COMMERCE CLAUSE (ARTICLE I, SECTION 8, CLAUSE 3), AND ON MAY 27, 1884, THE J. P. TOLMAN COMPANY BECAME THE FIRST U.S. COMPANY TO FORMALLY REGISTER ITS TRADEMARK: A DEPICTION OF OLD TESTAMENT STRONGMAN SAMSON, WHICH BRANDED ROPES MADE BY THE FIRM. (TO THIS DAY, THE COMPANY OPERATES UNDER THE 1884 TRADEMARK, AS SAMSON® ROPE TECHNOLOGIES, INC.)[5]

The Dukes not only produced various brands of cigarettes, they ventured into other tobaccos, including pipe and chewing tobacco. The latter was an especially popular category of merchandise, and American Tobacco entered a marketplace so fiercely competitive that consumers and retailers alike referred to "plug wars" among rival tobacco companies. Using a combination of aggressive branding (American Tobacco chewing tobaccos were marketed under such names as Horseshoe and Battle Axe); saturation advertising (including paying farmers to allow the company to paint billboards on the sides of barns); free-sample distribution; aggressive merger and acquisition practices; and predatory pricing that undercut smaller competitors, American Tobacco became the Standard Oil of its industry.

THE ART OF THE BRAND

By the height of the Gilded Age, American Tobacco had hooked Americans on two addictions. The first was to tobacco itself—although the nearly universal adoption of cigarettes would not truly sweep the nation until the end of World War I in 1918. The second, even more enduring habit, was the American addiction to brands. Consumers became "loyal" to certain brands partly because the *merchandise* was good or effective or priced for value, but mostly because they identified the *brand*—the identity of the product created through packaging and advertising—as good, effective, or priced right. As standardized mass production in a growing array of industries flooded consumer markets with very similar products, brands were often the only component that distinguished one offering from another.

Branding brought products to national attention, persuading consumers to trust and to purchase a mass-produced, nationally distributed item of merchandise as if it had been made by a local, long-familiar, and personally trusted craftsman. As branding became instrumental in selling products to the largest possible market, so advertising became essential to defining and disseminating the brand. Like branding, advertising dates to earliest recorded history, but the advertising agency—a business dedicated to creating and delivering advertising messages—came into being in London during the late eighteenth century and, in the United States, in 1850, with the founding of Volney B. Palmer's Philadelphia-based advertising business. In 1869, Francis Ayer founded N. W. Ayer & Son, also in Philadelphia, which is generally acknowledged as the first dedicated, full-service advertising agency.

While N. W. Ayer & Son was growing in Philadelphia, a young man from Pittsfield, Massachusetts, named James Walter Thompson was seeking his for-

> *"As branding became instrumental in selling products to the largest possible market, so advertising became essential to defining and disseminating the brand."*

tune in New York City working for Carlton and Smith. Established in 1864, the company specialized in selling advertising space in religious magazines. Its senior partner, William James Carlton, hired the twenty-one-year-old Thompson in 1868 as a bookkeeper, only to discover that his new hire's real talent lay in selling ad space. Indeed, Thompson soon became the modest firm's leading salesman. Recognizing that he had become indispensable to the company, Thompson, in 1877, offered to buy out Carlton and Smith. William James Carlton sold it to him for all of $500, along with all the office furniture for an additional $800.[6] After changing the name of the company to J. Walter Thompson®, the new owner soon transformed it into the go-to agency for any advertiser who wanted to buy space not just in religious publications, but in almost any periodical or magazine. By 1889, J. Walter Thompson was placing some 80 percent of *all* print ads in the United States.[7] In 1899, the company went international by opening a London office. Today, the firm operates in more than ninety countries and is an icon of the advertising industry.

J. Walter Thompson's dominance of American advertising during the Gilded Age earned him the enduring title of the "father of advertising." In addition to Thompson's own extraordinary talent as a salesman, two other qualities were responsible for the agency's remarkable development. First, Thompson started providing more than his services as a buyer of space and a placer of ads.

The pioneering ad agency J. Walter Thompson believed so strongly in advertising that it advertised itself in the *Blue Book of Trade Marks and Newspapers* in 1889. That year, "80% of the advertising in the United States" was placed by Thompson.

He hired writers and illustrators and offered to create the ads he placed for his clients. What he produced was invariably far more compelling and persuasive than anything his clients could put together themselves. From here, Thompson went even further, designing product packaging, conducting market research on their behalf, and, most notably, developing trademarks, which Thompson believed was the very core of creating an effective brand. By 1900, the J. Walter Thompson agency was advertising itself as the master of trademark creation, and in 1911 literally wrote (and published) the book on the subject.[8]

One of the biggest names of the Gilded Age had no need of J. Walter Thompson to convince him of the power of branding and trademarks. Thomas Edison, whom the popular press proclaimed the "Wizard of Menlo Park," proved himself a precocious wizard of branding as well. Edison identified himself personally with all the merchandise he marketed. He presented *himself* as a brand, and his characteristic signature, executed with a flourish and duly filed with the U.S. Patent and Trademark Office on May 27, 1899, became one of the most recognizable logos in American manufacturing history.[9]

"He presented himself as a brand, and his characteristic signature became one of the most recognizable logos in American manufacturing history."

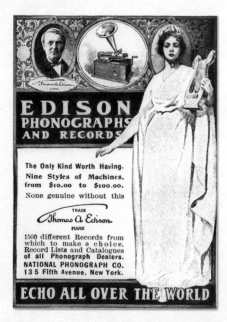

The "Thomas A. Edison" signature trademark prominently adorned Edison phonographs and recordings as well as other consumer products—and ads such as this one from 1901. The signature trademark became a logo familiar "all over the world."

The Edison signature logo represented the identity Edison's achievements had built for him. Consumers were eager to invest in his innovations because they felt that they were investing in no less than Thomas Alva Edison himself. The promotion of one invention after another became that much easier for Edison's companies, thanks to the personal identification of each innovation with the inventor behind it. Attach his name to a product, and it was bound to sell. Edison so valued his signature trademark that when his own son, Thomas A. Edison Jr., sold the use of his name to promote a bogus electromechanical medical device—an item of expensive quackery—Thomas A. Sr. paid the young man a stipend for life in exchange for his promise never to use *his own name* in connection with any product.

BIRTH OF THE RETAIL EXPERIENCE

The post–Civil War explosion in manufacturing, especially of consumer goods, both drove and was driven by a revolution in American retailing. Philadelphia merchant John Wanamaker set the pattern for the modern department store when he moved his men's clothing store to a remodeled Pennsylvania Railroad depot in 1876, a move that coincided with the great Centennial exhibition (see chapter 1). Before the nineteenth century closed, all the principal American cities had great department stores, which became even greater at the opening of the

In 1876, Philadelphia men's clothier John A. Wanamaker moved his store to a vacant Pennsylvania Railroad depot, which he remodeled to create the modern American department store. Photograph c. 1896.

new century. From 1910 to 1911, Wanamaker redesigned and enlarged the iconic Philadelphia store, commissioning Daniel H. Burnham, the Chicago architect who drew up the master plan for improving that city's post–Great Fire lakefront. Retailer Rowland Hussey Macy built four dry goods stores in Massachusetts between 1843 and 1855 before opening a larger store in New York City in 1858. Over the years, he expanded this establishment into adjacent buildings. In 1895, brothers Isidor and Nathan Straus bought the Macy company but retained its valuable name and, in 1902, moved into a five-story building on Herald Square, which was extensively expanded over the years and advertised as the "World's Largest Store."[10]

In Chicago, Massachusetts-born Marshall Field worked for Cooley, Wadsworth & Co., the city's biggest dry goods merchant, beginning in 1856. By 1862, Field was a partner in the firm and, by the 1880s, became a spectacular suc-

From left: Wanamaker's majestic interior court (photograph c. 1968) houses the largest operational pipe organ on the planet, making it a true cathedral of commerce; Chicago's Marshall Field's on State Street (c. 1908) reigned as the city's most elegant department store until 2006, when the company was purchased by Macy's; a photograph of Macy's New York flagship department store (c. 1908), which claimed the title of "biggest store in the world."

cess in dry goods. Like Wanamaker in Philadelphia, however, Field recognized that retailing had fallen badly out of step with the middle class—the consumer class—rising in Gilded Age America. Before the Civil War, retail business was conducted overwhelmingly by individual proprietors of dry goods stores, "general stores," butcher shops, grocer's shops, and by an array of specialized tradespeople—shoemakers, tailors, craftspeople in various fields. The success or failure of these businesses depended on reputations, which were built on word of mouth within the community. As American cities grew and more of the population became not only urban but more transient, moving from city to city or from one neighborhood to another within the same city, retail businesses became larger but also lost much of the personal connection. There was both less motivation and less opportunity for building a local reputation, and, increasingly, the governing principle in retail transaction became "caveat emptor," let the buyer beware. In

other words, instead of merchants having an implied obligation to stand behind their products, the burden was on the consumer to practice due diligence and thereby avoid being deceived or disappointed. Like Wanamaker, Field saw that increasingly empowered post–Civil War consumers expected merchants to treat them very well indeed. Like Wanamaker, he was determined to appeal to and satisfy this expectation—partly by standing behind his merchandise with a no-questions-asked refund policy and also by providing a friendly, courteous, even luxurious shopping environment in which merchandise would be helpfully *presented* to customers, never *forced* on them. Importantly, Field recognized that women were the major shoppers in most families, and so he designed his Chicago store with women in mind and trained his employees to appeal to them. His business motto was "Give the lady what she wants."[11]

> *"The Woolworths recognized an underserved segment of the vast American consumer market."*

THE RISE OF FIVE-AND-DIME AMERICA

Access to a wide array of appealing goods as well as possession of the financial wherewithal to purchase them became both a symbol of middle-class status and a feature of economic life in the Gilded Age. Merchants like Wanamaker, Field, and others saw their mission as not just selling merchandise, but creating and offering a retail experience of luxury and self-indulgence. Yet that came at a cost. Department store goods were not cheap. Moreover, prices—which reflected the "overhead" of all the amenities the stores offered—were nonnegotiable. Whereas shoppers could haggle with the general store owner, they could not argue with a price tag. Although the productivity of the Gilded Age substantially fostered the American middle class, whose members had sufficient disposable income, it also enlarged the class of low-skilled and unskilled labor, families that barely scraped by and had to make every penny

While the department store was at the high end of the Gilded Age retail spectrum, the Woolworth "five-and-ten" was at the low end. Entrepreneur Frank W. Woolworth created chain-store retailing and offered an array of goods anyone in possession of a spare dime could afford. Photograph c. 1925.

count. Common sense suggests that merchants had little incentive to address a market that could afford so little. The Woolworth brothers, Frank and Charles, thought differently, however. Where most retailers saw no business opportunity in the sub-middle class, the Woolworths recognized an underserved segment of the vast American consumer market.

Frank W. Woolworth opened the first five-cent store in Lancaster, Pennsylvania, on June 21, 1879. (Business histories and textbooks often call this type of modest commercial emporium a "variety store," but they are more commonly known as the "five-and-ten," "five-and-dime," "five-cent store," or just plain "dime store.") The very next month, he brought his brother into the business and, together, they opened another store in Harrisburg, Pennsylvania. The stores had been inspired by the success Frank had had when his employer, a Watertown, New York, dry goods merchant, allowed him to set up a five-cent table in his store. The table immediately became the busiest part of the store. The stores Frank and Charles opened expanded the five-cent table to the entire store (the price ceiling was eventually increased to ten cents).

Price was the great driver of the Woolworth business concept, but it was not the only ingredient in the brothers' formula. First and foremost, they created an economy of scale with a chain-store concept. Both the village general store and the palatial department store were one-offs. The five-and-dime store, by contrast, would be standardized nationally. As with many of the products it sold, the chain itself would be a brand, with a reputation for low price and high value. In contrast to other merchants who specialized in cheap goods, Woolworth stores would be pleasant, new, clean, and brightly lit. The sawdust-covered rough wooden floors of the small-time general store were replaced by clean wood, polished to a high sheen. Small goods—and much that the stores sold was small—were featured either in gleaming glass cases or open gondola displays, which allowed customers to pick up, handle, and closely examine the goods. There was an emphasis on self-service. Unlike the old general store, where the goods were put on floor-to-ceiling shelves behind a continuous counter, so that customers had to ask a clerk or proprietor for service, Woolworth stores encouraged customers to pick out what they wanted for themselves and, as they were preparing to leave the store, to bring their purchases to the clerk behind a well-designed, shiny mahogany counter. If a customer needed assistance, an employee was there to help—but most customers were content to serve themselves. This reduced the number of employees required as well as the level of training and experience needed. The result? Lower overhead costs. Best of all, far from perceiving this as a corner-cutting reduction in service and convenience, customers truly enjoyed browsing and selecting without the intervention of an impatient or pushy salesperson.

The Woolworth business model proved highly successful, and other chains joined the originator of the five-and-dime, most notably Ben Franklin Stores, W. T. Grant, S. S. Kresge Company, and S. H. Kress & Co. All were successful for a long time, but none more than Woolworth, which operated 596 stores nationwide by 1912. Together, however, the dime-store companies built thousands of stores across the nation, and although there was nothing gilded about these modest and efficient establishments, most of them prospered through more than three-quarters of the twentieth century and linger today as perhaps the most affectionately remembered institutions of the Gilded Age.

THE TRIUMPH OF MAIL ORDER

The department stores provided a magnificent sales platform for many of the products post–Civil War manufacturers turned out, and the dime stores served consumers who were priced out of the department store offerings. Not that dime stores appealed exclusively to lower-income shoppers, however. Even consumers with the means to patronize department stores needed the everyday products purveyed by Woolworth and the like. True, many of these five-and-dime items could be purchased in a department store as well, but those emporiums were generally located "downtown" and required public transportation to get there. The dime stores were neighborhood establishments, with many within walking distance of the customers they served. In short, they offered not only value for money, but convenience as well.

Yet one group of consumers was still left out, namely the majority of Americans who lived in rural America, mostly on farms. In 1870, 25.7 percent of Americans lived in urban areas. By 1900, as the Gilded Age ended, 39.6 percent were urban residents.[12] In 1872, Chicago merchant A. Montgomery Ward took a step toward addressing the roughly 75 percent of American consumers who lived far from either department stores or dime stores or, for

Mail-order retailing—pioneered by Montgomery Ward— reached consumers wherever they lived, thanks to the U.S. Mail's RFD (Rural Free Delivery) service.

that matter, traditional general stores. He reasoned that there was one way a merchant could easily reach these potential but hitherto underserved customers—via the U.S. mail. Accordingly, he created a 280-page catalog and mailed copies to thousands of farmers in the Midwest. With this, Montgomery Ward and Company became the nation's first mail-order house.

Montgomery Ward—affectionately known as Monkey Ward—became highly successful and inspired imitators. At least one of these took the mail-order concept well beyond Ward's model. Richard W. Sears began his mail-order operation in 1889 as a way of selling watches to customers who had little or no access to merchants who handled this specialized item, but still needed good watches.[13] To watches, Sears soon added jewelry and, from this base—in partnership with

Although Ward "invented" mail-order merchandising, Richard Warren Sears and his partner Alvah C. Roebuck created the most popular and plentiful mail-order catalog anywhere in the world. Not only did it promise variety, it promised value as the "Cheapest Supply House on Earth," as noted on this 1899 catalog cover.

Alvah C. Roebuck—he built a general mail-order business. Like Ward, Sears advertised his products in catalogs sent to farm families. Sears was the Amazon of the turn of the century. Among the company's merchandise were food, clothing, machinery, tools, stoves, and much more, even a complete kit for building your own Sears Craftsman Bungalow. The Sears Catalog became legendary for making available anything and everything a family, especially a farm family, might possibly need or want. And since most farmhouses lacked indoor plumbing, back copies of the catalog served both as reading matter for the outhouse and toilet paper, too. Sears printed it on soft, smooth paper stock. By 1893, mail-order sales exceeded $400,000, and by 1895 were at $750,000.[14]

Wards and Sears were joined by the National Cloak & Suit Co. just before the turn of the century, and by Spiegel in 1905. Other, smaller mail-order houses also sprang up late in the nineteenth century. Together, the catalog companies changed the lives of American consumers and none more than farm families across the country. Isolated in rural areas and often with limited funds, these families could afford neither the time nor the expense of shopping for goods in towns and cities. The catalogs extended what might be called the consumer franchise to every corner of the country, no matter how remote. Retail mail order brought the Gilded Age to the farm. In the country, as in the city, the mass of Americans had entered the post–Civil War era as seekers of little more than the means of subsistence. Urban or rural, they all emerged from the Gilded Age as avid consumers, united not only by the flag and other traditional patriotic symbols of the republic, but by the colorful and varied brand iconography of corporate America.

"The catalogs extended what might be called the consumer franchise to every corner of the country, no matter how remote."

LOWS JERSEY LILY
FOR THE HANDKERCHIEF

CHAPTER 6

STATUE AND ISLAND

The first that Americans saw of what would be the most iconic symbol of the Gilded Age was part of a right forearm and all of a hand, which grasped a giant torch surmounted by a gracefully sculpted flame. Together, the partial forearm and hand piece was perhaps 25 feet (7.6 m) high, rising out of the ground from a small building that served as its base. The torch, from bottom to flame tip, was about 38 feet (11.6 m). The hand alone was 16½ feet (5 m) long, including its index finger, which was 8 feet (2.4 m) long.

As big as it was, this work was a mere fragment that was exhibited in Philadelphia's Fairmount Park as part of the great Centennial Exposition. The big show opened on May 10, 1876, but the sculpture did not arrive until August— too late to be included in the official catalog. For this reason, it did not bear the name that its creator, the French sculptor Frédéric Auguste Bartholdi had given it, *Liberty Enlightening the World*. Instead, it was known simply as "The Colossal Arm" or the "Bartholdi Electric Light." (The titanic fragment was unlit, but was advertised as part of a planned "illuminated statue.")[1]

What most Centennial visitors who saw the sculpture liked most about it was that they could climb up to the balcony at the base of the torch flame and get a lovely view of the fairgrounds. After the Centennial closed on November 10, the arm was transported to New York City, where it was

A chromolithographic ad for "Low's Jersey Lily for the Handkerchief" (see bottom of base) featuring Frédéric Auguste Bartholdi's *Liberty Enlightening the World*. It appeared in 1884, two years before the statue was dedicated. The monument soon became universally known as the Statue of Liberty.

displayed in Madison Square Park for a number of years before it was returned to France, its country of origin.

There was, in fact, nothing American about this massive fragment of sculpture, which Bartholdi intended to serve as a harbinger of what an American poet, Emma Lazarus, would later call "The New Colossus"—an allusion to the great statue of Helios, Greek titan of the sun, erected in 280 BCE on the island of Rhodes. An earthquake destroyed the statue in 226 BCE, but at a reported 108 feet (33 m) high, it was about 50 feet (15 m) shy of the Statue of Liberty as measured from the top of its base to the tip of its torch. Still, as the tallest statue of its age, the Colossus of Rhodes is considered one of the Seven Wonders of the Ancient World.

Frédéric Auguste Bartholdi, pictured here, intended his Statue of Liberty to be accepted as a gift from France to the United States, its comrade in revolutionary liberty, equality, and fraternity.

LADY LIBERTY

The idea for a *new* Colossus is said to have originated in a conversation between Bartholdi, already famed as a creator of monumental sculpture, and his friend Édouard René de Laboulaye, a poet, a jurist, and a passionate abolitionist. The two men are supposed to have discussed the matter over dinner at Laboulaye's house in Versailles in 1865, a month or two after the end of American Civil War. Inspired by the Union's victory, which brought with it an end to slavery in America—in effect belatedly perfecting and completing the great American Revolution against tyranny—the abolitionist told his sculptor friend, "If a monument should rise in the United States, as a memorial to their independence, I should think it only natural if it were built by united effort—a common work of both our nations."[2] Not everyone agrees that this is how the Statue of Liberty began. U.S. National Park Service researchers date its origin five years later, in 1870, but they still credit Laboulaye with having inspired the project as a commemoration of the end of slavery and, therefore, the realization of the full promise of American independence.[3]

But the path from inspiration (whether in 1865 or 1870) to execution was neither quick nor easy. Bartholdi and Laboulaye were liberal idealists. The government of France under Emperor Napoleon III was, by contrast, downright repressive. The two men were under no illusion that the monarchy would support in any official, let alone financial, way a French monument to celebrate the overthrow of a monarchy. If we believe the traditional chronology of Bartholdi's inspiration—that it came in 1865, rather than the more recent revision of the time line—Bartholdi, perhaps discouraged by the prospects for *Liberty Enlightening the World* in the prevailing political climate, journeyed to Egypt toward the end of the 1860s to propose to that nation's ruling khedive that he commission a massive lighthouse in the form of an ancient female fellah (peasant farmer). This figure, to be erected at Port Said, the Mediterranean entrance to the Suez Canal, would be robed and would hold aloft a giant torch—though (based on surviving drawings) the actual lighthouse beacon may have been intended to emanate from a band encircling the statue's forehead. In some sketches, the figure's face is veiled. One modern scholar, Edward Berenson, writes that Bartholdi "produced a series of drawings in which the proposed statue began as a gigantic female fellah . . . and gradually evolved into a colossal goddess[4] In any event, Bartholdi presented to the khedive something vaguely resembling the Statue of Liberty, an echo of an ancient monument to serve the practical purpose of guiding modern ships to the entrance to the one of the great wonders of the *modern* world, the Suez Canal, which was nearing completion when the sculptor called on the khedive. Bartholdi proposed to call the work *Egypt Brings Light to Asia*.[5]

The Egyptian ruler turned the project down, but the idea and perhaps even the drawings may have found their way into the design for the Statue of Liberty. Long-accepted tradition holds that the model for the American statue was the artist's mother, Augusta Charlotte Bartholdi, but if the work celebrating American independence was actually recycled from a proposed lighthouse on the Suez Canal, it is possible that the icon of American liberty was created by a French sculptor from an Egyptian model, who was quite likely a Muslim and may even have been a Muslim black woman. At least one of the models for the Egyptian project was described as a "statue of a Nubian woman," and, in 2000, Dr. Leonard Jeffries Jr., a professor of African American studies at City College, in New York, "said his research showed that early models of the statue 'were more Negroid,' adding that 'the idea of the black Statue of Liberty has been kept out' of historical accounts."[6]

A NATION OF IMMIGRANTS

That the precedent for a modern symbol of the New World came from a Colossus of the Old, was created by a Frenchman, and was modeled after a French woman (or an Egyptian or black peasant woman—presumably Muslim) makes the Statue of Liberty all the more American. The United States is, after all, a nation of immigrants. This has always been true, but it was never truer than during the Gilded Age. In 1850, the U.S. immigrant population stood at 2,444,600, which was 9.7 percent of the total U.S. population. In 1870, the threshold of the Gilded Age, the number was 5,567,200—14.4 percent of the general population. In 1880, the number rose to 6,679,900, although the percentage of immigrants in the total population dipped to 13.3. By 1890, 9,249,500 Americans were immigrants (14.8 percent of the population), and by 1900, the figure reached 10,341,300 (13.6 percent). At end of the Gilded Age, in 1910, the U.S. immigrant population was 13,515,900 (back up to 14.7 percent). At the start of the twentieth century's third decade, 1920, the graph lines tracing the number of immigrants and the percentage of immigrants crossed: there were 13,920,700 immigrants in America, representing 13.2 percent of the total population. Ten years later, in 1930, the immigrant population reached an apogee of 14,204,100, which, however, was only 11.6 percent of the U.S. population. From 1930 to 1970, both the number of immigrants and their share of the U.S. population declined significantly, hitting a low of 9,619,300, just 4.7 percent of the population. Since 1970, however, the trend has sharply reversed, with immigrant numbers rising to 43,290,400 (13.5 percent of the population) in 2015.[7]

By the numbers, the conclusion is inescapable. The economic, industrial, and political climate of America in the Gilded Age encouraged immigration, which makes the period from 1870 to 1910 much more like our current America than, say, 1930 to 1970. So much is clear—from the numbers. But history and nations are more than numbers. As is true today, frightened and strident voices arose in opposition to the influx of immigrants.

Rejected by Egypt's khedive, Bartholdi decided to return to the American project, but was almost immediately stymied by the outbreak of the Franco-Prussian War in 1870. This not only created a logistical obstacle, it demanded Bartholdi's service when his militia unit—in which he served as a major—was called up. The war was of especially intense concern to Bartholdi because he was a native of Alsace, the province bordering Prussia. Fighting began at the end of July 1870 and, by September 1, 1870, Napoleon III—who had assumed personal command of French forces—lost the Battle of Sedan and surrendered himself as a prisoner of war. The so-called Government of National Defense, which overthrew the Second Empire, continued to fight, but, for all practical purposes, the Franco-Prussian War was over, Alsace was soon ceded to Prussia (which became the center of the new German Empire), and the monarchy was replaced by the Third French Republic. The loss to Germany of his home province must have been a hard blow for Bartholdi, but the establishment of the republic was a blessing for him. It created the liberal political and cultural climate in which a statue dedicated to liberty could find support. Bartholdi sailed for the United States in June 1871, bearing letters of introduction from Laboulaye, whose reputation as a pro-Union abolitionist made him popular in Washington political circles.

When he embarked, Bartholdi was simply interested in promoting a monumental statue to the cause of American independence, a cause in which France had played so central a role during the American Revolution. As his ship glided into New York Harbor, however, Bartholdi's attention became riveted on *Bedloe's Island,* which instantly struck him, for reasons both topographical and symbolic, as the ideal site for his statue. Any ship entering the harbor had to sail past the island. It was impossible to miss it. A statue raised upon it would welcome all who entered America through this port. After he himself had landed, Bartholdi made inquiries about Bedloe's Island (renamed Liberty Island by an act of Congress in 1956). The news was auspicious. It was owned by the federal government, having been ceded to the United States in 1800 as a site for harbor fortifications. The land belonged to no individual, no city, no state. It belonged to the people of the United States of America. As Bartholdi saw it, this was perfect.

Thanks to his letters of introduction, Bartholdi got the ears of movers and shakers in New York, and he even had a sit-down with President Ulysses S. Grant, who saw no problem in obtaining Bedloe's Island for the statue. Thus encouraged, Bartholdi stumped the country, traveling coast to coast by train in two round-trips, buttonholing influencers and opinion makers everywhere. Concerned that this top-down approach would not be sufficient to win popular support, he decided to return to France and, with Laboulaye's aid, plotted out a comprehensive public relations campaign. The two men also discussed elements of the design, and the sculptor enlisted the participation of the distinguished Beaux Arts architect Eugène Viollet-le-Duc to address the structural engineering aspects of the statue, including the construction of the base, the pier to which the skin of the sculpture would be attached, and the material—sheet copper—that would be used. As Bartholdi solved the essential problems of fabrication, the French economy began to reap the benefits of republican government. Although the nation was obligated to pay costly war reparations to the German Empire, there was a new spirit in France, a new productivity, and a strengthening economy. Indeed, it was one of those rare instances in which losing a war actually improved the welfare of the nation.

In 1875, Bartholdi observed the growing interest in the upcoming Philadelphia Centennial Exposition and realized that this would be a natural platform from which to gain the support of the American public for his statue. He and Laboulaye founded the Franco-American Union as a fund-raising organization, and Bartholdi went ahead with the fabrication of the arm and torch and part of the head. While the arm and torch were exhibited at the Centennial and afterward resided for a few years in

Bartholdi sculpted the arm and the head of the Statue of Liberty on spec, while he was still raising funds for the statue. The head was exhibited in New York's Madison Square Park before it was returned to Paris, where it resided in a city park until it was dismantled and shipped to the United States, along with the rest of the statue. Taken in Paris, this photograph dates from 1883.

New York's Madison Square Park, the head, completed in 1877, was displayed at the 1878 World's Fair in Paris.

Directed by the Franco-American Union, various fund-raising organizations were put into operation, the most important of which, in the United States, was the American Committee, which included among its members a young Theodore Roosevelt. On his last full day in office, March 3, 1877, President Grant signed a joint resolution of Congress, authorizing the chief executive to accept the statue from France (whenever it was finished) and to select a site for it. Grant's successor, Rutherford B. Hayes, took his recommendation of Bedloe's Island as the site of choice.

* ———— ✦ ————— *

ON SEPTEMBER 17, 1879, SIXTY-FIVE-YEAR-OLD VIOLLET-LE-DUC, succumbing to illness, died in his villa in Lausanne, Switzerland. This was a blow to the ongoing construction of the statue. Although he had directed the construction of the arm and the head, Viollet-le-Duc died before preparing plans for the main engineering. This seemed like a major setback; however, in 1880, Bartholdi hired no less a figure than Gustave Eiffel, renowned designer of extraordinary ironworks, the most famous of which, the Eiffel Tower (completed in 1889), was nearly a decade in the future. Eiffel quickly abandoned Viollet-le-Duc's idea of a rigid masonry pier and instead, in collaboration with Maurice Koechlin, a structural engineer, designed a truss tower built entirely of wrought iron. Mindful of the tremendous stress to which the copper skin would be subjected, Eiffel and Koechlin devised a system of internal bearings and couplings that allowed the truss tower to move as the copper skin contracted and expanded with changes in temperature. The support system also moved with the winds that were often strong over the harbor. The Gilded Age would see the birth of the modern skyscraper (see chapter 8), which depends on steel-cage and curtain-wall construction, in which the outer structure of the building is effectively attached to and suspended from an inner structure. This outer "curtain wall" bears no structural load, which is carried entirely by the steel cage. The armature of the Statue of Liberty was the very first example of the engineering that produced the skyscraper. Thus, while the statue was a

The Statue of Liberty under construction in Paris, about 1883. Bartholdi stands second from right.

symbol of political revolution, its construction itself exemplified a revolution in engineering and architecture.

◆

FUND-RAISING, PRIMARILY TO BUILD THE PEDESTAL FOR THE STATUE, proved to be a challenging endeavor. Both the New York State government, under Governor Grover Cleveland, and the U.S. Congress refused to appropriate funds. Among those scrambling to raise private funds was a group of artists and writers who auctioned off paintings and literary manuscripts. Among the manuscripts on offer was a sonnet written in 1883 by Emma Lazarus, titled "The New Colossus":

> *Not like the brazen giant of Greek fame,*
> *With conquering limbs astride from land to land;*
> *Here at our sea-washed, sunset gates shall stand*
> *A mighty woman with a torch, whose flame*

Is the imprisoned lightning, and her name
Mother of Exiles. From her beacon-hand
Glows world-wide welcome; her mild eyes command
The air-bridged harbor that twin cities frame.

"Keep, ancient lands, your storied pomp!" cries she
With silent lips. "Give me your tired, your poor,
Your huddled masses yearning to breathe free,
The wretched refuse of your teeming shore.
Send these, the homeless, tempest-tost to me,
I lift my lamp beside the golden door!"

Despite the efforts of Lazarus and many others, it appeared that a lack of funding would halt construction of the pedestal on Bedloe's Island and might even prevent the United States from accepting the statue from France. This predicament spurred the cities of Boston and Philadelphia to make rival bids for the monument, each offering to take delivery of the statue for its relocation in their town. Publishing mogul Joseph Pulitzer did not want New York to lose the statue and so responded to the funding crisis by mounting a drive to raise $100,000 by promising to publish in his *New York World* the name of every person who contributed—regardless of the size of the contribution. The result was a torrent of donations, many in pennies, nickels, and dimes from American children. Fully funded, pedestal construction finally proceeded apace. In order to test the fit of all components, the statue had already been put together in Paris. Bartholdi now ordered that it be dismantled (each component carefully numbered; there were approximately 350 pieces) and loaded aboard the French cargo steamer *Isère*. When that vessel arrived in New York with its cargo on June 17, 1885, American enthusiasm for the statue had become a phenomenon, and an estimated 200,000 people jammed the docks to greet the arrival. The dismantled statue had made the transatlantic crossing in about two hundred crates, which were offloaded but remained unopened until April 1886, when the pedestal was finally completed. The pedestal, a truncated pyramid in shape, was too wide to permit the construction of scaffolding. Workers were therefore obliged to place and attach the statue's copper skin,

The statue is obscured by smoke from the massed artillery fired to salute the arrival of President Grover Cleveland, who came to dedicate the monument.

section by section, while dangling from ropes. As precarious as this was, there were no fatalities—something that all concerned took as a blessed omen.

A week before dedication day, slated for October 28, 1886, the U.S. Army Corps of Engineers intervened with an objection to Bartholdi's proposal to illuminate the torch with powerful floodlights. The Corps feared that this would blind harbor pilots negotiating the busy waters of New York and New Jersey. As designed and built, the torch was sheathed in opaque gold leaf to reflect the sun during the day and floodlights at night. With astonishing improvisational agility, Bartholdi accommodated the Corps of Engineers by ditching the floodlights. He then cut small windows or portholes in the torch, put electric lights inside the structure—Edison had patented the incandescent electric lamp just seven years earlier—and powered them from a generating plant built on the island.

President Grover Cleveland (yes, the very politician who had earlier, as New

York governor, vetoed a $50,000 appropriation to aid construction of the pedestal) presided over the dedication of the Statue of Liberty on October 28, 1886. Although a grand parade in Manhattan drew as many as a million onlookers, according to some sources, only a select audience of dignitaries were invited to Bedloe's Island to witness the dedication itself. Adding further insult to this injury was the absence of any women—save the granddaughter of Suez Canal developer Ferdinand de Lesseps and Jeanne-Emilie Baheux de Puysieux, Bartholdi's wife—at this ceremony dedicating a female representation of liberty. The official excuse for the omission was a fear that ladies might get hurt in the crowd.

None of the speakers at the event—not de Lesseps, New York senator William M. Evarts, President Cleveland, or the keynote speaker, politician and attorney Chauncey Depew—said anything that history remembers. Certainly, none mentioned the immigrants—the "huddled masses yearning to breathe free"— whom Emma Lazarus's sonnet explicitly identified with the statue. Indeed, her words are perhaps the only ones that have resonated down through the years. But the poem was not part of the dedication ceremony. Doubtless, those in charge of the event had no idea of the existence of the poem, which had been forgotten even before Emma Lazarus died, apparently of Hodgkin's lymphoma, in 1887 at the age of thirty-eight. Her friend, Georgina Schuyler, seeking some memorial for her, succeeded in getting a bronze plaque engraved with the sonnet affixed to an inner wall of the pedestal, but this did not happen until 1903. In 1986, the plaque was moved to a permanent Statue of Liberty exhibit inside the pedestal, and that is where visitors to Liberty Island can find it today.

YEARNING TO BREATHE FREE

There are three prominent but small islands in New York Harbor. Liberty Island, on the New Jersey side of the harbor, and the larger Governor's Island, on the New York side, are the first to greet travelers sailing into the port of New York. Just to the north of Liberty Island, on the New Jersey side of the harbor and, as it were, behind the Statue of Liberty, is Ellis Island, about a mile (1.6 km) off the tip of lower Manhattan.

It was originally a destination—first for the Algonquians and then for the Dutch and English—because of its rich oyster beds. Around 1679, the island

Ellis Island processed as many as fourteen million immigrants between 1892 and 1895 and 1954. The Main Building, an ornate Renaissance Revival structure, was designed by architects William Alciphron Boring and Edward Lippincott Tilton. It was completed in 1900.

was given to—and named after—William Dyre, who would become the thirteenth mayor of New York. In 1774, a merchant named Samuel Ellis bought Dyre Island and renamed it after himself. After Ellis died in 1794, ownership of the island was disputed until New York State bought it in 1808 and immediately sold it to the federal government for the purpose of building an arsenal and fort.

After the creation of the U.S. Bureau of Immigration in 1891, Ellis Island was deemed the best location for new immigration processing facilities. Since 1855, Castle Garden—a circular fort built of sandstone at the very tip of Manhattan in what is today Battery Park—had served as the "Emigrant Landing Depot," which was operated not by the federal government, but by the state of New York. Functioning as the processing station for incoming immigrants, it was woefully inadequate to cope with the Gilded Age influx. It had been built originally as a fort called West Battery in 1808–11; was renamed Castle Clinton in 1815; and was then repurposed, when the army left it in 1821, as a place of "public entertainment." In 1824, now called Castle Garden, it served as a combination beer hall, theater, and opera house until the state took it over in 1855.

The newly created Bureau of Immigration opened its first facilities on Ellis Island on January 1, 1892. The main building was three stories high and was complemented by a suite of outbuildings. The entire complex was built of Georgia pine. Predictably, the whole wooden thing burned down in 1897—miraculously, without loss of life—and a fireproof complex, built of brick in an almost playful Renaissance Revival style, was completed in 1900. For the next sixty-two years, Ellis Island served not only as the main point of entry for America's immigrants but also as a symbol of the hopes, aspirations, fears, and disappointments of all those who entered the country from foreign lands.

The main purpose of the island facility was as a cordon sanitaire, where masses of immigrants could be received, examined for disease, and, as deemed necessary, quarantined, admitted directly to the mainland, or deported. For millions, Ellis Island was either the portal to the New World or the locked gate from which they were sent back to the Old.

During the height of its activity at the end of the nineteenth century and the beginning of the twentieth, Ellis Island processed, in its flag-draped Great Hall, hundreds of thousands of people a year; at least 12 million—perhaps as many as 14 million or more—passing through the place between 1895 and 1954, when the facility was closed.[8]

While Ellis Island served a necessary practical purpose, it was also a symbol of the nation's attempt to assert control over an endless influx of immigrants. It was a reflection of the balancing act that was always part of the American experience, but never more so than during the Gilded Age. Government administrators strug-

This color postcard from 1908 shows the Great Hall, through which arriving immigrants were processed and given medical examinations. Depending on the state of an immigrant's health, he or she would be admitted to the country, held for quarantine, or rejected and put on the next available outbound ship.

gled to weigh the nation's fears of an assault on its "American identity" against the demands of industry, which sought cheap immigrant labor in ever-increasing numbers from the end of the Civil War through the early 1900s. Immigration was hardly new to America, of course; however, from 1866 to 1900, more immigrants arrived than in the preceding 250 years. Moreover, they were of different origin than those who arrived before the Civil War. Overwhelmingly, the first waves of U.S. immigrants were Western Europeans, mostly from the British Isles, Ireland, Scandinavia, and Germany. After the Civil War and throughout the Gilded Age, the predominant influx was still European, but most came from Southern and Eastern Europe—Italians, Eastern European Jews fleeing persecution, and other Slavic peoples. The era also saw a sharp rise in the immigration of Chinese and Japanese, especially on the West Coast.

None of these groups came uninvited. Industry demanded cheap immigrant labor, and the government homesteading initiatives begun during the Civil War and continuing into the 1890s were intended to populate the West, expanding the nation's agriculture while also creating new markets for the products of U.S. manufacturers. As for the immigrants, many did achieve what they sought by leaving their home countries—greater liberty, escape from persecution, and an opportunity to achieve a degree of material security and prosperity. Yet there was also a backlash against immigrants and immigration. While "native-born" Americans generally tolerated and even welcomed the early waves of immigrants, whose Western European cultural, religious, and linguistic profile was generally similar to their own, the immigrants of the Gilded Age came with differences that some found unnerving and even intolerable. Eastern European culture, language, and religion—especially in the case of the Jews and the Roman Catholics—struck many as too different, too "other," to ever be successfully assimilated into the American Protestant mainstream. Newspapers, the halls of Congress, and even some churches and university classrooms were filled with talk of an "immigrant problem" and an "immigrant threat." Both nationally and locally, anti-immigrant, anti-Catholic, and anti-Semitic organizations sprang up, most notably the American Protective League and the Immigration Restriction League. Such organizations rallied support to pressure members of Congress to enact legislation restricting immigration, at least from certain places deemed undesirable.

Generally, the more "alien" an immigrant group was perceived to be, the stron-

This undated photograph shows Eastern European immigrant arrivals on Ellis Island. These immigrants were looked on less favorably than those from Western Europe, but both were far more readily welcomed than immigrants from Asia or Africa.

ger the objections to it. Chinese immigration, which had been encouraged and welcomed during the western Gold Rush era of 1848 to the mid-1850s and the great western expansion of the railroads during the 1860s and early 1870s, elicited ugly anti-Chinese agitation and even violence during the middle and late 1870s. Growing anti-Chinese sentiment, especially among the working class, which feared competition for laboring jobs, resulted in the 1882 passage of "An Act to Execute Certain Treaty Stipulations Relating to Chinese"—universally known as the Chinese Exclusion Act. The first U.S. law specifically aimed against a racial or ethnic group, the act barred Chinese immigration into the United States for ten years. In 1892, the Geary Act renewed the ban for another ten years, and, in 1902, the ban was made permanent until its repeal, during World War II, by the Magnuson Act of December 17, 1943.

Unquestionably, of course, the Chinese Exclusion Act was anti-Chinese, but, even more to the point, it was anti-American. This tragic irony was made all the more poignant by its passage just four years before the Statue of Liberty was dedicated. When Joseph Pulitzer, himself a Jewish immigrant from Hungary, conducted in the pages of his *New York World* a campaign to fund the construction of the pedestal for the statue, one reader, Saum Song Bo, a Chinese immigrant living in New York City, wrote a letter of protest to the editor:

[T]HE WORD LIBERTY MAKES ME THINK OF THE FACT THAT THIS COUNTRY IS THE LAND OF LIBERTY FOR MEN OF ALL NATIONS EXCEPT THE CHINESE. I CONSIDER IT AN INSULT TO US CHINESE TO CALL ON US TO CONTRIBUTE TOWARD BUILDING IN THIS LAND A PEDESTAL FOR A STATUE OF LIBERTY. THAT STATUE REPRESENTS LIBERTY HOLDING A TORCH WHICH LIGHTS THE PASSAGE OF THOSE OF ALL NATIONS WHO COME INTO THIS COUNTRY. BUT ARE THE CHINESE ALLOWED TO ENJOY LIBERTY AS MEN OF ALL OTHER NATIONALITIES ENJOY IT? ARE THEY ALLOWED TO GO ABOUT EVERYWHERE FREE FROM THE INSULTS, ABUSE, ASSAULTS, WRONGS AND INJURIES FROM WHICH MEN OF OTHER NATIONALITIES ARE FREE?

IF THERE BE A CHINAMAN WHO . . . DESIRES TO MAKE HIS HOME IN THIS LAND, AND WHO, SEEING THAT HIS COUNTRYMEN DEMAND ONE OF THEIR OWN NUMBER TO BE THEIR LEGAL ADVISER, REPRESENTATIVE, ADVOCATE AND PROTECTOR, DESIRES TO STUDY LAW, CAN HE BE A LAWYER? BY THE LAW OF THIS NATION, HE, BEING A CHINAMAN, CANNOT BECOME A CITIZEN, AND CONSEQUENTLY CANNOT BE A LAWYER. . . .

WHETHER THIS [1882] STATUTE AGAINST THE CHINESE OR THE STATUE TO LIBERTY WILL BE THE MORE LASTING MONUMENT TO TELL FUTURE AGES OF THE LIBERTY AND GREATNESS OF THIS COUNTRY, WILL BE KNOWN ONLY TO FUTURE GENERATIONS.

LIBERTY, WE CHINESE DO LOVE AND ADORE THEE; BUT LET NOT THOSE WHO DENY THEE TO US MAKE OF THEE A GRAVEN IMAGE, AND INVITE US TO BOW DOWN TO IT.[9]

Industries in need of cheap manual labor successfully lobbied Congress to allow large numbers of Chinese laborers to immigrate to the United States. In China, so-called labor agents lured prospective immigrants to America with promises of good, clean work in a land of equality and law. The new arrivals were invariably disappointed and, often, horrified.

Saum Song Bo was not the only immigrant who felt betrayed by what late nineteenth-century America offered. Among European immigrants, many had been lured to the United States by recruiters, called labor agents, who promised high wages and steady employment in the Promised Land across the Atlantic. The Western railroads, which owned vast tracts of land along their rights of way, launched propaganda campaigns throughout Europe that advertised the easy availability of cheap land in the Golden West. The colorful pages of the railroad flyers led many immigrants to believe they would soon own farms in a Garden of Eden. In fact, most newcomers had to content themselves with factory jobs in the densely populated urban ghettos of the East Coast. Many immigrants found themselves relegated to the ranks of the working poor. As journalists and reformers of the era documented (see chapter 14), they lived in dark, squalid, airless tenements. Yet the "Chinatowns," "Little Italys," and "Greek Towns" that appeared in a number of larger U.S. cities also became centers of ethnic and national pride and prosperity. Even as most first-generation immigrants eked out their living with low-paying jobs as unskilled factory laborers, they managed to lay the foundation for their children's brighter future.

Not all immigrants chose to stay. About half of young, single, male Italians, Greeks, and Slavs who immigrated between roughly 1870 and 1900 remained in the States just long enough to earn the kind of money they could not hope for at home. Once they reached whatever monetary goal they had set, they returned to Europe. During the period of the Gilded Age, two of three Chinese immigrants went back to China, and while Mexico contributed many permanent immigrants, a large class of Mexican migrant laborers regularly moved back and forth across the border in rhythm with whatever employment opportunities presented themselves north or south of the Rio Grande.[10]

THE AGE OF IMMIGRANTS

By the numbers, the Gilded Age was the heyday of immigration in America. Behind the numbers, however, it was a period during which both the worst and the best of the immigrant experience emerged front and center in American civilization. The ugliness of anti-immigrant prejudice and, sometimes, even outright exclusion (as in the 1882 anti-Chinese law) hurt many and broke some. Most immigrants, however, never lost their faith in the promise of America. For them, the immigrant experience was a crucible that tested them and, in testing, made them stronger. Their endurance paid off for their children, who grew up American.

Daniel Griswold, director of the Center for Trade Policy Studies at the Cato Institute, a conservative American think tank, wrote in 2002 that, far from "undermining the American experiment," immigration has "kept our country demographically young, enriched our culture and added to our productive capacity as a nation, enhancing our influence in the world." Moreover, while many immigrants do "fill jobs that Americans cannot or will not fill" at the low end of the skill spectrum, they are also today "disproportionately represented in such high-skilled fields as medicine, physics and computer science."[11] The same was true during the Gilded Age. Immigrants took on many of the very dirty jobs "native-born" Americans spurned, but they also included in their ranks some of the nation's greatest achievers. The likes of newspaper publisher Joseph Pulitzer, telephone inventor Alexander Graham Bell, mathematician and electrical engineer Charles Steinmetz, physicist and futurist Nikola Tesla, naturalist John Muir, journalist Jacob Riis, Lincoln private secretary John George Nicolay, labor activist Mary Harris "Mother" Jones, Jewish immigrant author Abraham Cahan, and financier and philanthropist Andrew Carnegie are just a few of the immigrants who made their mark during the Gilded Age.

The Gilded Age pulled America in opposite directions.

As symbolized in the great Centennial Exposition of 1876—the first world's fair—post–Civil War Americans had an urge to reach out into the world and to project themselves onto the global stage. They also proudly drew the world to themselves, inviting visitors and immigrants alike. Politically, the drive to project American power and influence expressed itself in the birth of American imperialism and a desire for the nation to be acknowledged as a world power. Economically, the industrial development and the Western settlement of the United States required an influx of immigrants from all over the world—to do industrial labor in the cities and to settle and cultivate the vast expanses of the nation's West.

Even as the 1876 exposition in Philadelphia celebrated the technological present and future, it also looked back longingly on the previous one hundred years. In much the same way, the American nation opened itself to the world yet also sometimes recoiled in fear from it, retreating into an "America First" nativism that was both timid and brutal. The clash between the cosmopolitan and the parochial defined both the energy and the angst of the Gilded Age. Along with such material monuments as the Statue of Liberty and the buildings on Ellis Island, these dual motives of collective advance and withdrawal have survived beyond the end of the nineteenth century. Thus the history of American civilization in the twentieth century and into the first two decades of the twenty-first is marked by a national ambivalence that should be familiar to us by now, an urge to both strike out into the wider world and to retreat from it, to open up to others and to build walls against them, to embrace unfamiliar people and cultures and to push them away. As is true today, democracy in the Gilded Age was far from simple and never stood still for long.

Oftentimes. Chinese immigrants were subjected to prejudice and persecution. This 1871 *Harper's Weekly* cartoon shows Columbia—the personification of America—preparing to protect a downcast Asian immigrant from an intolerant American mob.

CHAPTER 7

HARD LABOR

On December 28, 1960, Theodore W. Schultz, chair of economics at the University of Chicago and future Nobel laureate economist, delivered the presidential address to the seventy-third annual meeting of the American Economic Association in St. Louis. Titled "Investment in Human Capital," it began: "Although it is obvious that people acquire useful skills and knowledge, it is not obvious that these skills and knowledge are a form of capital, that this capital is in substantial part a product of deliberate investment, that it has grown in Western societies at a much faster rate than conventional (nonhuman) capital, and that its growth may well be the most distinctive feature of the economic system."[1]

Schultz was born in 1902, during the latter days of the Gilded Age, and he died in 1998 at age ninety-five. Even in 1960, the Gilded Age was a fading memory. But the term Schultz coined, *human capital*, not only stuck in twentieth- and twenty-first-century economics and business, it can serve us now to identify the biggest and most consequential investment American capitalists (captains of industry or robber barons, as you will) made during the final quarter of the nineteenth century. They did not use the term, of course, but as the explosion in American immigration from 1870 to 1910

The Bethlehem Steel Works, 1881, by American artist and author Joseph Pennell. It is described as a "watercolor in sepia brown, white and gray." The colors are suited to the factory depicted here and to the entire industrial expansion throughout America in the Gilded Age.

testifies, the growth of investment in human capital outpaced any investments in factories, machinery, and physical infrastructure—great as these outlays were. The need for human capital during this period profoundly shaped business, politics, social policy, and the law, as various interests vied with one another to attract labor, especially immigrants, while also managing labor in ways that typically sought to suppress what tycoons and factory managers alike saw as the excessively costly demands of the laboring class.

POVERTY AMID PRODIGALITY

"Throughout the Gilded Age," historian Sean Dennis Cashman wrote, "The specters of poverty and oppression waited on the banquet of expansion and opportunity."[2] Instead of jealously husbanding their investment in human capital, business owners squandered it prodigally, seemingly bent on, one way or another,

Lewis Hine earned a high place in the annals of photography with his gritty yet majestic images of American workers in the early twentieth century, many showing child laborers. He titled this 1911 photograph *Noon hour in the Ewen Breaker. Pennsylvania Coal Co Location: South Pittston, Pennsylvania.*

THE GILDED AGE

working their employees to death. They did this in two ways—first, through wages compatible only with abject poverty and, second, by providing working conditions that threatened life itself.

According to economic historian Clarence Long, the mean hourly wage of male factory workers, age sixteen and older, was 16 cents in 1890, with a low of 11 cents for cotton mill workers and a high of 29 cents in the printing industry. For females, the mean was 9 cents an hour, with a low of 6 cents in the glass industry and in tanneries, and a high of 11 cents both in the cigar making and rubber industries. For males under sixteen years old, the 1890 mean was 6 cents an hour, with wages ranging between just 5 and 6 cents across all factory industries.[3]

Such wages ensured that much of the semiskilled and unskilled working class would always be the working poor. In many areas, industrial slums proliferated. In smaller mill towns, these were often neighborhoods of overcrowded row houses, detached housing of one or two rooms, or even shantytowns. In the larger cities, where most Gilded Age immigrant laborers made their homes, tenements were built, the worst of which were little more than warehouses for human beings. Nowhere were tenements more abundant than in New York City. The destination for many immigrants, New York saw its population double every decade from 1800 to 1880. As the immigrants of the pre–Civil War era became better established financially, they left the poorest neighborhoods on the city's Lower East Side and moved farther north. The single-family, low-rise, masonry row houses they vacated were bought up by a variety of landlords and speculators, who subdivided them to accommodate multiple families. The result was a neighborhood of narrow apartment buildings, overcrowded, poorly lit, and even less adequately ventilated. Many lacked indoor plumbing. By 1900, about 2.3 million people—two-thirds of the city's population—lived in tenements. By this time, of course, the original tenement buildings, those converted from single-family dwellings, were vastly outnumbered by new, purpose-built structures. Some 80,000 tenements were built in New York City between the end of the Civil War and 1900.

By 1880, the typical tenement building was five to seven stories high. Its walls were pushed out to very nearly the full extent of the lot it occupied, the typical tenement lot being 25 feet wide by 100 feet long (7.6 x 30.5 m). Along the street, most tenement buildings shared a common wall, which gave anyone walking along Lower East Side streets the sensation of moving through a narrow corridor with walls continuous on both sides. The front of the tenement looked out onto the street, but the back was often no more than a foot (30.5 cm) away from the back of the tenement that fronted the opposite street. For most occupants, this meant a life lived in little daylight and with little fresh air (although some apartments had small air shafts built directly into the room).[4]

Tenement living had become infamous even before the Gilded Age proper. A catastrophic cholera epidemic that swept New York in 1849 was largely concentrated in the Lower East Side tenement district. It claimed some 5,000 lives, although no one kept an accurate count. The widespread, costly, and even deadly riots that erupted in Manhattan in July 1863, mostly among Irish immigrants, were called the "Draft Riots" because they protested the injustice of conscription laws, which targeted men too poor to afford $300 to buy their way out of service during the Civil War. In fact, the rioters' grievances also included outrage over tenement living conditions. By the end of the Civil War, New Yorkers lived in fear of a renewed outbreak of protest violence and, in 1867, largely in response

to ongoing grassroots agitation, the city passed its first Tenement House Act. The law mandated rudimentary zoning regulations to provide fire escapes, as well as some light and air in living and sleeping rooms. A new building code specified inclusion of one toilet—or privy—for every twenty residents. As basic as these regulations were, most developers and landlords simply ignored them, paying off local officials to avoid enforcement penalties.

Slum conditions were grim and dangerous, but the demand for cheap "human capital" and the

A tenement "yard" on Manhattan's Lower East Side, photographed by the great chronicler of urban immigrant poverty, Jacob Riis, for his monumental *How the Other Half Lives* (1890)—a foundational document of the American Progressive movement.

consequent flow of immigrants only continued to increase, keeping the tenements continuously occupied. Astoundingly, a significant number of families in each new immigrant cohort managed to improve their lot enough to move uptown and out of the Lower East Side. Nevertheless, this just made room for the newcomers, of whom the Port of New York seemed to present a limitless supply. Throughout most of the Gilded Age, more privileged New Yorkers either deliberately turned a blind eye to conditions in Lower Manhattan or were somehow sufficiently insulated uptown to be unaware of the squalor in which so many of their neighbors lived.

This began to change in 1890, when journalist Jacob August Riis published *How the Other Half Lives*, a meticulously detailed exposé of life in the slums of New York. The author's unflinching documentary prose was complemented by his stark photographs, most often illuminated by the garish light of flash powder. The result was a combination of naked, sensational truth and deep compassion.

Riis was himself an immigrant, having come to New York from his native Denmark in 1870. His first seven years in the city were spent close to destitution, but, in 1877, he found a job as a police reporter, first for the *New York Tribune* and then the *Evening Sun*. His office, on lower Manhattan's Mulberry Street, was directly across from police headquarters, in the heart of the Lower East Side immigrant slums. He made it a practice to walk the streets of this district between two and four in the morning, determined to catch the neighborhood "off its guard," as he said. He peered into such colorfully named locales as Bandits' Roost, Bottle Alley, Bone Alley, Thieves' Alley, and Kerosene Row when no one was supposed to be looking.

At the time, the Progressive movement (see chapter 14) was gathering momentum, and in this developing context, Riis

"Mulberry Bend"—the name of this Lower Manhattan street—is evocative of a country lane. The urban reality behind the name, as captured by Riis, is altogether different. The journalist's newspaper office was located on this street.

was prepared to declare that the tenement district of the Lower East Side "was not fit for Christian men and women, let alone innocent children, to live in, and therefore it had to go." With camera, pen, and the trained eye and ear of a reporter who had seen and heard everything on the police beat, he went about documenting the neighborhood he had known intimately for nearly two decades.

What most affected Riis, and what he believed would grip his readers hardest, was what he saw among the children of the neighborhood:

> The problem of the children becomes, in these swarms, to the last degree perplexing. Their very number make one stand aghast. . . . I counted the other day the little ones, up to ten years or so, in a Bayard Street tenement that for a yard has a triangular space in the centre with sides fourteen or fifteen feet long, just room enough for a row of ill-smelling closets at the base of the triangle and a hydrant at the apex. There was about as much light in this "yard" as in the average cellar. I gave up my self-imposed task in despair when I had counted one hundred and twenty-eight in forty families. . . . Bodies of drowned children turn up in the rivers . . . whom no one seems to know anything about. When last spring some workmen, while moving a pile of lumber on a North River pier, found under the last plank the body of a little lad crushed to death, no one had missed a boy, though his parents afterward turned up. . . .
>
> A little fellow who seemed clad in but a single rag was among the flotsam and jetsam stranded at Police Headquarters one day last summer. No one knew where he came from or where he belonged. The boy himself knew as little about it as anybody, and was the least anxious to have light shed on the subject after he had spent a night in the matron's nursery. . . . He sang "McGinty" all through, with Tenth Avenue variations, for the police, then settled down to the serious business of giving an account of himself. The examination went on after this fashion:
>
> "Where do you go to church, my boy?"
>
> "We don't have no clothes to go to church." And indeed his appearance, as he was, in the door of any New York church would have caused a sensation.
>
> "Well, where do you go to school, then?"
>
> "I don't go to school," with a snort of contempt.

"Where do you buy your bread?"

"We don't buy bread; we buy beer," said the boy, and it was eventually the saloon that led the police as a landmark to his "home." It was worthy of the boy. As he had said, his only bed was a heap of dirty straw on the floor, his daily diet a crust in the morning, nothing else.[5]

BY THE SWEAT OF YOUR BROW

What hope for a better future did such children have? Perhaps they would live to work in a factory—very likely starting before they reached the age of sixteen. Judging from accounts published in *The Factory Inspector*, the unofficial journal of the International Association of Factory Inspectors, such a life might not last very long. The periodical routinely published horrifying accounts of industrial accidents extracted from the annals of state labor bureaus. The following, from 1907, as summarized from the periodical by the U.S. Department of Labor on its History home page, are typical:

> At a steel mill in Butler, Pennsylvania, a heavy pot of hot metal spilled molten steel onto wet sand, causing a huge explosion which destroyed part of the plant. Streams of hot metal poured down on the workmen, engulfing and literally cooking some of them. Four men died and 30 more were injured. The explosion shook buildings in the town and caused panic among the populace. Thousands turned out to watch the huge fire that ensued.
>
> Two employees at a steel plant in Youngstown, Ohio, were sent to clean out the dust underneath the blast furnaces. Suddenly there was a slippage of tons of molten fuel and ore inside the furnace, causing large amounts of very hot dust to fall on them. One of the men was completely buried in it and died in great agony. The other escaped with severe burns.
>
> A machinist got his arm caught in a rapidly moving belt. It was jerked from its socket, and he fell 50 feet to the floor. His fellow workers, aghast at the man's shrieks, ran in panic from the shop.
>
> A young boy working in a coffin plant was decapitated and had both arms and both legs torn off when he was caught on shafting rotating at 300 revolutions per minute.

A worker in a brick-making factory was caught in a belt and had most of his skin torn off.

A sawmill worker fell onto a large, unguarded circular saw and was split in two.

When a worker got caught in the large flywheel of the main steam power plant of a navy yard, his arms and legs were torn off and the lifeless trunk was hurled against a wall 50 feet away.

In plain sight of a hundred fellow workmen, Martin Stoffel was cut into small pieces at the Philadelphia Caramel Works. . . . He was dragged into the machinery and his head severed. . . . A second later both legs were cut off. Then one arm after the other fell into the lesser wheels below, both being cut into many parts. Before the machinery could be stopped, Stoffel had been literally chopped to pieces.[6]

This image, c. 1907, depicts steelworkers drawing slag on the lower level of a blast furnace at the Homestead (Pennsylvania) steel works. In this same year, journalist William B. Hard published an exposé of dangerous industrial working conditions, titled "Making Steel and Killing Men."

In a 1907 article in *Everybody's Magazine*, titled "Making Steel and Killing Men," journalist William B. Hard wrote of accidents at United States Steel's great South Works along the Calumet River in the South Chicago neighborhood of Chicago. Following the declarative sentence, "Steel is war," he estimated that, out of a workforce of ten thousand in the plant, twelve hundred were killed or injured every year. In one particularly gruesome accident, a worker was cooked alive when molten slag spilled down on him from a great ladle that had slipped while being transported by an overhead crane. On investigation, it was shown that the ladle lacked proper lugs, so the crane's hook was simply placed under the rim of the ladle. Citing incidents like this, instances of obvious negligence, Hard wrote that U.S. Steel and many other companies could easily take steps to reduce accidents, but felt no incentive to do so. For one thing, finding replacement workers was never a problem; fresh immigrants kept arriving. For another, there was no more than a one in five chance that U.S. Steel would even be compelled to pay compensation to the family of a man killed or injured.[7]

Nevertheless, there were federal and local laws on the books that governed factory safety. They were nowhere near comprehensive, and they were poorly enforced, but they did exist. Labor in and around tenements was not covered by such laws, inadequate though they were. Jacob Riis wrote extensively of how the tenements were not just overcrowded, filthy, dark, and airless places to live, they were also overcrowded, filthy, dark, and airless places to work. He documented the role of an individual known as a "sweater," a man "who drums up work among the clothing-houses," recruiting garment workers for makeshift factories—sweatshops—established in or adjacent to tenement buildings:

Jacob Riis photographed these garment workers laboring in a sweatshop run out of a Ludlow Street tenement on Manhattan's Lower East Side, about 1889.

Harper's Weekly featured a full-page engraving captioned "Cheap Clothing—The Slaves of the 'Sweaters'" for a story on sweatshop labor published in April 1890. Jacob Riis observed, "The bulk of the sweater's work is done in the tenements, which the law that regulates factory labor does not reach."

The bulk of the sweater's work is done in the tenements, which the law that regulates factory labor does not reach. To the factories themselves that are taking the place of the rear tenements in rapidly growing numbers, letting in bigger day-crowds than those the health officers banished, the tenement shops serve as a supplement through which the law is successfully evaded. Ten hours is the legal work-day in the factories, and nine o'clock the closing hour at the latest. Forty-five minutes at least must be allowed for dinner, and children under sixteen must not be employed unless they can read and write English; none at all under fourteen. The very fact that such a law should stand on the statute book, shows how desperate the plight of these people. But the tenement has defeated its benevolent purpose. In it the child works unchallenged from the day he is old enough to pull a thread. There is no such thing as a dinner hour; men and women eat while they work, and the "day" is lengthened at both ends far into the night. Factory hands take their work with them at the close of the lawful day to eke out their scanty earnings by working overtime at home. Little chance on this ground for the campaign of education that alone can bring the needed relief; small wonder that there are whole settlements on this East Side where English is practically an unknown tongue, though the people be both willing and anxious to learn. "When shall we find time to learn?" asked one of them of me once. I owe him the answer yet.

Take the Second Avenue Elevated Railroad at Chatham Square and ride up half a mile through the sweaters' district. Every open window of the big tenements, that stand like a continuous brick wall on both sides of the way, gives you a glimpse of one of these shops as the train speeds by. Men and women bending over their machines, or ironing clothes at the window, half-naked. Proprieties do not count on the East Side; nothing counts that cannot be converted into hard cash.[8]

One day in 1890, Theodore Roosevelt, an emerging progressive political leader who was a member of the U.S. Civil Service Commission and a prominent activist in New York social causes, called on Riis. Finding him unavailable at the time, he left a card on his desk. "I have read your book," he wrote on it, "and I have come to help." Later, after he had been president of the United States, Roosevelt wrote of *How the Other Half Lives* that it had been to him "both an enlightenment and an inspiration."[9] There is no doubt that this book and the work of other authors and journalists were instrumental in motivating and guiding the Progressive reform movement (see chapter 14), but it took a heart-wrenching catastrophe at the very end of the era—the Triangle Shirtwaist Factory fire—to draw the attention of the entire nation to the profligate waste of "human capital" that was business as usual in the Gilded Age.

Jacob Riis—Danish-American immigrant, journalist, social reformer, and documentarian of tenement life in Gilded Age New York. His impact on progressivism in the United States cannot be overstated.

TRIANGLE SHIRTWAIST FIRE

At the close of work on March 25, 1911, one of the five hundred employees of the Triangle Shirtwaist Factory on 23–29 Washington Place in Greenwich Village, New York City, smelled smoke. She noticed that a rag bin near her eighth-floor workstation was on fire. She yelled—for there was no alarm system of any kind—to summon her fellow workers, who unsuccessfully set about trying to extinguish the blaze. Factory manager Samuel Bernstein ordered his employees to unroll the fire extinguisher hose, only to discover that it was rotted and useless.

Escape was the only remaining option. There were just three ways out for the Triangle workers, who occupied the top three floors of the ten-story Asch Building. They could use the external fire escape, the stairways, or the freight elevators. To many, the fire escape seemed the most obvious way out, and they rushed it. It was narrow, rusty, and inadequate to bear any concentrated load. It ended at the second floor, above a small courtyard. Those lucky enough to get this far still faced a high drop to safety. In the crush, some of the young women—for the workers were overwhelmingly young female Eastern European immigrants—tumbled over the low railing, falling from one landing to the next.

Other employees made for the stairways. Those on the eighth floor discovered that the door to the stairway on one side of the building had been locked. When they rushed over to the stairway on the other side, they found it clogged with workers fleeing from the ninth and tenth floors. This left the eighth-floor workers with the freight elevators, which were still operating. In acts of incredible heroism, several of the cutters risked their lives taking turns operating the elevator to carry their coworkers to safety.

The seventy employees who worked on the tenth floor escaped via the staircases or, in desperation, climbed onto the roof. Some law students and their professor from New York University, located across the street, got ahold of ladders, which they desperately stretched across the street to the roof of the Asch Building. In this way, approximately fifty workers perilously crawled across the chasm separating the roofs of the two buildings.[10]

But it was the 260 workers on the ninth floor who were in greatest danger. A warning telephone call from the eighth floor never reached them. They were, therefore, the last to know about the fire, and by the time they discovered it, nearly all avenues of escape were blocked. Some workers desperately clung to the elevator cables and used them to climb down. Others crammed into the narrow staircase, and still others climbed onto the fire escape. By this time, however, the repeated loads and the heat of the fire had weakened the already spindly structure, which separated from the wall of the building, falling to the ground in a mass of iron splinters and shattered flesh and bone.

All that was left to the ninth-floor workers were the window ledges. To fight the blaze, the New York Fire Department sent thirty-five pieces of equipment, including ladder vehicles. The young women on the ninth-floor window ledge watched in horror as the ladders, fully extended, stopped short at the sixth floor. Firefighters therefore stretched a net about a hundred feet below on the street. Workers began jumping off the ledges, some of the young women holding hands and jumping in pairs. The weight of the repeated impacts was too much for the stout canvas fabric, which split as bodies ripped through it.

Over the next several days, streams of survivors filed through the building to identify the 146 bodies—mostly young, mostly immigrant, mostly female. There was a sustained public clamor for laws to regulate the safety of working conditions. The immigrant community of New York and other American cities was no longer the invisible "other half." To many people, they suddenly appeared as human beings in jeopardy and in need of justice.

Immigrant laborers employed by the Triangle Shirtwaist Company factory—most of them young women—leaped to their deaths rather than be consumed by flame. The broken bodies were placed in coffins at the scene of the fire, March 25, 1911.

"THE MOST PERFECT TOWN IN THE WORLD"

George Mortimer Pullman sought to control every aspect of the production of his patented railroad sleeping and dining cars—including the very lives of his workers. The company town he built south of Chicago and named after himself was intended as an urban utopia. It fell far short of this aspiration.

Born in Brocton, New York, in 1831, George Mortimer Pullman spent much of his childhood working. After he dropped out of school at fourteen, he clerked at a store for a time before he joined his father in a house-moving business, lifting and moving houses to accommodate the widening of the Erie Canal. This taught him a lot about civil engineering, and, as a young man, he moved to Chicago, joining two more experienced engineers in a partnership to build a major sewer system for the burgeoning city on Lake Michigan. Because of Chicago's low-lying, boggy location, the sewers had to be laid on top of the existing ground and then covered over by six to eight feet of earth. Pullman's engineering specialty—moving houses to new foundations—was indispensable to this operation. Not only did he make a fortune, he made a sensational name for himself in 1861 when he raised the six-story brick Tremont House Hotel by six feet (1.8 m) so that the sewers could be laid, the new soil added, and a new foundation built—all while the guests remained undisturbed in their rooms.

In 1864, Pullman used the proceeds from the Chicago project to create a new kind of railroad sleeping car, which he dubbed the Pullman Palace Car. The grandest of Pullman's early production was the *Pioneer*, which, Pullman would later claim, served as a railborne hearse for the body of President Abraham Lincoln, assassinated on April 14, 1865. This is a myth, likely publicity-enhancing, started at the time (although it is an assertion still widely accepted today).[11]

The martyred president was carried on a long, roundabout procession from Washington to his home in Springfield, Illinois, and it may well be that the many hundreds of thousands of mourners who gathered along the tracks believed they were looking at a train that included Pullman Palace cars, even though at least one modern source asserts that no Pullman rolling stock was included in the nine-car funeral train.[12] Perhaps it was the public exposure to a luxury train, with or without Pullman cars, that stimulated sudden demand for the Palace sleepers. From 1865 on, railroads ordered the innovation in great numbers. A visionary, Pullman saw the sleeper not as merely a piece of rolling stock, but as a travel experience, a way to bring luxury to the expanding American middle class. He soon added a kitchen-and-dining car to his line—and then he ensured that the food served aboard it would be prepared by some of the nation's best chefs. In 1868, he even made a deal with New York's celebrated Delmonico's restaurant to cater the car he christened the Delmonico.

A stereographic view of the *Palmyra*, one of Pullman's "Palace Sleeping Cars," which transformed long-distance rail travel in America and much of the world.

Inundated with orders, Pullman needed a huge, skilled, well-behaved, and loyal workforce to produce his cars. America was roiled by labor unrest at the time, but Pullman had a new vision. He was confident that he had the means to create harmony in the ranks of his human capital. Pullman decided to ensure that his workers did not suffer from the customary ills of life in an industrial slum. He would do this not by paying them particularly generous salaries, but by giving them a model town to live in—and, incidentally, making residence in that town a requirement for employment. On 4,000 acres (1,600 ha) south of Chicago along the right-of-way of the Illinois Central Railroad, he built a town from scratch: Pullman, Illinois. Within its precincts were a new factory as well as the homes, stores, theaters, churches, library, and hotel to serve the workforce. Everything was designed by a single architect/civil engineer, Solon Spencer Beman, who conceived it as a total environment, a first-of-its-kind industrial utopian community. Pullman employees were put to work constructing the town, which was fabricated entirely out of brick fired in a brickworks dedicated to the project. Work began in 1880 and, just four years later, a thousand homes and public

Pullman created a sumptuous travel experience—for those with the money to pay—that came to symbolize the Gilded Age. The quotation printed on the elegant cover of this 1901 Pullman dining car menu is from a Middle English carol: *"Man, be merie as Brid on berie and al thi Care let away."*

buildings had been completed. Most employees lived in houses of two to seven rooms, complete with stone ornamentation and pitched roofs of slate. Every home opened onto a private yard (with woodshed) and a paved alley. Each alley provided access for vendors as well as trash collectors, who hauled garbage away daily. Pullman, Illinois, was built to be the very antithesis of the immigrant slum.

The only trouble was that the workers, laboring in the Pullman plant, living in their rented Pullman homes, worshiping in Pullman churches, purchasing virtually everything in Pullman stores, and citizens of a Pullman town, were regulated and ruled, morning and night, by George Mortimer Pullman.

The average monthly rent for three-room apartments was $8.00 to $8.50; a five-room row house rented for $18.00 per month; and executive homes could be had for rents starting at $25.00 a month. All of this was above the average throughout the city—but the level of quality was also above average. Rents were deducted directly from salaries. Indeed, a portion of workers' pay was issued in scrip, which was redeemable only at the company stores located in town.[13] As if this level of intrusion into private life were not sufficiently oppressive, Pullman managers kept close tabs on workers, insisting on their church attendance, enforcing their children's school attendance (in a Pullman schoolhouse), and general policing the behavior of the entire family. One resident complained that "the company owns everything and it exercises a surveillance over the movement and habits of the people in a way to lead one to suppose that it has a proprietary interest in [their] souls and bodies." The *New York Sun* reported on October 11, 1885 that residents were "not happy and grumble at their situation. . . . They say that all this perfection costs too much in money and imposes upon them an untolerable [*sic*] constraint." The company "continues its watch and authority over them after working hours." Residents "declare they are bound hand and foot by a philanthropic monopoly."[14]

Then came the national Panic of 1893, which brought on a major economic depression. Pullman responded by slashing wages across the board—without, however, commensurately reducing rents or prices in company stores. In 1894, a committee of employees asked to meet with Pullman to air their grievances. When he refused even to sit down with the committee, the American Railway Union, under the leadership of the fiery labor leader and socialist Eugene V. Debs, called a boycott of the handling of all Pullman cars. Union workers would not allow them to move on the nation's railroads. By this time, Pullman Palace Cars were ubiquitous on the rails, and the boycott brought rail service in some regions nearly to a halt. Because this disruption interfered with the transit of the U.S. mails, President Grover Cleveland intervened, authorizing Attorney General Richard Olney to obtain a federal injunction barring union leaders from supporting the strike and ordering strikers to return to work or face dismissal. When strikers responded with violence, not only in Pullman, but in many towns and cities affected by the general shutdown of rail service, Cleveland sent some twelve thousand U.S. Army regulars and teams of federal marshals to put down the strike by force of arms. In the violence that ensued, thirty strikers were killed and fifty-seven injured. Nationwide, property damage was estimated at $80 million before the strikers were finally forced to surrender on July 10, 1894.

In the aftermath of the Pullman strike, Eugene V. Debs was convicted of conspiracy to obstruct the mail and other charges; he spent six months in prison. As for Pullman, while he lived to see his namesake municipality voted the "most perfect town in the world" by judges at the 1896 Prague International Hygienic and Pharmaceutical Exposition, he died of a heart attack the following year. His

"Residents 'declare they are bound hand and foot by a philanthropic monopoly.'"

The Pullman strike of 1894 began in Pullman, Illinois, but soon spread throughout the entire American rail network, crippling transportation and prompting President Grover Cleveland to dispatch 12,000 U.S. Army troops. The result was a violent confrontation, in which 30 strikers were killed and 57 more were wounded.

successor as company president was none other than Robert Todd Lincoln, son of the sixteenth U.S. president.

In 1898, the Illinois Supreme Court, ruling that operating the town was an activity beyond the purview of the company's corporate charter, ordered the Pullman Company to sell all its property that was not used directly for industry. In 1889, Pullman, Illinois, had been annexed to the city of Chicago, and, after the sale of its land, it became just another South Side neighborhood. The brief experiment in industrial utopia was at an end.

THE DREAM OF "ONE BIG UNION"

Nice, neat, clean company houses in a nice, neat, clean company town were clearly not the sovereign remedy for the ills of labor and management. The labor movement intensified during the Gilded Age, but most unions rose and fell in fairly short order, often the victims of employer and government suppression, and the movement would not hit its full stride until the 1930s. Yet one enduring and iconic union did emerge in 1886, the American Federation of Labor (AFL), which was led by a former cigar maker, a Jewish immigrant from London named Samuel Gompers (1850–1924). What set this union apart from the first great American union, the Knights of Labor—which had been founded in 1869 and flourished in the 1880s—was that the AFL did not attempt to lump together all trades, skilled and unskilled. Recognizing that working people had certain common interests but also differing needs, the AFL existed as a true "federation," a kind of coordinating body for groups representing separate trades. The AFL, which agitated for an eight-hour workday, workers' compensation, controls on immigrant labor, and protection from what it called "technological unemployment" (losing your job to a machine), continues to this day as the AFL-CIO.

But the AFL had its limitations. For all its diversity, it was essentially an organization of craft unions—of *skilled* laborers. The greatest difficulty American unions always had was in organizing unskilled labor, mainly because unskilled workers were, by definition, eminently replaceable. If they called a strike, they were summarily fired and others quickly hired in their place. At last, in 1905, William "Big Bill" Haywood presided over the founding convention of the Industrial Workers of the World (IWW)—or the "Wobblies," as they came to be called—which offered itself as "one big union" for everybody, especially the unskilled workers left out by the AFL unions. The IWW's ambition was to do nothing less than represent labor, all labor, as a class. This aligned it squarely with Marxism or Communism, a political orientation that made it by far the most radical labor union in American history.

Haywood was born in 1869 in Salt Lake City, Utah, the son of a former Pony Express rider. His father died when Bill was just three years old and, at fifteen, the boy went to work in the silver mines of Idaho. There he became active in the Western Federation of Miners, the era's preeminent radical labor union, and he developed an appetite for pushing confrontation with management to the edge of violence and beyond. Haywood was with the WFM in Colorado between 1903 and 1905, when its conflict with the owners of mining and smelting corporations flared into all-out class warfare, often pitting miners against state militia forces. His takeaway from this experience was that American workers were doomed to wage slavery if they failed to organize into "one big union." Management had both money and the government in its pockets. Labor? All labor had was numbers—and, if properly organized, that was a great deal indeed.

IWW leader William "Big Bill" Haywood (the tallest marcher, left of center, in derby hat and open coat) leads a strike parade in Lowell, Massachusetts, 1912.

With Socialist Party leader Eugene V. Debs, labor leader Daniel de Leon, and seventy-five-year-old United Mine Workers organizer Mary Harris "Mother" Jones, Big Bill Haywood founded the IWW. Its alliance with the Socialist Party came at a time when this was a powerful political force, rather than a fringe political party. If anything, the Socialist Party reined in the more anarchic tendencies of the Wobblies, and it encouraged them to organize groups no other union would touch—women, African Americans, and immigrants—practically as they came down the gangplank. In addition, the IWW worked to organize migrant laborers—unskilled and semiskilled alike—who were shunned by the AFL and other craft unions.

Under Haywood, the IWW struck mines in the Rocky Mountain states, lumber camps in the Pacific Northwest and the South, and the textile mills of the Northeast. Management routinely hired private security forces and out-and-out thugs, while also co-opting local and state police to intimidate, beat, and even kill IWW activists and organizers. Joe Hill—a Swedish immigrant born Joel Emmanuel Hägglund—was, after Big Bill Haywood himself, the most famous Wobbly. Regarded by management as the chief troublemaker in the mines, thirty-six-year-old Hill was framed for a murder in Salt Lake City, tried, and executed in 1915. He instantly became a martyr to the cause of labor.

The fact is that the "establishment"—the alliance between business and government—was genuinely frightened of the IWW as a political force willing to fight by any means necessary. IWW workers became symbolic of the unchecked social and political power of labor. Business-backed vigilantes, as well as federal agents, harassed them, and the district attorneys prosecuted them under any law they could find—espionage, sedition, even criminal conspiracy. In the end, it was the Russian revolutions of 1917 that did in the IWW. The association of some IWW activists with American "Reds" (that is, Communists) led to more prosecutions, even as those in the public who were inclined to join leftist political groups opted for membership in the bona-fide Communist Party, rather than join labor unions. IWW membership declined sharply through a combination of prosecution, persecution, and dwindling public interest.

As for Big Bill Hayood, he was acquitted of conspiracy in the alleged 1905 murder of former Idaho governor Frank Steunenberg (he died from wounds suffered when a bomb rigged to the front gate of his house exploded), but was entangled in a net of espionage indictments during the "Red Scare" of 1918. Tried and convicted in Chicago, along with one hundred other IWW leaders, Big Bill, suffering from diabetes and alcoholism, jumped bail after the Supreme Court rejected his appeal. He fled to Moscow, where, despite an appointment as a labor adviser to the Bolshevik government and marriage to a Russian woman (whose language he could not speak, nor she his), he became increasingly depressed and homesick. Alcoholism and untreated diabetes led to a fatal stroke in 1928. He was cremated, half his ashes enshrined in the Kremlin wall and half returned to Chicago, where they remain buried near the Haymarket Martyrs' Monument at Forest Home Cemetery in suburban Forest Park.

The fate of Big Bill Haywood was the most extreme example of the marginalization of organized labor during the Gilded Age. Only as industrial production became increasingly diversified, complex, and specialized between the world wars and then during the first twenty years of the post–World War II period, did organized labor enjoy real leverage over the captains of industry. Because their skills, training, and experience were in high demand, management was forced to deal with them as what they, at last, in the fullest sense had become: human capital of the highest value.

CHAPTER 8

GILDED MONUMENTS

Patrick and Catherine O'Leary were an Irish immigrant couple who scratched out a living for themselves and their five children on the corner of DeKoven and Jefferson Streets, in a dreary neighborhood southwest of downtown Chicago. Like many recent Irish immigrants in Gilded Age America, Patrick was an unskilled laborer. Catherine had a more unusual urban occupation. She kept five cows in a barn on their property, and they produced milk enough for the family with some left over to sell. On October 18, 1871—ten days after the infamous conflagration that started in her barn and which would soon become known forevermore as the Great Chicago Fire—the front page of the *Chicago Times* described Mrs. O'Leary, forty-four, as "an old Irish woman . . . bent almost double with the weight of many years of toil, trouble and privation."[1]

Non-immigrants in America often troubled themselves about immigrants as a group, but they rarely showed much interest in them as individuals. What accounted for Mrs. O'Leary being singled out by the *Chicago Times* was the editorial need for a scapegoat, and her story line was ideal: apparently, the O'Learys had illegally been collecting welfare, and, when this fraud was discovered by a county agent, they had been cut off. Bitter over the harshness of her lot in life, the "old hag swore she would be revenged on

Cornelius Vanderbilt II named his oceanside mansion in Newport, Rhode Island, "The Breakers." Designed by Richard Morris Hunt, it featured the picturesque "loggia" shown in this hand-colored lantern slide by photographers Frances Benjamin Johnston and Mattie Edwards Hewitt.

The Great Chicago Fire of 1871, which consumed more than two thousand acres (800 ha) of the city, was a tragedy (perhaps three hundred were killed) and a catastrophe—but also an unprecedented opportunity to build what became the first truly modern American city of the Gilded Age. Lithograph. c. 1871.

a city that would deny her a bit of wood or a pound of bacon," and so, the newspaper conjectured, she set fire to her own barn in the hope or the foreknowledge that doing so would set fire to the whole city on Sunday, October 8.[2]

By her own testimony later, before a board of police and fire commissioners, Mrs. O'Leary acknowledged that her barn had indeed caught fire sometime between eight and eight-thirty that Sunday evening. But the first she knew of it was when her husband roused her from bed: "Cate, the barn is afire!" A neighbor, Mrs. White, later told her that she saw a man in her barn, milking her cows. Someone identified him as Daniel "Peg Leg" Sullivan, a neighbor who was one of the first to call attention to the fire. It was assumed that he had been drinking and smoking his pipe in the barn, and somehow accidentally ignited the blaze. He denied it.[3] Another immigrant, a Prussian Jew named Louis M. Cohn, eighteen at the time of the fire, confessed to gambling in the O'Leary barn with one of the family's sons and other boys. When Mrs. O'Leary ran out at about nine to chase them away, a kerosene lantern was knocked over, igniting hay—though not before Cohn scooped up his winnings. This confession, however, did not emerge until 1944, seventy-three years after the Great Chicago Fire and two years after Cohn's 1942 death. In the fullness of time, the teen had matured into a successful importer, grown wealthy, and bequeathed $35,000 to the Medill School of Journalism of Northwestern University. The bequest was not delivered until 1944—along with Cohn's confession.[4]

After nine days, during which the board of commissioners questioned fifty people and produced a transcript of their testimony that ran to 1,100 pages, the board failed to reach a conclusion as to the definitive cause of the fire. "Whether it originated from a spark blown from a chimney on that windy night, or was set on fire by human agency, we are unable to determine."[5] The public, however, both within Chicago and nationally, had little doubt that Mrs. O'Leary was to blame, either through malice or negligence. Some believed she had committed arson, some thought Peg Leg Sullivan or others had accidentally set the fire, but the story that really caught on to be repeated through the generations was that one of her cows kicked over a kerosene lantern. In the end, it made no difference whether the fire had been intentionally set or not. As a poor, "old" Irish "hag," Mrs. O'Leary lived what the non-immigrant majority saw as the shiftless, irresponsible life of the immigrant, especially the Irish immigrant. She therefore made a compelling culprit.

There were other causes suggested. Ignatius Loyola Donnelly, a populist writer and congressman from Minnesota, was a colorful Gilded Age figure with opinions on everything from who "really" wrote the plays of William Shakespeare (that would be Francis Bacon) to what the "lost continent" of Atlantis really was (namely, the birthplace of an Aryan race whose descendants now populate Ireland). He wrote in 1883 that the Chicago conflagration had been caused by a meteor shower.[6] (There were several other major fires in the Midwest on the same day, although not as well-known because they were eclipsed by the Chicago fire story; a number in Michigan, and one in the lumber town of Peshtigo, Wisconsin—the deadliest fire in U.S. history, which claimed approximately two thousand lives.) This natural cause is highly unlikely,[7] but, given the severe drought prevailing at the time, spontaneous combustion is not out of the question.[8] Yet neither the possibility of a meteor shower nor spontaneous combustion have ever

Harper's Weekly, chronicler of the Civil War and civil disaster, published this engraving of the "rush of fugitives through the Potter's Field toward Lincoln Park" during the Great Chicago Fire of 1871.

succeeded in moving the accusing finger away from the Irish immigrant. Nor did the revelation of Louis Cohn's 1944 confession make a dent in the myth. As anyone who grew up in Chicago can attest, the cow story survives to this day.

BUILT TO BURN

As for the event itself, the results of the Great Chicago Fire are beyond doubt. Between 9 p.m. on October 8, 1871, and the evening of the following day, fire consumed an area some four miles (6.5 km) long and (on average) three-quarters of a mile (1.2 km) wide—more than two thousand urban acres (800 ha), 17,500 buildings, $222 million in property ($4 billion in 2016 dollars), accounting for some 30 percent of the city's total valuation. A total of 120 bodies were recovered from the ashes, but most historians believe the actual loss of life amounted to perhaps 300 people. One-third of the city's population were made instantly homeless—100,000 people out of 300,000.[9]

In a way, the Great Chicago Fire was a case of self-immolation. The rise of the city was an accelerated microcosm of the rise of the nation. European contact with the Native Americans on the site of Chicago came toward the end of the seventeenth century, and Jean Baptiste Point du Sable, an African American, probably of Haitian origin, became the first permanent resident in the 1780s. In 1803, the U.S. Army built Fort Dearborn at the juncture of the Chicago River and Lake Michigan. During the War of 1812, the fort was ordered to be evacuated, and on August 15, 1812, Potawatomi Indians attacked the evacuees, including soldiers and their families, killing 48 of 148. Just twenty-one years after this, Chicago was incorporated as a city, and a building boom followed.

"In 1871, the Chicago Fire Department consisted of just 185 men and seventeen horse-drawn steam-engine pumps."

Like most booms in frontier towns, this one was born of no planning whatsoever and no thought for the future. Balloon-frame wooden structures predominated, roofed with tar or tarred shingles. Even the sidewalks, where they existed, were wooden. In 1871, the Chicago Fire Department consisted of just 185 men and seventeen horse-drawn steam-engine pumps.[10] Given the tinder-box construction throughout the city and the small number of inadequately equipped firefighters, the conflagration spread very rapidly, whipped by thirty-mile-per-hour (48-km-per-hour) winds and a phenomenon called "fire whirl," heat-generated turbulence that spawned fire tornados.[11] Even the Chicago River failed as a firebreak, and when, late in the afternoon of October 9, a massive piece of flaming timber crashed through the roof of the city's waterworks, the outnumbered firefighters no longer had a supply of water at the mains.

Firefighters struggled helplessly as the flames consumed block after block until a heavy rain put most of the blaze out during the evening. In an effort to contain the panic, Mayor Roswell B. Mason declared the city under martial law, which put Chicago's immediate fate in the hands of Lieutenant General Philip Sheridan, who had served as a Union officer in the Civil War. He led troops in the dynamiting of unburned buildings in the path of the fire, hoping to create an effective firebreak. The impact was marginal at best.

As for Ground Zero, the O'Leary residence at 137 DeKoven Street, it survived the blaze—except for that barn. Today, the site (now renumbered 558 DeKoven Street) is occupied by the Chicago Fire Academy.

THE GREAT REBUILDING

Chicago rose from frontier stockade to thriving city fast, and it burned down even faster, but, almost before the last embers died, Chicagoans began to glimpse opportunity. One week after the fire broke out, the Reverend Robert Collyer addressed his Unitarian congregation assembled on Dearborn Street, outside the ruins of Unity Church: "We have not lost . . . our geography. Nature called the lakes, the forests, the prairies together in convention long before we were born, and they decided that on this spot a great city would be built."[12]

The fact is that while the central business district had been largely destroyed, much of the rest of what financed the city remained very much intact. The stockyards and the meatpacking plants were well west and south of the fire. The slaughter, processing, and shipping of beef and pork, unparalleled in volume anywhere else on the planet, continued unabated, as did operation of more than two-thirds of the city's grain elevators, its railroads, and its Lake Michigan dock and terminal facilities. Although much of Chicago was devoted to manufacturing, the core industries of this city in the middle of the nation's corn, grain, and cattle belt were dedicated to making, selling, and transporting food products. Those same tracks and wharves were open to receive shipments of aid, which poured in from

Photographer William Shaw assembled this panoramic view of "The Great Conflagration of Chicago" five days after the fire. Most of the North Side lay in ruins.

cities all over America and much of the rest of the world. (Among the goods that citizens of Great Britain sent were books—enough to start what became the Chicago Public Library, which opened just two years after the fire in a giant LaSalle Street water tank, which had come through the fire unscathed.)

From survival, the city moved on to what would be called the "Great Rebuilding." In fact, a better name would have been "Building Anew." In this effort, there was something of the same headlong rush that had produced the ramshackle wooden structures that proved so vulnerable. This time, however, the financiers, builders, and architects were guided by an avalanche of laws and regulations ushered in by the disaster. The use of wood as a building material was substantially restricted, and brick and stone were specified instead. For some buildings, limestone and marble were called for—both of which were available from quarries in neighboring Indiana.

The Great Rebuilding not only demanded fresh materials, it demanded fresh architects. Fortunately for the city, some of the world's greatest and most innovative were on call, the most prominent of whom were Henry Hobson Richardson, Louis Sullivan, Dankmar Adler, Daniel Burnham, William Holabird, William LeBaron Jenney, Martin Roche, John Wellborn Root, and Solon Spencer Beman. They came to be called the architects of the Chicago School, and they constitute a who's who of late-nineteenth-century architecture at its most original. Using materials dictated in part by new fire codes, these men created a vigorous and innovative architectural vocabulary.

Many of the new Chicago buildings today deemed as harbingers of twentieth-century American commercial architecture used innovative steel-frame construction, clad in masonry, especially terra-cotta. Traditional masonry buildings are limited in height by the load that brick construction can bear—well under a dozen stories. This did not present much of a problem until practical electric versions of the "safety elevator" Elisha Otis had invented in 1852 became widely available in the last quarter of the nineteenth century. The safety elevator employed a mechanism that locked the elevator cab in place in case the hoisting cables broke. Electric hoisting motors, which replaced those powered by steam, made possible long lifts and precise stops at each floor. Prior to these innovations, the height of buildings was limited by the number of stairs most human beings would tolerate. No one wanted to go above eight or nine floors. With efficient elevators, however, building into the sky became an attractive way to increase available, usable, revenue-generating space without having to expand the costly footprint of buildings in dense urban settings.

In 1872, Daniel Burnham and John Wellborn Root became friends while both worked at the Chicago architectural firm of Carter, Drake, and Wight. With the city's post-fire building business booming, the two men left the security of the established firm to start their own company, Burnham and Root. Taking advantage of the new elevator technology, they built Chicago's first "high-rise," the ten-story Montauk Building (1883), which combined conventional masonry construction with steel-frame construction. In 1888 came the twelve-story Rookery, again a hybrid of exterior load-bearing masonry walls and interior load-bearing steel-frame construction. With their next building, Burnham and Root stepped backward, in terms of engineering. The spectacular Monadnock Building, planning for which began in 1881, was braced by an interior frame of cast and wrought iron, but all the exterior load was carried by heavy masonry walls of contoured brown brick, three

Daniel Burnham, of the Chicago architectural firm of Burnham and Root, not only pioneered the skyscraper in post-fire Chicago, he also laid out a grand plan for rebuilding the city—much of which was adopted.

feet (1 m) thick at the base and tapering as the walls rose to the building's full seventeen-story height. Burnham and Root completed the north half of the building in 1891, and the firm of Holabird & Roche completed the south half in 1893. The result was the largest office building in the world: twelve hundred rooms accommodating more than six thousand people.

The Monadnock Building, like the Montauk Building and the Rookery, still stands in Chicago and, quite properly, continues to elicit admiration and awe. These three buildings were, however, the last of their kind, the apogee and swan song of load-bearing masonry construction. The high-rise buildings of Burnham and Root generally reduced exterior ornamentation to make way for more plentiful windows to admit more natural light. The windows themselves were larger, the "Chicago window" (as it was termed) consisting of

Burnham and Root's Monadnock Building (1891–93) still flourishes on the corner of Dearborn Street and Jackson Boulevard in Chicago's Loop. What was forward-looking in the 1890s was the severe absence of ornamentation. What looked back to even the most ancient architecture was the load-bearing masonry construction.

a large fixed piece of glass, flanked by narrow double-hung windows, all in a single opening. This became one of the distinguishing features of post-fire Chicago architecture.

Inspired by these structures, those who commissioned great commercial buildings began to demand even bigger windows and sleeker exteriors, more business-like and less ornamented. They also wanted taller buildings—partly to gain more space without having to buy more ground-floor footage, but also in a strictly competitive spirit, as height became associated with prominence and power. It was a trend that harked back to the city-states of Renaissance Italy, when rival towns competed with one another to build the tallest tower. In response to customer

THE CHICAGO BUILDING OF THE HOME INSURANCE CO.

OF NEW YORK

Although "only" ten stories high, the Home Insurance Building, completed in Chicago in 1884 by William Le Baron Jenney, is generally considered the world's first "true" skyscraper because it was supported both inside and outside by a steel frame from which the masonry walls were, in effect, suspended.

demand and the aesthetic aspirations of a new generation of architects, structural engineers elaborated on the early steel-frame structures present in the masonry-steel hybrids. From 1884 to 1885, William LeBaron Jenney built the Home Insurance Building in Chicago, the first tall building to employ a single steel frame both inside and out, so that the entire load of the building was borne by the steel, rather than the masonry. This enabled the architect to install unprecedented expanses of windows.

Although the Home Insurance Building was "only" ten stories in height, the structure (demolished in 1931), is generally considered the first true skyscraper because of its steel-cage framing. Nevertheless, Jenney took the aesthetic possibilities of the skyscraper only so far. The first major proponent of this new building form—America's single most important contribution to world architecture—was Louis Sullivan (1856–1924). Among the greatest, most original, and most thoughtful architects of the Gilded Age, Sullivan not only built innovative buildings, he wrote about them, becoming a highly influential theorist of modern architecture. Unlike Burnham and Root, who radically simplified ornamentation, Sullivan formulated two theories of architectural embellishment. The first was the idea that "form follows function." The form of a building, he argued, should serve the function of the building, not only in practical terms, but in expressing the aspirations and values of those who made use of the building. Sullivan wanted nothing spurious or superfluous added to his works. Instead, he wanted design

"The form of the skyscraper fulfilled the function of business better than any other."

The Wainwright Building—St. Louis, 1890–91—was designed by Louis Sullivan and his partner Dankmar Adler, the foremost architects of the so-called Chicago School. Possessed of architectural genius not seen since the Renaissance, Sullivan held that the *form* of a building should follow its *function*.

and ornament to appear as inevitable, natural, and organic developments of the underlying structure of the building, and he thus developed a wide range of active, naturalistic ornamentation to replace outworn imitations of classical, medieval, and Renaissance models.

In 1879, Sullivan was hired by Dankmar Adler and, the following year, became the German-born immigrant's full partner in what developed as a highly successful and innovative architectural firm. Their Chicago-based practice used the devastated city as a vast blank canvas for some of their finest work, including Chicago's Auditorium Building (1889) and the beautiful Carson, Pirie, Scott and Company department store building (1899), among others. But it was with the Wainwright Building, raised in St. Louis in 1890, that Sullivan and Adler produced the most influential prototype of the steel-cage skyscraper, which has been called "the first skyscraper that truly looked the part" and earned Sullivan the historical title of "father of skyscrapers."[13]

The Wainwright Building was distinguished not only by its height—just ten stories, yet made to look loftily majestic—but by the beauty of what Sullivan called its "vertical aesthetic," which he had developed expressly to suit this new and unprecedented style of building. As he designed it, the skyscraper claimed new expressive territory, beholden to no buildings of the past and therefore uniquely American and uniquely modern. The result was an architecture of great strength, practicality, honesty, and grace, which, in giving the skyscraper aesthetic validity, transformed first the American urban landscape and then that of the world. It also made permanent the exuberant capitalism of America's Gilded Age. For the *form* of the skyscraper fulfilled the *function* of business better than any other.

DETERMINATION AND EVEN GENIUS HAVE THEIR LIMITS, as Chicagoans and the rest of the nation discovered. Enacting new building codes and turning architects loose on the city accomplished much, but the fact was that many of the city's less affluent residents could afford neither the fireproof materials nor the skilled labor to use them in rebuilding. What is more, relatively few could afford fire insurance, and no bank would lend money to build without it. One of the cruel ironies of the Great Chicago Fire was that even Chicagoans who had valid insurance policies often could not force companies to make good on them. The reason? Their policy papers burned up with their houses and businesses.

As often happens when cities and neighborhoods are redeveloped on a grand scale, some thousands of residents and small businesspeople, lacking the means to rebuild, were forced out of the city. Others took advantage of another feature of Gilded Age ambition to circumvent the new laws—political corruption, which was endemic throughout America and downright rampant in Chicago. For a smaller investment than that required for brick, iron, and steel, many businesses simply ignored the new building code and went back to wooden balloon frames, wooden cladding, and wooden ornamentation. Yet another class of people resorted to that other representative building type of the Gilded Age, the urban tenement (see chapter 7). Although Chicago and other cities never built tenements in the same profusion as New York City, densely packed apartment blocks did begin to appear throughout urban America.

DEEP DEPRESSION AND CONSPICUOUS CONSUMPTION

Even for those who could afford to rebuild and rebuild properly, the opening phase of the Chicago rebuilding boom was interrupted by another reality—the essential brittleness and fragility of an almost thoroughly unregulated economic system. Back in 1869, a single man, Jay Gould, had wreaked national financial havoc with his failed attempt to corner the gold market (see chapter 3). The ripples of this economic riptide continued to roil markets, and, in September 1873, the bank and brokerage of Jay Cooke & Company, which was overextended by financing the Northern Pacific Railroad, collapsed. It was a cataclysm that sent shock waves throughout the markets. Cooke was widely regarded not only as one of the nation's most solid financiers, but even as a hero, whose company, founded in 1861, had done much to finance the Union cause in the Civil War. The buildings Burnham and others would soon design were intended to project the substantial solidity and permanence of American business. The case of Cooke & Company suggested that financial substance required more than great architecture. Cooke scored what he believed was a coup by becoming, in 1870, the exclusive bond agent for the Northern Pacific, only to encounter great difficulty coaxing investors to buy the bonds. In the end, Cooke & Company was forced to buy some three-quarters of the Northern Pacific, lest the railroad collapse even before it was completed. With his firm precariously overexposed, investors began withdrawing from his brokerage, a bank run ensued, and Cooke & Company suspended operations. News of this development exploded on the New York Stock Exchange, precipitating a market crash. With this, the Panic of 1873, already underway in Europe, swept America.

An 1873 illustration of the scene in front of Jay Cooke & Company's Wall Street office in September of that year; the company's collapse precipitated the Panic of 1873—an event all too typical of the Gilded Age boom-and-bust economy.

It was destined to drag down the American economy through 1879, creating a depression that would be unrivaled in depth and breadth until the Great Depression of the 1930s. Much of the reconstruction of Chicago was slowed or halted as a result. A second major fire swept the city in July 1874—much smaller than the Great Fire, but still devastating, razing more than eight hundred buildings across 60 acres (24 ha). This discouraged some builders, but, in other cases, actually revived building efforts as hard-pressed businesses felt spurred to begin earning again. Moreover, it taught the city and the nation a hard lesson about the consequences of cutting corners, and thus the second phase of rebuilding was marked by much stricter enforcement of "fireproof" building codes. Another by-product of the Panic of 1873 was the bringing to Chicago of a new major industry: finance. With businesses unable to secure sufficient investment and credit from the nation's traditional Wall Street firms in New York City, the demand for local money spurred new banks to open in Chicago, and the city's financial district became the first business district to be extensively rebuilt.

———— ◆ ————

ONE OF THE FORCES THAT FINALLY LIFTED the economic depression of 1873–79 and dispelled the lingering panic was the growth in the financing of property purchases as well as building using mortgage loans. Real estate made for highly reliable collateral, and the nation dug itself out of the hole. In any case, most of the great fortunes had by no means disappeared during the 1870s, and losses incurred during that decade were rapidly made up in the 1880s. A new class of wealth arose in the final quarter of the nineteenth century, which provoked a Wisconsin-born son of Norwegian immigrant farmers to write a most remarkable book.

Born in 1857, Thorstein Bunde Veblen grew up on his parents' farm in Cato, Wisconsin. Normally, such a beginning would have determined the life course of a rural immigrant child. Veblen should have been destined to become a farmer. Instead, his parents—whose diligence and hard work turned their farm into a source of relative prosperity—sent their son to Carleton College in Northfield, Minnesota, where he became interested in sociology, economics, and philosophy. Instead of returning to the farm after earning his baccalaureate, he pursued graduate studies at Johns Hopkins and then at Yale, from which he received a PhD in

1884. Unable to obtain a university position, he returned to the farm for a time, leaving it in 1891 to pursue postgraduate studies in economics at Cornell University. In 1892 he became a fellow at the University of Chicago.

While living in this intensely American city, he wrote *The Theory of the Leisure Class: An Economic Study of Institutions*, which was published in 1899. An apparently "theoretical" treatise by an iconoclastic sociologist/economist should not have been expected to draw much attention outside of the academic community. Yet, it became a best seller.

Veblen's thesis was explosive—even scandalous—and it was backed by plenty of sharp-witted, sophisticated, and cynical anecdotal evidence that was also abundantly amusing. He explained the current social and economic institutions as evolutionary products of technology and industry. He argued that, in the modern age and especially in the Industrial Revolution, the forces of advanced industrial technology that churned out the products of contemporary civilization were also often, to all appearances, deliberately wasted. Veblen went on to declare that the waste was only apparent. It served a sociopolitical purpose, enabling the establishment and maintenance of a stratified social order in which workers (Karl Marx called them the "proletariat") were compelled to be efficient and compliant ("productive") so that the owners—the captains of industry/robber barons, the class Marx called the "bourgeoisie" and Veblen called the "leisure class"—could focus on the accumulation of wealth *and* the extravagant public display of that wealth. Both activities—accumulation and display—were equally important. Veblen invented an enduring name for the combination of the two: "conspicuous consumption." The purpose of conspicuous consumption, Veblen explained, was to elevate the leisure class over the working class by placing on exploitation a higher value than on creativity and industry. Put another way, conspicuous consumption was the social proof of the right of the leisure class to control and exploit the working class.

For architectural examples to substantiate his theory of the leisure class, Veblen need only have pointed to the profusion of private architecture in the spectacular homes of the Gilded Age, designed by the likes of "high society" architects Frank Furness, Richard Morris Hunt, George B. Post, Charles Follen McKim, Henry Hobson Richardson, and Stanford White. These Gilded Age structures stood in counterpoint to the great public buildings that came to characterize Chicago and other American cities.

VANDERBILT MANSIONS

While Gilded Age mansions were built across America from New England and New York, through the Midwest, and to California, and while they belonged to many prominent families, none are more representative than those built for Vanderbilts. Those of the last quarter of the nineteenth century and the first few years of the twentieth include:

FOR CORNELIUS VANDERBILT II (1843–99)

Cornelius Vanderbilt II House (1883), 1 West 57th Street, New York; by George H. Post, with consultant Richard Morris Hunt (demolished).

The Breakers (1892–95), Newport, Rhode Island; by Richard Morris Hunt.

FOR MARGARET LOUISA VANDERBILT SHEPARD (1843–1927)

Mansion (1882) (part of the Vanderbilt "Triple Palace," one of three adjacent mansions built by Margaret's father, William Henry Vanderbilt [1821–85] off Fifth Avenue); 2 West 52nd Street, New York (demolished); by John Butler Snook and the Herter Brothers.

Woodlea (1892–95), Scarborough, New York; by Stanford White (McKim, Mead & White).

FOR WILLIAM KISSAM VANDERBILT (1849–1920)

Idle Hour (1878–79), Oakdale, Long Island, New York; by Richard Morris Hunt. Destroyed by fire in 1899, a new version was built in 1900–1901 by the architect's son, Richard Howland Hunt.

Petit Chateau (1882), 660 Fifth Avenue, New York; built in 1882, by Richard Morris Hunt (after the late-gothic Hôtel de Cluny, Paris) (demolished).

Marble House (1888–92), Newport, Rhode Island; by Richard Morris Hunt.

FOR EMILY THORN VANDERBILT (1852–1946)

Mansion (1882), 2 West 52nd Street, New York (part of the "Triple Palace"); (demolished).

Elm Court (1887), Lenox, Massachusetts; by Frederick Law Olmsted.

FOR FLORENCE ADELE VANDERBILT TWOMBLY (1854–1952)

Townhouse (1883), 684 Fifth Avenue, New York; by John B. Snook (demolished).

Florham (1894–97), Convent Station, New Jersey; by McKim, Mead & White.

FOR FREDERICK WILLIAM VANDERBILT (1856–1938)

Rough Point (1892), Newport, Rhode Island; by Peabody and Stearns.

Hyde Park (1896–99), Hyde Park, New York; by McKim, Mead & White.

Pine Tree Point (1901), Adirondack great camp on upper St. Regis Lake, New York; included buildings by Japanese artisans.

FOR ELIZA OSGOOD VANDERBILT WEBB, AKA LILA VANDERBILT WEBB (1860–1936)

Townhouse (1883), 680 Fifth Avenue, New York, by John B. Snook (demolished).

Nehasane (1893), great camp on Lake Lila in the Adirondacks, New York.

Shelburne Farms (1899), Shelburne, Vermont.

FOR GEORGE WASHINGTON VANDERBILT II (1862–1914)

Townhouse (1887), 9 West 53rd Street, New York; by Richard Morris Hunt (demolished).

Biltmore (1888–95), Asheville, North Carolina; by Richard Morris Hunt.

The Vanderbilt Houses on New York's Fifth Avenue, shown here in 1900, were known as the Triple Palace.

George Washington Vanderbilt Houses (1902–5), 645 and 647 Fifth Avenue, New York (645 was demolished; 647 houses a Versace store); by Richard H. Hunt and Joseph H. Hunt.

FOR CORNELIUS VANDERBILT III (1873–1942)
Beaulieu (1859), Newport, Rhode Island; by Calvert Vaux and A. J. Downing.

Townhouse (1882), 640 Fifth Avenue, New York (demolished); by John Butler Snook.

FOR GERTRUDE VANDERBILT WHITNEY (1875–1942)
The Reef (1885), Newport, Rhode Island; by Sturgis & Brigham.

Applegreen (1902), Old Westbury, New York; by McKim, Mead & White.

FOR ALFRED GWYNNE VANDERBILT I (1877–1915)
Sagamore Camp (1897), great camp in the Adirondacks, New York, by William West Durant.

Vanderbilt Hall (1909), Newport, Rhode Island.

FOR CONSUELO VANDERBILT (1877–1964)

Cara-Mia (1900), Southampton, New York.

FOR WILLIAM KISSAM VANDERBILT II (1878–1944)
Deepdale (1904), Great Neck, New York; by Horace Trumbauer and Carrère and Hastings.

Townhouse (1905), 666 Fifth Avenue, New York; by Stanford White (demolished).

FOR REGINALD CLAYPOOLE VANDERBILT (1880–1925)
Sandy Point Farm (1902), mansion and stables, Portsmouth, Rhode Island.

Townhouse (1910), 12 East 77th Street, New York, New York.

FOR HAROLD STIRLING VANDERBILT (1884–1970)
Rock Cliff (1870), Newport, Rhode Island; by George Mason Jr.

Emily Thorn Vanderbilt (Mrs. William Douglas Sloane), as painted in c. 1900 by Charles Auguste Émile Durand, better known as Carolus-Duran, a prominent French portraitist.

A photograph from 1893 of the Breakers in Newport—Cornelius Vanderbilt II's quintessential mansion of the Gilded Age.

George Washington Vanderbilt II, for whom Richard Morris Hunt built an 1887 townhouse (in New York) and Biltmore, a 250-room mansion near Asheville, North Carolina—the largest privately owned home in the United States.

Biltmore—with 250 rooms and grounds designed by Frederick Law Olmsted—is the largest privately owned home in the United States.

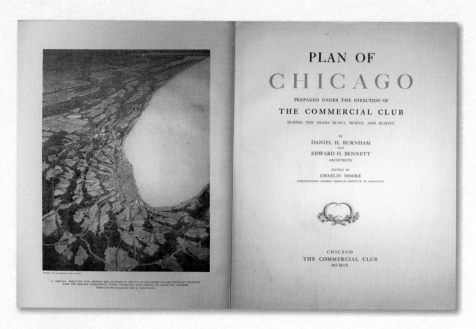

PLAN OF
CHICAGO

PREPARED UNDER THE DIRECTION OF
THE COMMERCIAL CLUB
DURING THE YEARS MCMVI, MCMVII, AND MCMVIII

BY
DANIEL H. BURNHAM
AND
EDWARD H. BENNETT
ARCHITECTS

EDITED BY
CHARLES MOORE
CORRESPONDING MEMBER AMERICAN INSTITUTE OF ARCHITECTS

CHICAGO
THE COMMERCIAL CLUB
MCMIX

Daniel Burnham's *Plan of Chicago* was a visionary redesign of a city devastated by fire. His idea was to create a metropolis that lived up to the Latin motto on its corporate Great Seal. *Urbs in horto*: "City in a garden."

THE GREENING OF THE CITIES

Architect Willis Polk often repeated an exhortation he attributed to his associate and colleague Daniel Burnham: "Make no little plans; they have no magic to stir men's blood. . . . Make big plans; aim high in hope and work. . . . Let your watchword be order and your beacon beauty."[14] As much as Burnham contributed to post-fire Chicago and the architecture of the Gilded Age, his most ambitious achievement came later, as a kind of coda to the Gilded Age, in 1909. It came not in the form of a single building, but as nothing less than a "Plan of Chicago," a coordinated, integrated system of projects that included new streets and widened streets, revised rail services, and extensive harbor development.

An outgrowth of work Burnham did for the city's 1893 World's Columbian Exposition (see chapter 15), the Plan of Chicago was an expression of Burnham's belief that, whatever else they achieved, architecture and design served a moral purpose for civilization. In this belief, Burnham may be accused of flirting with the ultimately self-serving industrial utopianism of George Mortimer Pullman

> *"The Plan of Chicago was an expression of Burnham's belief that, whatever else they achieved, architecture and design served a moral purpose for civilization."*

(see chapter 7), but the Chicago architect's vision was much wider than that of the creator of the Pullman Palace sleeping car.

Key to the Burnham plan was a system of city parks, integrated into the very fabric of Chicago in the spirit of the Latin motto that appears on the city's Great Seal: *Urbs in horto*—"City in a garden." This was an expression of Chicago's geographical location, a city set in a vast and fertile prairie. As the city lay in a garden, so Burnham proposed to bring the garden back into a city that, before the fire, had been, in fact, a landscape of grim industrial squalor.

Frederick Law Olmsted, the father of American landscape architecture, designed many of the nation's great urban parks, including Central Park in New York City. Perhaps more than any other single figure, Olmsted brought grace and natural beauty into the gritty industrial urban landscape of the Gilded Age.

Another visionary, Frederick Law Olmsted, is even more closely associated with a movement to introduce—or reintroduce—natural beauty into Gilded Age American cities in danger of becoming drab commercial and industrial purgatories. Whereas the skyscraper was a monument to enterprise, and the Gilded Age mansion a monument to what Veblen scorned as "conspicuous consumption," a city's

A view of Central Park, New York, about 1875. Olmsted married bucolic order with the spirit of wild beauty to create one of the world's great urban oases.

green spaces, Olmsted believed, could be great urban equalizers, available to, reinvigorating for, and ultimately uniting all social classes of city residents, rich and poor, owner and worker.

Where Burnham and the others worked with terra-cotta, stone, iron, and steel, Olmsted worked with the land and the landscape. He almost single-handedly created the profession of landscape architect in the United States. His greatest project, the work for which he is best known, was begun before the Gilded Age, before, even, the Civil War, when the city of New York hired the thirty-four-year-old in 1856 to supervise the clearing of more than a hundred acres (40 ha) of swampy, shanty-blighted land at what was then the northern fringe of the city. One year after Olmsted commenced what was a vast clearing and drainage project, city leaders announced a design competition for a new "Central Park" to occupy the site. In collaboration with prominent architect Calvert Vaux, Olmsted entered the contest with a design that incorporated a formal mall area lined by elm trees and acres of more rough, "natural" landscapes, planted with several million trees, shrubs, and plants. The Olmsted-Vaux design was selected from among thirty-three entries.

The Hartford-born Olmsted—who from 1848 to 1853 honed his skills on a 125-acre (50-ha) farm he purchased on the bucolic shore of southeastern Staten Island—was a student and champion of the Romantic, or picturesque, school of European garden design, which emphasized informal and natural settings. Yet the "natural" look he brought to New York City was the painstakingly studied product of meticulous design. "Every foot of the park's surface," he later wrote, "every tree and bush, as well as every arch, roadway, and walk has been fixed where it is with a purpose."[15] The work he did in Manhattan was carried over, after the Civil War and throughout the Gilded Age, in projects for Brooklyn (Prospect Park) and Chicago (Washington Park and Jackson Park) and projects in nineteen other states as well as Washington, DC, and Ontario and Quebec, Canada. Among these were parks, parkways, and the design of urban and suburban neighborhoods. He produced a generation of followers and acolytes, and he was the catalyst for park movements in many American cities as well as the national park movement, culminating in the creation of the first national park, Yellowstone (1872), and the National Park System. The nation's first great green spaces, like the skyscraper, were products of the Gilded Age.

Just as it is impossible for New Yorkers to imagine their city without Central Park—for Manhattan would be a brutal and unrelieved urban landscape without it—so it is difficult to imagine the American scene without the influence of Frederick Law Olmsted, who introduced into the industrial, commercial core of U.S. cities an element of the "wildness" the great pre–Civil War naturalist philosopher Henry David Thoreau believed to be "the preservation of the world."[16]

CHAPTER 9

AMERICAN REALISM

From Paris in 1780, where he served as U.S. commissioner to France and minister plenipotentiary, John Adams wrote to his wife, Abigail:

> I could fill Volumes with Descriptions of Temples and Palaces, Paintings, Sculptures, Tapestry, Porcelaine, &c. &c. &c.—if I could have time. But I could not do this without neglecting my duty. The Science of Government it is my Duty to study, more than all other Sciences: the Art of Legislation and Administration and Negotiation, ought to take Place, indeed to exclude in a manner all other Arts. I must study Politicks and War that my sons may have liberty to study Mathematicks and Philosophy. My sons ought to study Mathematicks and Philosophy, Geography, natural History, Naval Architecture, navigation, Commerce and Agriculture, in order to give their Children a right to study Painting, Poetry, Musick, Architecture, Statuary, Tapestry and Porcelaine.[1]

Folded into this passage from a letter between one formidable American intellect and another is a concise account of American high culture at the nation's founding. Both the liberal arts and the fine arts, Adams

American sculptor Daniel Chester French designed this majestic *Abraham Lincoln* (1920) for the Lincoln Memorial on the National Mall, in Washington, DC. It was carved by the Piccirilli Brothers, Italian immigrants whose Bronx studio was a center of American sculpture and stonework.

explains—with, it seems, sincere regret—must wait their turn behind the intellectual endeavors necessary to the survival and growth of an infant nation. First come politics and war. When these have done their job, mathematics, philosophy, "natural history" (i.e., science), and certain practical "arts" can be addressed. Then and only then, two generations forward, in the generation of Adams's grandchildren, will Americans earn the "right to study" the fine arts so abundantly present in Paris and elsewhere in the Old World.

In fact, there was important American literature and painting even during the American Revolution, but it was not until 1819–20, when Washington Irving (1783–1859) published *The Sketch Book*, containing (among other stories) "Rip Van Winkle" (written in a single night!) and "The Legend of Sleepy Hollow," that *American* literature began to earn fame beyond the ocean borders of the United States. Even so, in an essay published in 1820, the English clergyman, philosopher, critic, and all-around snarky wit Sydney Smith posed in the *Edinburgh Review* the rhetorical question, "In the four quarters of the globe, who reads an American book? Or goes to an American play? Or looks at an American picture or statue?"[2]

This state of affairs changed in August 1850, when Herman Melville, then an up-and-coming young writer in the midst of writing his greatest book, *Moby-Dick* (1851), wrote an extraordinary review of a collection of short stories titled *Mosses from an Old Manse* by Nathaniel Hawthorne, whose own greatest book, *The Scarlet Letter*, had recently been published.

MOSSES

FROM AN OLD MANSE.

BY

NATHANIEL HAWTHORNE.

EDINBURGH:
WILLIAM PATERSON.
1883.

Published in 1846, *Mosses from an Old Manse* put Nathaniel Hawthorne on the national literary map and soon drew international interest in American literature. Pictured here is an 1883 Scottish edition of the short story collection.

Believe me, my friends, [Melville wrote in his review, published in the *Literary Review*] that men not very much inferior to Shakespeare, are this day being born on the banks of the Ohio. And the day will come, when you shall say who reads a book by an Englishman that is a modern? The great mistake seems to be, that even with those Americans who look forward to the coming of a great literary genius among us, they somehow fancy he will come in the costume of Queen Elizabeth's day,—be a writer of dramas founded upon old English history, or the tales of Boccaccio. Whereas, great geniuses are parts of the times; they themselves are the time; and possess an correspondent coloring. . . . Nor must we forget, that, in his own life-time, Shakespeare was not Shakespeare, but only Master William Shakespeare of the shrewd, thriving business firm of Condell, Shakespeare & Co., proprietors of the Globe Theater in London. . . . Now, I do not say that Nathaniel of Salem is a greater man than William of Avon, or as great. But the difference between the two men is by no means immeasurable. Not a very great deal more, and Nathaniel were verily William.[3]

A remarkable group of American writers burst onto the scene in the decade leading up to the Civil War. Melville (1819–91) and Hawthorne (1804–64), as well as Edgar Allan Poe (1809–1849), Henry David Thoreau (1817–62), Walt Whitman (1819–92), and Ralph Waldo Emerson (1803–82) were the most notable among them. The twentieth-century literary historian F. O. Matthiessen christened the decade and a half leading up to the Civil War the "American Renaissance," and today we think of the writers of that period as our greatest American authors. They were highly original, each of them in their own way, but their work was also rooted in literary romanticism and philosophical idealism, both of which were linked to European traditions that had flowered earlier in the nineteenth century. By the time of the Gilded Age, the work of these writers—with the exception of Whitman, who still seemed radical, and Melville, who was largely forgotten, not to be rediscovered until the 1920s—was already regarded as classic, as opposed to contemporary. Perhaps it was the violence of the Civil War and the cynical corruption following it that made these authors seem like people of another, more poetic, more naive era, an age that dwelled in horse-drawn and moonlit imagination more than in the realm of dynamos and electric light.

THE WRITERS WHO MADE THEIR CAREERS in the post–Civil War Gilded Age rejected romanticism and instead took firm hold of the reality they found around them. Some even called themselves "realists," borrowing a term—*réalisme*—that had been used in France as early as the 1820s to describe literature that delivered something like a detailed transcript of the world as it "really" was. As realism developed in American literature during the last quarter of the nineteenth century, it ranged from "local color" fiction that depicted life in particular regions of the country, such as Cajun and Creole country (Kate Chopin, 1850–1904) or the hardscrabble life of the Midwestern prairie (Hamlin Garland, 1860–1940); to the "ordinary" middle-class life of successful men of business (William Dean Howells, 1837–1920); the exquisitely sensitive heroes and heroines of the privileged classes (Henry James, 1843–1916); and the harrowing vision of "naturalists" such as Stephen Crane (1871–1900). But no writer of the Gilded Age is more enduringly popular or more representative of his time and place than the one whose 1873 novel, *The Gilded Age: A Tale of To-day* (written with Charles Dudley Warner), gave that time and place its very name.

MARK TWAIN

As everyone knows, Mark Twain (1835–1910) was born Samuel Langhorne Clemens, and as *almost* everyone knows, his nom de plume (first used in 1863) was inspired by the cry of the "leadsman" aboard the Mississippi River boats Twain piloted. "Mark twain!" signified two fathoms' depth—twelve feet (3.7 m), safely navigable by a shallow-draft steamboat. To a pilot's ears, it was a joyous call.

Born in Florida, Missouri, Clemens moved with his family to Hannibal when he was four. He attended grade school there until he was twelve, then left to apprentice with a local printer. When he turned seventeen, he left home—forever—working first as an itinerant typesetter and then as an apprentice riverboat pilot. This profession consumed and captivated him. Learning the twists, turns, snags, sandbars, and other hazards of the ever-changing Mississippi was no small task, and Twain's mastery of it remained his proudest achievement. No figure plying the great river bisecting the nation was more universally admired than the riverboat pilot. Indeed, Twain saw himself as a kind of river god, whose occupation was not only to overcome the hazards of the muddy water but also to observe the incredible variety of humanity both aboard and ashore. It was as if the whole world came to him in a delectable cross section. Surely, no "realist" writer ever received better preparation for his craft.

Twain's idyllic career as a riverboat pilot spanned 1857 to 1861, including his apprenticeship. The outbreak of the Civil War cut it short, however, and the ex-pilot spent two weeks fighting the Civil War as an officer of a Confederate militia unit before giving up in disgust. He lit out for the territory, as the saying went, trying his hand at gold and silver mining in the Nevada Territory and California. He came up empty, except for appending his brand-new pseudonym to a short story called "The Celebrated Jumping Frog of Calaveras County," a deadpan comic version of a local folktale. Printed in the *New York Saturday Press* and the *Californian* in 1865, the little story made him nationally famous.

It was the kind of lucky strike that rarely happens in "real life," but one that Unitarian minister–turned–writer Horatio Alger (1832–99) celebrated in his series of rags-to-riches novels. Alger's stories—the most famous of which was *Ragged Dick* (1868)—typically featured a poor boy who, through hard work, simple piety, cheerful perseverance, and an indispensable dash of good luck, earns substantial material rewards. For Gilded Age boys and young men, Alger's fiction defined the "American dream." His variation on the rags-to-riches formula was presented in a series of books that sold more than 20 million copies. His influence was so pervasive that the phrase "Horatio Alger story" is still used to describe the life of any American man who rises from poverty to wealth through hard work—and good luck. A short story, "Poor Little Stephen Girard," often attributed to Twain, acidly satirized the Horatio Alger tale as all too typical of the kind of lies

> *"Twain saw himself as a kind of river god, whose occupation was not only to overcome the hazards of the muddy water but also to observe the incredible variety of humanity both aboard and ashore."*

that Americans reflexively told to deceive one another and soothe themselves.[4] Nevertheless, his own life nearly followed the Alger paradigm—albeit with many hard bumps along the way.

Twain made a name for himself as a Western journalist, and then took a steamship tour to Europe and the Holy Land, distilling the whole odyssey into a best seller titled *Innocents Abroad* (1869). In it, he discovered and offered to the world a blend of humane cynicism, humor, and meticulous attention to detail as well as an uncanny genius for hearing and transcribing a whole range of dialects and accents. Propelled by the success of the book, he became a touring lecturer and earned enough money to buy into a Buffalo newspaper. He multiplied his financial success by marrying the heir to an Elmira, New York, coal business, Olivia "Livy" Langdon. With this, he crowned his ascendency from humble Hannibal hayseed to cosmopolitan player on the vast stage of America's Gilded Age.

It was not an altogether comfortable transformation for him. Throughout his creative life, Twain was torn three ways. He wanted to be recognized not as a

The most American of American authors, Mark Twain, pictured c. 1900 with his wife, Olivia "Livy" Langdon Clemens, and their daughter, Clara. For better and often for worse, Livy regularly edited Twain's manuscripts, purging them of anything she found excessively cynical or irreverent.

THE GILDED AGE

mere humorist, but as a "serious" author, the equal of genteel New Englanders like Oliver Wendell Holmes Sr. (1809–94), James Russell Lowell (1819–91), and Henry Wadsworth Longfellow (1807–82). Yet he also yearned for popular acclaim and great wealth. It was a fine thing to be a successful author, but he envied even more the captains of industry and the robber barons. He craved major financial success—and this hunger drove him to make one ruinously foolish investment after another, repeatedly finding himself on the ragged edge of bankruptcy, and thereby perpetually forced to write something new—and eminently salable—which meant something funny. There was also a fourth dissonance in Twain's unharmonious three-note chord. His best-selling books were far from being his best writing. They were light, airy, and entertaining. Realistic? Yes, if by *realistic* you meant accurate in reflecting the surface of things. Twain longed to get beneath the surface. The trouble was that what he found there was usually ugly, even diabolical. The American reading public wanted—and was willing to pay for—more accomplished versions of Horatio Alger: happy and uplifting tales that uncritically celebrated American values in the Gilded Age. Twain could not stomach it, and were it not for the well-meaning censorship of his wife, Livy, to whom he showed everything he wrote, he would have begun to publish works steeped in the bitterness of someone who grew privately fond of the phrase "damned human race."

Nevertheless, he managed to create several enduring books and a few works of towering genius. His travel books, especially *Innocents Abroad* and *Life on the Mississippi* (1883) are delightful and addictive. His novels include two fascinating near-misses (*The Gilded Age* and *Pudd'nhead Wilson*), one minor masterpiece (*The Adventures of Tom Sawyer*), and one that is among the greatest works of American literature (*The Adventures of Huckleberry Finn*).

The Gilded Age: A Tale of To-day (1873), written in collaboration with Charles Dudley Warner, is a rather shapeless satire of the ruthless individualism and reckless speculation rampant in the Gilded Age. Beneath the broad satire lurks the biting bitterness Twain perpetually struggled to tamp down. *The Tragedy of Pudd'nhead Wilson* (1894) is a kind of detective story on which the author hangs a huge number of brilliantly subversive maxims in the name of the title character.

PUDDN'HEAD MAXIMS

"THE MAXIMS IN THE TRAGEDY OF PUDD'NHEAD WILSON PROVED SO POPULAR THAT TWAIN INCLUDED EVEN MORE IN HIS TRAVEL MEMOIR, *FOLLOWING THE EQUATOR* (1897). THOSE PUBLISHED IN THE LATTER WORK INCLUDE SOME OF TWAIN'S BITTEREST EPIGRAMS—SOME OF WHICH FOLLOW BELOW—THE PRODUCT OF WHAT HE CALLED (IN A SEPTEMBER 22, 1889 LETTER TO HIS FRIEND AND FELLOW NOVELIST WILLIAM DEAN HOWELLS) "A PEN WARMED UP IN HELL":[5]

"NOISE PROVES NOTHING. OFTEN A HEN WHO HAS MERELY LAID AN EGG CACKLES AS IF SHE HAD LAID AN ASTEROID."

"IT COULD PROBABLY BE SHOWN BY FACTS AND FIGURES THAT THERE IS NO DISTINCTLY NATIVE AMERICAN CRIMINAL CLASS EXCEPT CONGRESS."

"EVERYTHING HUMAN IS PATHETIC. THE SECRET SOURCE OF HUMOR ITSELF IS NOT JOY BUT SORROW. THERE IS NO HUMOR IN HEAVEN."

"THERE ARE THOSE WHO SCOFF AT THE SCHOOLBOY, CALLING HIM FRIVOLOUS AND SHALLOW. YET IT WAS THE SCHOOLBOY WHO SAID, 'FAITH IS BELIEVING WHAT YOU KNOW AIN'T SO.'"

"THERE IS A MORAL SENSE, AND THERE IS AN IMMORAL SENSE. HISTORY SHOWS US THAT THE MORAL SENSE ENABLES US TO PERCEIVE MORALITY AND HOW TO AVOID IT, AND THAT THE IMMORAL SENSE ENABLES US TO PERCEIVE IMMORALITY AND HOW TO ENJOY IT."

"PITY IS FOR THE LIVING, ENVY IS FOR THE DEAD."

"MAN WILL DO MANY THINGS TO GET HIMSELF LOVED, HE WILL DO ALL THINGS TO GET HIMSELF ENVIED."

"'CLASSIC.' A BOOK WHICH PEOPLE PRAISE AND DON'T READ."

THE GILDED AGE

The Adventures of Tom Sawyer (1876), Twain's most famous book, is a minor masterpiece because it mixes nostalgia and mythology with a realist's vision to produce a tale of antebellum boyhood that remains one the world's best-loved books. Far better because far more profoundly, joyously, and tragically human, however, is the sequel to *Tom Sawyer*. Ernest Hemingway wrote, "All modern American literature comes from one book by Mark Twain called *Huckleberry Finn*. American writing comes from that. There was nothing before. There has been nothing as good since."[6] Twain was clear in what he intended to accomplish in *Adventures of Huckleberry Finn* (1884): to "take a boy of twelve and run him on through life (in the first person)."[7] The life through which Twain runs Huck, along the pre–Civil War Mississippi, is hard and brutal, filled with sorry, slippery, and downright wicked adults, to whom the pure-hearted and naturally noble Huck proves himself morally superior, especially in his heroic loyalty to the fugitive slave Jim. The book is not only a portrait of American life before the Civil War, it is an expression of the tragic comedy that is the human condition and of humanity at its most soiled and most pure. In the midst of an age of gilded hypocrisy, Twain offered his readers something more precious than gold.

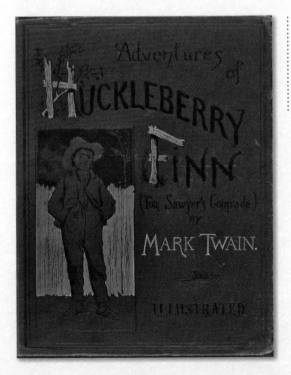

Twain's singularly *American* masterpiece, *Adventures of Huckleberry Finn*, was published first in Britain and Canada (1884) and then in the United States (1885). Here, the cover of the first U.S. edition, which was beautifully illustrated by E. W. Kemble.

The book is not only a portrait of American life before the Civil War, it is an expression of the tragic comedy that is the human condition and of humanity at its most soiled and most pure.

Mark Twain never surpassed the achievement of *Huckleberry Finn*—who could?—and his later years were plagued by business failures and near bankruptcy, as well as the sudden death of his favorite daughter and the chronic illness of his beloved wife. He secretly wrote bitter tales, which were not published until after his death, and in his despair he saw his personal rags-to-riches, obscurity-to-fame story as full of sound and fury, signifying nothing. In 1894, the Charles L. Webster & Co., the publisher in which he held a majority interest, failed, and Twain filed for an "Assignment for Benefit of Creditors," roughly the equivalent of bankruptcy. Yet Twain pledged to repay his creditors dollar for dollar. To make good on this, he embarked on an exhausting world lecture tour, through which he earned back his fortune and repaid his debts in full.[8] Concluded in 1900, the rigors of the tour wrecked Twain's health and underscored the contradictions in his heart. An exhibitionist who craved privacy, he was a would-be Gilded Age plutocrat who burned with a passion for social justice, a man who aspired to high literature but reveled in the American vernacular, a misanthrope who embraced all humanity.

KATE CHOPIN

Kate Chopin (1850–1904) wasn't the shortest-lived notable American author of the Gilded Age—that dubious honor may go to Stephen Crane (1871–1900), who died at age twenty-eight—but her life *as a writer* was nevertheless brief. It began in the early 1890s with some short stories and culminated in 1899 with a remarkably intense, courageous, and original novel, *The Awakening*.

Relatively obscure during her brief career, Kate Chopin was recognized as a major talent within a decade of her death at age fifty-four in 1904, only to recede back into obscurity until the 1960s, when the feminist movement "discovered" her. Her one full-length novel, *The Awakening* (1899), still has the power to move and to shock.

She was born Katherine O'Flaherty in St. Louis, Missouri. At age twenty, in 1870, she married Oscar Chopin and moved with him to New Orleans. There she had six children in eight years, the first in 1871, the last in 1879—the year her husband's business failed and they moved to rural Cloutierville in Natchitoches Parish. For many people, a major financial reversal is ruinous. For Kate Chopin, the forced move to Cajun and Creole country opened her eyes to the "local color" of the region. The untimely death of her husband in 1882 left her heavily in debt, and, after failing to revive his businesses, she and her children moved back to St. Louis, where her mother could give her financial assistance. Deeply depressed, however, Chopin took to heart the prescription of her physician, who suggested that she divert herself with writing. His advice unleashed roughly a hundred articles and short stories, most of them local color pieces set in Cajun and Creole Louisiana. Chopin was successful in finding magazines and periodicals that wanted her work, but they paid little. Still, it was clear that the nation had an appetite for local color fiction, and Chopin published two collections of her stories, *Bayou Folk* (1894) and *A Night in Acadie* (1897).

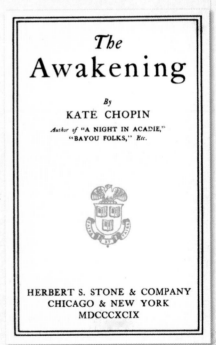

A common theme runs through many of her tales—rebellion against social convention, whether her protagonist is a woman refusing to settle into a dull marriage or a Creole lad embracing paganism over Christianity. Moreover, the best of her short stories exhibit a remarkable freedom from the Victorian conventions of language that tied down so many other writers. Chopin's prose is clean and economical, anticipating the work of such twentieth-century Americans as Ernest Hemingway.

But nothing in her brief career before 1899 suggested that she was capable of writing *The Awakening*, the story of Edna Pontellier, who rebels against her "duties" as a wife and mother after she falls in love with the

A first-edition title page of Kate Chopin's compact masterpiece. A quietly explosive novel, it broke through the sentimentality of conventional Gilded Age fiction to reveal the impersonal, utterly amoral power of sexual passion—not of some swashbuckling man, but of Edna Pontellier, a middle-class wife and mother.

handsome and charming Robert Lebrun, through whom she experiences a romantic awakening. After Robert breaks off the affair for a time, Edna seeks out a new sexual relationship with another man. With him, she undergoes an intense sexual awakening that has nothing whatsoever to do with love or romance. When Robert returns, Edna sees in him a chance to enjoy both romantic and sexual fulfillment, and she resolves to leave both her husband and her children. Robert, however, cannot bring himself to shake off the shackles of social convention, and, once again, he leaves her. In a scene of quietly intense sensuality, Edna chooses the ultimate escape by swimming into the Gulf of Mexico, going farther and farther from shore, to a destination of exhaustion and death:

> She went on and on. She remembered [another] night she swam far out, and recalled the terror that seized her at the fear of being unable to regain the shore. She did not look back now, but went on and on, thinking of the blue-grass meadow that she had traversed when a little child, believing that it had no beginning and no end.
>
> Her arms and legs were growing tired.
>
> She thought of [her husband] Léonce and the children. They were a part of her life. But they need not have thought that they could possess her, body and soul. . . .
>
> Exhaustion was pressing upon and overpowering her. . . . The shore was far behind her, and her strength was gone.
>
> She looked into the distance, and the old terror flamed up for an instant, then sank again. Edna heard her father's voice and her sister Margaret's. She heard the barking of an old dog that was chained to the sycamore tree. The spurs of the cavalry officer clanged as he walked across the porch. There was the hum of bees, and the musky odor of pinks filled the air.[9]

In some ways, *The Awakening* resembles the conventional melodramas of the era, which titillated readers with the prospect of sex, only to emphasize the terrible consequences of transgression consummated. But Chopin employs no breathless adjectives, no euphemisms, and none of the conventional literary circumlocutions. There is only feeling, a stream of thought, some sights, sounds, and smells, all calmly, sparely rendered. Nor does Chopin pass any moral judgments.

Edna does not choose to be a feminist. She can't help it, and her sexual liberation challenges the conventions of late nineteenth-century American society.

Gilded Age society rewarded not those who were morally true, but those who covertly indulged themselves while maintaining the appearance of moral righteousness. Edna refused to compromise who she discovered she was. Unable to find a sustainable way of living life authentically as a fully independent woman, she threw herself into the embrace of the vast Gulf.

Like the social thinkers and social critics of the era—Jacob Riis (see chapter 7), Thorstein Veblen (chapter 8), and Mark Twain—Kate Chopin dared to question the assumptions, conventions, and hypocrisies that passed for values in her time. But "her time" largely ignored her and, after her death, simply forgot about her. Kate Chopin was not "discovered" until the feminist movement of the 1960s set out in search of cultural heroes.

WILLIAM DEAN HOWELLS AND HAMLIN GARLAND

American literary realism proved to be a very big tent. In many respects William Dean Howells (1837–1920), whom most literary historians point to as the supreme exemplar of the realist approach, had so little in common with the likes of Kate Chopin that the two writers might have been inhabitants of different planets. Yet they were both dedicated to depicting a vision of what Howells called "ordinary life."

Like Mark Twain, who worshipped him as a literary figure and whose close friend and admirer he also became, Howells was very much a self-made man. He was born in Martins Ferry, Ohio, was largely self-educated, and found work as newspaper editor. While Kate Chopin took up writing as a form of psychotherapy, Howells just needed to make a living. In 1860, he was hired to write a campaign biography of Abraham Lincoln,

William Dean Howells. c. 1900. Known in his lifetime as the "Dean of American Letters," he set a high bar in the creation of American literary realism, holding a mirror to the nation's growing upper middle class.

for which Lincoln rewarded him with an appointment as U.S. consul in Venice (1861–64). It was by any measure a plum job, which broadened Howells's middle-American vision. In December 1862 he married Elinor Mead, the sister of noted American sculptor Larkin Goldsmith Mead, and of William Rutherford Mead, the preeminent Gilded Age architect who was one of the founders of the firm McKim, Mead, and White. The budding novelist in Howells was drawn to the romance of Venice and to the artistic personality of his bride. After he returned to the United States in 1865, he wrote some poems as well as two travel books, *Venetian Life* (1866) and *Italian Journeys* (1867). His European experience also produced his first novel, *Their Wedding Journey* (1872). Critics have called it more travelogue than novel, but, whatever it was or failed to be, the book included a literary manifesto in which Howells announced what he called a new kind of fiction based on the significance of ordinary middle-class experience and everyday life.[10]

What could be more dull? Howells countered by asking, *What could be more interesting?* Realism, after all, was about real life, which meant the lives Howells's readers lived. In this focus, he was very much in step with an era in which Americans were being transformed into consumers—consumers of manufactured goods, and, now, consumers of literature. The literature Howells offered was not fantasies about knights of old, but stories of his own readers' experience. Put it this way: Howells's novels made Americans consumers of themselves.

Howells was prolific; however, his best-known novel is also the most representative of his realist vision. The title character in *The Rise of Silas Lapham* (1885) puts the *ordinary* in "*ordinary life.*" He is not a soldier, explorer, poet, or adventurer, but a manufacturer of mineral-based paint. His business, when we first meet him, is booming—and has propelled the rise of the Lapham family in society. Silas is, in fact, a smallish-scale version of a Gilded Age captain of industry. Waking to their success, he and his wife overcome self-consciousness about their humble origins and decide to build their dream house in Boston's upscale Back Bay. As Silas oversees the design, construction, and furnishing of the house, he becomes caught up in making it a fashionable showcase. In the meantime, a former business partner calls on Silas to solicit his investment in several schemes. Silas has his doubts, but his wife persuades him to invest. The result is a major financial loss—which is made far worse when the Beacon Street house, still under construction, burns to the ground. These reversals of fortune compel the financially humbled family to leave Back Bay Boston and return to their roots in the Massachusetts countryside.

It is a deceptively conventional-seeming morality tale. In fact, the Laphams return to the source of the minerals from which the paint responsible for the family's all-too-vulnerable fortune is manufactured. Although Howells's realism details the ordinary features of ordinary life, it also finds in these features a penetrating symbolism. Silas Lapham's prosperity is built on the most superficial of products—paint—the thing we use to hide the truth of ugliness and imperfection. When misfortune strikes, he is forced to return to the earth, to confront the hard, solid substance deep beneath the surface. His humbling, it turns out, is his rise, and the book is thus a moral parable for the Gilded Age.

* * *

HOWELLS MAY HAVE DEFINED REALISM in *Their Wedding Journey* and embodied this definition in a long series of novels, but it was another writer—and friend—Hamlin Garland (1860–1940), who took realism to the next level. While Howells was a self-made man, he had not experienced the hardships of Hamlin Garland. The lad came of age in near poverty, on a succession of marginal Midwestern farms, beginning with the place of his birth near West Salem, Wisconsin. The focus of his realism was not "ordinary" middle class life, but "ordinary" hardscrabble Midwestern farm life, which was harsh, bitter, and life-threatening. To depict the hard lives of Midwestern farmers, Garland formulated his own version of realism, which he called "veritism." Garland raised issues Howells didn't touch—especially the brutal side of life lived on the ragged edge of desperate want. Living on this margin forced him to deal with essentials, so his veritism scratched at the surface of literary naturalism, an approach that was pioneered by the French novelist Émile Zola (1840–1902) and the British novelist Thomas Hardy (1840–1928), but that would see its fullest expression (during the Gilded Age) in the works of Stephen Crane. Naturalism emphasizes close, objective, even pitiless observation in emulation of the scientific method. The assumption of the naturalist writer is that a combination of a person's environment and character—what we might call genetic predisposition—determines the course of his life. As the naturalist saw things, people may boast about their freedom of will, but, in the end, they have very little.

Garland moved from the rural Midwest to Boston in 1884 and started to write. He saw the Midwestern farmer as implacably doing battle with the rising industrialism of the last quarter of the nineteenth century, and the novelist set out to tell the world that the pastoral idyll being peddled in popular literature was a sham. Farming was a struggle to the death. Although he considered himself primarily a novelist, his two best works were an autobiography and a biography. The autobiography, *A Son of the Middle Border* (1917), remains his most widely read book, although it was the sequel, *A Daughter of the Middle Border* (1921), a biography of his wife, that earned him a Pulitzer Prize. These works were the culmination of the veritism his fiction embodied: coolly factual, unblinking, and unrelievedly bleak—yet also celebratory of the Midwestern American character. Garland's farmers emerge as an antidote to the fast talkers and swindlers at the top of the Gilded Age socioeconomic food chain.

HENRY JAMES

In one American author of the era, the literary realism of Howells combines with Garland's naturalist desire to penetrate to the roots of human motivation and behavior. Henry James (1843–1916) reveled in the details, the furnishings, the fixtures, the costumes, the sights, and the sounds of life among the upper classes in America and Europe—especially American expatriates living in Europe. His depiction of these things and these characters, however, was aimed at getting beneath the surface to the dark mysteries of the head and the heart. Born in New York, he was the son of a celebrated Swedenborgian philosopher and the younger brother of the great psychologist/philosopher

The most sophisticated author of the Gilded Age, as portrayed by the greatest portraitist of the era: Henry James, painted by John Singer Sargent in 1913.

William James, founder of Pragmatism. This family milieu shaped Henry James's view of humanity. Muted and aloof in his own emotions, Henry James peered into the emotions of others, anatomizing feelings as a skilled pathologist might clinically dissect a cadaver.

But he rarely reached the level of raw emotion—as Chopin, Garland, and Crane did. Instead, he was the master of what is often called the novel of manners, a kind of Jane Austen transplanted into the Gilded Age. The "manners" he explored were the expression of intense emotion as it bubbled through the multiple layers of a hypersophisticated society in a hypersophisticated civilization.

James was educated in private schools in both the United States and Europe. He briefly studied law at Harvard (1862) and begin writing stories and articles for publication in 1864. His first novel, *Watch and Ward*, was serialized in *Atlantic Monthly* in 1871, and five years later, he sailed to Europe, settling briefly in Paris before moving permanently to London in 1876. He would live the rest of his life as an expatriate, and his main characters were typically Americans either visiting or living in Europe. He used his own distance from his native country to better understand how America shaped Americans.

The so-called "New York Edition" of James's fiction, the edition the novelist personally revised and approved in 1907–9, ran to twenty-four volumes of novels, novellas, and short stories. They reveal the evolving literary sensibility of a great artist whose genius consisted in an unrelenting passion for peeling back the layers of the social onion. His principal themes included the comparison of a raw and often naive America to a refined and devious Europe (*The American*, 1877; *The European*, 1878); the moral tenor of society as tested by the fate of innocent young women (*Daisy Miller*, 1878; *The Portrait of a Lady*, 1881; and *The Wings of the Dove*, 1902); outright good contending with outright evil in a social milieu that did its best to disguise the nature of both good and evil (*What Maisie Knew*, 1897; *The Turn of the Screw*, 1898; and *The Awkward Age*, 1899); and irony as a permanent condition of modern civilization (*The Bostonians*, 1886; and *The Spoils of Poynton*, 1897). Adultery was an obsession of this lifelong bachelor—less for its own scandalous self than for the challenges it posed to societies and nations founded on myths of family and fidelity. *The Ambassadors* (1903) and *The Golden Bowl* (1904), perhaps his greatest novels, were steeped in this theme.

At the heart of most of James's fiction is the absolute knowledge that humankind's most basic drives—sex and greed—were the most compelling, and that both in American and European society, they were managed through certain agreed-upon lies, lies that had become institutionalized to such a degree that they were the very substance of civilized life. As James saw it, irony, misdirection, and self-deceit were not aberrations in modern society. Rather, they were the critical scaffolding on which the whole social edifice had been raised. The chief difference between Americans and Europeans, James concluded, was that Americans denied this state of affairs or rebelled against it, whereas Europeans understood it, surrendered to it, and even embraced it.

◆

HENRY JAMES IS ALMOST UNIVERSALLY CONSIDERED a great writer today, and he certainly had a loyal following in his own time. But the truly popular acclaim he craved eluded him throughout his life. His point of view was simply too rarified for most readers of fiction, who may have enjoyed the odd intellectual challenge but, mostly, just wanted to be entertained. James used language in ways intended to demonstrate that words conceal as much as they reveal. It is a valuable insight, but it makes for demanding reading. Coming up behind the phase of realism that closed with James and Howell is a young writer who took the naturalism of Zola and Hardy and, yes, Hamlin Garland to a more universal and elemental level in a society into which James never ventured.

STEPHEN CRANE

Stephen Crane (1871–1900) was born in Newark, New Jersey, the ninth surviving child of straitlaced Methodists, whose narrow and moralistic view of life practically dared young Stephen to rebel. A child prodigy, he began writing at four and published his first newspaper articles by the time he was sixteen. He attended college briefly, but dropped out in 1891 to become a newspaper reporter—mostly on the tough police beat—and a fiction writer. In 1893, he published *Maggie: A Girl of the Streets*, a short novel about a Bowery girl driven to prostitution by a combination of privation and social isolation. When the manuscript was universally rejected by every publisher who saw it—they found its themes indecent—Crane paid for a private printing and then hired actors to ride the horse cars up and down Broadway, each ostentatiously reading a copy of the book. In

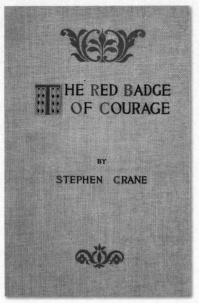

Stephen Crane created American literary naturalism and combined it with literary impressionism, which gave readers the uncanny sensation of *living* what Crane *wrote*. His best-known work, *The Red Badge of Courage* (1895), evoked Civil War combat so vividly that readers could not believe he was a ten-year-old New Jersey kid when Fort Sumter fell in 1861.

this way, he hoped to generate a groundswell of popular demand for the book. The strategy failed, but the book combines the cold, hard eye of a Jacob Riis with the touch of a distinctive literary voice. Literary historians regard *Maggie* as the first genuinely naturalistic American novel—Maggie is the inevitable product of her environment—and also as the first instance, anywhere, of literary impressionism.

While Crane had a fine ear for tough urban vernacular and did not shy away from precise description of low life, he often enhanced the emotional effect of a scene by emphasizing certain colors and images, rather than telling the reader what to feel. This mood-setting impressionism made his work all the more engaging. Nowhere is this truer than in his 1896 masterpiece, *The Red Badge of Courage*, a novel of the Civil War so realistic that readers assumed Crane was a veteran of the conflict. He proved that realism required imagination more than eyewitness experience, and American literature suffered one of its greatest losses when the novelist succumbed to tuberculosis in a German sanatorium at the age of twenty-eight.

REALISM IN PAINTING AND SCULPTURE

Among the writers of the Gilded Age, Stephen Crane had the nearest thing to a visual artist's sensibility, with his exquisite eye for color and image. The painting and sculpture most closely associated with the era was public art aimed at elevating the national taste with works of a noble and heroic nature.

Those artists who achieved the greatest popular success during the last quarter of the nineteenth century were formally trained, either in private studios, such as that of the painter William Merritt Chase (1849–1916) in New York, or in Europe, primarily at the École des Beaux Arts in Paris. Few Americans appreciated visual art that was as boldly innovative as the technological breakthroughs and innovations that characterized so much of the Gilded Age, but there is no denying that agreeable, skillfully executed, classically themed art became a highly sought-after, high-end consumer product during this period. In 1875, there were ten art schools in the United States. In 1882, there were thirty-nine—in addition to fourteen art departments in American universities and fifteen decorative art societies.[11]

The most popular subjects for painting and sculpture, especially during the early Gilded Age years, were drawn from mythology and poetry. Nudes were not only popular but morally acceptable, provided that they were at least somewhat idealized, looked antique, and were presented for a higher purpose, generally to personify such abstractions as Industry, Wisdom, Justice, Virtue, and the like. The prevailing tendency of the visual arts thus veered in the opposite direction from the literature of the period—with some important exceptions.

Thomas Eakins (1844–1916) was born, raised, and spent most of his life in Philadelphia. While he was interested in classical form and steeped himself in the techniques of such masters as Diego Velázquez, his subject matter was often starkly realistic, even shocking. *The Gross Clinic* (1875), for example, was a portrait of the eminent surgeon Dr. Samuel D. Gross—in the midst of a surgical procedure, with the patient, the incision, and the blood fully depicted. In the background, medical students sit in the operating theater, observing, while a woman just behind the standing figure of Dr. Gross recoils from the scene in abject horror.

Mary Cassatt (1844–1926) was the daughter of a prosperous stockbroker and the sister of Alexander Johnston Cassatt, president of the Pennsylvania Railroad. She began her art studies at the Pennsylvania Academy of the Fine Arts in Philadelphia when she was just fifteen, and moved to Paris in 1866—she was twenty-two—to study with Jean-Léon Gérôme. The great French artist also took on Eakins as his student, but whereas Eakins returned to the United States, Cassatt remained in Paris, studying with various masters, until the outbreak of the Franco-Prussian War in 1870 sent her back to Pennsylvania. While in the States, Cassatt exhibited and attempted to sell some of her paintings in Chicago, only to lose them in the Great Fire. She returned to France in 1871 and fell under the spell of the Impressionists. Her work in this style, however, steered clear of

Gathering Fruit (c. 1885), a print by the great American proponent of Impressionism, Mary Cassatt. Her gentle paintings and prints, depicting the intimacy between mothers and children, are some of the most intensely human documents of the Gilded Age.

the landscapes that were an Impressionist mainstay. Instead, she created extraordinarily intimate vignettes, mostly of women and children. In contrast to the stern stuff of Eakins's *Gross Clinic*, her work appealed to the domestic impulse of Americans and others in the closing years of the Victorian Age, which corresponded to the span, in America, of the Gilded Age. Cassatt's work is Impressionist, but, like the fiction of William Dean Howells, it depicts "ordinary" life in poignant and charming detail with a freshness entirely free of classical or idealizing convention.

Cassatt was an Impressionist whose works often celebrated the maternal aspects of femininity. Like Cassatt, John Singer Sargent (1856–1925) was also profoundly influenced by Impressionism, and he often painted portraits of women—but he did not celebrate them as mothers as much as the emerging sources of emotional power in American society. Born in Florence, Italy, to wealthy American parents, Sargent was given a European education and studied art at the École des Beaux Arts in Paris. His milieu was high society on both sides of the Atlantic, and the women he painted were, generally, the wives and daughters of the moneyed classes. He painted them exquisitely, lavishing loving attention on their faces and forms, as well as on their clothing and jewels. Sargent's masterful brushwork, influenced (as in the case of Eakins) by his study of the seventeenth-century Spanish painter Diego Velázquez as well as by the French Impressionists, charged these surface features with an exuberant, electric energy. Subtly, but unmistakably, Sargent also exaggerated the height of his female subjects, imparting to them a certain dominating quality that is of a piece, in spirit,

No painter captured Gilded Age high society with more exuberance, brilliance, and bravura technical mastery than John Singer Sargent. His 1883 *Margaret Stuyvesant Rutherford White (Mrs. Henry White)* exemplifies his portraits of the American aristocrats who commissioned them.

with the "Gibson Girls," the forthright, tall, slender, yet buxom beauties that illustrator Charles Dana Gibson (1867–1944) popularized during the late nineteenth century and early twentieth as a kind of composite of American young womanhood (see pages 262–65). Neither Sargent nor, even less, Gibson would have identified themselves as feminists, yet, in departing from earlier representations of American female beauty as either delicate and fragile or voluptuous and sensual to produce instead images of self-assurance, independence, and power, they both reflected and promoted the rise of women in the Gilded Age.

That said, Sargent's realism was not the realism of "ordinary" life, but of extraordinary life among the upper classes as well as among artists, writers, and intellectuals, all of whom represented the high culture of the Gilded Age. His portrait subjects both produced and enjoyed the fruits of the era, and his works are the art of what we might call the era's official culture. Sargent's portraits depict the private side of this culture, in contrast to the public side, which was represented in the work of such sculptors as Augustus Saint-Gaudens (1848–1907) and Daniel

Chester French (1850–1931). Saint-Gaudens's Civil War monuments include the *Admiral David Farragut Memorial* (1877–81), atop a pedestal designed by Stanford White in New York's Madison Square Park, and a bronze frieze in Boston memorializing Colonel Robert Gould Shaw, leading the 54th Massachusetts "Colored" Regiment (1884–97). French, a far more academic sculptor than Saint-Gaudens, created (among many other works) the monumental seated figure of Abraham Lincoln (1920) for the Lincoln Memorial in Washington, DC (see page 200). The emergence of Modernism early in the twentieth century has made the figurative work of Saint-Gaudens and French unfashionable. No matter; it is work that deserves to be looked at anew, as rare instances of celebratory public statuary that are genuinely moving, meaningful, and inspiringly aspirational, rather than dully retrospective.

The works of Eakins, Cassatt, Sargent, Saint-Gaudens, and French are eminently accessible, yet there is always, as the cliché goes, more to them than meets the eye. It is in this quality of "hidden" meaning, perhaps, that they are most fully representative of an era so often unfairly condemned as sufficiently superficial to merit the label Mark Twain and Charles Dudley Warner gave it. The creative wellsprings of the Gilded Age ran deep and strong.

The Shaw Memorial, a bronze frieze created by Augustus Saint-Gaudens during 1884–97 for placement in Boston Common, shows Union Army Colonel Robert Gould Shaw leading men of the 54th Massachusetts "Colored" Regiment into an assault on Confederate Fort Wagner, July 18, 1863.

The "official" bird's-eye view of the World's Columbian Exposition, Chicago, 1893.

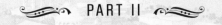

PART II

FORM AND REFORM

"Much has been given us, and much will rightfully be expected from us. We have duties to others and duties to ourselves; and we can shirk neither."

—THEODORE ROOSEVELT, INAUGURAL ADDRESS, MARCH 4, 1905

REPUBLICAN

NATIONAL CHART 1876

FOR PRESIDENT
RUTHERFORD B. HAYES.

FOR VICE PRESIDENT
WILLIAM A. WHEELER.

COPYRIGHT 1876

BY H.H. LLOYD & C?

SERVICE, AND DATE OF DEATH OF THE
HE UNITED STATES.

REPUBLICAN PLATFORM.

POPULAR VO

CHAPTER 10

RECONSTRUCTION ENDS

The centennial year that ushered in the Gilded Age with a grand world's fair in Philadelphia also brought into the White House the mild-mannered, unassuming governor of Ohio, Rutherford B. Hayes. In the most fraught presidential election prior to those of George W. Bush in 2000 and Donald J. Trump in 2016, leaders of the Republican and Democratic parties made the infamous "corrupt bargain" that elevated the Republican Hayes over the razor-thin electoral winner, Democrat Samuel Tilden, in exchange for Hayes's pledge that he would summarily end Reconstruction in the South as soon as he took office (see chapter 1).

Well-intentioned, in many respects noble, but also deeply flawed, coercive, punitive, inefficient, and politically corrupt, Reconstruction attempted to resolve the complex political and socioeconomic problems involved in readmitting the eleven states of the former Confederacy to the Union after the Civil War. The initial and chief feature of Reconstruction was the establishment of provisional military governments for the former Confederate states. Even before the war ended, such governments were installed in areas occupied by the U.S. Army. President Abraham Lincoln, anxious to begin healing the ghastly self-inflicted American wound, put forward in 1863 a

Detail of a "chart" with copious text (not shown) featuring everything the Republican Party wanted the public to know about the party's presidential and vice presidential candidates, Rutherford B. Hayes and William A. Wheeler, along with the Republicans' 1876 platform and some presidential statistics.

plan to reestablish civil governments in Union-occupied Southern states wherein at least 10 percent of the voting population had taken an oath of allegiance. Radical Republicans in Congress resisted this, protesting that this was not only far too lenient, but also an executive usurpation of legislative authority. In 1864, Congress passed the Wade-Davis Bill, which called for military government in each seceded state until a majority (not just 10 percent) of the state's white citizens swore a prescribed oath to the United States. At that point, the state was permitted to call a constitutional convention, but was constrained to frame a constitution that explicitly abolished slavery, repudiated secession, and disqualified Confederate officials from voting or holding office. Moreover, only persons who swore that they had never voluntarily aided the Confederacy would be enfranchised.

President Lincoln declined to sign the Wade-Davis Bill before the end of the congressional session. This "pocket veto" left the issue to Andrew Johnson, who

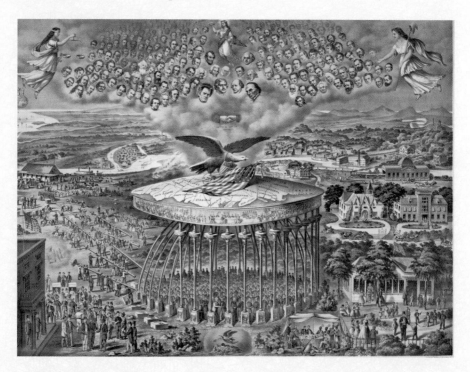

This remarkable print from 1867 attempts to explain Reconstruction as an allegory of the reform of the South and its reconciliation with the North. The old Southern foundation of slavery is replaced by Justice, Liberty, and Education as the faces of history's most notable reformers look on from above.

THE GILDED AGE

became president after Lincoln was assassinated on April 14, 1865. Johnson at first attempted to implement what he believed would have been Lincoln's moderate Reconstruction policies. But he was a crude and clumsy politician who lacked Lincoln's moral conviction, eloquence, political genius, and uncanny ability to make common cause. Johnson's conciliatory stance toward the South alienated the Radical Republican wing of Congress, even as his decidedly immoderate response to the South's rejection of the Fourteenth Amendment (which gave full citizenship rights to African Americans) alienated Southerners and provoked race riots in Dixie as well as passage of the reactionary "black codes."

THE BLACK CODES AND THE KU KLUX KLAN

Enacted in every state in the South after the Civil War, the black codes were laws expressly limiting the rights and liberties of the newly freed blacks. Most of the black codes compelled freedmen to work, subjecting unemployed African Americans to arrest and conviction for vagrancy. The codes also regulated hours of labor, permissible duties, and even specified how black agricultural workers were to behave in public. Most of the codes restricted African Americans either to agricultural labor or to domestic work, categorically barring them from other employment, except in cases where a special license (issued by a local judge) was obtained. The objective was to inhibit and even actively discourage self-sufficiency; for example, codes barred African Americans from raising their own crops. Property ownership was also typically restricted. In Mississippi, black codes prohibited black citizens from renting or leasing any land outside of cities or towns, thereby effectively preventing them from autonomously operating farms. Within cities and towns, black ownership of houses and other real estate was left to the discretion of local authorities.

Indeed, the black codes touched almost every aspect of daily life. Usually, African Americans were prohibited even from entering towns without written permission. Residency within many municipalities was made all but impossible, except in cases where a white employer agreed to assume responsibility for his black employee's conduct. In 1866, federal officials intervened to suspend black codes throughout the South, but the restrictions were variously and nefariously reinstated after Reconstruction was ended.

President Andrew Johnson's uncanny penchant for antagonizing and alienating both sides gave the Radical Republicans a large congressional majority in the 1866 election and thus put this uncompromising group in charge of Reconstruction. They quickly passed the Reconstruction Act of 1867, by which all the former Confederate states except Tennessee (which had been readmitted to the Union in 1866) were apportioned into five military districts for purposes of more efficient military government. As a requirement for readmission to the Union and the privilege of creating an elected civil government, each state was obliged to accept the Fourteenth Amendment (explicitly declaring freed slaves citizens and guaranteeing equal protection of the laws) and the Fifteenth Amendment (prohibiting states from denying anyone the right to vote on account of race or "previous condition of servitude") (see also page 44). Formed under supervision of the U.S. Army, the new state governments created between 1868 and 1870 were dominated by newly freed slaves who were totally unprepared to govern, by carpetbaggers (Northern opportunists who had gone into the South), and scalawags (Southerners who collaborated with the former slaves and the carpetbaggers). The majority of Southern whites regarded the black-dominated Reconstruction governments as both repugnant and illegitimate, humiliations imposed on them by Northern tyrants. They also despised the Freedmen's Bureau, which Congress created to look after the welfare and education of the former slaves in order to facilitate their transition to independent life.

Southern resistance to the institutions of Reconstruction promoted the formation of white shadow governments in each state. Their authority was chiefly supported by terrorism perpetrated by white supremacist secret societies, the largest and best known of which was the Ku Klux Klan (KKK). In its first incarnation, the KKK was founded in Pulaski, Tennessee in 1866, as a secret society and social club consisting of Confederate veterans. The origin of the name is uncertain, but it is believed that the "Ku Klux" is derived from the word *kyklos*, Greek for "circle." As for "Klan," it added an alliterative punctuation to the name. The KKK became the chief instrument by which Southern whites resisted and undermined Reconstruction. To this day, apologists for the group assert that members were frequently called upon to defend their homes and those of their neighbors from vengeful Northern whites as well as marauding blacks. White women, these apologists claim, were especially vulnerable to attack. Some more neutral historians agree that the KKK may indeed have played a necessary defensive role, but they also point out that it was, from the beginning, dedicated to restoring white supremacy in the South. To that end, the KKK engaged in campaigns of violence and intimidation against ex-slaves and any whites who aided or simply refused to condemn them.

In 1867, the KKK convened in Nashville, where it officially constituted itself as the "Invisible Empire of the South." Its first leader, called the grand wizard, was the ruthless and highly skilled ex-Confederate cavalry general Nathan Bedford Forrest. Like many other secret societies of the day, the KKK rapidly evolved a seemingly bizarre hierarchy of offices, from the grand wizard, to grand dragons, grand titans, and grand cyclopes. KKK members arrayed themselves in robes, hoods, and sheets, which were intended not only to disguise their identity from federal authorities, but also to terrorize uneducated and often superstitious former slaves. By the late 1860s, KKK "night riders" staged raids throughout the South, whipping, beating, and lynching freedmen as well as any whites who dared support them. The objective was to keep the newly freed blacks "in their place."

It is likely that the KKK was chiefly responsible for restoring white Southern rule in North Carolina, Tennessee, and Georgia; however, the organization's methods became so brutal that Forrest himself ordered the KKK to dissolve itself in 1869 and renounced his association with it. While the central organization thus ceased to exist, local "klaverns" (branches) continued to operate independently. This moved Congress to pass the Force Act of 1870 and the Enforcement, or Ku Klux Klan, Act of 1871, legislation authorizing the president to suspend habeas corpus and to use federal forces to suppress and punish "terrorist" organizations.

Terrorism and shadow government worked to circumvent the authority of the federal government and the authority of the Freedman's Bureau, effectively

An illustration from 1874 by Thomas Nast, the great political cartoonist of reform, depicts an unholy alliance between Southern white supremacists in a campaign of post–Civil War racial oppression Nast labels "Worse Than Slavery."

suppressing black efforts to achieve a voice in government and gain any measure of autonomy. Even under Reconstruction, therefore, African Americans received little protection—probably because a majority of white America, even in the North, paid little attention to their fellow citizens of color. In the Gilded Age, it was as if black people were socially invisible, and the era's optimistic and glittering surface mostly hid from view the oppression, humiliation, and outright crimes perpetrated against them. Only when the KKK and other domestic terrorist organizations brazenly defied federal authority in the South did Congress respond with the Force and Ku Klux Klan Acts. Otherwise, until President Hayes took office in 1877 and ended Reconstruction, withdrawing the last federal troops from the South, the abuse of black Southerners was a "dirty little secret" of the Gilded Age. There was never anything "little" about it, however, and, after 1877, there was nothing secret about it, either. The relegation of African Americans to the status of a permanent underclass in the South was widely accepted—normalized, really as a feature of American life in the South.

Adding insult to injury, the Supreme Court in its 1882 decision in the case of *United States v. Harris*, declared the Ku Klux Klan Act unconstitutional. By this time, however, the Klan had become dormant. Since the federal government no longer intervened in relations between state and local governments and Southern black citizens, there was no need for shadow state governments supported by shadow enforcers to circumvent the law and intimidate blacks.

The KKK would not resurface until 1915. In that year, director D. W. Griffith's silent-film epic, *The Birth of a Nation*, was released to almost universal acclaim. Like the 1905 novel on which it was based, Thomas Dixon Jr.'s *The Clansman*, the film romanticized, eulogized, and mythologized the Reconstruction-era KKK. On Thanksgiving of 1915, William Joseph Simmons, a failed Georgia physician, revived the Ku Klux Klan at a rally held at Stone Mountain, near Atlanta. By the early 1920s, driven by post–World War I xenophobia and nativism, in addition to a belief in white supremacy and nostalgia for the "Old South," the KKK expanded rapidly throughout mostly small-town Protestant America, especially in the South and Midwest. Membership rose to more than four million, and it was during the 1920s that the burning cross became a pervasive Klan symbol. The organization declined during the Great Depression of the 1930s and became virtually nonexistent during World War II in the 1940s. The African Ameri-

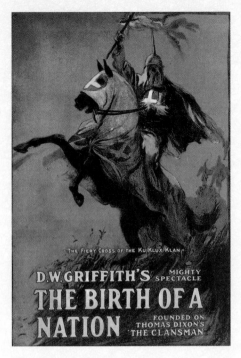

Film pioneer D. W. Griffith directed and produced *The Birth of a Nation* in 1915, a racist epic that helped initiate the rebirth of the KKK, which terrorized the black South during the 1920s and 1930s.

can civil rights movement prompted a new Klan revival during the 1960s, when, in the South, the organization again became a weapon used to intimidate blacks as well as white civil rights activists from the North. Today, the KKK continues in fragmented, typically surreptitious units, some of which are aligned and allied with the Aryan Nation and other far-right extremist groups.

"THE NADIR"

Throughout the Gilded Age, racial segregation and discrimination against non-Caucasian citizens was hardly confined to the South. For the most part, however, discrimination was *de facto* (an informal if widespread practice) in the North, but de jure (an official matter of law) in the South. Even though Reconstruction had largely failed to provide "equal protection of the laws" as guaranteed by the Fourteenth Amendment, the abrupt end of Reconstruction seemed to give Southern state governments tacit but unrestricted national license to legislate on the basis of racial bias. While the record of Reconstruction was poor, the abandonment of Reconstruction spelled the end of hope for many African Americans as well as for white Americans who favored the creation of a more just society. Even if it largely failed, Reconstruction had represented a certain idealism, and passage of the Fourteenth and Fifteenth Amendments were at least the embodiment of an aspiration to help the nation's freedmen. In practical terms, the Gilded Age did see the establishment of public education and welfare institutions available to blacks as well as whites. The federal government also took steps to alleviate the worst of post–Civil War Southern poverty—again, for both blacks and whites. It is true that, thanks in no small measure to Reconstruction, black Southerners were never formally or completely disenfranchised. They voted, and they did so in sufficient numbers to meaningfully affect the results of at least some elections. They also attended schools, so that literacy among African Americans, both in the North and the South, rose significantly during the last quarter of the nineteenth century, with a substantial majority becoming literate by 1900. Finally, African Americans served in elective offices at the local, state, and federal levels throughout the Gilded Age.

Still, in the very subtitle of his 1954 history, *The Negro in American Life and Thought: The Nadir, 1877–1901*, the African American historian and Howard University professor Rayford Whittingham Logan identified the Gilded Age as the nadir of American race relations.[1] Subsequent scholars, both black and white, have tended to agree with Logan's judgment. The metrics on which his thesis is based include the number of lynchings and instances of other violence directed against black Americans; both de facto and de jure segregation and racial discrimination; and open advocacy of white supremacy.

In the South, following the end of Reconstruction, a coalition of populist politicians—some white, some black—briefly enjoyed a period of biracial influence before conservative Democrats took over during the 1880s. These politicians used a variety of methods to suppress black voting in the "black belts," regions and districts where African Americans were in the majority. Poll taxes were levied in an effort to circumvent the Fifteenth Amendment ("The right of citizens of the United States to vote shall not be denied or abridged by the United States or by any State on account of race, color, or previous condition of servitude"). Many poor Southern African Americans could not afford to pay the poll tax and, as a result, were barred from voting. Of course, many Southern whites were also too poor to afford the poll tax. To ensure that the poll tax would not disenfranchise poor whites, voting registrars demanded that blacks produce poll tax receipts prior to registration, but required no such documentation from white voters.

Other late nineteenth-century voter suppression methods in the South included property ownership requirements and the use of tests to prove literacy as a prerequisite for voting. In 1890, Mississippi became the first state to require that prospective voters take and pass a literacy test. Other Southern states soon followed suit. Since many former slaves were illiterate, the requirement effectively barred a significant proportion of black Americans from voting. However, many Southern whites were also illiterate. To avoid disenfranchising illiterate whites, the laws of seven Southern states included a so-called grandfather clause, which provided that those who had had the right to vote prior to 1866 or 1867 (and the descendants of these individuals) were exempt from all literacy, property, and tax requirements for the franchise. Former slaves, naturally, had been excluded from the franchise until the ratification of the Fifteenth Amendment; therefore, they were not "grandfathered" in. The grandfather clause dodge was declared unconstitutional by the Supreme Court in 1915, but in 1900 the infamous U.S. senator from South Carolina, "Pitchfork" Ben Tillman, boasted of how he and his fellow Democrats were earnestly doing their "level best" to keep blacks from voting. He said, "We have scratched our heads to find out how we could eliminate the last one of them. We stuffed ballot boxes. We shot them. We are not ashamed of it."[2]

The most insidious and enduring suppressive and segregationist measures applied in the South were the so-called Jim Crow laws, passage and enforcement of which spanned roughly 1880 to the 1960s. "Jim Crow" was the name of a song and dance, as well as a character, created in 1829 by Thomas "Daddy" Rice, one of the white originators of the blackface minstrel show tradition. The Jim Crow image represents an extreme and belittling racial stereotype. While Jim Crow laws were by far most numerous and persistent in the South, they were also present on the books of many Northern states and municipalities. Most of the laws barred miscegenation (racially mixed marriage) and required business owners and public institutions to provide separate accommodations for black and white customers. In many cases, this requirement imposed an intolerable financial hardship on businesses, which could not afford to provide separate facilities; therefore, many white businesses simply turned away black job applicants and refused to serve black patrons.

Examples of Jim Crow laws include an Alabama statute barring hospitals from requiring white female nurses to work in "wards or rooms" in which black men were placed; mandating the partition of railroad passenger cars into white and black sections; requiring the separation by room or partition of white and black restaurant patrons; and even prohibiting blacks and whites from playing "together or in company with each other at any game of pool or billiards." Florida law barred interracial marriage as well as nonmarried cohabitation and mandated that "the schools for white children and the schools for negro children shall be conducted separately." In Georgia, "No colored barber shall serve as a barber [to] white women or girls," and the "officer in charge shall not bury, or allow to be buried, any colored persons upon ground set apart or used for the burial of white persons." Georgia parks were segregated: "It shall be unlawful for colored people to frequent any park owned or maintained by the city for the benefit, use and enjoyment of white persons . . . and unlawful for any white person to frequent any park owned or maintained by the city for the use and benefit of colored persons."[3]

Most Southern states and some Northern states excluded African Americans from serving on juries, and, without question, both federal and state justice systems frequently treated blacks and whites differently. Throughout the nation, but especially in the South, vigilante "justice" in the form of lynching—execution (usually hanging) by mob action—became common during the final quarter of the nineteenth century and well into the twentieth. According to many authorities, the practice of "lynching" got its name from Virginia militia colonel Charles Lynch, who, during the American Revolution, meted out summary "justice" to local British loyalists. Moreover, lynch law prevailed in many American frontier communities during the eighteenth and early nineteenth centuries. By about 1880, however, victims of lynching were most often African Americans. Typical offenses meriting such mob executions were variations on "stepping out of place," typically by violating social custom, demanding basic rights, talking "improperly" to a white woman, and so on. The first reliable statistics on lynching date from 1882. Between that year and 1968, when lynching (but not all racially motivated violence) virtually disappeared, 4,743 persons were killed by lynch mobs. Of this number, 3,446 were African Americans.[4] Lynchings were sometimes carried out by stealth, in the dark of night, the body left hanging for others to discover come daylight. Often, however, lynchings were performed openly, as public spectacles. In extreme cases, local newspapers even announced an upcoming lynching. Various forms of torture and mutilation were frequently part of the lynching, and, in some cases, the corpse of the victim was dismembered, with various parts distributed as souvenirs.

JUST AS THE GILDED AGE was a heyday of foreign immigration to the United States, it was also a period of intensive internal migration. In 1879, "some 40,000 Negroes virtually stampeded from Mississippi, Louisiana, Alabama, and Georgia for the Midwest."[5] The exodus to the North became even greater at the close of the Gilded Age and afterward. Between 1900 and 1960, in what is often called the Great Migration, some five million African Americans resettled in the North, moving mostly from the rural South to Northern cities.[6]

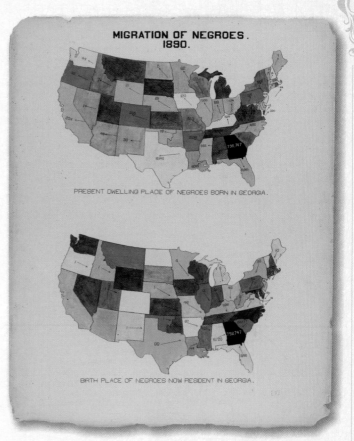

"Migration of Negroes, 1890" shows the net exodus of African Americans from Georgia to the Northern states.

"Between 1900 and 1960, in what is often called the Great Migration, some five million African Americans resettled in the North."

JIM CROW LAW.

UPHELD BY THE UNITED STATES SUPREME COURT.

Statute Within the Competency of the Louisiana Legislature and Railroads—Must Furnish Separate Cars for Whites and Blacks.

Washington, May 18.—The Supreme Court today in an opinion read by Justice Brown, sustained the constitutionality of the law in Louisiana requiring the railroads of that State to provide separate cars for white and colored passengers. There was no interstate commerce feature in the case for the railroad upon which the incident occurred giving rise to case—Plessey vs. Ferguson—East Louisiana railroad, was and is operated wholly within the State, to the laws of Congress of many of the States. The opinion states that by the analogy of the laws of Congress, and of many of states requiring establishment of separate schools for children of two races and other similar laws, the statute in question was within competency of Louisiana Legislature, exercising the police power of the State. The judgment of the Supreme Court of State upholding law was therefore upheld.

Mr. Justice Harlan announced a very vigorous dissent saying that he saw nothing but mischief in all such laws. In his view of the case, no power in the land had right to regulate the enjoyment of civil rights upon the basis of race. It would be just as reasonable and proper, he said, for states to pass laws requiring separate cars to be furnished for Catholic and Protestants, or for descendants of those of Teutonic race and those of Latin race.

An unidentified 1896 newspaper article on the Supreme Court's decision in *Plessy v. Ferguson*, which upheld the constitutionality of the "separate but equal" doctrine. *Plessy* enforced racial segregation until it was overturned by the High Court in *Brown v. Board of Education*, 1954.

Northerners did not necessarily greet the internal migrants with open arms. In the Midwest and the West especially, so-called sundown towns posted signs warning blacks "not to let the sun go down on them" in their town.[7] Many Northern towns and cities were rigorously segregated, not by law, but by custom and "gentlemen's agreements" among landlords and realtors. Parts of town were informally designated black only, while other parts were tacitly reserved for whites. For the most part, public accommodations in the North were integrated. This included public schools. Southern states and municipalities skirted the equal protection clause of the Fourteenth Amendment by providing what they called "separate but equal" public accommodations for whites and blacks, including public schools.

As a defense of segregation in public accommodations, the "separate but equal" doctrine found itself under examination by the Supreme Court. On June 7, 1892, in New Orleans, Homer Plessy, a thirty-year-old African American shoemaker, was arrested, convicted, and jailed for sitting in the "white" car of an East Louisiana Railroad passenger train. Plessy was one-eighth black and seven-eighths white, but, under Louisiana law, he was considered black and therefore required to sit in the "colored" car. Plessy took his case to court and argued, in *Homer Adolph Plessy v. The State of Louisiana*, that the state's Separate Car Act violated the Thirteenth and Fourteenth Amendments to the Constitution. The trial judge was John Howard Ferguson, a lawyer from Massachusetts, who had previously declared the Separate Car Act "unconstitutional on trains that traveled through several states." In Plessy's case, however, he ruled that Louisiana could regulate railroad companies that operated exclusively within its boundaries, and, therefore, he found Plessy guilty of refusing to leave the white car. Plessy appealed to the Supreme Court of Louisiana, which upheld Judge Ferguson's decision. From here, Plessy took the case to the United States Supreme Court. The majority opinion in *Plessy v. Ferguson*, handed down in 1896, upheld both Plessy's conviction and the constitutionality of Louisiana's segregationist law. The case was cheered by Southern segregationists, who used it to defend the legality of segregation of public facilities, most notably including those provided for public education. Only as late as 1954 did the Supreme Court decision in *Brown v. Board of Education of Topeka* overturn *Plessy v. Ferguson* by holding that "separate educational facilities are inherently unequal."[8]

Racism was not the exclusive province of the South or even of ignorant prejudice. During the closing quarter of the nineteenth century, many academics, including the father of modern anthropology, Professor Franz Boas, threw the weight of "race science" behind theories of black inferiority and white supremacy. Many Gilded Age scientists, physicians, sociologists, and politicians were believers in eugenics—the "science" of improving the human race through controlled breeding—and advocated various theories of the comparative inferiority and superiority of the races. Almost always, the prevailing thesis was the superiority of the white race.

REFORM

Starting from a "nadir," there is only one direction in which to go. While racial injustice roiled beneath the surface of the Gilded Age, so did racial reform and progress. Just after the end of the Civil War, white members of the First Congregational Society of Washington decided to fund a seminary for the training of African American clergymen. The idea quickly grew into a project to found a high-quality university for African American students. In 1867, General Oliver Otis Howard—a Union hero of the Civil War and, during Reconstruction,

Howard University, Washington, DC, was chartered in 1867 under the auspices of the Freedmen's Bureau to educate African American "youth in the liberal arts and sciences."

commissioner of the Freedmen's Bureau— took an active role in establishing the institution in Washington, DC. The First Congregational Society named it after him—Howard University—and in 1869 he became Howard's president. Through the end of the nineteenth century and to this day, Howard University has enjoyed a reputation as the premier African American institution of higher learning. Historically, it led the way for the establishment of other black colleges, which are today known as historically black colleges and universities (HBCUs).

Despite the success of Howard University, there were many in both the white and the black communities who believed that institutions emulating traditional "white" universities could not adequately serve the needs of most African Americans in the United States. Among those who believed this was Booker T. Washington (1856–1915), who had been born a slave in Franklin County, Virginia, and rose to become the foremost black educator and reformer of his time. After emancipation, he moved with his family to Malden, West Virginia, where, at age nine, he was put to work at a salt furnace and then in a coal mine. His life and

The faculty of Tuskegee Institute in Alabama with its first president, Booker T. Washington (seated third from left), and the industrialist-turned-philanthropist Andrew Carnegie beside him, 1906. Washington advocated "gradualism," the eventual attainment of racial equality through the establishment of African American economic autonomy.

career took a critical turn in 1872, when he enrolled at the Hampton Normal and Agricultural Institute in Virginia, supporting himself by working as a janitor. After graduating in 1875, Washington returned to Malden and taught school during the day and adult education classes at night. In 1878, he enrolled at Wayland Seminary in Washington, DC, and in 1879 was appointed to the faculty of Hampton Normal. Two years later, Alabama state officials chose Washington to serve as principal of a newly established state normal school (teachers' college) for blacks at Tuskegee. Called Tuskegee Normal and Industrial Institute, the underfunded school had only two buildings and almost no educational equipment of any kind. Nevertheless, for the next thirty-four years, Booker T. Washington developed it into a multifaceted training center dedicated less to "higher education" than to developing economic self-sufficiency in its fifteen hundred students. Indeed, in the institution's formative years under Washington, Tuskegee was a vocational school that emphasized the manual arts and agriculture.

By training African Americans to be economically autonomous, Booker T. Washington believed that, eventually, they would also achieve social, political, cultural, and legal equality with whites; however, until that time came, he was willing to postpone equality. This viewpoint was called "gradualism" by some and "accommodation" by others, because it frankly accommodated white racist conceptions of African Americans. Washington parried the criticism that he was reinforcing white supremacist views by arguing that "accommodation" was unavoidably necessary to obtain the immediate economic support of the white community. In fact, his approach was largely successful in garnering that support; Tuskegee Institute became a handsomely endowed institution.

Booker T. Washington gave succinct voice to his gradualist philosophy in his landmark speech, "An Address Delivered at the Opening of the Cotton States and International Exposition," commonly known as the "Atlanta Compromise Speech," which he delivered on September 18, 1895, to a mixed-race audience at the Atlanta Exposition. Holding up his hand and spreading his fingers, he declared: "In all things that are purely social we can be separate as the fingers, yet one as the hand in all things essential to mutual progress."[9] The speech and the position it articulated outraged many in the rising generation of progressive black leaders, the most vigorous and eloquent of whom was William Edward Burghardt Du Bois—better known as W. E. B. Du Bois (1868–1963). Born in Great Barrington, Massachusetts, he did not seek a vocational education at Tuskegee, but became the first African American to receive a PhD from Harvard University in 1896. Between 1897 and 1914, Du Bois went on to write several pioneering sociological studies of black America.

Briefly, at the start of the twentieth century, he was a supporter of black capitalism and economic equality as precursors to social equality—the very position outlined in the Atlanta Compromise Speech. Du Bois soon broke with Booker T. Washington, however, arguing that any willingness to accept segregation and to hold in abeyance broader questions of social equality was irreparably destructive to the black cause. Du Bois hoped that, through the application of social science, he could begin to offer solutions to racial inequality in America. In the course of his career, however, he became convinced that racism was so deeply ingrained and virulent in American culture and institutions that only vigorous social activism, including agitation and protest, could begin to improve the condition of American Americans.

The founders of the Niagara Movement, forerunner of the National Association for the Advancement of Colored People, photographed in 1905, superimposed over an image of Niagara Falls. W. E. B. Du Bois is seated in the middle row, second from right.

In the summer of 1905, Du Bois and a group of twenty-nine other social activists, including African Americans and whites, met secretly in Fort Erie, Ontario, across the Niagara River from Buffalo, to hammer out an organized response to "accommodation." The result was a set of resolutions that led to the founding of the Niagara Movement and the drawing up of a formal manifesto demanding full civil liberties for African Americans, an end to racial discrimination, and acknowledgment of brotherhood among all races. The movement spread quickly, with thirty branches established nationally. However, it almost as quickly began to fall apart, suffering from inadequate funding and weak organization. Then, in August 1908, thousands of white residents of Springfield, Illinois, descended upon the black community of that town—the state capital—after two black prisoners—one charged with the rape of a white woman, and another charged with murdering a white engineer—were being transferred to another prison. The white mob assaulted black residents, burned blacks' homes and businesses, and lynched two elderly black men, Scott Burton and William Donigan, before the Illinois state militia succeeded in restoring order, by which time five whites were also dead, some shot by black home and business owners.

After the riot, local whites not only showed no remorse, but were vocal in their approval of an action that might serve to keep blacks "in their place." In all, 117 indictments were brought, but most charges were dropped because witnesses were not forthcoming or claimed they were unable to identify perpetrators. White or black, prospective witnesses clearly feared retribution from the white community. In the end, the few brought to trial were "people with little community standing," including "a Jewish immigrant from Russia who was acquitted of all charges except petty larceny." As for George Richardson, the African American man accused of rape, charges were dropped against him when his accuser, Mabel Hallam, confessed to a grand jury two weeks after the riot that she had lied.[10]

This shocking "Race War of the North" (as the press called it) prompted a number of prominent white liberals to join with members of the Niagara group to found the National Association for the Advancement of Colored People (NAACP) in 1909. The following year, the Niagara Movement formally disbanded, leaving the NAACP as the chief national vehicle for activism in furtherance of racial justice.

From its inception, the NAACP was interracial, its membership including whites as well as African Americans. It was conceived as an organization dedicated to ending segregation and discrimination in such areas as education, housing, employment, transportation, and voting, and it set as a more general goal advocacy to ensure that blacks enjoyed all constitutionally guaranteed rights. Founding member Du Bois was most directly active as the organization's director of publicity and research during 1909–34 and as editor of the association's national magazine, the *Crisis*. In large part through Du Bois's communications outreach, NAACP became the single most influential organization advocating for civil rights, and as the twentieth century unfolded, it became an increasingly powerful force in congressional lobbying and in crafting and promoting civil rights legislation while also managing civil rights litigation in the courts.

THROUGHOUT HIS OWN CAREER, W. E. B. DU BOIS continued to wrestle with issues of black integration into the white mainstream versus black separatism. Black nationalism became of increasing interest to Du Bois, and he was an early advocate of Pan-Africanism, the doctrine that all people of African descent had common interests and therefore should work together toward common goals. Du Bois led the first Pan-African Conference in London in 1900 and was the motivating force behind four others convened between 1919 and 1927.

The Gilded Age had begun in an era of institutionalized and even legalized oppression of the very people—black Americans—so recently liberated from slavery. Most of the era was marked by the hardening of African American second-class citizenship. Yet new approaches and social movements also developed during the period, from Booker T. Washington's gradualism and black capitalism to the full social equality W. E. B. Du Bois and those of the Niagara Movement and the NAACP advocated. Yet, at the very end of the Gilded Age, Du Bois questioned both the feasibility and the desirability of black integration into American society and looked instead toward Pan-Africanism and black separatism. This transformation in his thinking coincided with the rise in influence of Marcus Garvey (1887–1940), who, during 1919–26, founded and organized the first major black separatist/black nationalist movement in the United States.

GARVEY WAS BORN IN JAMAICA AND, although he attended school through age fourteen, he was mostly self-taught. After traveling in Central America, Garvey settled in London, living there from 1912 to 1914, and then returned to Jamaica, where, with others, he founded the Universal Negro Improvement and Conservation Association and African Communities League, or Universal Negro Improvement Association (UNIA). The principal goal of the organization was to create, in Africa, a black-governed nation. Garvey took the organization to the United States in 1916, establishing UNIA branches in New York's Harlem and black neighborhoods in other Northern cities. In the States, UNIA attracted great interest, and Garvey was hailed as the "Black Moses." He claimed a following of some two million, although this figure is very much in dispute.

After a few years, Garvey's movement toward black nationalism retreated into a version of black capitalism, and in 1919, Garvey established the Negro

Jamaican-born Marcus Garvey, shown here in 1924, founded the Universal Negro Improvement Association (UNIA) and led a remarkable American black nationalist movement before he was convicted of mail fraud and deported to Jamaica.

Factories Corporation and an African American steamship company, the Black Star Line. He also opened a chain of restaurants and grocery stores, laundries, a hotel, and a printing establishment. Mismanagement soon led to outright fraud, however, and in 1922, he and other UNIA members were indicted for mail fraud in connection with the sale of stock for the Black Star Line. Convicted, Garvey served two years of a five-year federal sentence before President Calvin Coolidge, in 1927, commuted the balance of his prison term to deportation to Jamaica as an undesirable alien. There were no significant protests to this action, the UNIA was in collapse, and Garvey was never able to resurrect the movement. He lived out the rest of his life an obscure and forgotten exile, dying in London in 1940 at age fifty-two.

Yet this sad end was by no means the sum total of the African American journey in the Gilded Age. Whatever the failings of his movement, Garvey had given African Americans a reason to be proud of their heritage. He instilled this pride not through rhetoric alone, but by publishing in UNIA's newspaper, *Negro World*, stories of black achievement and heroes. Like Booker T. Washington before him, Garvey offered a model for black entrepreneurship, even as his example finally revealed that the problems of race relations were rooted more deeply than surface economics. As for the NAACP, more than any other social institution born during the Gilded Age "nadir" of race relations, it went on to become the foundation of an enduring civil rights movement in America.

The Black Star Line, an African American-owned steamship company, was the economic centerpiece of Garvey's black nationalist movement. Mismanaged and probably sabotaged by agents of J. Edgar Hoover's Bureau of Investigation (precursor of the FBI), Black Star Line collapsed in 1922, leading to Garvey's conviction for mail fraud.

CHAPTER 11

A WOMAN'S PLACE

It isn't Everest, the highest mountain on the planet, but the German-speaking Swiss nevertheless called the Matterhorn the *Berg der Berge*, the mountain of mountains. Straddling the Alpine Swiss-Italian border, it rises 14,692 feet (4,478 m), a remarkably symmetrical pyramid presenting four incredibly steep faces. Although the Alps are hardly a remote mountain range, the Matterhorn defied climbers well into the nineteenth century. It was 1857 before a first ascent was even attempted. It failed, as did sixteen more through 1865. The first successful ascent, on July 14, 1865, ended in the deaths of four of the climbers on their way down from the summit. Others succeeded in climbing it through the years since, but the north face of the mountain was not conquered until 1931 and the west face, highest of the Matterhorn's four faces, was not completely scaled until 1962. It is believed that the mountain has claimed the lives of more than five hundred climbers, an annual average of three to four.[1]

On July 22, 1871, Lucy Walker (1836–1916), a Canadian-born Briton, became the first woman to climb the Matterhorn when she accompanied her father, Frank Walker, and others in an ascent. In 1896, an American woman, Annie Smith Peck (1850–1935), wrote about her own ascent the year before in *McClure's Magazine*:

A colorized photograph of a women's suffrage parade down Fifth Avenue in New York City, May 6, 1911. More than three thousand women marched.

Soon after, we reach what would be the most dangerous part of the journey, if the whole distance were not hung with ropes. I had received various reports of its difficulty, some declaring that there were chains to be mounted hand over hand; others, that it was all as easy as possible. My own experience was that this was the nicest part of the climb. The ropes, with two exceptions, seemed new and strong, and in two places there were iron chains in addition. Then I had always the additional support of the rope around my waist, if one of the others had broken or the fastening staple gave way. So one at a time we scrambled up the rocks with ease and rapidity, though the incline was from forty to eighty degrees, mostly eighty. . . . Now we advance over an easier grade of rocks, more or less sprinkled with snow, until we arrive about half-past nine at the summit. It was indeed a moment of satisfaction to stand at last upon this famous peak, fourteen thousand seven hundred and five feet above the sea.

Annie Smith Peck earned a measure of fame as a female mountaineer—but an only slightly smaller measure of scorn for daring to scale the Matterhorn wearing trousers in 1895. She is shown here in trousers, c. 1900.

"The most dangerous and tiresome part of the journey was yet before me, but . . . I felt no apprehension."

—ANNIE PECK

Peck wrote of passing, on the way down, the spot from which "that young Hadow fell" in 1865, "dragging three of his companions to death four thousand feet below." She noted that "the most dangerous and tiresome part of the journey was yet before me, but . . . I felt no apprehension," and she went on to observe that climbing the Matterhorn had been "enjoyable, not simply for the exercise, varied and exciting though it may be, and for the elation that victory inspires but also for the intimate acquaintance thus gained with the mountain."[2]

By any measure and in any era, Annie Peck would be considered an accomplished woman. She attended Rhode Island Normal School, a teacher's college that had long welcomed young women, but she graduated from the University of Michigan in 1878, just seven years after it had become coeducational. Her major was Greek and Latin languages, and she went on to earn a master's in Greek, also from Michigan, in 1881. While subsequently studying in Europe, she discovered her enthusiasm for mountaineering. She became an educator and a writer of works about her adventures. Unsurprisingly, she was also a suffragist and a feminist—but, publicly, these interests took second place behind her mountaineering and adventuring. And that fact says something about her time and place. American women of the Gilded Age challenged male-dominated social order not only in the legal, political, and ideological realms, but in the arena of physical risk, courage, and achievement. They pushed against the boundaries not only of "feminine" behavior and appearance, but of aspiration, performance, and achievement as well.

TO OWN AND TO VOTE

Throughout the Gilded Age, the last quarter of the nineteenth century, the lives of most women, especially those of the middle class and above, were tightly controlled, lived out according to a well-established social script. There was little room for improvisation. Married American women, for instance, were mostly barred from owning real property in their own right. In 1839, Mississippi became the first state to allow such ownership—but strictly subject to the husband's permission. In 1845, New York became the first state to give married women rights to any patents they might secure, including earnings from them. Three years later, New York's Married Women's Property Act (1848) gave married

Elizabeth Cady Stanton and her daughter, Harriot. from a daguerreotype 1855.

Lucretia Mott.

Susan B. Anthony

Top left: Elizabeth Cady Stanton organized, with Lucretia Mott, the 1848 Seneca Falls (New York) Conference, which launched the women's suffrage movement in the United States. Stanton is pictured here in 1856, with one of her two daughters, Harriot.

Above: As co-organizer of the 1848 Seneca Falls Conference, Lucretia Mott shares credit with Elizabeth Cady Stanton for having founded the American women's suffrage movement.

Left: Along with Stanton, Susan B. Anthony fought for the adoption of constitutional amendments to enfranchise African Americans and women—two classes from whom the vote was long withheld in the United States. This photograph is by Mathew Brady, 1870.

women substantial independent control over all property held in their name, but it was not until 1900 that all other states enacted legislation that gave married women some degree of control over their own money, earnings, and property.

Women's suffrage—the right to vote—was even slower to gain ground during the Gilded Age, a fact that is all the more remarkable in view of the long history of the suffrage movement in the United States. During the American Revolution, New Jersey briefly permitted women to vote, but only because it had carelessly drafted its voting law, specifying that all "individuals" worth fifty pounds or more were eligible to cast ballots. New Jersey women who met the fifty-pound criterion voted in 1777, but the law was hastily reworded, changing the gender-neutral "individuals" to "men," and the loophole was closed before the next election. It was not until 1848, when the Seneca Falls Conference was held in the heart of New York's Finger Lakes district, that a formal American women's suffrage movement began. As organized by Elizabeth Cady Stanton (1815–1902) and Lucretia Mott (1793–1880), both also active in the abolitionist movement, the Seneca Falls meetings were reconvened annually.

In the years before the Civil War, the suffrage movement was increasingly subordinated to the abolitionist movement, and, after the Civil War, women suffragists became divided over whether to tie the campaign for women's rights to a campaign intended to ensure the enfranchisement of former slaves. Stanton and Susan B. Anthony (1820–1906) fought strenuously for constitutional amendments to enfranchise both blacks and women, and in 1866, Mott was elected chair of an Equal Rights Association. When the Fourteenth Amendment (intended to make freed slaves citizens) and the Fifteenth Amendment (extending the vote to black men) failed to address women's rights, Stanton and Anthony broke with Mott's group in 1869 to form the National Woman Suffrage Association, which opposed ratification of the Fifteenth Amendment (unless it also gave women the

> "During the American Revolution, New Jersey briefly permitted women to vote, but only because it had carelessly drafted its voting law."

"The National American Woman Suffrage Association (NAWSA) parade" of March 3, 1913, jammed the streets of Washington, DC. Note the onlookers perched atop the trolley cars.

Suffragettes
Parade 1913
Was. D.C. 2 M.

vote) and accepted only women as members. Another splinter group, the American Woman Suffrage Association, supported the Fifteenth Amendment as a necessary first step in the broadening of voting rights. They pointed out that while it did not give women the vote, at least it did not explicitly bar them from voting.

The early national suffrage groups were joined in the later years of the nineteenth century by federations of women's clubs, which, since the late 1860s, had devoted much attention to women's issues. Members of the Woman's Christian Temperance Union (WCTU, founded in 1873) also joined the crusade for women's suffrage. At last, in 1890, the National Woman Suffrage Association and the American Woman Suffrage Association ended their rivalry by merging to form the National American Woman Suffrage Association. While the merger had been guided by Anna Howard Shaw and Carrie Chapman Catt, it was Elizabeth Cady Stanton who was elected as the first president of the merged organization, with

The cover of the program for the NAWSA parade in Washington. A herald with bobbed hair, incongruously in medieval dress, sits atop a white horse (the parade was led by labor lawyer Inez Milholland dressed in white on a white horse).

THE GILDED AGE

Susan B. Anthony as vice president. Anthony's influence effectively eclipsed that of Stanton, who retired in 1892, leaving the field to Anthony, who was elected president that year. When Anthony retired as president in 1900, she positioned Catt to replace her, and it was at this point, from 1900 to 1920, that NAWSA mounted its most ambitious popular and political effort in the cause of woman suffrage, creating a unity of purpose that had earlier eluded the movement.

In 1890, Wyoming became the first state (discounting the eighteenth-century New Jersey aberration) to give women the vote, and a number of Western states followed suit. On the national front, Theodore Roosevelt's Progressive ("Bull Moose") Party endorsed women's suffrage in 1912. But it was not until well after the Gilded Age, after U.S. entry into World War I, that President Woodrow Wilson somewhat grudgingly endorsed a constitutional amendment granting women the right to vote. He considered it a vitally necessary war measure. The Nineteenth Amendment was passed by Congress on June 4, 1919 and was ratified by the states on August 18, 1920: "The right of citizens of the United States to vote shall not be denied or abridged by the United States or any State on account of sex." This, at long last, supplied the missing piece of the Fifteenth Amendment.

"BASKET-BALLS" AND CORSETS

Even though politics, business, and the profession of law remained largely masculine domains during the Gilded Age, the culture was changing. Women like Annie Peck were still sufficiently remarkable to be worth writing about. By 1896, when she published her account of her Matterhorn ascent, enough men were regularly climbing that mountain that no climb was especially newsworthy. But even though Peck was not the first woman to climb the Matterhorn, the idea of *any* woman mountain climber attracted readers. Her feat was neither an aberration nor, in itself, a scandal committed against social propriety—although the ascent did spark a debate among newspaper readers as to whether Peck should be arrested for wearing pants to make the climb. In an era in which many communities had laws barring women from wearing male attire, the debate was not entirely frivolous. Nevertheless, it was the climb itself that was considered most notable and even deserving of admiration, perhaps even emulation.

Female athletes and adventurers like Peck were beginning to enter the American cultural mainstream by the last quarter of the nineteenth century. They were part of what today might be termed a lifestyle movement, which no less a figure than Theodore Roosevelt, at the time governor of New York, called "The Strenuous Life." This was the title of a speech he delivered in Chicago, at the Hamilton Club, on April 10, 1899:[3]

> In speaking to you, men of the greatest city of the West, men of the State which gave to the country Lincoln and Grant, men who preëminently and distinctly embody all that is most American in the American character, I wish to preach, not the doctrine of ignoble ease, but the doctrine of the strenuous life, the life of toil and effort, of labor and strife; to preach that highest form of success which comes, not to the man who desires mere easy peace, but to the man who does not shrink from danger, from hardship, or from bitter toil, and who out of these wins the splendid ultimate triumph.

Perhaps no American political leader packed within himself a more capacious store of high-potency testosterone than TR. For him, the "strenuous life" was *mostly* a man's life:

> A life of slothful ease, a life of that peace which springs merely from lack either of desire or of power to strive after great things, is as little worthy of a nation as of an individual. I ask only that what every self-respecting American demands from himself and from his sons shall be demanded of the American nation as a whole. Who among you would teach your boys that ease, that peace, is to be the first consideration in their eyes—to be the ultimate goal after which they strive? You men of Chicago have made this city great, you men of Illinois have done your share, and more than your share, in making America great, because you neither preach nor practise such a doctrine. You work yourselves, and you bring up your sons to work. . . .
>
> In the last analysis a healthy state can exist only when the men and women who make it up lead clean, vigorous, healthy lives; when the

children are so trained that they shall endeavor, not to shirk difficulties, but to overcome them; not to seek ease, but to know how to wrest triumph from toil and risk. The man must be glad to do a man's work, to dare and endure and to labor; to keep himself, and to keep those dependent upon him. The woman must be the housewife, the helpmeet of the homemaker, the wise and fearless mother of many healthy children. In one of Daudet's powerful and melancholy books he speaks of "the fear of maternity, the haunting terror of the young wife of the present day." When such words can be truthfully written of a nation, that nation is rotten to the heart's core. When men fear work or fear righteous war, when women fear motherhood, they tremble on the brink of doom; and well it is that they should vanish from the earth, where they are fit subjects for the scorn of all men and women who are themselves strong and brave and high-minded. . . .

Let us therefore boldly face the life of strife, resolute to do our duty well and manfully . . . to uphold righteousness by deed and by word.

Yes, the strenuous life was *mostly* a man's life—and Roosevelt's speech left no doubt that, in his view, a man's place was on the job and a woman's place was in the home. "Fear of maternity" was a terrible social sin that betrayed a rottenness at the very heart of any nation whose women felt this fear. Yet the governor declared that a "healthy state can exist only when the men *and women* who make it up lead clean, vigorous, healthy lives." Thus while Roosevelt's gender-specific division of labor between breadwinning and housekeeping reflected the prevailing social and cultural reality of late nineteenth-century America, so did his more inclusive sentence concerning clean, vigorous, and healthy living. For he was speaking to an audience who could afford leisure but whose leisure was increasingly devoted to strenuous recreation. The Gilded Age saw the rise of such sports as bicycling—which was by far the most popular participant sport of the 1890s—and tennis. And it was also the period in which professional and college football as well as community-based and professional baseball became national pastimes. The YMCA (Young Men's Christian Association) and YWCA (Young Women's Christian Association) were founded in Europe in 1844 and 1855, respectively, and by the 1870s they had become very popular and highly influential throughout the United States.

In 1891, the head of the YMCA's physical training staff, Dr. Luther H. Gulick, asked Dr. James A. Naismith, an instructor at the YMCA's International Training School in Springfield, Massachusetts, to create an indoor winter game with the objective of stimulating YMCA attendance during cold weather. Naismith came up with "basket-ball," an indoor sport using a round ball and two peach baskets. If you look very, very hard, you may find basketball's ancestor in a game played by the Mayans and possibly the Olmecs, from whose culture the Mayans adopted their calendar. The ancient pastime involved throwing a ball through a basket with a vertical-facing hoop attached to a wall. Naismith himself, however, claimed no such lineage. He was just trying to solve the problem of creating a highly physical game that could be played indoors. He knew that it had to have a ball, for the simple reason that all games did. Because play was confined within four walls, players shouldn't be allowed to run with the ball, as they did in football, or kick it, or tackle other players, or knock them down. With these constraints in mind, Naismith settled on a rounded goal, rather than uprights, as in football, to keep players from charging at it, and he stuck it above their heads to keep defense from clustering around it. He found his peach baskets, threw in a soccer ball to play with, came up with half a dozen simple rules, and he knew he had his answer to the YMCA's winter doldrums.

Because it was simple, easy to learn, and did not require an army of specialists, the game caught on quickly. The first game was played by two nine-player teams—mainly because Naismith had eighteen students in the YMCA phys ed class he taught. His original thirteen rules did not specify team size, and the accepted number waned and waxed before settling in 1897 at five, the current on-court contingent.[4] No matter what the numbers, basketball became a phenomenon. By 1894, three years after Naismith invented it, the game was being officially administered by the Amateur Athletic Union as well as the YMCA. A professional league, with teams in Brooklyn, Philadelphia, southern New Jersey, and New York City, formed in 1898 but lasted only a couple of seasons. An exhibition game was played at the 1904 Olympics, and after several pioneering seasons of play by Yale and the University of Pennsylvania, playing rules were officially established in 1909 by the Intercollegiate Athletic Association of the United States (renamed the National Collegiate Athletic Association, or NCAA, in 1910). Soon, basketball was attracting crowds in high schools and colleges around the country. In a 1902 article written for *Harper's Weekly*, Naismith wrote:

Female students playing basketball at Western High School, Washington, DC, 1899. Generally conservative—even hidebound—when it came to the rights and social roles of women, the Gilded Age nevertheless fostered the remarkable rise of the American woman as athlete.

In the gymnasiums of the majority of girls' colleges and schools, basket-ball is one of the principal methods of pastime and exercise. In the cities like New York and Brooklyn, the winter is, in fact, the regular playing season, and more than the usual number of matches have already taken place. But in the larger [women's] colleges throughout the country, such as Vassar, Wellesley, Bryn Mawr, Newcomb, Smith, and others, the winter gymnasium practice is only preliminary to the class games and matches that are played out-doors in spring and early summer. These games are largely attended by the relatives and girl friends of the teams, but are in no sense public gatherings like the football contests of the girls' brothers.

The college girl who goes in for athletics is just as much in earnest as her big brother, but she goes about the matter in a different way. The boy is proud of his athletic inclinations and ability, and fond of displaying his prowess to an admiring public. His sister may be no less conscious of her skill and strength, but it is not good form to court notoriety, and thus it is that we hear much less of the girl athlete. Nevertheless, in college circles and among the girl's intimates, her reputation as a star player is as well known and discussed as are the feats of her sturdier relative.[5]

As its name suggests, the Gilded Age was enamored of surfaces, appearances—image. Even as the male dominance of the era seemed unshakable, the very image of womanhood was changing. Whether climbing mountains or playing "basket-ball," American women were no longer Victorian shrinking violets. The era's signature image of femininity emerged as the "Gibson Girl." The brainchild of illustrator Charles Dana Gibson (1867–1944), the Gibson Girl was probably inspired by the artist's own wife, Irene Langhorne, and her four sisters, all of whom were celebrated society beauties. Gibson himself said that he intended the Gibson Girl, which made its first appearance in the 1890s, to be an American composite:

I SAW HER ON THE STREETS, I SAW HER AT THE THEATRES, I SAW HER IN THE CHURCHES. I SAW HER EVERYWHERE AND DOING EVERYTHING. I SAW HER IDLING ON FIFTH AVENUE AND AT WORK BEHIND THE COUNTERS OF THE STORES. . . . [T]HE NATION MADE THE TYPE. WHAT [ZIONIST AUTHOR AND PLAYWRIGHT ISRAEL] ZANGWILL CALLS THE "MELTING POT OF RACES" HAS RESULTED IN A CERTAIN CHARACTER; WHY SHOULD IT NOT ALSO HAVE TURNED OUT A CERTAIN TYPE OF FACE? . . . THERE ISN'T ANY "GIBSON GIRL," BUT THERE ARE MANY THOUSANDS OF AMERICAN GIRLS, AND FOR THAT LET US ALL THANK GOD. . . .

THEY ARE BEYOND QUESTION THE LOVELIEST OF ALL THEIR SEX. . . . IN THE UNITED STATES, OF COURSE, WHERE NATURAL SELECTION HAS BEEN GOING ON, AS ELSEWHERE, AND WHERE, MUCH MORE THAN ELSEWHERE, THAT HAS BEEN A GREAT VARIETY TO CHOOSE FROM. THE EVENTUAL AMERICAN WOMAN WILL BE EVEN MORE BEAUTIFUL THAN THE WOMAN OF TO-DAY. HER CLAIMS TO THAT DISTINCTION WILL RESULT FROM A FINE COMBINATION OF THE BEST POINTS OF ALL THOSE MANY RACES WHICH HAVE HELPED TO MAKE OUR POPULATION.[6]

THE GILDED AGE

Gibson thus explained his "all-American" girl as the product of an immigrant melting pot, which he further defined in Darwinian terms. The United States, destination of so many people from so many places, was the scene of "natural selection" that produced the Gibson Girl and was destined to produce an even more beautiful woman in years to come.

The illustrator's application of Darwin is intriguing, but it is far more likely that Gibson's interpretation of American beauty was more a product of cultural values than natural selection. The ideal woman of the Gilded Age, as he pictured her, was neither a fragile flower nor a Rubenesque model, but a new vision of health, athleticism, and sex. Buxom and full in the hips, she could have been described as "voluptuous" were she not somehow too "healthy" and "athletic" for that word. Moreover, she was tall and slender, and her expression more aloof and independent than alluring. If you needed a single word to describe the Gibson Girl, that word was *formidable*.

To the modern eye, the one feature of the Gibson Girl that seems a caricature impossible in real life—perhaps even incompatible with life itself—is her wasp waist, which, in profile, creates an S-curve torso. The fact is that this was no caricature. By the latter part of the Gilded Age, many young women actually looked like this. They wore "swan-bill" corsets, which featured a busk (made of bone, ivory, or wood) that was inserted at the center front of the corset, so that it forced the torso to lean forward, pushing the bust forward while thrusting the hips and buttocks backward. Makers of this undergarment claimed that it was healthier than traditional corsets because it did not constrict the abdomen as severely. They failed to point out that it did force the wearer into a markedly abnormal

14065—Detroit Publishing Co.   Copyright, 1901, by Life Pub. Co.

GIBSON'S TYPICAL AMERICAN GIRL.

Brainchild of famed American illustrator Charles Dana Gibson, the "Gibson Girl" came to symbolize the "ideal" American woman of the late nineteenth century.

> "*If you needed a single word to describe the Gibson Girl, that word was formidable.*"

EFFECT OF AN **OLD STYLE CORSET**

THE NEW FIG-URE

The Gibson Girl's most remarkable feature was her unnatural "S-curve torso." The effect was created by a new type of "swan-bill" corset, for which its designers claimed health benefits as extravagant as they were dubious. This corset ad appeared in *Ladies' Home Journal*, October 1900.

forward bend. Throughout the Gilded Age, women and their doctors argued over the health effects of tight corsets. One of the early uses of x-rays at the beginning of the twentieth century was to demonstrate how tightly laced corsets damaged the body,[7] and in 1890 even the esteemed British medical journal the *Lancet* published an article titled "Death from Tight Lacing."[8]

Whatever the health risks, American women who aspired to the silhouette of the Gibson Girl endured their corsets, even as others, who admired the athleticism of the Gibson Girl, spurned the corset as incompatible with freedom of movement. The early American feminist author Elizabeth Stuart Phelps Ward (1844–1911), for example, urged women to "Burn up the corsets! . . . No, nor do you save the whalebones, you will never need whalebones again. Make a bonfire of the cruel steels that have lorded it over your thorax and abdomens for so many years and heave a sigh of relief, for your emancipation I assure you, from this moment has begun."[9] The protest against the corset was, in a most literal—that is, physical—sense, a precursor of what the 1960s would call "women's liberation." The corset became a symbol of the oppression male-dominated society imposed on women to compel their conformity to an ideal of sexual beauty, dictated mainly by men. In the Gilded Age, the Gibson Girl brought the new ideal of the healthy, athletic—and liberated, independent, even aloof—woman into direct conflict with Gibson's own corseted ideal of the S-curve torso. Women would have to choose. And they did. It is no accident that the end of the Gilded Age coincided with the end of tightly laced corsets, as women's dress turned toward simpler and more comfortable designs that made a fashion virtue of liberating the female figure and, metaphorically at least, freeing the whole woman.

THE "MATERNAL COMMONWEALTH"

The fact is that ordinary people—not just politicians, physicians, preachers, academics, suffragists, and advocates of women's rights generally—were increasingly questioning the role of women in American society. In an 1881 editorial, *Scribner's Magazine* noted: "We often hear it said that there are many men engaged in work women could do as well, and that women ought to be in their places." It is an opening sentence at once narrow and provocative. Its focus is less on the welfare of women than on the prospect of women taking jobs from men. The opening argument is identical to the complaint many Americans lodged against abolition in the Civil War (freed slaves will take jobs from white workers) and against large-scale immigration during the Gilded Age (immigrants will take jobs from "American" workers). The editorial asserted that women are constitutionally, physiologically, or anatomically unfit for certain types of work: "Woman is endowed with a constitution and charged with a function which makes it quite impossible for her to do certain classes of work for which her mind and her hands, if we consider them alone, are entirely sufficient. Not impossible, perhaps, for she undoubtedly does much that inflicts infinite damage upon her, and those that are born of her." The author of the editorial was particularly concerned about employment that required either too much standing or too much sitting. In the end, however, he conceded that a "woman has a right to do everything she can do," subject to a single restriction:

> . . . provided she does nothing which will unfit her for bearing and rais-
> ing healthy children. The future of the nation and the race depends upon
> the mothers, and any woman who consents to become a mother has no
> moral right to engage in any employment which will unfit her for that
> function. . . . We have a theory, which, we regret to say, is not only unpop-
> ular among a certain class of women, but exceedingly offensive to them,
> viz., that every one of them ought to be mistress of a home. Women have
> a fashion in these days of rebelling against the idea that marriage is the
> great end of a woman's life. They claim the right to mark out for them-
> selves and achieve an independent career. We appreciate the delicacies of
> their position, and we bow to their choice and their rights; nevertheless,
> we believe that in the millennium women will all live in their homes, and
> that men will not only do that which is regarded as their own peculiar
> work, but much of that which is now done by women. There has been in
> these late years a great widening out of the field of women's employments.
> We have been inclined to rejoice in this "for the present necessity," but we
> are sure the better time is to come when man, the real worker of the world,
> will do the work of the world, or all of it that is done outside of home, and
> that woman will, as wife and daughter and domestic, hold to the house
> and to that variety of employments which will best conserve her health
> and fit her for the duties and delights of wifehood, and the functions of
> motherhood. Quarrel with the fact, as she may, woman's rights must all
> and always be conditioned on her relations to the future of humanity.[10]

The *Scribner's* argument would be quite unacceptable to most women and men in the twenty-first century. Today, it comes across as a narrow-minded, intellectu-ally bankrupt evasion, based on easily discredited assumptions about the nature of work. The chief function of women is to bear children; work outside of the home endangers that function; therefore, women should content themselves with being "wife and daughter and domestic."

Narrow and intellectually bankrupt the argument is. Nevertheless, during much of the nineteenth century and especially during its later years, many American crusaders for women's rights eagerly embraced motherhood as the primary role of their gender. A case in point is the suffragist movement as it entered the Gilded Age. In 1872, a group of suffragists challenged the prosecution of Susan B. Anthony for illegally voting in the election that year. They hoped an appellate court would overturn the conviction by arguing that the definition of citizenship contained in the recently ratified Fourteenth Amendment implicitly gave women the right to vote. The court challenge failed, and the case also failed to reach the Supreme Court, but in 1875, the Supreme Court did hear *Minor v. Happersett*, only to unanimously reject the argument that the Fourteenth Amendment extended the vote to women.[11]

Defeated in the courts, the suffragists sought a legislative solution, proposing in 1878 a constitutional amendment consisting of a single sentence: "The right of citizens to vote shall not be abridged by the United States or by any State on account of sex." For the next forty-one years, this amendment would be introduced and reintroduced in every session of Congress.

In 1890, suffragists tried yet another approach. After the National Woman Suffrage Association merged with the American Woman Suffrage Association to form the National American Woman Suffrage Association, under the presidency of Elizabeth Cady Stanton (1815–1902), the group shifted from their constitutionally based demand for the same rights and responsibilities as men to a biologically based appeal. It was, in fact, the very rationale so many men (and women)—including the writer of the *Scribner's* editorial—used to argue *against* any change in the role and rights of women. Stanton and her followers argued that women deserved the vote not because they were *like* men, but because they were *uniquely different from* them. They and only they were capable of motherhood. So far, this was a very conservative position. The women took it a step further, however, arguing that their gender-specific contribution to the republic should consist of more than simply birthing healthy babies and raising them right. Given the opportunity for full political, social, and professional expression, women could fashion American into a cleaner, healthier, more moral "maternal commonwealth." It was a phrase that came to be heard repeatedly during the last decade of the nineteenth century.

Many suffragists no longer campaigned exclusively for the right to vote. They

The headquarters of the National American Woman Suffrage Association, a merger of the rival National Woman Suffrage Association and the American Woman Suffrage Association, was located on the ground floor of a humble Washington, DC building. Photograph, 1913.

added temperance—a campaign against the manufacture, sale, and consumption of alcoholic beverages—and initiatives to improve the lot of America's destitute families, especially in the nation's urban slums.

The temperance movement had begun well before the Civil War, and by 1855, the manufacture and sale of alcoholic beverages was against the law in thirteen of the thirty-one states. During the Civil War and Reconstruction, however, the Republican Party, fearful of weakening its grip on government at both the state and federal levels, was reluctant to take a stand on what many citizens, women especially, now clearly wanted: national prohibition of a drink that, women persuasively argued, brutalized, impoverished, and even destroyed families, thereby undermining the future of the republic itself. In the 1870s, groups of women mobilized against alcohol consumption and in 1873 formed the Woman's Christian Temperance Union (WCTU); in 1895, members of the newly created Anti-Saloon League were successful in influencing numerous state and local elections in favor of "dry" candidates.

The most colorful of the temperance women was Carrie Nation (1846–1911), who, in 1889, joined the WCTU branch in Medicine Lodge, Kansas, where she preached the gospel in a local church and ran a successful hotel. Nation's anti-alcohol campaign in Medicine Lodge took the form of harassing saloon patrons and owners, mostly by singing hymns at them while they were just trying to have a good time. One day, acting in response to what she called the voice of God, she suddenly graduated to another tactic. Nation began raiding saloons throughout Kansas, physically assaulting them—first with rocks and then with a hatchet. Often accompanied by a chorus of women singing hymns, she would burst into an establishment, announce to the patrons that she had come "to save you from a drunkard's fate," and then wield her hatchet against the bar, fixtures, liquor bottles, and beer barrels. (She avoided hitting the imbibers themselves.)

Carrie toured the nation, delivering paid temperance lectures and using the proceeds to pay the cost of bail and the many fines levied against her. Nothing could stop her, including what many considered simple decency. When President William McKinley was mortally wounded by an assassin's bullets in 1901, she declared her suspicion that the slain president had been a "secret drinker" and had thus gotten "what he deserved."[12]

Carrie Nation took her anti-alcohol campaign to the saloons. At first, she annoyingly sang hymns to the patrons. Later, she wielded a hatchet against liquor bottles, beer barrels, and bar fixtures. Her efforts paved the way for national Prohibition.

> *"Nation's anti-alcohol campaign in Medicine Lodge took the form of harassing saloon patrons and owners, mostly by singing hymns at them."*

While Carrie Nation attracted national attention, it was Frances Willard (1839–98), one of the founders, in 1873, of the WCTU, who emerged as the most influential and credible advocate of national temperance. Willard was a suffragist and educator—the first dean of women at the Woman's College of Northwestern University—and she inserted the campaign for prohibition into a social-improvement initiative that included prison reform, labor reform (including legal establishment of the eight-hour workday), and laws to establish minimum ages of consent for marriage. Her approach to temperance was to "Do Everything," which meant moving beyond a narrowly religious anti-alcohol argument (drinking is sin) to social and medical appeals. Through her efforts, the WCTU established soup kitchens as well as medical clinics in the skid row neighborhoods of America's cities.

The "Do Everything" approach of Willard's WCTU suggests comparison with another aspect of the "maternal commonwealth." Jane Addams (1860–1935) was born and raised in Cedarville, Illinois, the daughter of a prominent family that included five brothers and sisters. The death of Mrs. Addams (when Jane was two) and the subsequent remarriage of her father brought two stepbrothers into the family. Addams's father instilled in his daughter the values of tolerance, philanthropy, and a strong work ethic. After graduating from the all-female Rockford Seminary, she decided to pursue a degree in medicine. Seeking to divert her from what was widely considered an inappropriate goal for a young lady, however, her father and stepmother sent her on a two-year "grand tour" of Europe. The result was a bout of severe depression, which was deepened by the death of Addams's father shortly after her return from Europe. The young woman became a virtual invalid, barely able to walk. Diagnosed with curvature of the spine, she underwent surgery and was compelled to remain in a confining back harness for nearly a year. The enforced inactivity induced her to reflect on her life and goals, and, after she recovered, she embarked on a second trip to Europe in 1887, but this time she and her traveling companion, Ellen Starr, went far beyond the itinerary of the conventional grand tour. They were fascinated by Toynbee Hall, a "settlement house" in the slums of London.

Suddenly, Jane Addams's life had direction. In 1889, she and Starr purchased Hull House on Halsted Street, in an impoverished immigrant section of Chicago. They took up residence in the facility on September 8, 1889, offering community members hot meals, child-care services, tutoring in English, and many classes in vocational and other subjects. Hull House also sponsored neighborhood clubs and cultural and recreational activities. The goal was not simply to dispense charity, but to address the physical and intellectual needs of a disadvantaged community as well as to lift its morale and create a neighborhood spirit in which residents worked together to improve the conditions in which they lived. Hull House became a center of community activism, which successfully petitioned the city for improvements to the streets, for the creation of public baths, parks, and playgrounds.

Within a few years, Hull House was enjoying a steady flow of large donations from many philanthropic sources. Eventually, the center offered medical care and legal aid, in addition to its various educational and social programs. At the height of what was now the Progressive Era, Addams began to focus as much on attacking the sources of poverty as on remedying its results. She led successful campaigns to reform child-labor laws, the laws for the factory inspection system, and the juvenile justice system. Her efforts were

Jane Addams launched the American settlement house movement by founding Hull House in the gritty immigrant community of Chicago's Near West Side in 1889. Her objective was to root out poverty by attacking the sources of poverty, changing lives, not just economic fortunes.

An early postcard of Hull House, 800 South Halsted Street, Chicago, a mansion built in 1856 and named for its first owner.

instrumental in bringing about legislation to protect immigrants from exploitation, to limit the working hours of women, to enforce mandatory schooling for children, to afford legal recognition and protection for labor unions, and to provide for industrial safety. Addams was also active in the women's suffrage movement, first on the local level, working for Chicago municipal suffrage, and then as the first vice president of the National American Women Suffrage Association in 1911. She was a vigorous campaigner for Theodore Roosevelt and the Progressive ("Bull Moose") Party in 1912.

The example of Hull House inspired the establishment of community centers and "settlement houses" across America. Hull House itself became a kind of social laboratory, which drew educators, reformers, and social philosophers who explored a wide range of social and political issues. Her 1910 memoir, *Twenty Years at Hull-House*, was read as a handbook of social activism.

Jane Addams's advocacy of social justice encompassed a passionate belief in pacifism. She was an outspoken opponent of U.S. entry into World War I and was a founder of the Women's Peace Party, which not only sought an end to the war, but worked to establish a permanent international peacekeeping organization. A founding member of both the NAACP and the American Civil Liberties Union, Addams went on to earn the Nobel Peace Prize in 1931—the first American woman to do so.

THE GILDED AGE WAS PULLED BY CONTRADICTORY IMPULSES: toward innovation and radical forward thinking yet also toward a reactionary and retrospective longing for return to a golden age in which everyone knew his— and her—place. The idea of the "maternal commonwealth" did not reconcile this contradiction so much as it synthesized the opposing forces, in the process giving women a place in the forefront of the Progressive movement. The most profound revisions of "a woman's place" would not occur until years after the Gilded Age, but the foundations of these revisions were discovered or created during the final quarter of the nineteenth century in America.

THE GREAT WEST

COPYRIGHTED 1885 BY GAYLOR

CHAPTER 12

THE FRONTIER CLOSES

With good reason, we think of the Gilded Age as playing out largely in America's big, mostly Eastern cities. The economic power of those cities, however, the driver of their productivity and growth, is to be found in the markets created by America's westward expansion and by the raw materials of the West—from cattle and crops to oil and ore—that fed, fueled, and built the major cities. In this sense, Gilded Age enterprise and politics were ultimately the offspring of a national ethos that had been articulated as early as the run-up to the US-Mexican War (1846–48). In its 1844 presidential platform, the Democratic Party wrote of effecting the "re-occupation of Oregon and the re-annexation of Texas," even though the United States had never previously occupied these places.[1] By the word *re-occupation*, however, the party asserted a nonexistent right, advancing an imperialist agenda without risking a charge of imperialism. The idea was to court the support of expansionists without alienating more reticent or scrupulous voters. A year later, in July 1845, *New York Post* editor John L. O'Sullivan echoed the Democrats' platform in an article titled "Annexation," published in the *United States Magazine and Democratic Review*. "It is our manifest destiny," O'Sullivan declared, "to overspread and possess the whole of the continent which Providence has given us for the development of the great experiment

Published in New York by lithographers Gaylord Watson and Tenney & Weaver about 1881, "The Great West" presents an idealized, quasi-allegorical image of the increasingly settled American frontier—its industries, its mineral and agricultural wealth, and its dramatic landscape.

of liberty and federated self-government entrusted to us."[2] He thus expressed a sentiment held by many Americans since the days of the Pilgrims and the Puritans: that America was a chosen land and that it was the providential destiny of white, Christian Americans to possess the entire American continent. The implication was that any war fought to realize this "manifest destiny" would be a just war—indeed, a holy war. Moreover, there existed a deeply held American belief that the acquisition of land was part and parcel of the "unalienable right" to life, liberty, and the pursuit of happiness mentioned in the Declaration of Independence.

From the beginning, the leaders of the American republic had been determined to avoid the fate of Europe, with its small elites addicted to luxury and its huge, discontented, and therefore inherently rebellious landless majorities. Even the privileged class in America argued that the nation's great "experiment" in government depended on the prosperity of individual property holders. Widely distributed land ownership was a safeguard against dangerous concentrations of power. As citizens of a young country, its history but brief when compared with the histories of Old World nations, Americans developed what historian Drew McCoy called "a vision of expansion across space—the American continent— as a necessary alternative to the development through time that was generally thought to bring with it both political corruption and social decay."[3] This vision blended manifest destiny with manifest innocence—together, the very essence of what many have called "American exceptionalism." It was the vision that moved journalist John Babson Lane Soule in 1851 to editorialize in the *Terre Haute Express*, "Go west young man, and grow up with the country."[4]

Somewhere in the mix of divine mission and sheer romanticism, westward expansion was also driven by a growing feeling that the nation simply needed somewhere to put the influx of foreign immigrants, as packing them into cities was resulting in the creation of slums and the social misery that goes along with them. In any event, some combination of spiritual vision, a romantic yearning for the open spaces of the frontier, and the perception of demographic necessity motivated the United States to go to war with Mexico, and to acquire thereby most of what is now the American Southwest. The war effectively ended with General Santa Anna's defeat at the Battle of Huamantla (October 9, 1847), and the Treaty of Guadalupe Hidalgo (February 3, 1848) formally concluded hostilities.

This 1873 chromolithograph was made by George A. Crofutt after an 1872 painting by John Gast titled *American Progress* (and also *Westward Ho!*). It features an allegorical figure representing the spirit of "manifest destiny"—the idea that the American nation was providentially destined to spread from Atlantic to Pacific.

That was convenient timing, because on Monday, January 24, 1848, James Marshall, an employee of Northern California rancher John Sutter (1803–80), found gold in Sutter's millrace, a discovery that triggered the great California Gold Rush later that year.

GOLD RUSH

Sutter had been born Johann August Sutter in Germany. Bankrupted there, he immigrated to America in flight from his creditors. He did not stop when he reached an East Coast port, but traveled overland, westward, in search of fortune. After going bust twice, he scraped together enough money to buy a ranch in California's fertile Central Valley. Sadly, Marshall's discovery of gold did Sutter no good at all. Not only did all his employees run off to look for more of what Marshall had found, but his ranch was soon overrun by gold seekers, who destroyed nearly everything in sight. So, once again, the luckless immigrant lost money, and he spent his last days fruitlessly petitioning Congress for restitution over losses he suffered in the Gold Rush.

Among those who unleashed the hordes on Sutter was a Mormon elder and newspaperman named Samuel Brannan. At the time of Marshall's discovery, Brannan was staying the night at Sutter's ranch while traveling. He collected a quinine bottle full of gold dust, returned with it to San Francisco—at the time a modest village called Yerba Buena—and ran through the dusty streets waving the bottle and bellowing, "Gold! Gold! Gold from the American River!"

Almost overnight, Yerba Buena's population fell from a few thousand to a few dozen, as men threw down their tools or shuttered their shops and lit out for the Central Valley. Come midsummer, Brannan joined them—not to look for gold himself, but to make his fortune by selling picks, shovels, pans, and provisions from a brand-new ramshackle store he built right next to Sutter's Mill. Before 1848 ended, about a quarter-million dollars in ore was taken from California streams and topsoil. It arrived in San Francisco in bottles and buckskin bags, old tins and beat-up shoes, and much of it was shipped East around the tip of South America in vessels that stopped along the way at ports of call in Hawaii, Mexico, Peru, and Chile. Experienced South American miners set sail up the coast, and by 1849, the mining population has swelled to ten thousand or so. Tales of golden nuggets

In 1851, when this photograph of Portsmouth Square was made, San Francisco was a rough-and-ready Gold Rush boomtown of ramshackle buildings.

THE GILDED AGE

just waiting to be gathered by the handful and riverbeds paved with gold spread throughout the rest of the United States. "Forty-niners," as hopeful prospectors came to be called, gushed out of Atlantic seaboard cities, Midwestern villages, and Southern plantations—eighty thousand to a hundred thousand of them in 1849 alone. Yerba Buena exploded from a semideserted village to San Francisco, suddenly a major seaport. Prices for everything soared, as newcomers filled some five hundred bars and a thousand gambling dens. Life was counted cheap, but eggs went for $6 a dozen in town, and three bucks each in the gold fields.

Few prospectors struck it rich, and most eventually limped back East, discouraged and broke. By 1852, when gold production soared to an annual high of $81 million, most of the "placer" (surface) gold was gone and large-scale, well-funded, mechanized mining companies had pushed out most of the individual prospectors. But many of those who established businesses to serve the forty-niners quickly grew wealthy, purveying merchandise and real estate at vastly inflated prices. Collis Huntington and Mark Hopkins made their money cornering the market in shovels and blasting powder, taking most of what prospectors hadn't spent on gambling, drink, and loose women. Teamed with prospector-turned-shopkeeper Charles Crocker and mining-camp storekeeper Leland Stanford, they would become California's Big Four, financial backers of the Central Pacific, the western portion of America's first transcontinental railroad (see page 78).

While the Big Four were the biggest success stories to come out of the Gold Rush—the precursors of the robber barons, others also laid the foundations of Western fortunes that rose higher and higher during the Gilded Age. John Studebaker earned enough cash making wheelbarrows for miners to expand his family's small-time, Indiana-based wagon works into the nation's biggest and best-known carriage maker. A Bavarian immigrant, named Levi Strauss, patented the use of copper rivets to reinforce the seams of the indestructible trousers he made for forty-niners out of canvas tent fabric dyed blue. Philip D. Armour was a laborer who saved enough to open a butcher shop in the gold fields, slaughtering and selling meat at exorbitant prices—and earning more than enough to take back with him to Milwaukee, where he built the nation's biggest and best meatpacking plant. And then there were Henry Wells and William G. Fargo, two Easterners who had no intention of settling in the West, but who knew there was money to be made by running mule trains to keep miners supplied.

They ended up creating the country's premier stagecoach freight and passenger business before expanding into banking.

SODBUSTERS, COWBOYS, AND RAIL GANGS

The Gold Rush did not last long—scarcely a decade—but it nevertheless helped to make the West a destination for millions. In quest of overnight fortunes, the forty-niners were the advance guard of subsequent legions of farmers and tradespeople, looking not to get in, get a fortune, and get out, but to settle and build lives on the West Coast. On May 20, 1862, President Abraham Lincoln gave them a major incentive to do just that when he signed the Homestead Act of 1862. The law authorized any citizen (or immigrant who intended to become a citizen) to select any surveyed but unclaimed parcel of public land, up to 160 acres (64 ha), settle it, improve it, and, by living on it for five years, gain title to it.

With the nation torn apart by the Civil War, Lincoln hoped that the accelerated settlement of the West would strengthen what was left of the Union by creating an unbroken link between East and West. The Homestead Act, and several acts that followed, were also formulated to encourage orderly settlement by families, instead of the abusive exploitation by land speculators, large ranchers, and others. As an alternative to living on the land for five years, a homesteader could "preempt" the land after just six months' residence by purchasing land for $1.25 per acre (0.4 ha). The homesteader could also exercise preemption to augment his basic 160-acre (64-ha) claim, though few settlers could ante up the $50 for the minimum purchase of 40 acres (16 ha) the government required. Another option for adding to the original grant was to make a "timber claim" by planting 10 acres (4 ha) of timber-producing trees. This entitled the homesteader to an additional 160 acres (64 ha)—an important incentive on the mostly treeless Western prairies, where the hard-packed soil was not naturally conducive to timber growth. Indeed, were it not for John Deere's recently developed steel plow, the unyielding prairie soil would have been largely worthless for farming, and the Homestead Act might have had few takers. As it was, the homesteaders soon earned a nickname born of the soil. They were called "sodbusters," and they farmed the prairie.

The sodbusters were not the only agricultural workers who plied the Western Plains. The Civil War converted many Texas ranchers into Confederate soldiers, and when they went off to fight, a lot them left their livestock to fend for them-

TITLE.

The First Homestead in the United States, U. S. A.

This rare photograph documents the first homestead claim made under the Homestead Act of 1862. The claimant was Daniel Freeman; the location was Gage County, Nebraska. The photograph was made in 1904, some four decades after the claim was staked.

selves. By the end of the war, millions of head of cattle ranged free across the state. Hearing of this, a fair number of Southern young men, their region ravaged by combat and paid employment hard to find, went west to round up Texas strays, brand them, and drive them to market up North. That was how the trail cattle drive industry began, and if any one man can be said to have started the enterprise, it was former Texas Ranger Charlie Goodnight (1836–1929).

He was born on a southern Illinois farm and came to the Brazos River country of Texas with his family in late 1845. There, in a land of longhorns running wild, he learned how to be a cowboy, to gather the animals and drive them to market for local ranchers. With his stepbrother as his partner, he gradually amassed a small herd of his own, but, like many other Texans, left ranching to fight for the Confederacy. Mustered out of the Texas Rangers a year before the Civil War ended, Goodnight and his stepbrother found that their original herd, numbering 180 head at the outbreak of the war, had grown to 5,000—a figure they supplemented by appropriating cattle on the open range. At this time, most ranchers were starting to drive their cattle to Kansas railheads for shipment to Eastern markets. With Oliver Loving, an old-time cattleman, Goodnight decided to move in the other direction, pioneering a trail to Colorado, where mining operations and Indian-fighting military outposts were creating a tremendous demand for beef. In 1866, Goodnight and Loving gathered 2,000 head of longhorns and, with eighteen riders, followed the Southern Overland Mail route to the head of the Concho River, where they liberally watered their stock for the long, dry trip across the desert. They lost some 400 head on the trail—300 of thirst, 100 trampled to death in the stampede that ensued whenever they reached a watering

Painters and photographers never tired of portraying cowboys and cattle drives. Titled "Round-up Scenes on Belle Fouche [sic] in 1887," this print was made by South Dakota photographer John C. H. Grabill. (Today Belle Fourche is the seat of Butte County, South Dakota.)

THE GILDED AGE

hole—but the first drive along the Goodnight-Loving Trail netted the partners $12,000 in gold.[5]

The Goodnight-Loving Trail was one of four principal Western cattle trails, which also included the Chisholm (from Brownsville, Texas, to the Kansas railheads of Dodge City, Ellsworth, Abilene, and Junction City), the Shawnee (from Waco to Kansas City, Sedalia, and St. Louis, Missouri), and the Western (from San Antonio, Texas, to Dodge City and then on to Fort Buford, at the fork of the Missouri and Yellowstone Rivers, deep in the Dakota Territory). Between 1866, when Loving and Goodnight cut their trail, and 1886–87, when a single terrible winter nearly wiped out the range-cattle industry, many millions of beeves had been driven on these great trails.

———◆———

WHILE THE SODBUSTERS RAISED WHEAT AND CORN, the trail drive was all about beef. But the industry also spawned the trail-drive cowboy, perhaps the single most beloved and mythologized worker in American history. He was America's knight-errant; his image was noble, brave, and pure, surviving even the cynicism of the Gilded Age. The truth was that most cowboys were the poorest of the poor—many of them Confederate veterans dispossessed of family, friends, and all they had owned, and many others African Americans, Indians, and

A photocrom print from Detroit Publishing Company, this image of a cowboy throwing a lariat dates from between 1898 and 1905, when the "Wild West" was rapidly slipping into memory and legend.

Mexicans, all standing on the lowest rungs of the American socioeconomic ladder. Nevertheless, the mythology proved resilient and well-nigh indestructible. It made exciting reading for consumers of the pulp fiction known as dime novels, brightening the dreary day of innumerable Eastern factory workers.

In the early days of the trail drives, cowboys drove the cattle directly to market, traversing great distances on horseback. As the nation's western railroad network developed, the drives were shorter. Cattle were rounded up and driven to the nearest railhead. The Lincoln administration stimulated the building of western railroads for the same reason it encouraged western settlement through home-steading. The president wanted to expand the Union westward, and that meant promoting settlement, which, in turn, required reliable transportation. The Pacific Railway Act of 1862 (see pages 5 and 74) and subsequent legislation granted huge tracts of land to the railroads, which used some of the land for rights-of-way and sold some of it to help finance rail construction. Federally backed loans were also made available, and in 1865, when even this generous funding proved inadequate to keep construction moving on the rail line to the Pacific, President Lincoln called on the Massachusetts congressman, Oakes Ames (1804–73). Known as the

Oakes Ames, 1860. Known as the "Ace of Spades" because he had amassed his first fortune by making and marketing shovels, Ames masterminded Crédit Mobilier, the corrupt banking enterprise that financed the transcontinental railroad.

THE GILDED AGE

"Ace of Spades" because he had amassed his initial fortune by making and marketing shovels, Ames recruited investors—his fellow legislators, who were offered discounted stock—in a corporation created by Union Pacific Railroad vice president Thomas Durant and named after the company that had financed the French railway system a decade earlier, Crédit Mobilier. It was an offer that couldn't be refused—a masterpiece of quasi-legal corruption created on the cusp of an age in which corrupt bargains would become business as usual. Crédit Mobilier, run by the directors of the Union Pacific, was paid by the Union Pacific to build the Union Pacific. The directors (who were the principal investors) made a profit on the operation of the railroad as well as on the cost of building the railroad. In essence, therefore, they were investing in themselves. This led to monumentally padded construction bills and a national scandal that, however, was not exposed until 1872. When the scandal broke, the Crédit Mobilier Scandal rocked the administration of Ulysses S. Grant and gave Oakes Ames a new nickname. No longer "King of Spades," he was now "Hoax Ames."

Scandalous though it was, Crédit Mobilier got construction of the transcontinental railroad moving. Under the leadership of Grenville Mellen Dodge, a U.S. Army engineer, the Union Pacific made prodigious progress, east to west, across the plains, despite the hostile climate and, often, hostile Indians, whose land was being gobbled up. Building from west to east, the Central Pacific moved more slowly through the mountainous terrain of the Sierras. Immigrant laborers—especially Irish on the Union Pacific and Chinese on the Central Pacific—were hired in unprecedented numbers. Casualties among the hard-driven work gangs were numerous, especially among Chinese laborers, who were put to work blasting out mountain passages.

Despite the profiteering, exploitation, corruption, and waste, on May 10, 1869, at Promontory Summit in Utah Territory, Leland Stanford drove the final ceremonial spike, painted shiny gold, into the last tie of America's first transcontinental railroad. With this, the eastbound line of the Central Pacific was joined to the westbound rails of the Union Pacific. The ceremony did not go smoothly. As Chinese workmen, who had endured much persecution at the hands of their Caucasian employers and coworkers, lowered the final length of rail in place, a photographer hired to commemorate the moment hollered, "Shoot!" The workers instantly dropped the five-hundred-pound rail and ran.

Promontory Summit, Utah, May 10, 1869. Here the eastbound tracks of the Central Pacific were ceremonially joined to the westbound rails of the Union Pacific with a "Golden Spike" made of 17.6-karat copper-alloyed gold. The photograph shows CPRR's Samuel S. Montague (center left) shaking hands with UPRR's chief engineer, Grenville M. Dodge (center right).

THE "INDIAN WARS"

Immigrant laborers were not the only targets of racism in the westward rush. The story of the European settlement of America is also the story of Native American dispossession, displacement, and war. Virtually the entire span of the Gilded Age was marked by more or less continuous low-intensity warfare between the U.S. Army and many Indian tribes in the West. The most intense period of conflict began in 1866, when the Teton Sioux, the Northern Cheyenne, and the Northern Arapaho attempted to close the Bozeman Trail in Montana and Wyoming in a violent effort to stanch the flow of white settlers onto their lands. Beginning with the so-called War for the Bozeman Trail or Red Cloud's War, the army waged fourteen major military campaigns, culminating in operations against the Sioux and ending in the Battle (or Massacre) of Wounded Knee, South Dakota, on December 28–29, 1890.

In so many ways both tragic and immoral, United States Indian policy is a staggeringly complex subject far beyond the scope of a few paragraphs in a

The United States Office of Indian Affairs issued this map of U.S. Indian reservations (highlighted in red) in 1892, the year after the Sioux Wars (1854–91) ended.

book. It is all too easy to broadly condemn the policy as genocidal. Without a doubt, some military operations targeted entire villages, combatant and noncombatant—men, women, and children. Nevertheless, if any single approach can be identified as national policy, it was not genocide but "concentration"—the gathering together and relocation of Indian groups on lands "reserved" for them. By law, once consigned and confined to a reservation, Indians became wards of the federal government, which pledged to provide them with rations and other necessary goods. The execution of official policy was, however, rife with corruption and incompetence, and, in many cases, reservation tribes suffered from privation, starvation, and deliberate abuse. These conditions incited rather than prevented "uprisings" and "rebellions."

The objective of most military action against Indians during the Gilded Age was to force them onto reservations and keep them there. During 1870–90, the U.S. Army rarely topped 28,000 officers and men. It was essentially a frontier police force—poorly paid, poorly fed, poorly equipped, poorly trained, and often poorly led—very thinly spread across a vast area. The "enemy" it faced included—especially among the Plains tribes—warriors raised in a culture that valued and cultivated skill at arms, combat-effective horsemanship, and what today would be called guerrilla tactics. Possessed of a definite tactical edge, warrior tribes also had the advantage of defending a homeland they loved and knew intimately against "foreign" invaders. Threatened with impoverishment, dispossession, and death, the Indian warriors were highly motivated. This was in sharp contrast with the soldiers of the U.S. Army, who were often given ambiguous orders and who were themselves ambivalent about their mission. While some soldiers looked on Indians as a brutal, even subhuman enemy, many respected them and were revolted by the injustice and abuse to which poorly conceived and indifferently, incompetently, or maliciously executed federal policy had subjected them. Such ambivalence also reached to the highest levels of government. The halls of Congress rang with condemnation of military activity in the West, yet legislators struggled and failed to devise just alternatives.

For all their tactical advantages, Indian combatants were fatally handicapped in warfare by the very features of their culture, which prized individual strength, cunning, skill, endurance, courage, and honor. War chiefs were not generals. They did not command their fighters, but led them by charisma, reputation, and example. Rarely could large numbers of warriors be led in coordinated, disciplined operations. Even more rarely did tribes act with unity or form intertribal strategic alliances. Most of all, by the Gilded Age, the white population in the West massively outnumbered the Native American population—on average by a factor of ten. Against such demographic odds, no warriors could long prevail.

The western "Indian Wars" of 1866–90 were wars of attrition, and by the end of the nineteenth century, there were 187 reservations—181,000 square miles (468,788 km²) of land—in the United States. Of the 248,253 Native Americans counted in the 1890 U.S. Census, most were domiciled on reservations. This was the culmination of four centuries of Indian-white warfare in North America. And at this point, there arose from the despair and misery of the reservations a shamanistic Paiute prophet named Wovoka. Having spent part of his youth with a white rancher's family, he was the product of both Native American and white Christian religious traditions. This moved him to prophesy to the reservation Indians the coming of a new world, in which only Indians dwelled and in

The Wounded Knee Massacre of December 29, 1890, made international news. This wood engraving, titled "The Ghost Dance of the Sioux Indians," was published in the *Illustrated London News* on January 3, 1891.

SITTING BULL.

Copyrighted by D. F. Barry, 1885,
BISMARCK, DAK.

D. F. BARRY,   BISMARCK, DAKOTA.

No Native American was more famous or more revered—by whites and Indians alike—than the Hunkpapa Lakota chief Sitting Bull. He poses here adorned with a crucifix and holding a "peace pipe." Five years later, he enthusiastically espoused the Ghost Dance religion—and was killed by Native American reservation police sent to arrest him on December 15, 1890.

which the bison were again plentiful on virgin plains. To promote the advent of this world, Wovoka urged all Indians to perform a sacred Ghost Dance and, in the meantime, to faithfully practice the ways of peace.

Ghost Dancing soon swept through many of the Western reservations. While the Teton Sioux embraced the Dance, they rejected the ways of peace. Two Ghost Dance leaders among the Tetons, Short Bull and Kicking Bear, called for hastening the day of deliverance through a bloody campaign to obliterate the white man. For warriors in this cause, they fashioned a "ghost shirt," which, they claimed, was impervious to white men's bullets.

The Ghost Dance alarmed white Indian agents in charge of the reservations, who summoned army reinforcements. In a climate of increasing fear and distrust, the revered Hunkpapa Sioux chief Sitting Bull (c. 1831–90) took up the Ghost Dance religion. Knowing that many Sioux would follow Sitting Bull's example, the agent in charge of the chief's reservation dispatched Native American reservation police officers to arrest him on December 15, 1890.

The arrest went very badly. A riot broke out and, in the melee, whether deliberately or by accident, Sitting Bull was killed. Word of the "murder" spread like flame across the Sioux reservations, and a new war seemed inevitable. The most militant chiefs and warriors made a stand in a part of the Pine Ridge Reservation called the Stronghold. Chief Red Cloud, a Pine Ridge leader friendly to the whites, asked Spotted Elk ("Big Foot"), chief of the Miniconjou Sioux, to come

Renowned Western artist Frederic Remington published his depiction of "The Opening of the Fight at Wounded Knee" in the January 24, 1891, edition of *Harper's Weekly.*

to the reservation and use his influence to persuade the Stronghold party to surrender. Tragically, the army commander in the region, General Nelson A. Miles, knew nothing about this. All he knew was that the Sioux were near rebellion and that Big Foot, a prominent Sioux leader, was on his way to meet with the leaders of that rebellion. He therefore ordered his troops to pursue and intercept Big Foot and any other Miniconjous.

So, on December 28, 1890, a squadron of the 7th Cavalry located the chief and about 350 of his followers camped near a South Dakota stream called Wounded Knee Creek. By morning, some five hundred soldiers, under Colonel James W. Forsyth, surrounded Big Foot's camp. In defiance, a medicine man, traditionally identified as Yellow Bird but probably Stosa Yanka ("Sits Up Straight"), began dancing, urging his people to fight. A shot was fired—no one knows by whom— and the soldiers opened up on the camp with deadly Hotchkiss guns, small rapid-fire cannon that delivered one 42-millimeter round per second. The troops mowed down men, women, and children, killing Big Foot and at least 153 other Miniconjous in less than an hour. Others, who were wounded, crawled or limped away and therefore went uncounted among the slain. Estimates put the total death toll at 300 of the 350 who had been camped at Wounded Knee Creek.

Miles was appalled by Wounded Knee, but he nevertheless used the "battle" as the opening move in the final suppression of the Sioux "uprising." The chiefs surrendered on January 15, 1891.

SPANISH-AMERICAN WAR

University of Wisconsin historian Frederick Jackson Turner delivered his famous paper on the significance of the frontier in American history just two years after the surrender of the Sioux (see page 13). Based on the 1890 census, Turner concluded that the frontier had been fully settled—conquered, as it were—and therefore "closed." He predicted that the "restless, nervous energy," which had so long driven American westward expansion, would now "demand a wider field of exercise." Without what he called the "safety valve" of an open frontier—his implied analogy to a steam engine was significant in an age of steam—American energy would propel expansion overseas. The United States would become an imperialist power.[6]

Recent historians question whether the frontier, as Turner imagined it, ever really existed. And if it did not exist, how could it "close"? Nevertheless, Turner was correct in his prediction that American policy would suddenly look beyond the ocean-bound borders of the United States. In February 1896, the Spanish government sent General Valeriano Weyler to restore order in Cuba, its increasingly rebellious island possession. Among the military governor's first acts was to build "reconcentration camps" for the incarceration of rebels as well as other citizens accused of supporting or even sympathizing with the rebels. Although both U.S. presidents Grover Cleveland and his successor William McKinley stoutly resisted calls from some in Congress to intervene against Spanish "atrocity" in Cuba, American popular sentiment, whipped up by lurid stories of Spanish cruelty published in the rival New York papers of Joseph Pulitzer and William Randolph Hearst, at last moved McKinley to order the battleship USS *Maine* into Havana Harbor to protect American citizens and property there.

The onset of war fever in the United States was not exclusively caused by a humanitarian concern for Cuban suffering. By the late nineteenth century, large and powerful American business concerns had made major investments in the island, especially in sugar plantations. Revolutionary unrest posed a threat to these investments; however, a successful revolution, if properly supported by the United States, could create a nominally independent Cuban government that would be an obedient U.S. client. Alternatively, the United States might simply annex the island.

On February 9, 1898, Hearst created a sensation by publishing a purloined private letter in which the Spanish minister to the United States insulted President McKinley. With the nation now fully infected with war fever, news broke on February 15 that the armored cruiser *Maine*, moored in Havana Harbor, had suddenly exploded and sunk, with the loss of 266 crewmen. Today, most historians believe that the ship's powder magazine spontaneously ignited through no hostile action, but a naval court of inquiry at the time concluded that the ship "was destroyed by the explosion of a submarine mine."[7] The court did not assign responsibility for the explosion—was it a rebel mine or a Spanish one?—but the Hearst and Pulitzer papers most certainly did. Each pointed a finger at Spain, and the United States soon rang with the battle cry of "Remember the *Maine* . . . to hell with Spain!"

Spain wanted no war, and obligingly began accelerating its withdrawal from Cuba. President McKinley therefore delayed a decision throughout the early spring, but, yielding at last to popular pressure, he requested congressional authorization for an invasion. The legislators gave him more than he asked for, voting to recognize Cuban independence from Spain. In response, Spain declared war on the United States, on April 24, 1898.

The diminutive U.S. Army was entirely unprepared to fight an "expeditionary campaign"—an overseas foray against a foreign adversary. But the far more formidable U.S. Navy was prepared, and it made the first move—not in Cuba, but in the Spanish-occupied Philippine Islands. After receiving word of the declaration of war, Rear Admiral George Dewey steamed his Asiatic squadron from Hong Kong to Manila Bay. On May 1, 1898, he fired on the Spanish fleet, destroying all ten ships in the bay. President McKinley dispatched eleven thousand troops to the Philippines, and that force, along with pro-independence Filipino irregulars commanded by Emilio Aguinaldo, defeated Spanish forces in Manila, the archipelago's capital city, on August 13.

In the meantime, the U.S. Army delayed and blundered as it struggled to transport its soldiers from the American mainland to Cuba aboard a ragtag fleet of chartered commercial vessels. Yet once military action did start, the army moved decisively. On May 29, the U.S. fleet blockaded the Spanish fleet at Santiago Harbor on the eastern end of Cuba. The following month, seventeen thousand

The Rough Riders pose around their commanding officer, Lieutenant Colonel Theodore Roosevelt, atop San Juan Heights (also known as San Juan Hill or Kettle Hill), which they had captured on July 1, 1898, during the Spanish-American War. It was the make-or-break battle of the brief war's even briefer land phase.

troops were finally positioned to invade Cuba at Daiquiri. Despite severe illness ravaging the ranks—Cuba was plagued by yellow fever—the invaders advanced on Santiago.

The regular army forces were supplemented by numerous hastily raised volunteer units, including the 1st U.S. Volunteer Cavalry. When its commander, Colonel Leonard Wood, was given command of the entire 2nd Cavalry Brigade, his second in command, Theodore Roosevelt, assumed operational command of the 1st USVC, better known by its nickname, the Rough Riders. Roosevelt had stepped down from McKinley's cabinet, in which he had been serving as assistant secretary of the navy, to accept a commission as lieutenant colonel, and he had personally selected the men of the Rough Riders. Thanks to a transportation snafu, the unit arrived in Cuba without most of its horses. So, when Roosevelt led the Rough Riders in the assault on Kettle Hill during the Battle of San Juan Hill on July 1, the attack was largely on foot. They not only took Kettle Hill, but fended off a determined counterattack. This victory enabled the American forces to surround Santiago de Cuba, and, from San Juan Heights (as the combination of San Juan Hill and Kettle Hill were called), the American forces attacked Santiago de Cuba while also firing on the Spanish cruiser fleet in the city's harbor, which had been blockaded by the U.S. Navy. Under withering fire from the Heights, Spanish Admiral Pascual Cervera decided that he had no choice but to run the blockade. In a four-hour naval battle, the American fleet destroyed all of Cervera's ships while sustaining minor damage and the loss of just a single American sailor.

On August 12, Spain agreed to withdraw from Cuba and to cede Puerto Rico and the Pacific island of Guam to the United States. Formal peace negotiations in Paris resulted in Spain's also selling the Philippine Islands to the United States for $20 million.

The United States set up a territorial government in Puerto Rico without much difficulty, but U.S.-Cuban relations proved far more tenuous. In 1899, President McKinley installed a military government and pondered annexation of Cuba, mainly to protect substantial American investments there.

Meanwhile, McKinley ran for reelection in 1900, winning a second term, with Theodore Roosevelt as his vice president. TR assumed the presidency himself on September 14, 1901, following McKinley's assassination (see

Theodore Roosevelt takes the oath of office as president of the United States, September 14, 1901, at the home of his friend, lawyer Ansley Wilcox, in Buffalo, New York. The ceremony took place hours after President William McKinley died of septic shock from wounds sustained during the Leon Czolgosz shooting.

pages 310-11). In May 1902, the United States renounced annexation. Roosevelt withdrew federal troops from the island, and instead authorized Cuban leaders to draft a constitution for an independent Cuba. The document, which was subject to U.S. approval, included clauses establishing American military bases on the island and guaranteeing the right of the United States to intervene in Cuban affairs to "preserve" the island's independence.

BECOMING A WORLD POWER

Riding a wave of popularity gained as a result of his heroism in what John Hay (U.S. ambassador to the United Kingdom and then secretary of state) famously called "that splendid little war,"[8] Theodore Roosevelt was elected president in his own right in 1904. As president, he took steps that certainly seemed to bear out Professor Turner's predictions about the rise of American imperialism.

> *"Roosevelt established a policy toward the Caribbean islands and Latin America that determined U.S. behavior in the region for decades to come."*

Roosevelt established a policy toward the Caribbean islands and Latin America that determined U.S. behavior in the region for decades to come. Known as the Roosevelt Corollary to the Monroe Doctrine, the policy called for the United States to act as an international police force in the region. In this way, for better or worse, the nation shunned the isolationism that had dominated its policies ever since George Washington warned against foreign entanglements. The nation began to assume a position as both a regional and a global power. The trend had begun during McKinley's administration when, in January 1899, following the conclusion of the Treaty of Paris with Spain, the United States announced annexation of the newly acquired Philippines. Pro-independence Filipinos, under Emilio Aguinaldo, responded by proclaiming Philippine independence on June 12, 1898. This touched off the bitter Philippine-American War of 1899–1902, which brought an end to the First Philippine Republic and made the Philippines an unincorporated U.S. territory.

This portrait of the Empress Dowager Cixi was made c. 1890. It was hand-colored by painters of the Imperial Court. The regent who presided over Qing dynasty China from 1861 to 1908, she threw her support behind the so-called "Boxers" in the Boxer Rebellion. shooting.

In 1899, Secretary of State Hay proposed to the governments of France, Germany, Great Britain, Italy, Russia, and Japan that they all endorse an "Open Door Policy" (first suggested by a British customs official, Alfred E. Hippisley) with regard to China. The United States, all European nations, and Japan, he argued, should have equal access to Chinese trade. Although Japan balked, the proposal met with universal approval among the nations of the West, but China—the very subject of the policy—had not been consulted on the matter. An ancient empire in acute decay, China was torn by internal tensions and was barely held together by Cixi, the empress dowager. Seeing an opportunity to gain much-needed popularity by uniting the divided country against the foreigners, the empress dowager issued a proclamation on January 11, 1900, encouraging an uprising of a militant secret society called the Yihequan, the "righteous and harmonious fists," which the Westerners called the "Boxers."

In response to Boxer violence, the United States participated in a military coalition that also included England, France, Russia, Austria-Hungary, Germany, Italy, and Japan. Their mission was to protect their nationals in China by suppressing the so-called "Boxer Rebellion." The coalition's victory gained the United States little other than a measure of international prestige. As for China, the defeat of the Boxers brought down the Qing, or Manchu, dynasty, which had ruled since 1644. It would be decisively overthrown in the Chinese Revolution of 1911.

ROOSEVELT'S BOLDEST STEP TO PROMOTE AMERICAN IMPERIALISM was his conclusion of the Hay-Bunau-Varilla Treaty, signed in 1903 and approved by the U.S. Senate in 1904, which cleared the way—diplomatically—for a canal joining the Atlantic and Pacific Oceans through the Isthmus of Panama. The idea of building a canal to create a passage between the Atlantic and Pacific Oceans was not new. In the 1840s, the United States negotiated an agreement with New Granada (a nation consisting of present-day Panama and Colombia) for rights of transit across the Isthmus of Panama, which separates the Caribbean Sea from the Pacific Ocean. Although the isthmus jungle was dense and disease-ridden, it was nevertheless preferable to making the long and hazardous sea journey all the way down one side of the South American continent and up the other. Moreover, the 1849 California Gold Rush prompted the United States to fund the Panama Railroad across the isthmus. The ultimate goal—of the United States as well as Great Britain—was to build a *canal* across the isthmus. In 1850, the two nations concluded the Clayton-Bulwer Treaty, agreeing that neither would assert exclusive control over the canal.

Drawing up an agreement for a canal was a long way from actually digging one. It was 1881 before a French firm, under the direction of Ferdinand de Lesseps, began work on an isthmus canal, only to quickly succumb to bankruptcy and the diseases endemic to the Panamanian jungle—yellow fever and malaria. Twenty years later, still bathed in the afterglow of victory in the Spanish-American War, Theodore Roosevelt's State Department persuaded Great Britain to relinquish its claim to joint control of a Central American canal. In that same year, 1901, an American commission recommended building the canal in Nicaragua instead of Panama, but the New Panama Canal Company, successors to de Lesseps's defunct firm, persuaded Roosevelt to build through Panama by offering

A stereograph of the SS *Panama* steaming through the Culebra Cut on February 7, 1915; it was one of the first passenger ships to pass through the completed Panama Canal.

the rights it held to the canal route not for the original asking price of $109 million, but for the bargain-basement price of $40 million. Congress authorized construction early in 1902, and the next year ratified the Hay-Herrán Treaty, by which Colombia (of which Panama was then a part) granted the United States a ten-mile (16-km) wide strip of land across the isthmus in return for a $10 million dollar cash payment and, after nine years, an annual annuity of $250,000.

Everything looked rosy until the Colombian Senate delayed ratification in the hope of increasing the price offered by the United States. Then, on August 12, 1903, that body flatly refused to ratify the treaty, partly over money, but mostly in response to a popular movement to resist "Yankee imperialism." Roosevelt now turned to Philippe Bunau-Varilla, the French engineer who had worked on the original French canal project, joined the successor company, and gave the American president a good deal on the rights to the canal route. The president commissioned Bunau-Varilla to work with advocates of Panamanian independence to organize a revolt against Colombia. The Frenchman rallied and led a group of railway workers, firemen, and disaffected Colombian government officers and soldiers at Colón, Panama, in an uprising on November 3–4, 1903. The rebels proclaimed Panamanian independence. In the meantime, just offshore, the U.S.

Navy cruiser *Nashville*, dispatched by President Roosevelt, interdicted an attempt by Colombian general Rafael Reyes to land troops to quell the rebellion.

On November 6, President Roosevelt officially recognized Panamanian independence and greeted Bunau-Varilla as minister from the new republic. With this new minister, Secretary of State Hay concluded the Hay-Bunau-Varilla Treaty on November 18, which provided for the acquisition of a canal zone and the right to build and control a canal in exchange for the same monetary terms that had been offered Colombia. The U.S. Senate approved the Hay-Bunau-Varilla Treaty in 1904, and actual construction began in 1906, after Colonel William Gorgas of the U.S. Army Medical Corps defeated the twin scourges of yellow fever and malaria by waging a successful war against mosquito infestation. In 1914, after eight years, almost $400 million, and the excavation of 240 million cubic yards (183,493,166 m³) of earth, the Panama Canal was opened to shipping. The magnitude of this project, which changed the face of the Earth itself, was extraordinary. For Theodore Roosevelt, *that* was precisely the point. A great world power should take on nothing less.

Copyright, 1900, by Keppler & Schwarzmann.

"What Fools these Mortals be!"

Puck

Entered at N. Y. P. O. as Second-class Mail Matter.

"TAMMANY IS GREAT AND CROKER GETS THE PROFIT."

COPYRIGHT 1900 BY KEPPLER & SCHWARZMANN.

DIRTY POLITICS

While its "gilded" moniker implied an era of fraud, the progress in production, technology, innovation, the building of wealth, and the rise of a prosperous middle class during the last quarter of the nineteenth century were all real. As for the plutocrats—the Carnegies, Vanderbilts, Rockefellers, Morgans, Fricks, and their like—no era before the Gilded Age had seen so many great fortunes piled so high so fast. Even the immigrants, coming in their millions and subjected to sweatshop labor conditions, tenement living, discrimination, and general struggle, often actually found, on American shores, hope as well as its fulfillment.

Such progress was all the more remarkable for what had preceded it. For the Gilded Age was hardly the crowning glory of an era of enlightened leadership by visionary political leaders presiding over a green and pleasant land. On the contrary, it was a period of recovery from a bloody and ruinous Civil War that had pushed the American people, government, and economy far beyond what anyone had ever contemplated as possible. At the end of the war, the South was an economic ruin and, in some cities, a physical ruin as well. As for the North, by 1865 the national debt had been raised some 1,505 percent,[1] mostly in the effort to build a military—the Union Army

A November 1900 *Puck* cover depicts a smug-looking Richard Croker—the corrupt head of Tammany Hall from 1886 to 1902—holding a knife labeled "Tammany Vote" behind his back. Hobbling down the road is a wounded William Jennings Bryan.

alone had soared from a handful to a million men—and the nation was left with the task of putting itself back together again. Under the best of circumstances, this would have been an incredibly daunting task. But circumstances were far from the best. The one truly visionary, compassionate, yet pragmatic political leader of the Civil War era, Abraham Lincoln, had been assassinated, leaving the executive branch to the well-meaning but inept, intolerant, and unpopular Andrew Johnson.

AN ERA OF POLITICAL MEDIOCRITY

The hard truth about the period from the end of the Civil War to the elevation of Vice President Theodore Roosevelt to the White House following the assassination of William McKinley in 1901 (shot on September 5, dead on September 14) is that it was an age of political mediocrity, including a series of what the irascible Harry S. Truman would have described as "non-entity presidents."[2] Andrew Johnson (1865–69), Ulysses S. Grant (1869–77), Rutherford B. Hayes (1877–81), James A. Garfield (1881), Chester A. Arthur (1881–85), Grover Cleveland (1885–89), Benjamin Harrison (1889–93), Cleveland again (1893–97), and William McKinley (1897–1901)—ask anyone who is not an American historian or a hard-core history buff to attach one significant or memorable event to each of these men, and you might get responses for Johnson (was impeached), Grant (ran an incredibly corrupt administration, but got nothing out of it himself), Hayes (was elected by fraud), Garfield (was assassinated), McKinley (provoked a war with Spain—and, the bonus answer, was assassinated). The others would likely yield nothing more than blank stares.

In fairness, poor Garfield, nominated by the Republican National Convention of 1880 as the darkest of dark horses on the thirty-sixth ballot and narrowly elected following an extremely subdued "front-porch" campaign against Democrat and Civil War hero Winfield Scott Hancock, showed every indication of high ethics and maybe near-greatness. He had hardly begun a program of genuine political reform before Charles J. Guiteau, a delusional seeker of political patronage, shot him in the back on July 2, 1881, four months into his presidency. He lingered, conscious but prostrate, for eleven weeks before succumbing to sepsis from a wound that certainly would have proved nonlethal today. In fairness as well to his vice president and successor, Chester A. Arthur defied all predictions that he would quickly steer the administration out of the progressive path on which Garfield was putting it. Arthur was a hack product of the New York Republican political machine known as the Stalwarts, who owed his allegiance to the exuberantly corrupt party boss, Senator Roscoe Conkling. His inclusion on a ticket with Garfield, a member of the party's rival progressive wing, had been a political compromise to secure nomination in a badly divided party. To everyone's amazement—and Conkling's sublime consternation—Arthur rose to his office and embraced reform, most notably passage of the Pendleton Civil Service Reform Act of 1883 (see chapter 14), which created the foundation for the modern, merit-based, nonpartisan civil service system.

But Garfield and Arthur were exceptions, and while politics was very much in evidence during the Gilded Age, the politicians themselves were by and large notoriously unproductive. If the White House sheltered largely unremarkable occupants, Congress was outrageously boisterous yet singularly inefficient. The legislative halls were a sort of rowdy men's club, suffused in cigar smoke and lined with cuspidors, a place in which the business of the *nation* was typically neglected in favor of the business of the *Congress*, which was the trading of political power, influence, and favors. Until ratification of the Seventeenth Amendment in 1913, senators were appointed by state legislatures rather than directly voted into (and out of) office by the people. Throughout the Gilded Age, the autocracy that was the Senate domineered not only over the House of Representatives but over the president as well.

From all appearances, the senators were princelings and barons, but the titans of big business and finance played them like marionettes. National direction came less from the three constitutional branches of government than from the robber barons and captains of industry for which the era was famed and infamous. What the humorist Will Rogers said in the 1920s applied even more literally to the post–Civil War political scene: "America has the best politicians money can buy."[3] The prevailing mediocrity of politicians during this period meant that the real doers in the public sphere were the business tycoons, who used their financial resources to buy both political support and the politicians themselves—at municipal, state, and national levels, purchasing mayors, governors, and senators by the bushel basket. The result was the emergence of an oligarchic class and an unholy alliance between government and business that may be fairly described as the triumph of crony capitalism. Indeed, not until the forty-fifth president stocked his cabinet with billionaires would the United States government flirt so brazenly with outright oligarchy, government by and for those on the topmost rung of the socioeconomic ladder.

Arguably, given the lackluster quality of political leadership talent after the Civil War, government by big business produced some genuine benefits. Industrial innovation and production exploded, raising the general standard of living and creating a demand for well-paid skilled labor, including a new echelon of white-collar managers. There is no denying that the massive deficits of the Civil War period were rapidly erased. Under Garfield/Arthur, Cleveland (first term), and Harrison—that is, between 1881 and 1893—the national debt became a national surplus, although overproduction helped set the stage for the Panic of 1893 (see chapter 14), the worst American economic depression before the Great Depression of the 1930s.

The fact is that economic instability—whipsaw cycles of boom and bust—were one consequence of turning over government to Wall Street movers and shakers. Another cost was the poverty among the ranks of semiskilled and unskilled laborers and their families as well as the unconscionable exploitation of labor, including child labor, under unsafe working conditions (see chapters 6 and 7). The nation would not again see so vast a divide between the lowest and highest levels of the economy until the twenty-first century. The financial violence of economic boom and bust was accompanied by the kind of labor violence discussed in chapter 7, by political violence, and by racial violence.

AN ERA OF POLITICAL ASSASSINATION

That two American presidents were assassinated during the Gilded Age is no coincidence. Abraham Lincoln's assassin, John Wilkes Booth, may have been deranged, but there is no question that he was also a Confederate sympathizer. The murder of the sixteenth president was therefore the work of a madman or, in the broadest sense, an act of war.[4] The assassins of Garfield and McKinley certainly exhibited signs of mental illness, but, just as certainly, both were also politically motivated. Garfield's assailant, Charles J. Guiteau, had written an unsolicited campaign speech for Garfield. He convinced himself that the speech (never delivered and never used by the campaign, but printed at Guiteau's own expense) had been instrumental in the candidate's victory, and he therefore demanded

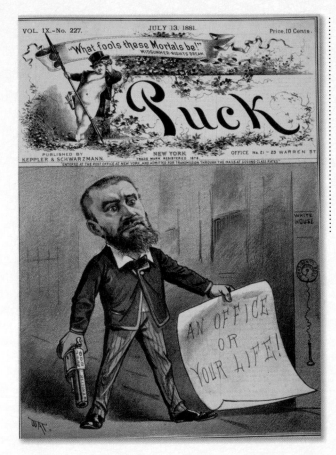

VOL. IX.—No. 227.   JULY 13, 1881.   Price, 10 Cents.

"What fools these Mortals be!"
MIDSUMMER-NIGHTS DREAM.

Puck

PUBLISHED BY
KEPPLER & SCHWARZMANN.   NEW YORK   OFFICE No. 21 - 23 WARREN ST
TRADE MARK REGISTERED 1876.
ENTERED AT THE POST OFFICE AT NEW YORK, AND ADMITTED FOR TRANSMISSION THROUGH THE MAILS AT SECOND CLASS RATES.

AN OFFICE OR YOUR LIFE!

WHITE HOUSE

Garfield seemed committed to a program of much-needed political reform when he was shot by Charles J. Guiteau, characterized by the media as a spurned seeker of a political patronage appointment. *Puck* portrayed him as a "Model Office-Seeker," the inevitable product of a spoils system run amok.

from the administration a political reward in the form of appointment as U.S. consul to Vienna or (fallback choice) Paris. Turned away by both the president and, repeatedly, by his staff, Guiteau became obsessed, borrowed $15 from an in-law, purchased a revolver, and shadowed Garfield throughout June 1881. On July 2, after reading a newspaper story revealing that the president was leaving on his summer vacation, Guiteau waited for him at the Baltimore & Potomac Railroad terminal in Washington, approached him from the back, and, at point-blank range, shot him twice, grazing his shoulder with one round but hitting him solidly in the lower back with the second. Guiteau fled the station to board a cab he had waiting, but, out the door, blundered into a Metropolitan police officer, who arrested him. "I am a Stalwart of the Stalwarts!" Guiteau told the cop. "I did it and I want to be arrested! Arthur is president now!"[5]

Following a failed insanity defense, Guiteau was convicted of murder and, on June 30, 1882, hanged. The political press had its own slant on the tragedy. A popular political cartoon, published shortly after the assassination over the caption "Model Office Seeker," shows Guiteau holding his revolver in one hand and, in the other, a note that says "AN OFFICE OR YOUR LIFE!"

The assassin of William McKinley, Leon Czolgosz, was a steelworker who lost his job during the Panic of 1893, when unemployment reached 18.4 percent in 1894.[6] He consoled himself among fellow jobless first in a socialist workingman's club and, later, in a more aggressive socialist political group. Unable to get steady employment, he went, in 1898, to live with his father and stepmother on their farm in Warrensville, Ohio. Czolgosz became interested in anarchism, a movement that was rapidly gaining followers in an America gripped by a seemingly intractable economic depression. Interest would turn to obsession after Czolgosz discovered Emma Goldman.

A Jew born in Lithuania (then part of the Russian Empire) in 1869, Goldman immigrated to the United States in 1885. She was drawn to anarchism after the Haymarket Riot in Chicago, and its aftermath—an event we are about to discuss—and thereafter became a radical lecturer and author on that political philosophy as well as on women's rights and other social issues. Her presence on a lecture platform was electrifying. She attracted thousands—including Czolgosz, who met and spoke with her at a lecture in Cleveland in May 1901. They had a longer conversation, in July, at the Chicago home of an anarchist newspaper publisher, Abraham Isaak. While Goldman considered Czolgosz a sincere radical in the making, Isaak took him for a U.S. government spy and even published a warning about him to fellow anarchists in his paper.

As for Goldman, there was a dark side to her anarchism, for she was no mere theorist. A believer in what some anarchist writers called "propaganda of the deed," she planned with her lover and fellow anarchist Alexander Berkman an 1892 attempt on the life of Carnegie Steel president Henry Clay Frick. Berkman carried out the "deed," walking into Frick's Pittsburgh office armed with a sharpened steel file and a revolver. Frick was seated at his desk. Berkman, standing, fired at point-blank range. The downward trajectory of the shot nicked Frick's earlobe, penetrated his neck, and lodged in his back. Berkman squeezed off a second shot before Carnegie Steel vice president, John George A. Leishman,

The most extreme alternative to the unbridled capitalism of the Gilded Age was not Socialism or even Communism, but anarchy. Emma Goldman and her lover, Alexander Berkman, were the most famous, influential, and reviled anarchists in America.

present in the office at the time, grabbed Berkman's arm, preventing a third shot. Wounded though he was, Frick lunged at Berkman, and the three men—Frick, Leishman, and the would-be assassin—struggled on the office floor. Berkman used his file to stab Frick four times in the leg before more Carnegie employees rushed into the office and subdued the assailant. Frick survived and recovered. Berkman, who was tried and convicted of attempted murder, was sentenced to twenty-two years. Although Goldman was not charged in this crime, she did not disavow her role in it.

Perhaps we may assume that Czolgosz imbibed more than the theory of anarchy from Emma Goldman. We know for certain that he was also inspired by another assassination attempt—this one successful. On July 29, 1900, anarchist Gaetano Bresci shot and killed King Umberto I in Monza, Italy. This instance of "propaganda of the deed" emboldened the United States anarchist movement and prompted an Italian-American New York City police lieutenant, Joseph Petrosino, to warn President McKinley that his life was almost certainly in danger. McKinley's private secretary, George B. Corelyou, urged the president to heed Petrosino's warning that he make use of bodyguards. McKinley, who enjoyed public contact, dismissed these concerns.

When newspapers announced that President McKinley would be visiting one of the great expositions of the Gilded Age, the Pan-American Exposition in Buffalo, New York, as part of a six-week cross-country presidential tour, Czolgosz took the train to Buffalo, rented a hotel room, and purchased a revolver. On September 6, 1901, he took his place in a line of well-wishers inside the exposition's Temple of Music. In his right hand, he held his brand-new .32 cal-

LESLIE'S WEEKLY
McKINLEY EXTRA

Vol. XCIII—EXTRA NUMBER   New York, September 9, 1901   PRICE 10 CENTS

LEON F. CZOLGOSZ, THE ASSASSIN.
FIRST PHOTOGRAPH OF THE WRETCHED ANARCHIST WHO SHOT THE PRESIDENT AT NOON F. M. SEPTEMBER 6TH, 1901, AT THE PAN-AMERICAN EXPOSITION.—(Photographed by Senor Edwards, 1901.)

iber Iver Johnson revolver, wrapped in a handkerchief that made it look as if his hand were bandaged. The line advanced toward the president. One by one, people shook the chief executive's hand. When it was Czolgosz's turn, McKinley reached out to him, Czolgosz batted the proffered hand aside with his left hand, raised the weapon in his right, and discharged two shots, point blank, into McKinley's ample abdomen.

Remarkably, the first round ricocheted off a coat button, but the second penetrated. "Go easy on him, boys,"[7] the victim called out to the members of the crowd that had piled on the assassin.

The wounded president was taken to the Exposition Hospital, which had been set up to attend to whatever presumably minor medical emergencies might arise

Among Goldman's admirers was Leon Czolgosz, who shot President William McKinley on September 6, 1901. This image, published in *Leslie's Weekly*, chillingly embodied the dark menace of anarchy stalking the nation as the Gilded Age drew to a close.

among those attending a large international fair. Surgeons administered morphine and strychnine to sedate McKinley as they probed the wound in a vain effort to locate the bullet. Although a working X-ray machine was on display at the exposition, the conservative doctors attending the president believed it would be of no use. They sewed up an entry and exit wound in the man's stomach and left the unlocated bullet wherever it was—presumably, they thought, lodged harmlessly in a back muscle.

Indeed, McKinley rallied and seemed to be destined for recovery. Hopeful telegrams were dispatched daily to the press. Eager to help, no less a figure than Thomas Edison—at the time working on improvements to X-ray technology—sent one of his own machines to Buffalo. Once again, it was not used—and may have been shipped missing a key component. In the meantime, despite the apparent improvement in the stricken man's condition, gangrene set in, and the twenty-fifth president of the United States succumbed early in the morning of September 14. At his arraignment for murder, Czolgosz entered a guilty plea, which the judge rejected, sending him to trial, at the end of which a jury convicted him on September 26, after a single hour of deliberation. He was executed on October 29 by means of a device Thomas Edison had not personally invented but had financed and endorsed. It was the electric chair. The assassin's final words were unremorseful: "I killed the president because he was the enemy of the good people—the good working people. I am not sorry for my crime."[8]

Emma Goldman, who had published a political defense of Czolgosz, was arrested and imprisoned a number of times between 1901 and 1917, mostly on charges of inciting a riot and once for illegally distributing information on birth control. In 1906, she founded *Mother Earth*, an influential anarchist journal, which ceased publication in August 1917, after she and Berkman (released from prison after serving fourteen years of his twenty-two-year sentence for attempted murder) were convicted and imprisoned for inducing persons not to register for the military draft after the United States entered World War I in April 1917. Released in 1919, the two anarchists were deported to their native Russia. Initially enthusiastic about the Bolshevik Revolution, Goldman was soon profoundly disillusioned. She left Russia and lived in England, France, and Canada. Her two-volume autobiography, *Living My Life* (1931 and 1934) became a classic study not only in anarchy, but of the immigrant experience during the Gilded Age and of that era's political violence.

THE EVENT THAT WAS THE TIPPING POINT in Emma Goldman's conversion to anarchism took place in Chicago, on May 4, 1886, during a strike against the McCormick Harvesting Machine Company—a strike that was part of a much larger national labor union campaign to secure an eight-hour workday. The day before, on May 3, a clash between strikers and police resulted in the death of one striker, possibly two, and the injury of others as officers moved to protect strikebreakers ("scabs"). In protest against what they deemed police brutality, the strikers convened a mass demonstration in Haymarket Square on the city's Near West Side. The demonstration was reasonably peaceful until a contingent of police were called in to break it up. During this action, someone—no one knows who—hurled a dynamite bomb, the explosion of which killed eight officers and four demonstrators, and injured about sixty other people—police and civilians.[9] The rest of the police contingent opened pistol fire on the strikers,

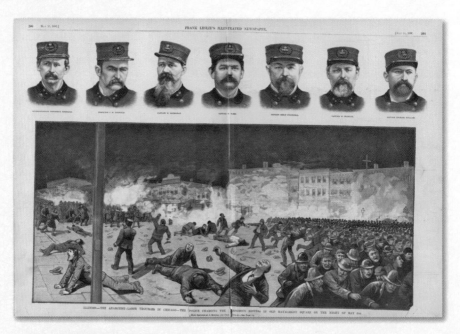

A *Frank Leslie's Illustrated* feature depicts the "Haymarket massacre" in Chicago, published a week after the riot of May 4, 1886. The top row shows the police officers involved in the arrests.

some of whom were armed and exchanged shots with law enforcement officers.

Although the bomb thrower was never identified, eight alleged anarchist labor leaders—including August Spies, a radical labor activist and anarchist—were tried for and convicted of murder on the prosecution's theory that they had conspired with, aided, and/or abetted the unknown bomb thrower. The theory was tenuous, as were the grounds for conviction. No connection between the unidentified bomber and those convicted was demonstrated in court. Nevertheless, amid public hysteria over the apparent rise of anarchism, compounded by hostility toward militant labor organizers, Spies and three others were hanged on November 11, 1887. Another condemned man committed suicide in prison. As far as democracy, the rule of law, and the guarantees of the Constitution are concerned, the only positive outcome of the Haymarket affair was the action of Illinois Governor John Peter Altgeld, who, in 1893, after reviewing the convictions of the other three condemned men, pardoned them. An act of moral and ethical courage all too rare among Gilded Age politicians, it was hailed by progressives and organized labor, but it ended Altgeld's political career.

Just as the Haymarket tragedy revealed the American nexus of labor, politics, and violence, the Colfax Riot, years earlier, on April 13, 1873, revealed the intersection of politics, racism, and violence. In this case, the magnitude of the violence was unspeakable.

Perhaps more than any other state, Louisiana was torn apart by post–Civil War Reconstruction. With the Democratic Party decimated, Radical Republicans assumed control of state government. Despite this, resistance to the Fourteenth and Fifteenth Amendments, granting freed slaves citizenship and the vote, respectively, was fierce among Louisiana whites, who feared that the former slaves, enfranchised and empowered, would turn against their former masters. The gubernatorial election of 1872 was disputed, ending in the "election" of two governors, a Republican and a Democrat, each claiming legitimacy. The federal government supported the Republican governor and sent U.S. Army soldiers to Louisiana to enforce his installation in office. This provoked many of the state's whites to coalesce around a combination shadow government and citizen militia dubbed the White League. The White League committed acts of intimidation and violence against white Republicans as well as blacks. On Easter morning, April 13, 1873, in the town of Colfax, a White League militia clashed with a

Harper's Weekly published this engraving of the aftermath of the bloody clash between men of Louisiana's White League "militia" and African American residents of Colfax on April 13, 1873. Some 150 African American men were killed—many by summary execution after surrendering to the militia.

contingent of Louisiana state militia, which was predominantly African American. The ensuing combat resulted in the deaths of some 150 African American men and three white men. Of the black casualties, 20 to 60 (one account reported 48) were shot after surrendering.[10]

President Ulysses S. Grant responded by sending federal troops to restore order in Louisiana and elsewhere in the South, and federal indictments were handed down against ninety-seven White League members on charges of violating the Enforcement Act of 1870. Of these, just nine were brought to trial and only three were convicted. The convictions were subsequently overturned by the Supreme Court in 1876 (*United States vs. Cruikshank*) on the grounds that the government had failed to prove a racial motive for the killings.

DIVISION AND STALEMATE

Amid the intense, urgent, even violent social, economic, and labor climate roiling the nation, American political life during the last quarter of the nineteenth century was so evenly divided between the two major parties, Republican and Democrat, that legislative stalemate was the norm—a situation not unlike recent American politics. The razor-thin balance between the Republican and Democratic electorate made legislators reluctant to take any strong stand that might alienate any segment of voters, no matter how small. The political parties were unwilling occupants of the same boat, which neither side wanted to rock. Instead of relying on bold political action to earn votes, they fell back on machine politics, cronyism, political patronage, and general corruption, which included naked electoral fraud and manipulation.

Interestingly, the presidents of the era seem to have been largely oblivious to the corruption even within their own administrations. The range of scandals during the two presidential terms of Ulysses S. Grant (1869–77) is staggering. There were:

- The Gold Panic of 1869, kicked off by Jay Gould (see chapter 3);

- The New York Custom House ring of 1871–72, in which customs collectors Moses H. Grinnell and Thomas Murphy, Grant appointees whose monetary compensation depended on the amount of revenue they collected, gave importers preferential treatment in exchange for exorbitant fees;

- The Star Route fraud (1872–76, and then again from 1878–80 during the Hayes administration), in which the U.S. Post Office Department paid contractors huge fees for servicing so-called Star Routes (leased inland mail routes) in remote parts of the country;

- The Salary Grab of 1873, in which Grant failed to veto a law that massively raised the salaries of the president and members of Congress;

- The Fort Laramie Treaty Breach of 1875, by which gold miners were allowed to prospect the Black Hills in violation of a treaty with the Lakota Sioux;

- The Sanborn incident of 1874, in which John D. Sanborn, a private agent hired by Secretary of the Treasury William A. Richardson to collect delinquent taxes, inflated his commission fees by collecting both delinquent and nondelinquent taxes;

> *"American political life... was so evenly divided between the two major parties, Republican and Democrat, that legislative stalemate was the norm."*

- The Delano affair of 1875, in which Secretary of the Interior Columbus Delano took bribes in exchange for making fraudulent grants of public lands;

- The Pratt & Boyd affair of 1875, in which Attorney General George H. Williams took bribes in exchange for declining to prosecute certain cases, including one against the merchant house of Pratt & Boyd;

- The Whiskey Ring of 1875 (see page 33), in which distillers evaded massive federal excise taxes by paying somewhat less massive bribes instead.

All of this happened under the president's nose, but, apparently, without his knowledge. Except for the Salary Grab, he derived no tangible benefit from any of the schemes.

As numerous as the Grant scandals were, the single most spectacular, brazen, and sinister instance of corruption at the executive level was the "stolen election" of 1876, which traded occupancy of the White House for Rutherford G. Hayes's pledge to end Reconstruction (see chapter 1). From that point on, through the next five presidential administrations—presidential activity picked up under William McKinley, elected in 1896—remarkably little was accomplished by Congress. Between 1875 and 1896, just five major bills made it to a president's desk for signature. For most politicians, the focus was less on governing the nation than it was on maintaining themselves in office. At every level—municipal, state, and federal—votes were routinely bought, sometimes for cash, but more often by patronage—the distribution of politically appointed employment. When Benjamin Harrison narrowly defeated Grover Cleveland in his bid for election to a second term in 1888, he publicly gave thanks to "Providence" for his victory. Senator Matthew Quay of Pennsylvania privately scoffed: "Providence didn't have a damn thing to do with it!"[11] Indeed, Harrison, who, like Grant, was personally above reproach, later discovered that his faith in Providence had been grossly naive. Belatedly realizing that it was the Republican machine that had purchased

PUCK.

THIS IS NOT THE NEW YORK STOCK EXCHANGE, IT IS THE PATRONAGE EXCHANGE, CALLED U. S. SENATE.

The satirical *Puck* on the state of machine politics in the republic, 1881: "This is not the New York Stock Exchange, it is the patronage exchange, called U.S. Senate."

his election, the president famously remarked: "I could not name my own cabinet. They had sold out every position in the cabinet to pay the expenses."[12]

As far as complex but much-needed legislation on tariffs and other money matters was concerned, both congressional and executive action was excruciatingly slow, as politicians on all sides embraced what, from the perspective of history, appears to have been an unspoken version of the prime directive of the ancient Hippocratic Oath: "First, do no harm." But whereas, for the physician, the harm in question was to the patient, for politicians it was to the politicians themselves. Inaction in support of the status quo unquestionably did great harm to farmers, laborers, and *small* businesspeople. At the lowest level of politics, in city government, the urban bosses and their machines were all-powerful. Local politicians were responsive to their constituents, but almost exclusively on a quid pro quo, pay-as-you-go basis. City governments had an array of lucrative jobs to award. The bosses eagerly awarded them in exchange for votes, plus monetary kickbacks from patronage wages earned.

THE CORRUPTIBLE BOSS TWEED

William Magear Tweed—"Boss" Tweed—made a profession of what he called "honest graft" in New York City government. He and his "Tweed Ring" set the corrupt pattern for urban machine politics in the Gilded Age.

Urban political corruption was exposed in the run-up to the Gilded Age when, in 1871, Tammany Hall's "Boss" Tweed was arrested for failing to audit contractors' bills submitted to New York City for projects connected with construction of the "Old" New York County Courthouse (52 Chambers Street, New York City), better known as the Tweed Courthouse. The scandal marked the beginning of the end for the organizer of the infamous Tweed Ring, which would become a synonym for the corrupt political machines that dominated Gilded Age urban America. Nevertheless, Tweed's arrest did not end machine politics. On the contrary, Tweed emerged as the paradigm and prototype of the big city boss.

Starting out his political life in the 1850s as a New York City alderman, William Magear Tweed (1823–78) cadged an appointment as chief of the Department of Public Works, a position from which he controlled most of the city's patronage jobs; this meant that he owned huge voting blocs. The heyday of Boss Tweed was also the heyday of foreign immigration into New York City, with newcomers from Ireland and Italy forming the majority of immigrants. Tweed made a play for their loyalty by throwing his support behind their labor unions and their Roman Catholic Church. He traded political favors, including city jobs, for votes and thereby became the city's most important power broker. During the economic boom that followed the Civil War during the second half of the 1860s, Tweed built a network of city officials, Democratic politicos, and private contractors. Paying them all piled titanic debts upon the city, but Tweed enriched himself from what he brazenly dubbed "honest graft": fraudulent contracts, political patronage, kickbacks, and phony payment vouchers. His hand was in some of the city's most ambitious and consequential projects, including the building of the Brooklyn Bridge and the purchase of land for Central Park.

A hostile press branded his circle of confederates the "Tweed Ring," and by the time the famous crusading editorial cartoonist Thomas Nast began lampooning it in *Harper's Weekly*, Tweed could afford to offer Nast a half-million-dollar payoff to withdraw an especially scathing cartoon. Nast turned him down. The Tweed Ring was at its zenith when the Boss was finally arrested for graft in 1871. (After several trials, imprisonment, a foiled escape, and re-imprisonment, Tweed died of pneumonia in a New York City federal prison in 1878.) But Tammany Hall, New York's Democratic Party machine, had been around since 1789 and would remain in action far after the passing of Boss Tweed, surviving all opponents except for Mayor Fiorello La Guardia, who succeeded in ending Tammany political power by the 1930s. Tammany-like machines dominated Gilded Age urban politics, and big city bosses dominated the machines. When Tweed left Tammany Hall, men such as John Kelly and Richard F. Croker took over, but none ever achieved the breadth and depth of Tweed's influence. In Philadelphia, the archetypal boss was "King James" McManes; in Boston, it was "Czar" Martin Lomasney; and in St. Louis—where the political machine was exposed by reformer Lincoln Steffens in his 1904 *book The Shame of the Cities* (see chapter 14)—the monarch was "Colonel" Ed Butler.

Political machines had such remarkable staying power because they served the urban poor—the Irish, Italian, and German immigrants, the unorganized working people, and the African Americans—as no formal political body did. In many municipalities, while kickbacks funded bribes, they also created a rich slush fund from which local officials distributed cash to help the poorest of their constituents. Cities became de facto, ad hoc welfare states. In exchange for a vote, the machine offered food when a poor man was hungry, rent and clothing when he was down and out, legal help when he was in trouble, and, for many, a decent job.

A GROUP OF VULTURES WAITING FOR THE STORM TO "BLOW OVER."—"LET US PREY."

In one of the most famous political cartoons in American journalism, Thomas Nast portrayed the Tweed Ring as a "group of vultures," with Tweed himself the fattest of them all. Their watchword? "Let us *prey*." The cartoon appeared in *Harper's Weekly* in September 1871, a month before Tweed's arrest. Commenting on Nast's work, Tweed reportedly said, "Stop them damned pictures. . . . My constituents don't know how to read, but they can't help seeing them damned pictures!"

THE ALMIGHTY TARIFF

As Sir Isaac Newton stated in his Third Law of Motion, for every action in nature there is an equal and opposite reaction. As in nature, so in the dirty politics of the Gilded Age. Corruption eventually provoked a reaction—opposite, if not always equal—in the reforms of the late nineteenth and early twentieth centuries. Two of the three major political issues that dominated late Gilded Age politics were reforms of currency and of the civil service. As reforms, they are properly subjects for the next chapter, which is devoted to the Progressives. But the third of the great issues of the age was the tariff.

In a time before income taxes, tariffs were important sources of revenue for the federal government. Nobody paid much attention to them as long as they were nothing more than modest taxes on foreign imports, the proceeds of which were used mainly to fund the agencies that managed customs and immigration. Thanks to tariffs, these agencies were self-supporting.

But there is another use of tariffs. So-called protective tariffs are levied not primarily to raise revenue, but to make certain that imported goods are more expensive and therefore less competitive with their domestically produced counterparts. In the infancy of the republic, President James Madison (in office 1809–17) used protectionist tariffs to encourage the development of embryonic American industries. Protectionist tariffs are rarely modest taxes. They are, after all, intended to force significant boosts in the retail price of imports. While they are not taxes levied directly on U.S. consumers, their cost, ultimately, is borne by them in the form of higher prices for goods. Congress, recall, was averse to rocking the boat by offending constituents; also recall, however, that many legislators were in the pocket of big business, and big business favored protectionist tariffs that kept foreign imports out of domestic American markets. When tariffs are high, it is the consumer who pays, and consumers in the Gilded Age resented this mightily.

Yet American consumers were not just consumers. They were also workers—and increasing numbers of them were becoming workers in companies that produced consumer products. Since their jobs depended on demand for their employers' goods, they could be persuaded that they, too, benefited from protectionist tariffs. Among the great concerns of the Gilded Age was the perpetual battle to achieve some balance between the political demands of big money, big business, and big industry on the one hand, and consumers/workers on the other. A growing slice of the electorate came to believe that it was a battle stacked against them. For if the Congress and the White House were bought and paid for by business and industry, a very heavy fist was pushing down on the scales of economic and political justice. Some Americans responded to the inherent unfairness with violence, others with grim acquiescence, but many—more and more as the Gilded Age marched on—began to demand political, moral, and economic reform. The Tariff Act of 1890, often called the McKinley Tariff, after Representative (and future president) William McKinley, raised import duties from 38 to 49.5 percent,[13] and ignited massive popular opposition. The Republicans lost their House majority in the election of 1890, and in 1892, Democrat Grover Cleveland trounced Republican Benjamin Harrison. The Democratically sponsored Wilson-Gorman Tariff Act of 1894 drastically lowered import duties.

PUCK.

"LOVE ME, LOVE MY DOG."
Uncle Sam—Well, you 're a nice girl; but I don't keer fer yer pet !

This *Puck* cartoon championed passage of the Wilson-Gorman Tariff Act of 1894 to lower import tariffs and instead raise needed federal revenue with an income tax. The young lady resists the blandishments of Uncle Sam by telling him, "Love me, love my dog," who wears a collar labeled "Income Tax."

OUR NATION'S CHOICE.

HARMONY, PEACE AND PROSPERITY.

OUR COUNTRY FOREVER

OUR NATION'S HONOR WILL BE PRESERVED.

Gen. JAMES ABRAM GARFIELD,
Republican Candidate for President.

Gen. CHESTER A. ARTHUR,
Republican Candidate for Vice-President.

THE PLATFORM OF THE REPUBLICAN PARTY,
ADOPTED AT THE
Convention in Chicago,
JUNE 2-8, 1880.

DEVOTION TO THE UNION.

The Star Spangled Banner in Triumph shall Wave

OVER the Land of the Free and the Home of the Brave.

Electoral Vote for President and Vice-President since 1864.

SUMMARY OF THE BALLOTING.

CHAPTER 14

THE PROGRESSIVES

The victory of dark horse nominee James A. Garfield over James G. Blaine on the thirty-sixth ballot of the incredibly rancorous Republican National Convention of 1880 marked the victory of the party's progressive wing (this faction had yet to earn a capital "P") over the Stalwart faction led by New York senator Roscoe Conkling, the nation's preeminent machine politician. Garfield represented social change and clean politics. He was a major advocate of efficient government, including civil service reform, which was intended to replace political patronage (the "spoils system")—by which government appointees and employees were chosen for their demonstrated party loyalty—with nonpartisan, merit-based appointments. Conkling represented the old way of doing things; Garfield the new and "progressive" approach, which was widely seen as part of the modernization trend evident in all aspects of American life during the Gilded Age.

After Charles J. Guiteau gunned down the president at the start of his fifth month in office (see chapter 13), he proclaimed to police, "I am a Stalwart of the Stalwarts! I did it and I want to be arrested! Arthur is president now!"[1] Vice President Chester A. Arthur (1829–86), a Conkling protégé and, judging by his record, a machine hack, was indeed a Stalwart. Those who believed that Garfield's election meant real change for the nation were heartbroken. All they could do was pin their fragile hopes on the wounded

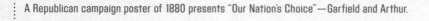

A Republican campaign poster of 1880 presents "Our Nation's Choice"—Garfield and Arthur.

Bloated and bewhiskered, Vice President Chester A. Arthur looked every inch the comfortably corrupt Republican "Stalwart." On the death of President James A. Garfield, Arthur stunningly defied expectations by carrying out the slain president's program of reform. No American political figure has ever redeemed himself more remarkably.

man's recovery, and when Garfield succumbed to infection on September 19, 1881, their hopes vanished. For Arthur was indeed president now.

A soft, round man, whose mutton chop whiskers only drew more attention to his turkey neck, Chester "Chet" Alan Arthur looked every inch the well-fed part of the typical Stalwart politician. Doubtless, with his succession to office, Conkling and his cronies looked forward to unexpected good times. But Arthur himself was anything but exultant. When news of the president's death reached him, all he could manage to stammer was "I hope—my God, I do hope it is a mistake."[2] His sole function as Garfield's running mate had been to balance the ticket. Garfield was a Midwestern progressive, Arthur an Eastern Stalwart. Mostly, he was a functionary, obedient and submissive. In 1877, President Rutherford B. Hayes, in a rare spasm of reform, had fired Arthur from his lucrative post as New York customs collector. Since then, presumably fearful of losing another patronage sinecure, he did whatever Conkling told him to do.

Miraculously, on the death of the president, Chet Arthur found within himself a reserve of character he had never before tapped. Installed in the executive mansion, he did not miss a beat in taking up the cause of reform exactly where the slain president had left it. He morphed from Stalwart to progressive. His signal action was to sign into law the Pendleton Civil Service Reform Act of 1883, which laid the foundation of the modern nonpartisan, merit-based civil service system (see page 305). This sent shock waves through Stalwart ranks. Of subtler significance was his espousal of naval reform by authorizing the building of three steel "protected cruisers," *Atlanta*, *Boston*, and *Chicago*, cutting-edge forerunners of the modern battleship and the heralds of another progressive theme—the United States's claim to a position as world power.

DOWN ON THE FARM

The social and economic abuses rampant in the Gilded Age—the reign of the robber barons (see chapter 3), the abuse of immigrants (see chapter 6), the oppression of labor (see chapter 7)—had all triggered calls for reform, sometimes violent reform. Discrete acts of reform were generally associated with the cities, but the broader movement toward large-scale political reform began during the 1880s and the early 1890s with the complaints of the nation's beleaguered farmers.

The farmers felt left out. After the Civil War, the industrialists and financiers

The photographs of Solomon Butcher chronicle the hard life of the prairie sodbuster, far from the gilded cities of the late nineteenth century. Here are the Rawlings, "a farming family of Custer County, Nebraska," 1886.

usurped from them the language by which they had formerly defined themselves. Democratic ideals, such as democracy, liberty, equality, opportunity, and individualism, which Thomas Jefferson and Andrew Jackson had associated with the noble agrarian—the independent farmer who boldly pushed American civilization to the western frontiers of the continent—were now the terms by which Rockefeller and Carnegie and Morgan and others of their frock-coated ilk pushed a program of laissez-faire economic policies that effectively put government in the hands of big capital.

In truth, industry was invading agriculture with more than words. Innovative machinery, including sulky plows with wheels and a driver's seat, corn planters, end-gate seeders, spring tooth rakes, binders, threshing machines, hay balers, hoisting forks, and corn shellers, had been essential to the recovery (still very imperfect) of Southern farmers from Civil War devastation. Such machinery was even more critical to farmers on the frontier, especially on the Plains, where the unyielding soil did everything possible to defeat mere human muscle. In the days of Jefferson and Jackson, self-sufficiency may have been for farmers both the idea and the rule. In the Industrial Revolution, however, farmers produced not for themselves and the villages surrounding them, but for "the market" as a whole, and the increased yields, combined with innovations in communications and transportation, ended agrarian isolation forever. The farmer now had access to a national, even international market, but was also obliged to compete in that market without government protections or regulation over production. Lacking the advantages of an urban tycoon's capital reserves, the farmer found himself bound to the wild swings of business and price cycles over which he had no control and into which he had very little insight. The farmer did not actually *see* this marketplace, but he was keenly aware of its impact on him. Even as his productivity increased, the prices he received for his commodities declined. There was terrible injustice in a system that earned him less the harder he worked and the more he grew. Moreover, the less he earned, the more he needed to spend to increase production. The gap between income and expenses widened with each passing season, and soon the farmer became a debtor, forced to mortgage his land or borrow against future harvests to cover debts.

With many of the same business forces that impinged on urban labor now encroaching on them as well, farmers across the country overcame their bias toward going it alone and began forming unions and alliances that passed through

"Gift of the Grangers," an elaborate chromolithograph of c. 1873, decorated the farmhouses of thousands of members of the Grange during the heyday of this powerful agricultural advocacy and lobbying organization.

several incarnations before emerging in 1891 as the People's Party, which was also called the Populist Party or simply the Populists. The two most important Populist precursor parties, the Farmers' Alliance (1870s) and the Greenback Party (1874–89), were largely rural and agrarian. A third forerunner was made up of an amalgam of urban labor groups, the most important of which were four small parties with the word *Labor* in their names: Union Labor Party, United Labor Party, Industrial Labor Party, and Labor Reform Party. These drew mainly on members of the Knights of Labor union and disaffected members of the waning Greenback Party. This agglomeration of political organizations became regional, rather than national, election influencers, electing a number of candidates to local offices in 1886.[3]

In addition to the Knights of Labor, the National Grange of the Order of the Patrons of Husbandry—more simply called the Grange—a fraternal order of farmers founded in 1867, had a major role in expanding the Populist Party. As for the Greenback Party (also known as the Greenback Labor Party), its name reveals the chief concern of its members. "Greenbacks" were the paper currency, not backed by gold, issued during the Civil War. Greenbacks were intended to increase the money supply to facilitate payment of the tremendous expenses incurred by the war. The driving concern of the Greenback Party was its opposition to the postwar return to a fully gold-backed monetary system because it contributed to deflation and a lowering of prices paid to farmers. Unbacked currency, the party believed, would be a boon to farmers by raising prices and making their debts easier to pay. From the perspective of the government, greenbacks had been strictly an emergency expedient during the Civil War. From the perspective of farmers in dire straits, this fiat money represented salvation. For them, the "emergency" had never ended.

On February 22, 1892, a total of 860 delegates from twenty-seven reformist organizations, including the National Farmers' Alliance, the Industrial Union, the Knights of Labor, and others, met in St. Louis at what was billed as the Industrial Conference. With 246 delegates between them, the National Farmers' Alliance and the Industrial Union formed a single bloc and proclaimed their support for the new People's Party, which many persisted in calling the Populist Party. Under either name, it was the most radical third party in American history.

The Populist Party proposed some of the most radical economic and political innovations of the late nineteenth century. Call it socialism "lite": government ownership of railroads and utilities, a progressive (graduated) income tax, voting by secret ballot (which was not universally adopted in the United States until 1891), women's suffrage, and Prohibition. The central issue, however, was the "the free coinage of silver," which was the use of both silver and gold ("bimetallism") as currency at the ratio of 16:1—sixteen ounces (454 g) of silver assigned the value of one ounce (28 g) of gold. The idea was to inflate the value of money to raise farm and other commodity prices, free up credit, and increase employment. Doing this also meant an end to unregulated laissez-faire economics and required federal manipulation of the money system. Such intervention rested on the proposition that government properly had some responsibility for the social well-being of its citizens. Urban—especially East Coast—capitalists were terrified.

The People's Party held its first national convention on July 4, 1892, in Omaha, Nebraska, nominating former Iowa congressman James B. Weaver as its presidential candidate. Both Weaver and the Republican nominee that year, James G. Blaine, lost to Democrat Grover Cleveland. Undaunted, the Populists continued to promote a program of radical reform. The new party filled the vacuum between the Democrats and the Republicans and narrowed the gaps separating regions of the country, races, and classes. For the first time in American political history, this third party staked out viable common ground on which reformers of every stripe could join hands. By far, the widest gulf bridged was the long-standing division between the interests of farmers and labor. In 1896, the Populists took what they saw as their best shot at gaining national power. They showed up in full force at the Democratic National Convention in July 1896 in Chicago and snatched the party's nomination from Cleveland, who was looking to run for an unprecedented third term. In his place, the Populists offered William Jennings Bryan (1860–1925), congressman from Nebraska's 1st District, and already nationally famous as the "Boy Orator of the Platte."

"For the first time in American political history, this third party staked out viable common ground on which reformers of every stripe could join hands."

The nation was in the depths of what was still being called the Panic of 1893, but which had become an intractable depression, the like of which would not be seen again until the Great Depression of the 1930s. It had begun when the Philadelphia and Reading Railroad went bankrupt, triggering the biggest sell-off the New York Stock Exchange had experienced up to that point. Banks called their loans. Credit dried up. The Erie, the Northern Pacific, the Union Pacific, and the Santa Fe railroads all failed, one after another. Mills, factories, furnaces, and mines shut down everywhere. Before it was over in 1897, roughly 500 banks had failed, at least 15,000 businesses were shuttered, and uncounted numbers of farms were simply abandoned. In 1892–93, the unemployment rate shot up from 3 percent to 11 percent. In New York City alone, it hit a staggering high of 35 percent.[4]

Amid financial chaos and sheer terror, the Populist agenda, which many had dismissed as the ravings of a lunatic fringe, now appeared supremely rational.

True, the notions of a progressive income tax and votes for women were still too much for most voters to swallow, but they were now at least open to serious public discussion. In droves, voters exited the Democratic as well as the Republican mainstream and embraced Populism. Looking to save their party, the Democrats, jealously eying the outflow of votes, summarily ejected the conservatives, the so-called Bourbon Democrats, and that meant ditching President Cleveland himself. Invited to the convention rostrum, William Jennings Bryan electrified the Democratic National Convention with a speech advocating the whole Populist agenda, including bimetallism. "I would be presumptuous, indeed, to present myself against the distinguished gentlemen to whom you have listened if this were a mere measuring of abilities," Bryan quietly began, "but this is not a contest between persons. The humblest citizen in all the land, when clad in the armor of a righteous cause, is stronger than all the hosts of error. I come to speak to you in defense of a cause as holy as the cause of liberty—the cause of humanity." He later made the case for a *second* American revolution:

> It is the issue of 1776 over again. Our ancestors, when but three millions in number, had the courage to declare their political independence of every other nation; shall we, their descendants, when we have grown to seventy millions, declare that we are less independent than our forefathers? No, my friends, that will never be the verdict of our people. Therefore, we care not upon what lines the battle is fought. If they say bimetallism is good, but that we cannot have it until other nations help us, we reply that, instead of having a gold standard because England has, we will restore bimetallism, and then let England have bimetallism because the United States has it. If they dare to come out in the open field and defend the gold standard as a good thing, we will fight them to the uttermost.

And, with this, he let fly his final arrow: "Having behind us the producing masses of this nation and the world, supported by the commercial interests, the laboring interests, and the toilers everywhere, we will answer their demand for a gold standard by saying to them: 'You shall not press down upon the brow of labor this crown of thorns; you shall not crucify mankind upon a cross of gold.'"[5] Nor did he rely on words alone. Pressing the fingers of both hands to his temples, he suddenly extended both arms outward from his body in a pose of crucifixion. He stood thus for some five seconds, while the audience, transfixed, was silent. He then lowered his arms, stepped down from the podium, and, as he did, the applause began, slowly, before erupting in delirium.

That delirium, however, did not translate into a victory against Republican William McKinley, who received 271 electoral votes to Bryan's 176. While Bryan remained a popular figure in American politics and a presidential hopeful in 1900 and 1908, his defeat by McKinley in 1896 heralded the demise of the Populist Party. Bryan became a successful lecturer—mostly on subjects of Christianity and general morality—from 1900 through 1912 on the Chautauqua circuit. A phenomenon of the Gilded Age, the Chautauqua movement began in 1874 with a camp meeting organized by Methodist minister John Heyl Vincent and a businessman, Lewis Miller, on the shore of Chautauqua Lake in upstate New York. It spawned Chautauqua assemblies nationwide, which variously featured speakers, educators, musicians, preachers, and others in what is best described as a mass, popular, adult-education movement.

Bryan kept his hand in politics and supported Woodrow Wilson for president in 1912, becoming his secretary of state in 1913 but resigning two years later in protest against what he deemed the president's drift toward entry into the Great War (World War I). At the end of his career and his life, Bryan passionately advocated for Prohibition and against the teaching of Darwinian evolution in public schools. This culminated in his testimony for the prosecution in the sensational Scopes Trial of 1925, in which Tennessee schoolteacher John T. Scopes was convicted of violating state law by teaching human evolution. Bryan was humiliated on the witness stand by Scopes's attorney, the legendary Clarence Darrow, and died five days after the trial ended. The often-brilliant, always incendiary journalist, social critic, and self-appointed enemy of intolerance H. L. Mencken gleefully published Bryan's obituary the day after the man's death. He claimed that Bryan had "committed suicide" upon "Clarence Darrow's cruel hook," having "writhed and tossed in a very fury of malignancy, bawling against the veriest elements of sense and decency like a man frantic. . . . He staggered from the rustic court ready to die, and he staggered from it ready to be forgotten, save as a character in a third-rate farce, witless and in poor taste."[6] Except for Mencken's *Baltimore Sun*, the nation's newspapers reported the cause of Bryan's death as "apoplexy," a stroke, but it is most likely that diabetes was a contributing factor.[7]

FROM POPULISM TO PROGRESSIVISM

The Populist Party came to an end, but Populism did not so much die as it was remolded into a more cohesive progressive movement, which may be described as Populism ratcheted up from the farmers and laborers to the middle class. There was less emphasis on improving the lot of the masses than on raising the level—and the moral "tone"—of American civilization. Progressivism was associated with "progress" in all its guises, including an embrace of education and science as applied to creating a more just and a more efficient society. "Taylorism," the high-efficiency management ideas Frederick Winslow Taylor published in his 1911 *Principles of Scientific Management*, transformed the American workplace as well as the bureaucracies of American government (see chapter 4).

In the run-up to the founding of a Progressive Party in 1912, the most important reforms in national politics and policy were currency reform and civil service reform. The Greenback Party and, later, the bimetallism advocated by Bryan, led to pressure for congressional action. The admission of six new Western states in 1889–90, during the administration of President Benjamin Harrison, tipped the balance toward demand for silver coinage to increase the money supply. The Sherman Silver Purchase Act of 1890 required the U.S. Treasury to purchase 4.5 million ounces (128 million g) of silver per month to be converted into coins and silver certificates (paper money backed by and redeemable as silver). This emboldened Bryan in 1896 to ask for even more—a transition from the gold standard to a combined gold and silver standard, which would release yet more money into the economy. But, in electing McKinley, thereby installing in the White House a more probusiness administration in 1896, a substantial majority of voters rejected this lurch toward Populism.

As it turned out, the election of 1896 did not swing the policy pendulum permanently back toward the era of the robber barons. Under Theodore Roosevelt, who would succeed the slain McKinley in 1901, Populism would continue to morph into progressivism, and big business would find itself facing a new reformer. The reforms President Roosevelt championed had their predicates in two important pieces of Gilded Age legislation. The Interstate Commerce Act of 1887 was passed in response to abuses by railroad monopolies, including price fixing among monopolistic rivals and discriminatory shipping rates that forced farmers to use grain elevators and other storage facilities controlled by particular railroad operators. The act required "charges made for any service rendered or to be rendered in the transportation of passengers or property . . . to be reasonable and just" and prohibited as unlawful "every unjust and unreasonable charge."[8] What this meant was that the federal government now had regulatory and oversight power over interstate commerce. The idea that government had a proper role in the regulation of business was thus laid as a cornerstone of future progressivism. Three years later, another law, the Sherman Antitrust Act, was passed, barring businesses from employing monopolistic practices or otherwise acting in restraint of trade, including taking unfair advantage of competitors.[9] With this,

OUT OF THE SILVER FLOOD!

The Sherman Silver Purchase Act (1890) put more silver coins and paper "silver certificates" into circulation, creating an inflationary "flood" that (according to this 1893 *Puck* cartoon) threatened to drown "Business Interests." Uncle Sam comes to the rescue with an effort to climb the rope of "Public Opinion" to the high ground of a proposed repeal of the act.

the reign of laissez-faire big business was doomed—at least once a president willing to wield the government's new powers came into office.

In the meantime, civil service reform took a giant—and unexpected—leap in 1883 when Chester A. Arthur, catapulted into the presidency by Garfield's assassination in 1881, supported the Pendleton Civil Service Reform Act.[10] The act was the beginning of the end of the old spoils system, by which nonelective government positions were distributed to party faithful as the "spoils" of electoral victory. Under the act, the United States Civil Service Commission was established to create and administer a civil service system to ensure that government personnel would be hired—and maintained and promoted or dismissed—on the basis of merit and performance, not because of political connections. The process of reform extended throughout the last twenty years of the Gilded Age, so that, by the turn of the century, approximately half of all federal employees were classified under civil service rules. Today, the overwhelming majority of unelected government employees are civil servants, although high-level policy positions continue to be filled by political appointees serving at the pleasure of the president.

ROUGH RIDER

Senator Mark Hanna of Ohio was one of the Republican "Old Guard"—an updated name for the faction called the Stalwarts twenty years earlier. When word reached him of the death of President McKinley on September 14, 1901, he cried out: "Now look! That damned cowboy is president of the United States."[11]

He was referring, of course, to Theodore Roosevelt (1857–1930), who had, in fact, owned and personally worked a ranch in the Dakota Territories, but who was far better known for his relentlessly reformist record as a former member of the U.S. Civil Service Commission and the former president of the New York City Police Board of Commissioners. As governor of New York, before being tapped as McKinley's second-term running mate in 1900, he introduced bold reforms in Albany. His energy and zeal were inexhaustible, and he would now apply both to the presidency. The Old Guard—everywhere—had reason to mourn the passing of McKinley.

As a progressive rather than a Populist, TR saw capitalist enterprise as the great and essential engine of the American economy and the American claim to economic and political leadership in the world. Nevertheless, he believed that the Old Guard Republican policy of uncritical support for laissez-faire business, even at the expense of labor and consumers, was not only bad for the nation, but ultimately fatal for the party. Business should be allowed to prosper, but under the watchful eye and regulatory hand of enlightened government.

Enlightened government—*that*, Roosevelt believed, could not be entrusted to the legislative branch. He resolved to end the Gilded Age reign of weak presidents by refashioning the presidency as the office of the people's steward and tribune. Persuaded that too many members of Congress were in the pocket of big business and no longer represented the interests of the people, Roosevelt decided that he would both represent *and* guide the electorate. He therefore proclaimed what he termed a "New Nationalism," in which the entire administrative machinery of the federal government would be geared toward promoting the public welfare. The states would be obliged to subordinate themselves to federal direction, and the president, as tribune for all the people, would lead Congress in crafting laws to serve them.

President Theodore Roosevelt speaks at Freeport, Illinois, June 3, 1903, at the dedication of a monument to the second of Abraham Lincoln's antislavery debates with Stephen A. Douglas. TR saw in Lincoln an ancestor in the cause of progressive reform.

Theodore Roosevelt packaged his progressive domestic agenda as the "Square Deal." This included policies intended to curb the abuses of big business, especially monopolistic trusts, while also curbing the "outrageous" demands of radical labor. The newspapers hailed the president as a "Trust Buster" after his Department of Justice used the Sherman Antitrust Act of 1890 to force the breakup of Rockefeller's Standard Oil. At the same time, TR became the first president to proactively engage with labor by articulating labor's legal rights as well as the limits of those rights. When necessary, he intended to intervene in labor-management disputes directly.

Among the most innovative and far-reaching of Roosevelt's progressive reforms was his promotion of what was called, in the early twentieth century, "conservation"—today's environmentalism. He championed an array of conservation legislation, including laws that set aside millions of acres of national forest to be protected either entirely or in part from commercial exploitation. His signature environmental legislation, the 1906 American Antiquities Act, established 150 national forests, fifty-one federal bird reserves, four national game preserves, five national parks, and eighteen national monuments. When his legislative zeal collided with the interests of farmers and industrialists, their lobbyists goaded Congress into enacting legislation in 1908 that transferred from the president to the Congress authority to create future national forests in some Western states. Undaunted, Roosevelt resorted to executive orders to instantly implement many of his conservation initiatives. In all, by law and by executive action, TR protected some 230 million acres (92 million ha) of public land during his presidency.[12]

On the world stage, Roosevelt bolted far ahead of Congress. While many presidents before him deferred to the legislature on key matters of foreign policy, TR assumed quasi-autocratic authority in matters of international relations, barely consulting with Congress. In his first annual address to Congress on December 3, 1901, he asserted that U.S. victory in the Spanish-American War (1898)—in which he had fought as lieutenant colonel of the legendary Rough Riders—meant that the United States now had "international duties no less than international rights."[13] Roosevelt's redefinition of America as a world power would find expression in the nation's 1917 entry into the Great War that had begun in 1914—when most Americans disdainfully called it the "European War." Except for a span of isolationist Republican administrations during the 1920s and into the first three years of the 1930s, the United States would henceforth define itself as a great world power with great privileges and even greater responsibilities.

A stereograph of President Roosevelt with Sierra Club founder John Muir, the Scottish-American naturalist instrumental in molding the president's passion for the environment. This photograph was made at Glacier Point on a trip to Yosemite Valley, California, in 1903.

TR'S WAR OF 1912

As unconventional as Theodore Roosevelt was, he could not bring himself to break the tradition, started by George Washington, that no president would serve more than two terms. In 1908, there was no Twenty-Second Amendment to legally bar a president from seeking a third term, and, had he chosen to run, TR could have argued that it would be, after all, only his second *elected* term. In the end, he erred on the side of tradition and bowed out of consideration, deferring, however, to a candidate he himself handpicked to succeed him. William Howard Taft (1857–1830), TR's secretary of war, was a committed progressive, and the president trusted him to carry forward the executive agenda he had established. Indeed, Taft dutifully laid down a full program for legislative action—some of which was enacted—but Taft, ponderous in deliberation as he was ponderous in weight (at 355 pounds [161 kg], he was by far the heaviest U.S. president), never goaded Congress, let alone defied it, as Roosevelt often had. Nor did he go around the legislature to use what TR famously called the executive's "bully pulpit" to appeal directly to the people. Taft preferred to quietly propose legislation, present a logical argument for it, and then let Congress take its course.

Taft was not a great president, but he was an admirable chief justice of the Supreme Court, to which President Warren G. Harding appointed him in 1921. It was a job Taft relished far more than the presidency. Here, an undated photograph of Taft.

That course was not uniformly progressive, and in March 1910, Republican progressives in the House united with Democrats to strip Speaker Joseph Cannon, an unapologetic Old Guard Republican, of much of his power. This created legislative chaos that a President Teddy Roosevelt would have seized on to aggrandize executive power. But Taft wanted no such thing, and the result was a dysfunctional Congress, a drifting presidency, and a profoundly discontented electorate.

As for Roosevelt, he had bitter reason to regret his decision against seeking a third term. In 1912, Taft was on course for the Republican nomination to run for a second term. Roosevelt was undecided about challenging him—until Robert M. LaFollette, senator from Wisconsin, a man who had earned his progressive reputation as the daringly innovative governor of Wisconsin, challenged Taft. Believing that neither Taft nor LaFollette could prevail against Democrat Woodrow Wilson, Roosevelt rather belatedly announced "My hat's in the ring. The fight is on, and I'm stripped to the buff."[14] In the primaries, TR emerged the clear victor, winning 278 delegates to Taft's 48 and LaFollette's 36. But because thirty-six states did not hold primaries, the convention was very much up for grabs. Although most of LaFollette's delegates deserted him for Roosevelt, Taft nevertheless prevailed. Roosevelt charged that some of the Taft delegations had been seated fraudulently, and he walked out of the convention, declaring himself the presidential candidate of the brand-new Progressive Party, which he and his supporters founded right then and there. It was quickly nicknamed the Bull Moose Party after newspapers reported that candidate Roosevelt said he now felt "fit as a bull moose."[15]

PUCK

THE CROWD AS IT LOOKS TO THEODORE.

In 1912, Theodore Roosevelt was the presidential nominee of the Progressive Party, but when he told reporters that he felt "fit as a bull moose," the party got a more colorful nickname that stuck, and TR became the "Bull Moose candidate."

The Bull Moose platform is remarkable, even by modern standards:

- Political campaign contribution limits

- Disclosure of contributors to political campaigns

- Registration of lobbyists

- All congressional committee proceedings to be recorded and the minutes published

- Creation of a National Health Service

- Creation of "social insurance," to provide for the elderly, unemployed, and disabled

- Limits on legal injunctions against labor strikes

- A minimum wage law for women

- An eight-hour workday

- Creation of a federal securities commission

- Farm relief programs

- Creation of a fund for workers' compensation for work-related injuries

- A federal inheritance tax

- Women's suffrage

- Popular election of senators (at the time, senators were appointed by state legislatures)

- Required primary elections for state and federal nominations[16]

It was a tough three-way campaign that year among Taft, Wilson, and Roosevelt—who very nearly didn't survive it. On October 14, 1912, while TR was campaigning in Milwaukee, John Schrank, a local saloonkeeper by trade, shot the candidate at close range just as he was about to enter an auditorium to deliver a speech. The bullet hit Roosevelt's steel eyeglass case in the inner pocket of his frock coat, penetrating it before tearing through the fifty-page manuscript of the evening's speech, which was folded—thereby doubling its thickness—in the same coat pocket. These two obstacles significantly slowed the projectile, which nevertheless lodged in Roosevelt's capacious barrel chest.

Roosevelt neither lost consciousness nor was even knocked off his feet. A renowned big game hunter, the Bull Moose candidate pronounced the wound minor, mainly because he was breathing well and was not coughing up any blood. Waving off everyone's insistence that he, for the love of God, allow himself to be rushed to the hospital, Teddy Roosevelt insisted on delivering a speech.

Taking his place at the podium, he dramatically threw open his coat and vest to reveal his blood-soaked shirt.

"Ladies and gentlemen," he began, "I don't know whether you fully understand that I have just been shot; but it takes more than that to kill a Bull Moose."[17] He then spoke for an hour and a half before finally consenting to go to the hospital. There, x-rays revealed that the bullet had passed through three inches (7.5cm) of

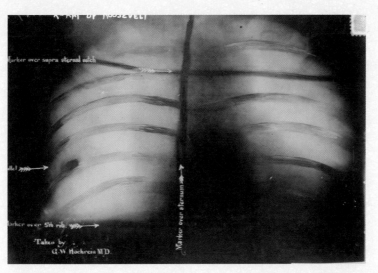

Shot in the chest at point-blank range on October 14, 1912, just before he was to deliver a campaign speech in Milwaukee, Roosevelt refused medical attention and delivered a ninety-minute oration before he allowed himself to be hospitalized. This X-ray shows the bullet lodged in the candidate's chest (second arrow from bottom). It remained there for the rest of his life.

chest tissue, coming to rest in a muscle before it could hit any vital organs. Surgeons decided to leave the slug where it was, rather than risking an operation to remove it. TR carried the bullet for the rest of his life.

Hospitalization took Roosevelt off the campaign trail for a week, during which both Taft and Wilson suspended their campaigns, agreeing that it was the only gentlemanly thing to do. In the end, TR drew 27 percent of the popular vote, to 42 percent for Wilson and a miserable 23 percent for the incumbent Taft. Socialist Eugene V. Debs polled 6 percent. Roosevelt's tally remains the best third-party performance in American electoral history. While his defeat marked the end of the Progressive Party as a significant political force, it hardly signaled the end of Progressivism. On the contrary, Woodrow Wilson, a prolific author of works on American political history, a distinguished PhD professor of political science, former president of Princeton University, and reform governor of New Jersey, was perhaps the ultimate Progressive and, in every possible way, the exact opposite of the old-style Gilded Age politician.

CHAPTER 15

WHITE CITY

The fracture of the Republican Party in 1912 gave the Democratic Party an opportunity that had eluded them for years. Populism had failed to lead the Democrats to the White House, but Progressivism, it turned out, crossed party lines. The conservative, or Bourbon, Democrats were still influential in the party, and they would bolt if William Jennings Bryan or anyone like him were nominated again. Canny party strategists realized that most Democratic Populists and many Bourbon Democrats would likely accept a Progressive candidate—and, as luck would have it, one was available.

Thomas Woodrow Wilson (1856–1924) was unlike any other candidate in the history of the American presidency. He held a doctorate and was a professor of political science, who had, as president of Princeton University from 1902 to 1910, single-handedly transformed that sleepy school into a world-class institution. That achievement put Wilson in the news, and New Jersey Democrats decided to recruit him as their candidate for governor. While the Progressives saw Wilson as one of their own, Democratic machine bosses saw him as inexperienced, naive, and eminently malleable. They were wrong. Wilson proved tough, stubborn, and boundlessly energetic. Once elected, he declared war on the machine with a program of Progressive reform that commanded national attention.

An illustration from 1893, of an illuminated Court of Honor, the architectural highlight of the forward-looking World's Columbian Exposition held in Chicago that year. Woodrow Wilson, at the time a Princeton professor, delivered a speech there in praise of liberal education (see page 355).

Woodrow Wilson, so far the only American president with a PhD, is shown here a few hours after his nomination by the Democratic National Convention on July 2, 1912. He considered the primary duty of the president to be the "brain" of the nation.

Come the 1912 national convention, Wilson was put up against old-school Populist party boss and speaker of the House Champ Clark of Missouri. William Jennings Bryan, who received a nondecisive bloc of delegate votes, was expected to throw his support behind his fellow Populist. Instead, he enthusiastically backed Wilson, who became the party's nominee on the forty-sixth ballot.

Against both incumbent Republican William Howard Taft and third-party candidate Theodore Roosevelt, Wilson prevailed by a plurality (see chapter 14). Significantly, Taft, who had fallen short as a progressive, came in third in this three-way race. Roosevelt, Wilson's fellow Progressive, came in second—as mentioned previously, it was the only time a third-party presidential candidate has bested a major-party contender, let alone the incumbent. As for Wilson, he may have been the most radical major-party candidate ever in American history. As early as 1879, before he had graduated from college, Wilson published an academic paper calling for a constitutional amendment to end the separation of powers between the legislative and executive branches—transforming American government into a British-style parliamentary cabinet government by allowing the president's cabinet to sit in Congress, where they could directly instigate and shape legislation. Later, in 1885, at the graduate school of Johns Hopkins University, he elaborated on this idea in a book titled *Congressional Government.*

By the early 1900s, he argued more simply for what Theodore Roosevelt was already doing: fully assuming the mantle of national leadership by initiating legislation and then driving its passage through direct appeal to the American people. But Wilson was resolved to do more than merely imitate TR. The logical culmination of Progressivism was to transform politics itself into the *science* of governing. As a political *scientist*—the only one this nation ever installed in the White House—Wilson was the perfect president to effect this apotheosis of Progressivism. He set about rationalizing the TR model in both theory and practice. He intended to remold the office of president and institutionalize its expanded power for all time. Moreover, if Roosevelt regarded the president as the people's steward and tribune, Wilson saw himself as nothing less than the people's brain. Yes, he had to appeal to the people, but his first and foremost duty was to *think for them* and, by thinking, *solve* all national problems. The ideal president—which is precisely what Wilson believed himself to be—formulated policy and then educated the people as to that policy. Properly instructed, the people would enthusiastically back their president, and Congress would have no choice but to implement the policy.

Woodrow Wilson attempted to unitize two of the three constitutional branches of government. Instead of attempting to amend the Constitution, as he had theorized in his student days, he approached Congress as one partner to another, telling senators and representatives in his first address to a joint session, that he regarded himself as "a human being trying to cooperate with other human beings in a common service."[1] And while his natural tendency was to impose his point of view on others—Why? Because he knew he was right, that's why!—Wilson was eminently collegial, meeting with legislators on key bills and stunning them by actually leaving the White House to visit the Capitol, where he called on *them* in *their* offices.

The approach proved incredibly productive. Whereas TR had often locked horns with Congress and then bypassed the legislature altogether by issuing one executive order after another, Wilson skillfully co-opted Congress, leading it to enact sweeping reforms that included the lowering of tariffs across the board (in defiance of big business), passing the Federal Reserve Act of 1913 (giving the federal government unprecedented regulatory powers over the economy),

Among President Wilson's boldest progressive reforms was, in defiance of big business, the lowering of protectionist tariffs on imports. *Puck* approved, putting a cartoon on its October 2, 1912, cover showing the new president handling the live wire of "The Tariff" with gauntlets insulated by "fearlessness" and "common sense."

HE DARES TO TOUCH IT.
The Live Wire and the Man with the Rubber Gloves.

enacting currency and banking reforms, passing the Federal Trade Commission Act and the Clayton Anti-Trust Act (both of which greatly increased the government's power to regulate and break up monopolistic trusts), passing the Adamson Act (which gave railway workers an eight-hour workday), and passing the Child Labor Act (curtailing children's working hours). Perhaps the greatest Progressive reform customarily associated with the Wilson administration was ratification of the Sixteenth Amendment, which introduced the graduated federal income tax. In truth, the amendment was passed in 1909 during the Taft administration. Nevertheless, Wilson enthusiastically endorsed its ratification by the states during his presidential campaign. Ratification was completed on February 3, 1913, a month before Wilson's March 4 inauguration. The income tax was implemented entirely during Wilson's first term.

Roosevelt had wrapped his reforms in a couple of neat packages—the Square Deal and the New Nationalism. The bow Wilson tied around his Progressive measures was labeled the "New Freedom." Its most innovative feature was a new approach to federal action against monopolies. Whereas TR had wielded the Sherman Anti-Trust Act of 1890 against egregious vertical monopolies—such as Standard Oil, in which a trust not only crushed competition, but controlled all industries related to its principal business—Wilson used an array of new economic legislation to create a national business environment in which companies would simply be unable to create trusts. TR busted trusts. Wilson set out to create a world in which there would be no trusts to bust. The Underwood Tariff Act (1913), the Clayton Anti-Trust Act (1914), and the Federal Trade Commission Act (1914) were not cudgels for smashing monopolies, but laws against the unfair competition that made monopolies possible to begin with. In addition, the creation of a Federal Reserve system to regulate and stabilize currency had the effect of leveling the playing field by freeing up credit and making it available to more businesses, big *and* small.

Amid all this, Wilson established the president's identity as the leader of the Democratic Party—a role that others, typically a cabal of bosses, had usurped during most of the post–Civil War era. Because he saw himself as the leader of legislation, Wilson stressed the importance of enforcing party discipline. Democrats were supposed to follow and support the president in the passage of key legislation. By way of undermining the old Democratic Party machine, Wilson promoted the spread and institutionalization of the primary system. This would effectively take the nomination out of the hands of party bosses and give it to the people, to whom a presidential hopeful could make his case directly.

In one important regard, Wilson's impulse to embrace Progressivism clashed with Wilson's desire for party discipline. As a Progressive rationalization of government, the New Freedom enlarged the bureaucracy and thus created slots for many more federal administrative appointees. The president's Progressive ethos dictated that these appointments be made on a rigorously nonpartisan, merit basis. Wilson quickly recognized, however, that one advantage of the bad old spoils system was that it enforced party discipline by rewarding party loyalty with tangible government jobs. Wilson awarded a number of high-profile federal appointments to the Democratic Party faithful. This created party loyalty and discipline, but it also severely undercut any support congressional Republicans might be inclined to offer him. A time would come when he would need this support desperately—and he would not get it.

President Wilson followed President Roosevelt's lead in making the United States a world power, but he also put a more intellectual and idealistic spin on American global leadership. As chief executive of the nation that the world looked considered an exemplar of freedom and prosperity, Wilson believed that the president of the United States could wield powerful moral influence over other national leaders and thereby directly enhance the peace and prosperity of the world.

It was an inspiring theory. In practice, however, Wilson could be overbearing and even violent in his approach. Concerned that the chronic revolutionary turbulence of the nation's southern neighbor, Mexico, threatened American borderlands, Wilson withheld U.S. recognition and aid to the government established under President Victoriano Huerta until that government demonstrated to his sole satisfaction what Wilson deemed "constitutional legitimacy" by adhering to its own constitution. Wilson explained to Congress that he intended to "teach" Latin America's would-be leaders how to govern. This attitude moved him to order a U.S. military occupation of Veracruz, Mexico, in 1914 and to invade Mexico in a fruitless pursuit of the Mexican social bandit and revolutionary leader Pancho Villa in 1916.

Such international adventurism was the kind of thing Professor Frederick Jackson Turner had warned against in his famous "frontier thesis" paper of 1893 (see chapter 12), and it was a grotesque irony that the apostle of rational, even scientific Progressivism should resort to acts of war in 1914 and 1916 in furtherance of it. Wilson ran for reelection to a second term in 1916 on the slogan, "He Kept Us Out of War," referring to his strict first-term policy of neutrality in the "Great War" (World War I), which had been shattering European civilization and destroying the very flower of its youth since July 1914.

Narrowly reelected in November 1916 and inaugurated in March 1917, Wilson asked Congress for a declaration of war against Germany and the other "Central Powers" on April 2 of that year. He argued—and a prematurely aging

Theodore Roosevelt enthusiastically agreed—that entry into the war was an American duty. Wilson bolstered this argument by citing German outrages against America's freedom to navigate the high seas and the attempt of the German foreign minister to make common cause with Mexico in a war against the United States. German U-boats attacked and sank ten U.S.-flagged merchant ships before America entered the war,[2] but it was the sinking of the British liner *Lusitania* on May 7, 1915, that figured in the American popular mind as the greatest atrocity. Among the 1,201 passengers drowned, 128 were U.S. nationals.[3] As for the German-Mexican outrage, early in 1917, British intelligence presented President Wilson with an intercepted telegram from Germany's foreign minister, Alfred Zimmermann, to the German ambassador to Mexico. Transmitted on January 16, 1917, the "Zimmermann Telegram," as it came to be called, authorized the ambassador to propose to Mexican president Venustiano Carranza a joint German-Mexican war on the United States, in return for which Mexico would receive Germany's support in a campaign to recover for Mexico the territory it had lost in the Mexican-American War of 1846–48. Carranza declined the outlandish proposal, but its revelation was the proverbial last straw. Wilson asked Congress for a declaration of war on April 2, 1917.[4]

Yet the causes for war Wilson cited did not alter the fact that the United States was not directly threatened by any of the belligerents. No, the true cause was ideological, rather than existential. Famously, Wilson told Congress, the United States had to "make the world safe for democracy."[5] Winning public support for entry into what most Americans called the "European War" required a concerted effort to "educate" the people. A major propaganda campaign was therefore mounted, and, thanks to it, a national war fever was stirred up. The temperature of that fever was raised by the addition of a strange bedfellow for a Progressive apostle: big business and big banking. By 1916–17, America's financial and industrial firms were heavily invested in producing arms and making loans to the Allies (principally Britain, France, and Italy). Anxious to protect their investments, they urged President Wilson to do all that he could to ensure the defeat of the Central Powers (Germany, Austria-Hungary, the Ottoman Empire, and Bulgaria). That meant not only going to war, but going all-in on war.

One month after Wilson's second inauguration, in April 1917, he asked Congress for a declaration of war. His administration ginned up war fever among the reluctant American people by demonizing Germany and its allies as "mad brutes" in need of extermination, as shown in this propaganda poster.

LOOKING TO THE FUTURE

Total, universal, "world" war, in which an average of 6,046 soldiers died every day for four years,[6] was not the future America had imagined for itself back in 1893, the year of the most ambitious international exposition of the Gilded Age. It was called the World's Columbian Exposition, and while it was officially a celebration of the 400th anniversary of the arrival of Christopher Columbus in the New World in 1492, it was really a celebration of the future. This fact distinguished it from the first great world's fair of the Gilded Age, the Philadelphia Centennial of 1876 (see chapter 1). A commemoration of American independence, that exposition featured forward-looking displays of the latest products of mostly American industry and technology, but it was also a nostalgic plunge into American history since colonial times. To a nation recovering from Civil War, flooded by immigrant newcomers, and living through a rapid transformation from an agrarian to an industrial civilization, the "old days" looked to be nothing but "good."

Not so in Chicago just seventeen years later. In contrast to Philadelphia, which was founded in the seventeenth century, Chicago was incorporated as a frontier town in 1833, within the lifetime of many of the older visitors to the fair. Moreover, the Great Fire of 1871 (see chapter 8) had destroyed most of the old urban core, much of it ramshackle, so the best of the city was indeed brand-new, some of it built by America's greatest and most innovative architects, including Daniel Burnham and John Wellborn Root, two of the Columbian Exposition's principal designers.

Not that what Burnham, Root, and others built for the exposition was futuristic or even modern. The fair's prevailing look was French neoclassical, the style taught at the École des Beaux-Arts in Paris. But this "traditional" style was part of the forward-looking message. In contrast to the 1876 Philadelphia fair, which celebrated America's birthday, the Chicago exposition was not focused on the United States. Rather, its focus was global, bringing to the middle of the country exhibits and buildings representing forty-five nations in addition to America. The buildings were intended to convey an international look, and French neoclassicism was considered both worldly and timeless.

The so-called White City of the World's Columbian Exposition, built of "staff" (a temporary building material consisting mainly of plaster of Paris) in Jackson Park on Chicago's gritty South Side, was a dream of a technological utopia.

There were fourteen "great buildings"—major structures—but also nearly two hundred lesser buildings, all set in 690 acres (276 ha) of Jackson Park, on Chicago's South Side. This acreage had been landscaped for the fair under the supervision of Frederick Law Olmsted, chief designer of New York's Central Park and the creative force behind city parks in many American cities as well as the city beautiful movement, which sought to soften and humanize the nation's burgeoning industrial urban landscape. Stately and tranquil lagoons, faux-sVenetian canals, and bucolic meadows looked as if they had always been a part of this rough-and-ready prairie city. In fact, the landscaping was temporary, as were almost all the buildings.[7] They were constructed of powdered gypsum and plaster of Paris, blended with cement, glycerin, and dextrin; mixed with water; and strengthened with hemp or jute. Called *staff*, this material had been developed in France in 1876, where it was used for temporary structures in the Paris Expositions of 1878 and 1889.

THE GILDED AGE

Dedicated to the future, the World's Columbian Exposition was a vision, temporary and ephemeral, the staff structures left mostly in their naked color, a chalky plaster white. The effect was that of a mirage, which fairgoers—some 27,300,000 of them between May 1 and October 30, 1893—referred to as the White City. It shone spectacularly in daytime and, thanks to an elaborate electrical generating and lighting system, was even more magical at night. The companies of Thomas A. Edison and George Westinghouse engaged in a bidding war for the contract to electrify the exposition. Victory meant more than a lucrative assignment, since Edison and Westinghouse were locked in a titanic battle over the use of direct current (DC; Edison's system) versus alternating current (AC; Westinghouse's system). In the end, Westinghouse underbid Edison, but then discovered that he was obliged to create a new type of incandescent lamp to avoid a massive patent infringement lawsuit from Edison. Plans specified the installation of 93,000 lightbulbs throughout the exposition, and because Westinghouse

ELECTRICAL BUILDING—WORLD'S COLUMBIAN EXPOSITION.

The "Electrical Building" at the World's Columbian Exposition featured "the most brilliant and novel exhibits" of the world's fair. Inside, displays looked back to Benjamin Franklin flying his kite in a lightning storm and looked forward to anticipated new electrical wonders from Thomas Edison, George Westinghouse, and Nikola Tesla.

> ## *"The White City, its purity shining out across Chicago's own South Side, was an expression of hope and of real possibility."*

had had to rush his bulbs through design and production, they had a very short life span. His company was forced to overproduce bulbs and then dispatch an army of workers daily to replace burnouts. Indeed, Westinghouse lost a great deal of money on his cut-rate contract—but his company gained far more. The fair became a demonstration of the superiority of AC infrastructure over DC, and, ultimately, it was alternating current technology that became the standard for electrification worldwide.

"White City" implied more than the color of a building material. The fact was that urban industrial America at the close of the nineteenth century presented a vista mostly gritty, sooty, and even filthy. The pervasive political corruption, commercial venality and vulgarity, and economic injustice of the era seemed to be embodied in the physical squalor of many turn-of-the-century American cities and towns. These qualities were all aspects of what New York crusading journalist Lincoln Steffens, in the title of his 1904 exposé of corrupt urban political machines, called *The Shame of the Cities*.

New as it was, Chicago shared in that urban shame. But the White City, its purity shining out across Chicago's own South Side, was an expression of hope and of real possibility. If Gilded Age America was a time and place of greed and corruption, it was also a time and place of philanthropy and reform. If some of its buildings were shoddy and dismal, the best new structures soared to the very sky. If people readily slipped into moral hypocrisy and narrow, corrosive religiosity, many sincerely wanted to make life better, more equitable, kinder, and—through science and the humane application of technology—more intelligent, productive, and fulfilling. Ultimately, the White City was an aspiration. Yet it was an aspiration that, based on the progress being made in so many areas of business, invention, consumer goods, the arts, and, yes, philanthropy, seemed within grasp. A few more years, perhaps. A decade or two at most . . .

Still, present reality could be stubbornly heedless of aspiration. For one thing, there was anxiety in the very air, it seemed, as the nation slipped deeper into recession during the Panic of 1893 (see pages tk and tk). Then, on October 28, 1893, just two days before what was to be the joyous celebratory closing of the exposition, Carter Henry Harrison Sr., the magnificently bearded and mustachioed five-term mayor of Chicago, was awakened by his maid. There was a man to see him, she said. Mayor Harrison rose from a divan, left the room in which he had been dozing, entered the hallway of his home, and was promptly confronted by a stranger.

When the stranger later surrendered to police, he identified himself as Patrick Eugene Prendergast, an Irish immigrant and newspaper distributor by trade. He believed that the mayor had promised to appoint him to the post of Chicago corporation counsel—the city's lawyer—if Harrison won reelection. In fact, Harrison had never met Prendergast, and the promise was a wild delusion—much like the belief Charles J. Guiteau had harbored that President Garfield owed him an appointment as consul to Vienna or Paris. As Prendergast saw it, Harrison had been reelected, but had broken his promise, and so it was time to pay the mayor a call and settle the score.

Prendergast came armed. Leveling a .38-caliber revolver at the mayor, he squeezed off three shots, more than enough to kill him. A half-hour later, Prendergast presented himself at the Desplaines Street precinct house and confessed to having murdered the mayor.

The shooting cast a pall over the last day of the fair, prompting cancellation of the closing ceremony, so that, instead of a triumphal celebration, the lights of the White City were simply switched off and the staff buildings were torn down, the pale dust of their remains carted away.

———— ◆ ————

WOODROW WILSON, AT THE TIME A DISTINGUISHED PRINCETON university professor, delivered a speech at the 1893 World's Columbian Exposition on the importance of a liberal education to the future of civilization itself. "Our professional men are lamed and hampered by that partial knowledge, which is the most dangerous form of ignorance," he said. He condemned "the empiric"—the person whose education was narrowly empirical rather than broadly liberal—as "the natural enemy of society" and declared it "imperative that everything should be done, everything risked, to get rid of him. Nothing sobers and reforms him like a . . . liberal education."[8]

Wilson believed education—the right education, a complete, all-encompassing *liberal* education—was the key to achieving something like a utopian future, the kind of future to which the 1893 Chicago fair aspired. Yet the immediate future following the close of the fair was very far from utopian. The Panic of 1893 brought a severe economic depression, followed by the Spanish-American War, which some thought a great and glorious thing for the United States, while others feared it would lead America down the Old World's path of error through a lust for imperialist conquest. Singularly atavistic violence marred American politics. The assassination of President McKinley in 1901 was followed by the attempted assassination of Theodore Roosevelt in 1912.

On the other hand, the presidency of Roosevelt, from 1901 to 1909, had brought breathtaking reforms that stirred high hopes for American progressivism, and while the William Howard Taft interregnum following TR was dull and disappointing, the first term of Woodrow Wilson seemed to promise fulfillment of the very aspirations that had been embodied in the White City. Indeed, Wilson set out to be not merely a great president, but *the* great educator—and not of America alone, but of the whole world.

Wilson was an eloquent, intense, and earnest man. Many Americans allowed themselves to be persuaded that the Great War, into which Wilson led the United States a month after his second presidential term began, was the horribly painful but absolutely necessary beginning of a better nation and a better world, a world in which democracy would rule supreme and war would be forever consigned to the sands of history. But after the Allied victory—a victory largely bought and paid for by the infusion of fresh American blood—Woodrow Wilson's affronts to the Republican legislators he disdained came back to haunt him. Wilson, in Paris, had been instrumental in drawing up the Treaty of Versailles that ended the Great War and that included the creation of a League of Nations, where national leaders would talk through their disputes instead of fighting over them. Never consulted about the treaty or the league, Senate Republicans refused to approve either one. Without American membership and support, the League of Nations sputtered, withered, and eventually died, and on September 1, 1939, a second

The "Big Four"—French Prime Minister and Minister of War Georges Clémenceau (left), President Wilson, and British Prime Minister David Lloyd George (receiving a handshake at right)—as they exit the Palace of Versailles after signing the Treaty of Versailles, formally ending the Great War (World War I) June 28, 1919. The fourth member of the Big Four, Italian Prime Minister Vittorio Emanuele Orlando, does not appear in the photograph. Silk hats were doffed in greeting, but the sentiments among the victorious Allies were by no means entirely cordial.

world war broke out in Europe. It would prove far deadlier than the first, and America would fight it, driving the victory, and claiming at last the international position that Theodore Roosevelt had wanted for the United States: economic, military, and moral preeminence as master of the world—a world the Gilded Age had helped to make, but a world that neither Roosevelt nor anyone else who came of age at the end of the nineteenth century would have easily recognized, let alone understood.

Today, near the close of the second decade of the twenty-first century, America seems to have entered a new Gilded Age—an age of technological wonders and enormous wealth, but an age divided between the wealthiest 1 percent of Americans and the rest by a chasm even wider than that of the final quarter of the nineteenth century. Yet more bewildering, distressing, and confounding is the new state of factual truth and moral values, commodities that have become even more fluid than they were a century and a quarter ago, during an age whose very name was coined to convey corruption. Could it be that we, too, are on the verge of reform and rediscovery?

ACKNOWLEDGMENTS

FOR ANITA AND IAN

———◆———

Mythology aside, authorship is never a solitary profession. It doesn't quite take a village to make a book, but it is an intense team effort. I want to thank all those at Sterling who created *The Gilded Age* with me. Executive Editor Barbara Berger and I have worked together for years. She asked me to write the book, and she developed it with me from concept to publication. Art Director Lorie Pagnozzi has created a stunning and highly effective interior design, using the inspired artwork selection of Photography Editor Linda Liang. More mythology aside, books really are judged by their cover, and David Ter-Avanesyan has given *The Gilded Age* a cover of great beauty. Let me offer special thanks to Production Editor Michael Cea; Senior Art Director, Covers, Elizabeth Lindy; and Senior Production Manager Fred Pagan for their essential contribution to this book.

—ALAN AXELROD
ATLANTA, GEORGIA

SOURCE NOTES

INTRODUCTION: ALL THAT GLITTERS

1. Henry Demarest Lloyd, *Wealth Against Commonwealth* (New York: Harper & Brothers, 1899), 496.
2. Janette Thomas Greenwood, *The Gilded Age: A History in Documents* (New York: Oxford University Press, 2000), 25; Jeanne Sahadi, "The Richest 10% Hold 76% of the Wealth," *CNN Money* (August 18, 2016), http://money.cnn.com/2016/08/18/pf/wealth-inequality/; Quote Investigator, "History Does Not Repeat Itself, But It Rhymes," http://quoteinvestigator.com/2014/01/12/history-rhymes/.
3. Erica Werner, "Harry Reid Warns of 'New Gilded Age' in Senate Farewell Speech," NBC News Chicago (December 8, 2016), http://www.nbcchicago.com/news/politics/Harry-Reid-Bids-Farewell-to-Senate-After-30-Years-405491516.html.
4. Paul Krugman, "Why We're in a New Gilded Age," *New York Review of Books* (May 8, 2014), http://www.nybooks.com/articles/2014/05/08/thomas-piketty-new-gilded-age/; Thomas Piketty, *Capital in the Twenty-First Century* (Cambridge, MA: Harvard University Press, 2014), http://www.nybooks.com/articles/2014/05/08/thomas-piketty-new-gilded-age/.
5. William Safire, *Safire's Political Dictionary* (New York: Oxford University Press, 2008), 237.
6. "Lifestyles of the Rich and Famous (1984–), IMDb, http://www.imdb.com/title/tt0086750/.
7. The term "robber baron" first appeared in the *New York Times* (February 9, 1859) to describe Cornelius Vanderbilt. Cited by T. J. Stiles in "Robber Barons or Captains of Industry," *History Now*, https://www.gilderlehrman.org/history-by-era/gilded-age/essays/robber-barons-or-captains-industry.
8. United States Census, *Bicentennial Statistics: Historical Statistics of the United States, Colonial Times to 1970,* part 1, chapter K, Agriculture, 437, http://www2.census.gov/library/publications/1975/compendia/hist_stats_colonial-1970/hist_stats_colonial-1970p1-chK.pdf.
9. Frederick Jackson Turner, *The Frontier in American History* (New York: Holt, 1921; e-Book reprint edition, Department of English, University of Virginia, 1996), chapter 1, http://xroads.virginia.edu/~HYPER/TURNER/home.html.

PART I: PEOPLE AND THINGS

1. J. S. Ingram, *The Centennial Exposition, Described and Illustrated, Being a Concise and Graphic Description of this Grand Enterprise, Commemorative of the First Centenary of American Independence* (Philadelphia: Hubbard Bros., 1876, 5.

CHAPTER I: CENTENNIAL

1. Stephanie Grauman Wolf, "Centennial Exhibition (1876)," in *The Encyclopedia of Greater Philadelphia*, http://philadelphiaencyclopedia.org/archive/centennial/.
2. Beth Swift, "From the Archives: Wielding Winged Lightning," *Wabash College Magazine*, http://www.wabash.edu/magazine/index.cfm?news_id=4795; Wolf, "Centennial Exhibition (1876)."
3. Ingram, *Centennial Exposition*.
4. Ibid., 40.
5. Ibid., 109–116.
6. Wolf, "Centennial Exhibition (1876)."
7. Ingram, *Centennial Exposition*, 157–298.
8. Wolf, "Centennial Exhibition (1876)."
9. Ibid.

10. Susanna W. Gold, *The Unfinished Exhibition: Visualizing Myth, Memory, and the Shadow of the Civil War in Centennial America* (Oxford, UK, and New York: Routledge, 2017), "Conflict on the Fairgrounds" Kindle ed.

11. Ari Hoogenboom, *Rutherford B. Hayes; Warrior and President* (Lawrence: University Press of Kansas, 1995), 273.

12. The account of Sickles during Election Night 1876 is drawn from Thomas Keneally, *American Scoundrel: The Life of the Notorious Civil War General Dan Sickles* (New York: Nan A. Talese/Doubleday, 2002); the account of Sickles in the Keys murder and the trial that followed is drawn from Keneally, *American Scoundrel,* and from Fletcher Pratt, *Stanton: Lincoln's Secretary of War* (New York: W. W. Norton, 1953), 81–85.

13. See Alan Axelrod, *The Real History of the Civil War: A New Look at the Past* (New York: Sterling, 2012), 266–271.

14. Quoted in Keneally, *American Scoundrel,* 261.

CHAPTER 2: THE DYNAMO, THE VIRGIN, AND THE BRIDGE

1. Henry Adams, *The Education of Henry Adams* (1907, 1918; reprint ed., Boston: Houghton Mifflin, 1973), 380, 379.

2. Ibid., 379–80.

3. Ibid., 380.

4. Ibid., 381.

5. Ibid.

6. Ibid., 383.

CHAPTER 3: TITANS, PLUTOCRATS, AND PHILANTHROPISTS

1. William Tecumseh Sherman, quoted in Major David F. Boyd, "Gen. W. T. Sherman. His Early Life in the South and His Relations with Southern Men," *Confederate Veteran* 18 (1910), 412.

2. Margaret E. Wagner, Gary W. Gallagher, and Paul Finkelman, *The Library of Congress Civil War Desk Reference* (New York: Simon & Schuster, 2002), 75.

3. Matthew J. Gallman, *The North Fights the Civil War: The Home Front* (Chicago: Ivan R. Dee, 1994), 26.

4. James A. Rawley, *The Politics of Union: Northern Politics during the Civil War* (Hinsdale, IL: Dryden Press, 1974), 28.

5. https://www.nps.gov/articles/industry-and-economy-during-the-civil-war.htm.

6. http://www.civilwarhome.com/civilwarindustry.htm.

7. Ibid.

8. Thomas Carlyle, *Past and Present* (1843), book IV, chapter IV; Kindle ed.

9. Quoted in T. J. Stiles, "Robber Barons or Captains of Industry," *History Now,* https://www.gilderlehrman.org/history-by-era/gilded-age/essays/robber-barons-or-captains-industry.

10. Mark Twain, "Open Letter to Com. Vanderbilt" (March 1869, reprinted in Milton Meltzer, *Mark Twain Himself: A Pictorial Biography* [1960; reprint ed., Columbia: University of Missouri Press, 2002], 202).

11. For the story of the sale, see Ron Chernow, "The Deal of the Century," *American Heritage* 49, no. 4 (July/August 1998), http://www.americanheritage.com/node/59682. For Carnegie as the "richest man in the world," see Carnegie Corporation of New York, "Andrew Carnegie's Story," https://www.carnegie.org/interactives/foundersstory/#!/.

12. Andrew Carnegie, "Wealth," *North American Review* 148, no. 391 (June 1889), 653, 657–62.

13. Andrew Carnegie, "The Gospel of Wealth," in *The Gospel of Wealth and Other Timely Essays by Andrew Carnegie* (New York: The Century Company, 1901), 1–46.

CHAPTER 4: SCIENCE AND INDUSTRY

1. Nathaniel Hawthorne, *The House of the Seven Gables* (1851), chapter 17, Kindle ed.

2. George Bernard Shaw, "Maxims for Revolutionists: Civilization," in *Man and Superman* (Cambridge, MA: The University Press, 1903), 241.

3. Tom Sandage, science correspondent for the *Economist, The Victorian Internet: The Remarkable Story of the Telegraph and the Nineteenth Century's On-Line Pioneers* (New York: Bloomsbury, 1998).

4. "Improvement in Telegraphy," UX 174465 A (March 7, 1876), https://www.google.com/patents/US174465.

5. Randy Alfred, "March 10, 1876: 'Mr. Watson, Come Here . . .'" *Wired* (March 10, 2011), https://www.wired.com/2011/03/0310bell-invents-telephone-mr-watson-come-here/.

6. Ibid.

7. Associated Press, "T. A. Watson Dead; Made First Phone," *New York Times* (December 15, 1934), http://www.nytimes.com/learning/general/onthisday/bday/0118.html.

8. Elon University School of Communications, *Imagining the Internet: A History and Forecast*, "1870s–1940s—Telephone," http://www.elon.edu/e-web/predictions/150/1870.xhtml.

9. Mohammed Rasooldeen, "5 billion mobile phone users in 2017: GSMA," *Arab News* (March 1, 2017), http://www.arabnews.com/node/1061261/business-economy.

10. "List of Edison Patents," Wikipedia, https://en.wikipedia.org/wiki/List_of_Edison_patents#1001_to_1084.

11. David A. Hounshall, *From the American System to Mass Production, 1800–1932* (Baltimore: Johns Hopkins University Press, 1984), 224.

12. R. E. Houston, "Model T Ford Production," http://www.mtfca.com/encyclo/fdprod.htm.

13. History Channel, "[February 17,] 1972: Beetle overtakes Model T as world's best-selling car," http://www.history.com/this-day-in-history/beetle-overtakes-model-t-as-worlds-best-selling-car.

CHAPTER 5: THE MARKETPLACE

1. Carnegie Corporation of New York, "Andrew Carnegie's Story," https://www.carnegie.org/interactives/founderss-tory/#!/.

2. Sean Dennis Cashman, *America in the Gilded Age*, 3rd ed. (New York: New York University Press, 1993), Kindle ed., 63–64.

3. Ray Stannard Baker, "What the United States Steel Corporation Really Is, and How It Works," published in *McClure's* (November 1901) and quoted in Albert Shaw, ed., *The American Monthly Review of Reviews: An International Magazine* 24 (July–December 1901), 614–16.

4. "Topics in Brief," *Literary Digest* (New York: Funk & Wagnalls Company, 1902), 635.

5. "SAMSON," United States Patent and Trademark Office, Trademark Search, http://tsdr.uspto.gov/#caseNumber=70011210&caseType=SERIAL_NO&searchType=statusSearch.

6. "J. Walter Thompson's History of Advertising," https://www.jwt.com/history/.

7. Edd Applegate, *The Rise of Advertising in the United States: A History of Innovation to 1960* (New York: Rowman and Littlefield, 2014), 134.

8. J. Walter Thompson Company, *Things to Know about Trade-Marks: A Manual of Trade-Mark Information* (New York: J. Walter Thompson Company, 1911).

9. Filed on May 27, 1899, the trademark was registered on July 18, 1899; Justia: Trademarks, "THOMAS A EDISON—Trademark Details," https://trademarks.justia.com/700/58/thomas-a-edison-70058571.html.

10. Macy's laid claim to the title of "world's largest" department store until the Shinsegae Centum City Department Store was opened in Busan, South Korea, in 2009. Barbara Farfan, "What is the World's Largest Retail Store?" *The Balance* (September 14, 2016), https://www.thebalance.com/largest-retail-stores-2892923.

11. Tradition as well as some authorities also attribute the more familiar maxim "The customer is always right" to Marshall Field, but there is compelling evidence that it originated with American-born British department store magnate Henry Gordon Selfridge. See "The customer is always right," *The Phrase Finder,* http://www.phrases.org.uk/meanings/106700.html.

12. United States Census 2010, *United States Summary: 2010* (September 2012), 20–26, http://www.census.gov/prod/cen2010/cph-2-1.pdf.

13. Sears Archives, http://www.searsarchives.com/catalogs/chronology.htm.

14. Sears Archives, http://www.searsarchives.com/history/history1890s.htm.

CHAPTER 6: STATUE AND ISLAND

1. Yasmin Sabina Khan, *Enlightening the World: The Creation of the Statue of Liberty* (Ithaca, NY: Cornell University Press, 2010), 130.
2. Jonathan Harris, *A Statue for America: The First Hundred Years of the Statue of Liberty* (New York: Four Winds Press, 1985), 7–9.
3. Rebecca M. Joseph with Brooke Rosenblatt and Carolyn Kinebrew, "The Black Statue of Liberty Rumor: An Inquiry into the History and Meaning of Bartholdi's *Liberté éclairant le Monde*" (Boston Support Office, National Park Service, September 2000).
4. Edward Berenson, *The Statue of Liberty: A Transatlantic Story* (New Haven, CT: Yale University Press, 2012), 21.
5. Agence France-Presse and DailyMail.Com Reporter, "Was the inspiration for the Statue of Liberty a Muslim woman? Researchers say French sculptor turned 'veiled peasant' designed for the Suez canal into Lady Liberty," *DailyMail.com* (December 1, 2015; updated December 2, 2015), http://www.dailymail.co.uk/news/article-3342140/Statue-Liberty-inspired-Arab-woman-researchers-say.html.
6. Glenn Collins, "Cracks Found in the Myths Around Statue; Park Service Librarian Writes Book to Clarify Lady Liberty's Origins," *New York Times* (October 28, 2000), http://www.nytimes.com/2000/10/28/nyregion/cracks-found-myths-around-statue-park-service-librarian-writes-book-clarify-lady.html?pagewanted=all. Also see Agence France-Presse and DailyMail.Com Reporter, http://www.dailymail.co.uk/news/article-3342140/Statue-Liberty-inspired-Arab-woman-researchers-say.html, and Sarah Birnbaum, "The Statue of Liberty was modeled after an Arab woman," *PRI* (February 1, 2015), https://www.pri.org/stories/2017-02-01/statue-liberty-was-modeled-after-arab-woman.
7. Migration Policy Institute (MPI), "U.S. Immigrant Population and Share over Time, 1850–Present," http://www.migrationpolicy.org/programs/data-hub/charts/immigrant-population-over-time.
8. The Statue of Liberty–Ellis Island Foundation, "Ellis Island History," http://www.libertyellisfoundation.org/ellis-island-history, puts the 1892–1954 total at more than 12 million; however, *the Annual Reports of the Commissioner General of Immigration* for 1892–1924 total about 14 million (National Park Service, "U.S. Immigration Statistics: Immigration Station at Ellis Island, NY," https://www.nps.gov/elis/learn/education/upload/statistics.pdf).
9. Saum Song Bo, *American Missionary* (October 1885), 10.
10. Janette Thomas Greenwood, *The Gilded Age: A History in Documents* (New York: Oxford University Press, 2000), 31–32.
11. Daniel Griswold, "Immigrants Have Enriched American Culture and Enhanced Our Influence in the World," *Insight* (February 18, 2002), republished by the Cato Institute, https://www.cato.org/publications/commentary/immigrants-have-enriched-american-culture-enhanced-our-influence-world.

CHAPTER 7: HARD LABOR

1. Theodore W. Schultz, "Investment in Human Capital," *American Economic Review* 51, no. 1 (March 1961), 1–17, http://la.utexas.edu/users/hcleaver/330T/350kPEESchultzInvestmentHumanCapital.pdf.
2. Sean Dennis Cashman, *America in the Gilded Age: From the Death of Lincoln to the Rise of Theodore Roosevelt*, 3rd ed. (New York: New York University Press, 1993), Kindle ed., 100.
3. Clarence D. Long, *Wages and Earnings in the United States, 1860–1890* (Princeton, NJ: Princeton University Press, 1960), 106, Table 48, http://www.nber.org/chapters/c2500.pdf.
4. See "Tenements," History.com, http://www.history.com/topics/tenements.
5. Jacob August Riis, *How the Other Half Lives: Studies among the Tenements of New York* (1890; reprint ed., New York: Charles Scribner's Sons, 1914), 184.
6. United States Department of Labor, "5. Progressive Era Investigations," https://www.dol.gov/dol/aboutdol/history/mono-regsafepart05.htm.
7. US Department of Labor, https://www.dol.gov/dol/aboutdol/history/mono-regsafepart05.htm.
8. Riis, *How the Other Half Lives,* 123–24.

9. Jacob August Riis, *Theodore Roosevelt, the Citizen* (New York: The Outlook Co., 1904), 131; *Theodore Roosevelt, An Autobiography* (New York: Macmillan 1913), 186.

10. Renamed the Brown Building, the Asch Building is now owned by New York University and serves as a science building. New York Landmarks Preservation Commission, "Brown Building (original Asch Building)" (March 25, 2001), Designation List 346, LP-2128, http://rememberthetrianglefire.org/images/brown.pdf. Also, http://www.law.nyu.edu/news/triangle_fire_centennial.

11. Today, the Pullman State Historic Site explains that the *Pioneer* was chosen by Colonel James H. Bowen, chairman of the Republican State Central Committee, for inclusion in the funeral train to accommodate the Lincoln family. (The Pullman State Historic Site, "Abraham Lincoln and the *Pioneer*" in "The Pullman Company," http://www.pullman-museum.org/theCompany/.) The president's remains were carried in "The President's Car," which was an ornate car built by the Alexandria, Virginia, car shops of the Military Railroad System in 1864. (See "Conventional Wisdom" and "Historical Fact" in "Pullmans Palace Car Co.-Page 2," http://www.midcontinent.org/rollingstock/builders/pullman2.htm.)

12. See Coachbuilt, Pullman entry, http://www.coachbuilt.com/bui/p/pullman/pullman.htm.

13. Pullman State Historic Site, "The Town of Pullman," http://www.pullman-museum.org/theTown/; Stanley Buder, *Pullman: An Experiment in Industrial Order and Community Planning, 1880–1930* (New York: Oxford University Press, 1970), Table 3: Rental and Type of Dwelling Units, 90.

14. Buder, *Pullman*, 99.

CHAPTER 8: GILDED MONUMENTS

1. Karen Abbott, "What (or Who) Caused the Great Chicago Fire?" Smithsonian.com, http://www.smithsonianmag.com/history/what-or-who-caused-the-great-chicago-fire-61481977/.

2. Ibid.

3. Richard F. Bales and Thomas F. Schwartz, *The Great Chicago Fire and the Myth of Mrs. O'Leary's Cow* (Jefferson, NC: McFarland, 2005), 127–30; Matt Soniak, "Did a Cow Really Cause the Great Chicago Fire?" Mental_Floss, http://mentalfloss.com/article/12864/did-cow-really-cause-great-chicago-fire.

4. "Louis M. Cohn—Biography," *Jew Age,* http://www.jewage.org/wiki/he/Article:Louis_M._Cohn_-_Biography.

5. Abbott, "What (or Who) Caused the Great Chicago Fire?"

6. See Ignatius Donnelly, *Ragnarok: The Age of Fire and Gravel* (1883), digital edition, part II, chapter 3, http://www.sacred-texts.com/atl/rag/index.htm.

7. Mica Calfee, "Was It a Cow or a Meteorite? *Meteorite Magazine* 9, no. 1 (February 2003), http://www.fireserviceinfo.com/cow-comet.html.

8. Bales and Schwartz, *Great Chicago Fire*, 111.

9. Donald Miller, *City of the Century: The Epic of Chicago and the Making of America* (New York: Simon & Schuster, 1996), 159.

10. Ibid., 146.

11. The "fire whirl" is discussed in Abbott, "What (or Who) Caused the Great Chicago Fire?"

12. Robert Collyer, quoted in Herman Kogan, "The Great Fire: Chicago 1871," *University of Chicago Magazine* (November–December 1971), http://mag.uchicago.edu/law-policy-society/great-fire-chicago-1871.

13. Rob Bear, "Mapping PBS' 10 Buildings That Changed America," *Curbed* (May 10, 2013), http://www.curbed.com/maps/mapping-pbss-10-buildings-that-changed-america.

14. Quoted in Sean Dennis Cashman, *America in the Gilded Age*, 3rd ed. (New York University Press, 1993), Kindle ed., 191–92.

15. Quoted in Daniel D. McLean and Amy R. Hurd, *Recreation and Leisure in Modern Society*, 10th ed. (Burlington, MA: Jones & Bartlett Learning, 2015), 43.

16. Henry David Thoreau, "Walking," 1862; reprinted in *Henry David Thoreau: Collected Essays and Poems* (New York: Library of America, 2001), 239.

CHAPTER 9: AMERICAN REALISM

1. Letter from John Adams to Abigail Adams, dated May 12, 1780, in Frank Shuffleton, ed., *The Letters of John and Abigail Adams* (New York: Penguin, 2004), 377–78.
2. Sydney Smith, "Review of Seybert's *Annals of the United States*," published in *Edinburgh Review*, 1820; reprinted in Evert A. Duyckinck, ed., *Wit and Wisdom of the Rev. Sydney Smith* (New York: Redfield, 1856), 190.
3. A Virginian Spending July in Vermont [Herman Melville]. "Hawthorne and His Mosses," *Literary World* (1850), http://www.eldritchpress.org/nh/hahm.html.
4. Mark Twain, "Poor Little Stephen Girard," in Anna Randall-Diehl, ed., *Carleton's Popular Readings* (New York: G. W. Carleton & Co., 1879), 183–84. The story was first published in the *New York Sun* on October 21, 1872, where it was credited to "John in Philadelphia." All subsequent publications of the story listed Mark Twain as the author. Twain never repudiated authorship, but Leslie Myrick, of the University of California's Mark Twain Project, makes a case for removing it from the Twain canon. See Barbara Schmidt, "Removing 'Poor Little Stephen Girard' from the Mark Twain Canon," http://www.twainquotes.com/StephenGirard.html.
5. Mark Twain, *Following the Equator: A Journey Around the World* (Hartford: American Publishing, 1897), http://www.gutenberg.org/files/2895/2895-h/2895-h.htm.
6. Myra Jehlen, "Banned in Concord: *Adventures of Huckleberry Finn* and Classic American Literature," in Forrest G. Robinson, ed., *The Cambridge Companion to Mark Twain* (New York: Cambridge University Press, 1995), 93.
7. Quoted in Stuart Hutchinson, ed., *Mark Twain: Tom Sawyer and Huckleberry Finn* [Columbia Critical Guides] (New York: Columbia University Press, 1998), 21.
8. An excellent, concise account of Twain's financial crisis was written by bankruptcy expert Leon D. Bayer, "Mark Twain Has Filed Bankruptcy!" The NACTT Academy (December 8, 2012), http://considerchapter13.org/2012/12/08/mark-twain-has-filed-bankruptcy/.
9. Kate Chopin, *The Awakening* (Chicago and New York: Herbert S. Stone & Co., 1899), 302–3, https://en.wikisource.org/wiki/The_Awakening_(Chopin)/Chapter_XXXIX.
10. See John E. Bassett, "Their Wedding Journey': In Search of a New Fiction," *Studies in the Novel* 19, no. 2 (Summer 1987), 175–86.
11. Sean Dennis Cashman, *America in the Gilded Age: From the Death of Lincoln to the Rise of Theodore Roosevelt*, 3rd ed. (New York: New York University Press, 1993), Kindle ed., 193.

CHAPTER 10: RECONSTRUCTION ENDS

1. Rayford Whittington Logan, *The Betrayal of the Negro: From Rutherford Hayes to Woodrow Wilson* (New York: Da Capo Press, 1997), originally published as *The Negro in American Life and Thought: The Nadir, 1877–1901* (1954).
2. Ibid., 91.
3. National Park Service, "Jim Crow Laws," https://www.nps.gov/malu/learn/education/jim_crow_laws.htm.
4. "Lynching Statistics," the Charles Chesnutt Digital Archive, http://www.chesnuttarchive.org/classroom/lynching-stat.html.
5. Logan, *Betrayal of the Negro*, 133.
6. Campbell Gibson and Kay Jung, "Historical Census Statistics on Population Totals by Race, 1790 to 1990 . . . ," Population Division, Working Paper No. 56 (Washington, DC: US Census Bureau, 2002).
7. James W. Loewen, "Sundown Towns: A Hidden Dimension of American Racism," http://sundown.tougaloo.edu/sundowntowns.php.
8. *Brown v. Board of Education of Topeka*, 347 U.S. 483 (1954), https://supreme.justia.com/cases/federal/us/347/483/.
9. Louis R. Harlan, ed., *The Booker T. Washington Papers*, vol. 3 (Urbana: University of Illinois Press, 1974), 583–87; http://historymatters.gmu.edu/d/39/.
10. Carole Merritt, *Something So Horrible: The Springfield Race Riot of 1908* (Springfield, Illinois: Abraham Lincoln Presidential Library Foundation, 2008), 7, 61–63, https://www.illinois.gov/alplm/museum/learning/documents/race_riot_catalog_2008.pdf

CHAPTER 11: A WOMAN'S PLACE

1. Dougald MacDonald, "10 Things You May Not Know about the Matterhorn," *Climbing* (July 14, 2015), http://www.climbing.com/news/10-things-you-may-not-know-about-the-matterhorn/.
2. Annie S. Peck, "A Woman's Ascent of the Matterhorn," *McClure's Magazine* (July 1896), 127–35.
3. Theodore Roosevelt, "The Strenuous Life," Speech before the Hamilton Club, Chicago, April 10, 1899, Bartleby.com, http://www.bartleby.com/58/1.html.
4. Hooptactics, "Basketball Basics: Heritage of the Game—The 13 Original Rules of Basketball," http://hooptactics.com/Basketball_Basics_Original_Basketball_Rules; and Hooptactics, "Basketball Basics: The Evolution of the Game—A Chronological Look at the Major Refinements," http://hooptactics.com/Basketball_Basics_History.
5. James A. Naismith, "College Girls and Basket-Ball," *Harper's Weekly* (February 22, 1902), 234–35.
6. Charles Dana Gibson, quoted in Edward Marshall, "The Gibson Girl Analyzed by Her Originator," *New York Times* (November 10, 1910).
7. Michelle Starr, "Vintage X-rays reveal the hidden effects of corsets," CDNET (February 25, 2015), https://www.cnet.com/news/vintage-x-rays-reveal-the-hidden-effects-of-corsets/.
8. "Death from Tight Lacing," *Lancet* 135, no. 3485 (June 14, 1890), 1316.
9. Elizabeth Stuart Phelps, *What to Wear?* (Boston: James R. Osgood and Company, 1873), 79.
10. Editorial, "Woman and her Work," *Scribner's Magazine* 21, no. 47 (February 1881), 633–34.
11. Legal Information Institute, *Minor v. Happersett* (88 US 162), https://www.law.cornell.edu/supremecourt/text/88/162.
12. Al Maxey, "A Bulldog for Jesus: Reflecting on the Life and Work of Carrie A. Nation," *Reflections*, no. 335 (February 8, 2008), http://www.zianet.com/maxey/reflx335.htm.

CHAPTER 12: THE FRONTIER CLOSES

1. Robert V. Hine and John Mack Faragher, *The American West: A New Interpretive History* (New Haven, CT: Yale University Press, 2000), 200.
2. Quoted in Sanford Levinson and Bartholomew H. Sparrow, *The Louisiana Purchase and American Expansion, 1803–1898* (Lanham, MD: Rowman & Littlefield, 2005), 39.
3. Drew McCoy, *The Elusive Republic: Political Economy in Jeffersonian America* (Chapel Hill: University of North Carolina Press, 1980), 9–10.
4. John Babsone Lane Soule, quoted in Hal Gordon, "'Go West, Young Man': Who Wrote It? Greeley or Soule," *Sakgit River Journal of History and Folklore, http://www.skagitriverjournal.com/us/library/newspapers/greeley1-gowest.html.* The phrase—as "Go West, young man, go West and grow up with the country"—is commonly misattributed to an editorial Horace Greeley published in July 12, 1865, in his *New York Tribune.* It was lifted from Soule.
5. B. Byron Price, "Goodnight, Charles," and Harwood P. Hinton, "Goodnight-Loving Trail," in Charles Phillips and Alan Axelrod, eds., *Encyclopedia of the American West* (New York: Macmillan Reference USA, 1996), vol. 2, 617–18, 618–19.
6. Frederick Jackson Turner, "The Significance of the Frontier in American History," in *The Frontier in American History* (1920; reprint ed., Bremen, Germany: Outlook, 2011), 24, 216.
7. "Official Report of the Naval Court of Inquiry into the Loss of the Battleship *Maine*," March 21, 1898, http://www.spanamwar.com/mainerpt.htm.
8. John A. Gable, "Credit 'Splendid Little War' to John Hay," *New York Times* (July 9, 1991), http://www.nytimes.com/1991/07/09/opinion/l-credit-splendid-little-war-to-john-hay-595391.html.

CHAPTER 13: DIRTY POLITICS

1. Alan Axelrod, *Full Faith and Credit: The National Debt, Taxes, Spending, and the Bankrupting of America* (New York: Abbeville Press, 2016), table published as front endpapers.

2. Harry S. Truman, "Making Up Your Mind," in Margaret Truman, ed., *Where the Buck Stops: The Personal and Private Writings of Harry S. Truman* (New York: Warner Books, 1989), 78. The essay was posthumously published in this volume.

3. "Will Rogers on Politics," Quotes by Will Rogers in "Will Rogers Today," http://www.willrogerstoday.com/will_rogers_quotes/quotes.cfm?qID=4.

4. Some even assert that Booth was an agent of the Confederate government. See, for example, John C. Fazio, *Decapitating the Union: Jefferson Davis, Judah Benjamin and the Plot to Assassinate Lincoln* (N.p.: Morris Gilbert Publishing Co., 2017).

5. Candice Millard, *Destiny of the Republic* (New York: Doubleday, 2011), 230.

6. Christina Romer, "Spurious Volatility in Historical Unemployment Data," *Journal of Political Economy* 84, no. 1 (1986), 1–37.

7. Theodore Roosevelt Inaugural National Historic Site, New York, "September 6, 1901," https://www.nps.gov/thri/september6.htm.

8. Quoted in "Survey of the World," *The Independent: A Weekly Magazine* (November 7, 1901), 2615.

9. "Haymarket and May Day," in *Encyclopedia of Chicago*, http://www.encyclopedia.chicagohistory.org/pages/571.html.

10. Richard Ruben, "The Colfax Riot," *The Atlantic* (July/August 2003), https://www.theatlantic.com/magazine/archive/2003/07/the-colfax-riot/378556/.

11. Quoted in William Loren Katz and Laurie R. Lehman, eds., *The Cruel Years: American Voices at the Dawn of the Twentieth Century* (Boston: Beacon Press, 2001), 20.

12. Quoted in H. W. Brands, *T.R.: The Last Romantic* (New York: Basic Books, 1997), 219.

13. Joanne Reitano, *The Tariff Question in the Gilded Age: The Great Debate of 1888* (University Park, PA: Pennsylvania State University Press, 1994), 129.

CHAPTER 14: THE PROGRESSIVES

1. Candice Millard, *Destiny of the Republic* (New York: Doubleday, 2011), 230.

2. Quoted in Stephen G, Yanoff, *The Second Mourning: The Untold Story of America's Most Bizarre Political Murder* (Bloomington, IN: AuthorHouse, 2014), 315.

3. Morris Hilquit, *History of Socialism in the United States* (New York: Funk & Wagnalls, 1903), 271, https://archive.org/stream/cu31924022571701#page/n7/mode/2up.

4. Gerald Parshall, "The Great Panic of '93," *U.S News & World Report* 113, issue 17 (November 2, 1992), 70.

5. William Jennings Bryan, "Cross of Gold Speech," July 8, 1896, Chicago, http://www.let.rug.nl/usa/documents/1876-1900/william-jennings-bryan-cross-of-gold-speech-july-8-1896.php.

6. H. L. Mencken, "In Memoriam: W. J. B.," *Baltimore Sun* (July 27, 1925), http://www.thephora.net/forum/showthread.php?t=39549.

7. Vikki L. Jeanne Cleveland, "William Jennings Bryan: The Most Influential Loser in American History," http://www.lib.niu.edu/2003/ih090311.html.

8. Interstate Commerce Act of 1887, chapter 104, 24 Stat. 379, approved February 4, 1887, https://www.ourdocuments.gov/doc.php?doc=49&page=pdf.

9. See Title 15 of the U.S. Code at https://en.wikipedia.org/wiki/Title_15_of_the_United_States_Code.

10. Pendleton Act (1883), https://www.ourdocuments.gov/doc.php?doc=48.

11. Quoted in Link Hullar and Scott Nelson, *The United States: A Brief Narrative History*, 3rd ed. (Wheeling, IL: Harlan Davidson, Inc., 2011), 118.

12. National Park Service, "Theodore Roosevelt and Conservation," https://www.nps.gov/thro/learn/historyculture/theodore-roosevelt-and-conservation.htm.

13. Theodore Roosevelt, "First Annual Message," December 3, 1901, http://www.presidency.ucsb.edu/ws/?pid=29542.

14. Quoted in William Safire, *Safire's Political Dictionary* (New York: Oxford University Press, 2008), 310.

15. Edmund Morris, *Colonel Roosevelt* (New York: Random House, 2010), 215.

16. Gary Murphy, "'Mr. Roosevelt Is Guilty': Theodore Roosevelt and the Crusade for Constitutionalism, 1910–1912," *Journal of American Studies* 36, no. 3 (2002), 441–57; American Presidency Project, "Progressive Party Platform of 1912, November 5, 1912," http://www.presidency.ucsb.edu/ws/?pid=29617.

17. Theodore Roosevelt Association, "It Takes More Thant That to Kill a Bull Moose: The Leader and the Cause," http://www.theodoreroosevelt.org/site/c.elKSIdOWIiJ8H/b.9297449/k.861A/It_Takes_More_Than_That_to_Kill_a_Bull_Moose_The_Leader_and_The_Cause.htm.

CHAPTER 15: WHITE CITY

1. Woodrow Wilson, "April 8, 1913: Message Regarding Tariff Duties," University of Virginia Miller Center, https://millercenter.org/the-presidency/presidential-speeches/april-8-1913-message-regarding-tariff-duties.

2. Rodney Carlisle, "The Attacks on U.S. Shipping That Precipitated American Entry into World War I," *Northern Mariner/Le marin du nord* 17, no. 3 (July 2007), 41–66, http://www.cnrs-scrn.org/northern_mariner/vol17/tnm_17_3_41-66.pdf.

3. V. E. Tarrant. *The U-Boat Offensive 1914–1945.* New York: Sterling Publishing, 2000), 21.

4. The best account of the Zimmermann Affair is Barbara Tuchman, *The Zimmermann Telegram* (1958; reprint ed., New York: Random House, 1985).

5. Woodrow Wilson, "Wilson's War Message to Congress, 2 April, 1917," https://wwi.lib.byu.edu/index.php/Wilson's_War_Message_to_Congress.

6. Micheal Clodfelter, *Warfare and Armed Conflicts: A Statistical Reference to Casualty and Other Figures, 1500–2000*, 2nd ed. (Jefferson, NC: McFarland, 2002), 479.

7. Only two of the exposition's buildings survive today in place (three other smaller structures were relocated to other states)—the Palace of Fine Arts and the World's Congress Auxiliary Building. The Palace housed the Field Museum of Natural History, until it moved in 1921 to its present building on Lake Shore Drive. The Palace was closed, but rebuilt in place with permanent materials in 1933 to house the Museum of Science and Industry. The other survivor, the World's Congress Auxiliary Building, was not built on the fair grounds proper, but downtown, in Grant Park, and became home to the Art Institute of Chicago.

8. Woodrow Wilson. "Should an Antecedent Liberal Education Be Required of Students in Law, Medicine, and Theology?," in Arthur S. Link, ed., *Papers of Woodrow Wilson*, vol. 8 (Princeton, NJ: Princeton University Press, 1970), 290–92.

FURTHER READING

Abrams, Richard M. *Issues of the Populist and Progressive Eras, 1892–1912.* New York: Harper and Row, 1969.

Ackerman, Kenneth D. *The Gold Ring: Jim Fisk, Jay Gould, and Black Friday, 1869.* New York: Dodd, Mead, 1988.

Adams, Henry. *The Education of Henry Adams.* 1907, 1918; reprint ed., Boston: Houghton Mifflin, 1973.

Aron, Cindy Sondik. *Ladies and Gentlemen of the Civil Service: Middle-Class Workers in Victorian America.* New York: Oxford University Press, 1987.

Bales, Richard F., and Thomas F. Schwartz. *The Great Chicago Fire and the Myth of Mrs. O'Leary's Cow.* Jefferson, NC: McFarland, 2005.

Beatty, Jack. *Age of Betrayal: The Triumph of Money in America, 1865–1900.* New York: Vintage, 2007.

Billington, Ray Allen, with James Blaine Hedges. *Westward Expansion: A History of the American Frontier.* 1949; reprint ed., New York: Collier Macmillan, 1974.

———. *The American Frontier Thesis: Attack and Defense.* Washington, DC: American Historical Association, 1971.

Boyer, Paul. *Urban Masses and Moral Order in America, 1820–1920.* Cambridge, MA: Harvard University Press, 1978.

Brands, H. W. *T.R.: The Last Romantic.* New York: Basic Books, 1997.

Bremner, Robert H. *From the Depths: The Discovery of Poverty in the United States.* New York: New York University Press, 1956.

Brian, Denis. *Pulitzer: A Life.* New York: John Wiley and Sons, 2001.

Bringhurst, Bruce. *Antitrust and the Oil Monopoly: The Standard Oil Cases, 1890–1911.* Westport, CT: Greenwood, 1979.

Bruce, Robert V. *1877: Year of Violence. Indianapolis and New York.* Bobbs-Merrill, 1959.

Buck, Solon J. *The Granger Movement.* 1913; reprint ed., Cambridge, MA: Harvard University Press, 1963.

Buhle, Marie Jo. *Women and American Socialism, 1870–1920.* Urbana: University of Illinois Press, 1981.

Burg, David. *Chicago's White City of 1893.* 1976; reprint ed., Lexington: University Press of Kentucky, 2009.

Calhoun, Charles W., ed. *The Gilded Age: Perspectives on the Origins of Modern America.* New York: Rowman & Littlefield, 2006.

Callow, Alexander B., Jr., ed. *The City Boss in America.* New York: Oxford University Press, 1976.

Campbell, Charles S. *The Transformation of American Foreign Relations, 1865–1900.* New York: Harper, 1976.

Carnegie, Andrew. *The Gospel of Wealth and Other Timely Essays by Andrew Carnegie.* New York: The Century Company, 1901.

Carwardine, William. *The Pullman Strike.* Chicago: Kerr Publications, 1973.

Cashman, Sean Dennis. *America in the Gilded Age: From the Death of Lincoln to the Rise of Theodore Roosevelt*, 3rd ed. New York: New York University Press, 1993.

Chandler, Alfred. *The Visible Hand: The Managerial Revolution in American Business.* Cambridge, MA: Harvard University Press, 1977.

Chen, Jack. *The Chinese of America.* New York: HarperCollins, 1981.

Chernow, Ron. *Titan: The Life of John D. Rockefeller, Sr.* New York: Random House, 1998.

Chidsey, Donald Barr. *The Gentleman from New York: A Life of Roscoe Conkling.* New Haven, CT: Yale University Press, 1935.

Chopin, Kate. *The Awakening.* Chicago and New York: Herbert S. Stone & Co., 1899.

Clark, Judith Freeman. *The Gilded Age.* New York: Facts on File, 2005.

Condit, Carl. *The Chicago School of Architecture.* Chicago: University of Chicago Press, 1964.

Davis, Allen F. *American Heroine: The Life and Legend of Jane Addams.* 1973; reprint ed., Chicago: Ivan R. Dee, 2000.

Degler, Carl N. *The Age of Economic Revolution, 1876–1900.* Glenview, IL: Scott, Foresman, and Company, 1977.

Diaz Espino, Ovidio. *How Wall Street Created a Nation: J. P. Morgan, Teddy Roosevelt, and the Panama Canal.* New York: Four Walls Eight Windows, 2001.

Dinnerstein, Leonard, and David Reimers. *Ethnic Americans: A History of Immigration and Assimilation*, 2nd ed. New York: Harper & Row, 1975.

Dobson, John M. *Politics in the Gilded Age: A New Perspective on Reform.* New York: Praeger, 1974.

Dubofsky, Melvyn. *Industrialism and the American Worker, 1865–1890.* Wheeling, IL: Harlan Davidson, 1996.

Edwards, P. K. *Strikes in the United States, 1881–1974.* New York: Palgrave Macmillan, 1981.

Fels, Rendigs. *American Business Cycles, 1865–1897.* Chapel Hill: University of North Carolina Press, 1959.

Fite, Gilbert C. *The Farmer's Frontier, 1865–1900.* New York: Holt, Rinehart and Winston, 1966.

Franklin, John Hope. *Reconstruction after the Civil War.* Chicago: University of Chicago Press, 1961.

Giggie, John M., and Diane Winston, eds. *Faith in the Market: Religion and the Rise of Urban Commercial Culture.* New Brunswick, NJ: Rutgers University Press, 2002.

Goldberger, Paul. *The Skyscraper*, 3rd ed. New York: Alfred A. Knopf, 1983.

Gordon, John Steele. *The Scarlet Woman of Wall Street: Jay Gould, Jim Fisk, Cornelius Vanderbilt, the Erie Railway Wars, and the Birth of Wall Street.* New York: Weidenfeld and Nicolson, 1988.

Graham, Otis L. *The Great Campaigns: Reform and War in America, 1900–1928.* Englewood Cliffs, NJ: Prentice-Hall, 1971.

Greenwood, Janette Thomas. *The Gilded Age: A History in Documents.* New York: Oxford University Press, 2000.

Hacker, Louis M. *The World of Andrew Carnegie, 1865–1901.* Philadelphia: Lippincott, 1968.

Handlin, Oscar. *Race and Nationality in American Life.* Boston: Little, Brown, 1957.

Harlan, Louis R. *Booker T. Washington: The Making of a Negro Leader, 1856–1901.* New York: Oxford University Press, 1975.

Harris, Jonathan. *A Statue for America: The First Hundred Years of the Statue of Liberty.* New York: Four Winds Press, 1985.

Hayter, Earl W. *The Troubled Farmer, 1850–1900: Rural Adjustment to Industrialism.* De Kalb: University of Northern Illinois Press, 1968.

Henry, David. *A History of the Haymarket Affair.* New York: Farrar & Rinehart, 1936.

Higgens-Evenson, R. Rudy. *The Price of Progress: Public Services, Taxation, and the American Corporate State, 1877 to 1929.* Baltimore: Johns Hopkins University Press, 2003.

Higham, John. *Send Them to Me: Immigrants in Urban America*, rev. ed. Baltimore: Johns Hopkins University Press, 1984.

Hine, Robert V., and John Mack Faragher. *The American West: A New Interpretive History.* New Haven, CT: Yale University Press, 2000.

Hofstadter, Richard. *Social Darwinism in American Thought, 1860–1915.* 1944; reprint ed., Boston: Beacon Press, 2016.

———. *The Age of Reform: From Bryan to FDR.* New York: Vintage, 1955.

Hoogenbaum, Ari A. *Outlawing the Spoils: A History of the Civil Service Reform Movement, 1865–1880.* Urbana: University of Illinois Press., 1960.

Howe, Irving. *World of Our Fathers: The Journey of the East European Jews to America and the Life They Found and Made.* New York: Schocken Books, 1997.

Hymowitz, Carol. *A History of Women in America.* 1978; reprint ed., New York: Bantam, 2011.

Ingram, J. S. *The Centennial Exposition, Described and Illustrated, Being a Concise and Graphic Description of this Grand Enterprise, Commemorative of the First Centenary of American Independence.* Philadelphia: Hubbard Bros., 1876.

Israel, Paul *Edison: A Life of Invention.* New York: John Wiley and Sons, 1998.

Jackson, Helen Hunt. *A Century of Dishonor.* 1881; reprint ed., N.p.: Amazon Digital Services, 2015.

Jackson, Stanley. *J. P. Morgan: The Rise and Fall of a Banker.* London: Heinemann, 1984.

Josephson, Matthew. *The Robber Barons.* 1934; reprint ed., San Diego, New York, London: Harcourt, 1962.

———. *The Robber Barons: The Great American Capitalists, 1861–1901.* New York: Harcourt, Brace, and World, 1962.

Katz, William Loren, and Laurie R. Lehman, eds., *The Cruel Years: American Voices at the Dawn of the Twentieth Century.* Boston: Beacon Press, 2001.

Kaufman, Stuart Bruce. *Samuel Gompers and the Origins of the American Federation of Labor, 1848–1896.* Westport, CT: Greenwood, 1973.

Keller, Morton. *The Art and Politics of Thomas Nast.* New York, 1968; reprint ed., New York: Oxford University Press, 1975.

Kirkland, Edward C. *Business in the Gilded Age: The Conservatives' Balance Sheet.* Madison: University of Wisconsin Press, 1952.

———. *Industry Comes of Age: Business, Labor, and Public Policy, 1860–1897.* New York: Holt, Rinehart and Winston, 1961.

Kraditor, Aileen. *The Ideas of the Woman Suffrage Movement, 1890–1920.* New York: W. W. Norton, 1981.

Kraut, Alan M. *The Huddled Masses: The Immigrant in American Society, 1880–1921.* 1982; reprint ed., Malden, MA: Wiley-Blackwell 2001.

Letwin, William. *Law and Economic Policy in America: The Evolution of the Sherman Anti-Trust Act.* New York: Random House, 1965.

Licht, Walter. *Industrializing America: The Nineteenth Century.* Baltimore: Johns Hopkins University Press, 1995.

Limerick, Patricia Nelson, Clyde A. Milner II, and Charles E. Rankin eds. *Trails: Toward a New Western History.* Lawrence: University of Kansas Press, 1991.

Link, William A., and Susannah Link, eds. *The Gilded Age and Progressive Era: A Documentary Reader.* Malden, MA: Wiley-Blackwell, 2012.

Livesay, Harold C. *Andrew Carnegie and the Rise of Big Business.* New York: Longman, 2000.

Lloyd, Henry Demarest. *Wealth Against Commonwealth,* New York: Harper & Brothers, 1899.

Logan, Rayford Whittington. *The Betrayal of the Negro: From Rutherford Hayes to Woodrow Wilson.* New York: Da Capo, 1997; originally published as *The Negro in American Life and Thought: The Nadir, 1877–1901* (1954).

Long, Clarence D. *Wages and Earnings in the United States, 1860–1890.* Princeton, NJ: Princeton University Press, 1960.

Lubove, Roy. *The Progressives and the Slums: Tenement House Reform in New York City, 1890–1917.* Pittsburgh: University of Pittsburgh Press, 1962.

Mackay, James A. *Little Boss: A Life of Andrew Carnegie.* Edinburgh: Mainstream, 1997.

Mandelbaum, Seymour. *Boss Tweed's New York. 1965*; reprint ed., Chicago: Ivan R. Dee, 1990.

Marcus, Robert D. *Grand Old Party: Political Structure in the Gilded Age, 1880–1896.* New York: Oxford University Press, 1971.

McCullough, David. *Mornings on Horseback.* New York: Simon & Schuster, 1981.

McGerr, Michael. *A Fierce Discontent: The Rise and Fall of the Progressive Movement in America, 1870–1920.* New York: Oxford University Press, 2005.

Melosi, Martin V. *Thomas A. Edison and the Modernization of America.* New York: HarperCollins, 1990.

Millard, A. J. *Edison and the Business of Innovation.* Baltimore: Johns Hopkins University Press, 1990.

Millard, Candice. *Destiny of the Republic.* New York: Doubleday, 2011.

Miller, Donald. *City of the Century: The Epic of Chicago and the Making of America.* New York: Simon & Schuster, 1996.

Montgomery, David. *The Fall of the House of Labor: The Workplace, the State, and American Labor Activism, 1865–1925.* New York: Cambridge University Press, 1987.

Morgan, Howard Wayne, ed. *The Gilded Age: A Reappraisal.* Syracuse, NY: Syracuse University Press, 1963; revised, 1970.

———. *America's Road to Empire: The War with Spain and Overseas Expansion.* New York: McGraw Hill, 1965.

Morris, Charles R. *The Tycoons: How Andrew Carnegie, John D. Rockefeller, Jay Gould, and J. P. Morgan Invented the American Supereconomy.* New York: Times Books, 2006.

Morris, Edmund. *Colonel Roosevelt.* New York: Modern Library, 2010.

———. *The Rise of Theodore Roosevelt.* New York: Modern Library, 2010.

———. *Theodore Rex.* New York: Modern Library, 2010.

Nasaw, David. *The Chief: The Life of William Randolph Hearst.* Boston: Houghton Mifflin, 2000.

Nevins, Allan. *Study in Power: John D. Rockefeller: Industrialist and Philanthropist,* 2 vols. New York: Charles Scribner's Sons, 1940, 1953.

Patrick, Rembert W. *The Reconstruction of the Nation.* New York: Oxford University Press, 1977.

Paul, Rodman W. *Mining Frontiers of the Far West, 1848–1880.* 1963; reprint ed., Albuquerque: University of New Mexico Press, 1980.

Prucha, Francis Paul. *Indian Policy in the United States: Historical Essays.* Lincoln: University of Nebraska Press, 1981.

Randal, William Pierce. *Centennial: American Life in 1876.* Philadelphia: Chilton Book Co., 1969.

Reitano, Joanne R. *The Tariff Question in the Gilded Age: The Great Debate of 1888.* University Park: Pennsylvania State University Press, 1994.

Riis, Jacob August. *How the Other Half Lives: Studies among the Tenements of New York*. 1890; reprint ed., New York: Charles Scribner's Sons, 1914.

———. *Theodore Roosevelt, the Citizen*. New York: The Outlook Co., 1904.

——— *Theodore Roosevelt, An Autobiography*. New York: Macmillan 1913.

Ritter, Gretchen. *Goldbugs and Greenbacks: The Antimonopoly Tradition and the Politics of Finance in America*. New York: Cambridge University Press, 1997.

Rozwenc, Edwin C. *The Entrepreneur in the Gilded Age*. New York: Heath, 1965.

Rydell, Robert W. *All the World's a Fair: Visions of Empire at American International Expositions, 1876–1910*. Chicago: University of Chicago Press, 1985.

Sandage, Tom. *The Victorian Internet: The Remarkable Story of the Telegraph and the Nineteenth Century's On-Line Pioneers*. New York: Bloomsbury, 1998.

Scully, Vincent. *American Architecture and Urbanism*. San Antonio: Trinity University Press, 1969.

Smith, Henry Nash. *Virgin Land*. 1950; reprint ed., Cambridge, MA: Harvard University Press, 2007.

Sproat, John. *The Best Men: Liberal Reformers in the Gilded Age*. 1966; reprint ed., Chicago: University of Chicago Press, 1982.

Standiford, Les. *Meet You in Hell: Andrew Carnegie, Henry Clay Frick, and the Bitter Partnership That Changed America*. New York: Crown, 2005.

Stanton, Elizabeth Cady, and Susan B. Anthony. *History of Woman Suffrage*, 6 vols. 1881–1922; reprint ed., N.p.: Amazon Digital Services, 2017.

Steeples, Douglas W., and David O. Whitten. *Democracy in Depression: The Depression of 1893*. Westport, CT: Greenwood Press, 1998.

Stover, John F. *The Life and Decline of the American Railroad*. New York: Oxford University Press, 1970.

Strouse, Jean. *Morgan: American Financier*. New York: Random House, 1999.

Swetnam, George. *Andrew Carnegie*. Boston: Twayne, 1980.

Tarbell, Ida M. *The History of the Standard Oil Company*. 1904; reprint ed., N. p.: CreateSpace Independent Publishing, 2015.

Trachtenberg, Alan. *The Incorporation of America: Culture and Society in the Gilded Age*. New York: Hill and Wang, 1982.

Trelease, Allen W. *White Terror: The Ku Klux Klan: Conspiracy and Southern Reconstruction*. 1971; reprint ed., Baton Rouge: Louisiana State University Press, 1995.

Truettner, William H. *The West as America: Reinterpreting Images of the Frontier, 1820–1920*. Washington, DC: Smithsonian Books, 1992.

Twain, Mark, and Charles Dudley Warner. *The Gilded Age: A Tale of Today*. 1873; reprint ed., New York and London: Harper & Brothers, 1915.

Unger, Irwin. *The Greenback Era: A Social and Political History of American Finance, 1865–1879*. Princeton, NJ: Princeton University Press, 1964.

Wall, Joseph F. *Andrew Carnegie*, 2nd ed. Pittsburgh: University of Pittsburgh Press, 1989.

Washburn, Wilcomb E. *The Indian in America*. New York: HarperCollins, 1975.

Weinstein, Allen. *Prelude to Populism: Origins of the Silver Issue, 1867–1878*. New Haven, CT: Yale University Press, 1970.

Wertheimer, Barbara. *We Were There: The Story of Working Women in America*. New York: Pantheon. 1977.

Wicker, Elmus. *Banking Panics of the Gilded Age*. New York: Cambridge University Press, 2000.

Wilson, Richard Guy, Dianne H. Pilgrim, and Richard N. Murray. *The American Renaissance, 1876–1917*. New York: Pantheon, 1979.

Wolff, Leon. *Lockout: The Story of the Homestead Strike of 1892*. New York: Harper & Row, 1965.

Woodward, C. Vann. *The Strange Career of Jim Crow*, rev. ed., 1974; reprint ed., New York: Oxford University Press, 2001.

Zunz, Oliver. *Making America Corporate, 1870–1920*. Chicago: University of Chicago Press, 1990.

PICTURE CREDITS

Alamy: © Ian Dagnall: 216; © Paul Fearn: 298; © Everett Historical: 144; © Interfoto: 118; © ITAR-TASS Photo Agency: 206; © Lebrecht Music and Arts Photo Library: 16; © Mary Evans Picture Library: 170; © North Wind Picture Archives: 126, 174, 248

Chris Bain: 105

Bridgeman Art Library: © Shelburne Museum: 195 right top

Duke University: James Buchanan Duke Papers, David M. Rubenstein Rare Book & Manuscript Library: 121; John W. Hartman Center for Sales, Advertising & Marketing History, David M. Rubenstein Rare Book & Manuscript Library: 125

Flickr/Preus Museum: 161

Getty Images: 92; © Bettmann: iv, vi; © Chicago History Museum: 133; © Museum of Science and Industry, Chicago: 342

Granger Images: 46, 60, 134, 210, 238

Internet Archive: 3, 22, 24, 202, 219

iStock: © CSA Images/B&W Engrave Ink Collection: 122 bottom, 301; © ilbusca: 54, 177, 273; © Diane Labombarbe: 215; © Man_Half-tube: 143; © Oak68: 200

Library of Congress: 4, 7, 9, 11, 12, 19, 20, 26, 27, 32, 33, 35, 38, 41, 43, 45, 49 right, 50, 51, 52, 59, 61, 63, 64, 66, 67, 68, 69, 71, 73, 74, 76, 79, 81, 83, 84, 86, 88, 89, 91, 94, 95, 97, 99, 107, 109, 112, 115, 119, 127, 128 right, 129, 131, 136, 142, 146, 151, 151, 153, 155, 156, 158, 164, 165, 166, 167, 169, 176, 178, 180, 184, 187, 188, 189, 191, 195 left and middle, 197, 198, 213, 221, 224, 226, 228, 231, 237, 240, 241, 243, 246, 250, 252, 254, 256, 261, 268, 269, 271, 274, 277, 281, 282, 283, 284, 288, 290, 291, 292, 295, 296, 300, 302, 307, 309, 310, 312, 314, 317, 318, 319, 321, 322, 324, 325, 327, 333, 335, 337, 338, 339, 341, 344, 346, 350, 352, 357, front and back endpapers

National Archives: 49 left, 57 left

National Gallery of Art: 222

National Park Service/Thomas Edison National Historic Park: 110

Courtesy of the North Carolina Department of Natural and Cultural Resources: 122

New York Public Library: 30, 103, 148, 149, 171, 172, 194, 209, 247, 263

Shutterstock: © Digiselector: throughout (ornaments); © Everett Historical: 116, 353; © Fotoluminate LLC: 195 right bottom; © Horenko: throughout (background); © ivgroznii: : throughout (ornaments); © julijamilaja: throughout (ornaments); © Tatiananna: throughout (ornaments); © Liubou Yasiukovick: throughout (ornaments)

Wellcome Library: 15, 55

Courtesy of Wikimedia Commons: 29, 48, 82, 106, 128 left, 160, 196, 211, 233, 264, 272; British Library: 25; Smithsonian Institution: 138, 186; © Soerfm: 278; © Beth Stiner: 223; © victorgrigas: 182; © Yale University Libraries: 286

INDEX